Business Competitor Intelligence

Business Competitor Intelligence

Methods for Collecting, Organizing, and Using Information

WILLIAM L. SAMMON
MARK A. KURLAND
ROBERT SPITALNIC

A RONALD PRESS PUBLICATION
John Wiley & Sons
New York • Chichester • Brisbane • Toronto • Singapore

This publication is designed to provide accurate and authoritative information in regard to the subject matter covered. It is sold with the understanding that the publisher is not engaged in rendering legal, accounting, or other professional service. If legal advice or other expert assistance is required, the services of a competent professional person should be sought. *From a Declaration of Principles jointly adopted by a Committee of the American Bar Association and a Committee of Publishers.*

ISBN 0-471-87591-0

Printed in the United States of America

10 9 8 7 6 5 4 3

Preface

The business world is an arena of competition. Like hustling baseball clubs, campaigning politicians, and battling armies, companies are in conflict with their counterparts. Yet managements' understanding of their competitors is often casual, cursory, and wrong. Unlike contenders in other fields of organized struggle, people in business are not inclined to monitor the moves, calculate the strengths, or study the strategies of rivals. This customary indifference to the competitive position and potential of the other side may be changing slowly in some corporate circles, but today most managers in most American companies regard "competitor intelligence" as one or more of the following:

Unethical behavior.

Illegal spying.

An invitation to antitrust litigation.

Unwarranted and costly research.

A minor aspect of marketing best done in an informal, intuitive fashion.

Despite increasing evidence that numerous foreign companies recognize the practical short- and long-term value of systematic competitor intelligence, American managers generally have a minimal understanding of the character and strengths of the firms they compete against for customers, market share, and resources.

Yet the corporate battleground is littered with wounded companies whose management kept their eyes on everything but the most dynamic variable in the strategic environment: competitors. Under a former chairman, RCA, one of the electronics industry's first-rank companies, focused its senior management's energy and attention on minute changes in quarterly financial results. In contrast, changes in competitor's strategies were dimly perceived and frequently ignored. CBS and other domestic competitors rapidly gained ground. Foreign manufacturers like Matsushita and Sony also exploited RCA's fixation on financial reports and were able to wrest major markets from the industry leader in a remarkably short time.

DuPont, one of the major producers of polyester tire cord fiber, turned that industry upside down when it developed a new fiber product (Kevlar) that caught its competitors napping. Monsanto, then a major producer of polyester fiber, based its tire cord strategy on expanding existing market share through aggressive promotion and manufacturing economies of scale. It followed duPont closely but failed to grasp the technological thrust of its competitor's strategy and erroneously concluded that duPont was vulnerable on price. Goodyear, a captive, "merchant" producer of polyester tire cord, naively regarded duPont as a nonthreatening supplier of fiber.

Upon completion of the introductory phase of Kevlar's market development, duPont not only commercialized the technologically advanced fiber for tire cord production but unexpectedly diverted its sizable polyester fiber capacity to other industrial applications. This double strategic switch enabled duPont to substantially enlarge its hold on the high-margin segment of the tire cord market while directing existing polyester fiber capacity to more profitable end-use markets—for example, aerospace, and sail cloth, in which its competitors were at best marginal suppliers.

In intelligence and football circles the technical term for duPont's devastating competitive maneuver is "blindsided." In some managerial circles it is called bad luck, the "unpredictability of the market place," "economic changes," or "industry trends," anything but what it really is—an intelligence failure.

The most superficial review of any industry quickly reveals that companies with comparable physical assets and similar strategic objectives often have widely different performance records. Some, like General Mills, do very well, and others, like Borden, struggle to catch up. In such cases—which are more common than many executives care to admit—the difference in competitive performance ultimately comes down to the quality of management. The quality of management is in turn determined by who has made the best executive decisions at the right time for the long term. This critical qualitative difference that makes one management team first rate and their counterparts "also rans" is reflected in their corporate strategies.

Business strategies embody the thinking and planning that frame the fundamental decisions executives must make. Many factors contribute to smarter corporate strategies and superior industry performance: relative cost position, corporate culture, management depth, executive continuity, product mix, business portfolio, and successful R&D, to name just a few. Sharper and timely "intelligence" on competitors' capabilities and intentions is another but perhaps less salient strategic factor that separates corporate leaders from laggards in the increasingly fast track of business competition in the 1980s. While many companies develop sound strategic plans, effective implementation requires a strategic intelligence resource that few possess.

CEOs frequently ascribe their companies' success to quality products and dedicated employees. But the artful strategies of top corporations like IBM, Johnson and Johnson, duPont, Gillette, and General Electric also reveal telltale traces of superior competitor intelligence. Intelligence is used to monitor competitors, identify emerging strategic opportunities, and then swiftly exploit opponents' mistakes with shrewdly timed competitive moves. Timing is often the keystone of effective strategies, and competitor intelligence gives leading companies the peripheral vision necessary to make the right move at the right time.

Hewlett-Packard, the number one company in precision instruments, achieved that rank in part because it understood the competitive dynamics of its markets and the strategic errors of its leading rivals. A major competitor, Texas Instruments (TI), based its strategy and manufacturing operations on the economics of the experience curve and priced and marketed its products accordingly. Hewlett-Packard carefully monitored its competitor's move and realized something significant—Texas Instrument was carrying a good strategy too far as it aggressively cut prices in anticipation of the volume benefits of learning-curve economics. Hewlett-Packard understood the flaw in its opponent's strategy, realized it would lead to strategic failure, and then used this intelligence to counter TI with a deft strategy keyed to high-quality products at premium prices. Customers reacted favorably to Hewlett-Packard's segmentation strategy and TI never achieved the volume levels it anticipated. Today TI is pulling itself together from this debacle while Hewlett-Packard moves smoothly ahead.

In an industry known for its fierce competition and impulsive management, Boise Cascade stands out as a company that carefully monitors its rambling competitors, discerns the strengths and weaknesses of their strategies, and deftly uses competitor intelligence to play chess to its opponents checkers. Better intelligence has made Boise's strategy anticipatory rather than reactive.

In the forest products industry, rapidly rising energy and fiber costs have made it increasingly difficult for companies with second-rate timber resources to compete in lower-margin commodity markets such as linerboard and plywood. Fortunately the explosive growth of business paper copying machines in the mid-1970s turned the industry's high-margin white papers market into a growth segment.

Hampered by poorly positioned and comparatively limited timber resources, Boise Cascade and Mead Corporation developed new strategies built around the expanding white papers market. At great expense, both repositioned their product mix to emphasize high-quality, high-margin business printing and publishing papers. Today Boise has a profitable, leading position in white papers and its management is rated among the best in the industry. Mead's strategy, however, was flawed by bad timing and poor implementation. Today the company's financial strength is in jeopardy, and management's previously strong reputation has been severly eroded. For Mead's $1.5-billion capital spending program gave it the right capacity at the wrong time—in the depths of the steep 1980–82 recession. With earnings down and expenses up Mead increased its borrowing to support the costly capacity expansion program. Corporate debt jumped from 46 percent of total capital in 1981 to 58 percent in 1982.[1] The norm in the capital intensive forest products industry is 30 to 35 percent. Recently Standard & Poors dropped Mead's credit rating from A to BBB+.

In a 1982 *Fortune* survey, major U.S. corporations were ranked by the reputations they held within their industry. The survey's respondents (industry executives, outside directors, and financial analysts) ranked Boise Cascade number three out of ten in the forest product industry, with a qualitative score of 6.14; Mead's aggregate score of 5.38 placed it in the number eight position.[2]

Within the forest products industry, Boise's current management is highly respected for developing and implementing a superbly timed strategy that gave the company the right growth capacity, at an economical cost, ahead of the competition. Like Mead, Boise spent a large sum—$1.4 billion—to upgrade its product mix. But unlike its competitors, Boise did it sooner and cheaper largely by buying old mills and quickly upgrading them.[3] When the faltering economy plunged the forest products industry into a depression, Boise's new production capacity was in place and the company was in a superior strategic position, having carved out a leading market share of the important white papers business.

The purpose of this book is twofold: (1) to outline the contributions competitor intelligence can make to more effective and less vulnerable business strategies, and (2) to delineate various practical methods and analytical techniques for obtaining and using competitor intelligence to support strategic planning.

Competitor intelligence is examined in the context of the "competitive analyses" that are increasingly recognized as one of the vital but frequently missing components of business strategies.[4] The subject of "competitive analysis" is getting more attention in executive circles because in the past decade too many well laid corporate and business unit plans have been torpedoed by the unanticipated countermeasures of aggressive competitors. Greater managerial emphasis on the hard fact that business rivals act and react in a highly dynamic, often volatile manner in most industries is beginning to close one of the more dangerous reality gaps in strategic planning. Yet as the strategic significance of competitive analysis is better understood, attention is rapidly drawn to the growing need for better competitor data and the practical difficulties companies have in trying to obtain relevant information about competitors in a timely and legal fashion.

All novel intellectual and professional themes usually reflect the real-world heat of new pressures that are in fact old pressures conveniently forgotten for awhile. Today in wide stretches of corporate America the rising interest in competitive analysis and competitor intelligence is flogged on by the reluctant and uncomfortable realization that the new economic era may be one of stagflation, recession, and weak recoveries. In this troublesome period of slow and slippery growth, managers must wrest their victories not from a growing marketplace powered by ballooning demand, but rather from their hungry, angry, and fiercely competitive rivals—domestic and increasingly foreign as well. In short, the brave gray business world of the late 20th century has become a harsh arena of economic combat characterized by increasingly volatile business cycles and declining profitability.[5] It is a treacherous strategic environment governed by the stern rules of a zero-sum game in which market share and higher profits are now won by exploiting another's strategic vulnerabilities and managerial lapses.

For many executives who came of age in the halcyon era of steady growth and inflation protected margins (1964–78), an unusual time when most companies were comfortable winners and management decisions had a wide margin of error (thanks to an expanding, if inflationary, pie), it is a rude awakening to discover that the rules of the game have changed in a rather fundamental way and now robust competition means winners and *losers.*

Competitors are now something more than genial fellow members of an industry trade association with common concerns and shared aims. Today they are frequently viewed as the main threat, the strategic opponent who gives and seeks no quarter in the serious game of business survival. Company executives who may once have known more about their home team's rivals than their own firm's competitors are now increasingly eager to learn more about their business rivals than the color of their corporate logos. This book addresses corporate management's new-found appetite for competitor intelligence.

The concept of "intelligence" is presented as a practical, proven, and analytical method that managers can use to minimize the competitor information gaps that result in sightless strategies. To improve strategic planning by the addition of systematic competitive analyses, a coherent and relevant competitor intelligence resource is required.

Intelligence does not equal information. Rather, it is a method for *identifying* the intelligence requirements of a company, systematically *collecting* relevant information on competitors, and then analytically *processing* that raw data into actionable knowledge about competitors' strategic capabilities, position, performance, and intentions. The major value of systematic competitor intelligence is that it helps managers focus on the key organizational and behavioral variables that reflect and drive competitors' strategies. This intelligence is crucial to the development of effective business strategies that engage the dynamic fundamentals of the competitive environment.

Although large corporations with their multiple businesses and complex strategies may have the greatest appetite for competitor intelligence, a company of any size that faces strong competition in the markets it serves has a practical need for organized competitor intelligence. For many small and medium-sized firms, competitor intelligence is very often the key to marketplace survival. Executives and managers of modest-sized and perhaps more nimble companies will recognize many of the intelligence techniques discussed at length in the text and may already have incorporated them—albeit in a less organized, more intuitive fashion—into their own decision-making routines. Although the book is oriented towards the complex intelligence problems that confront large-scale multinational corporations, most of the material can, with minor modification, be adapted to the more limited intelligence needs of smaller, single-industry companies. Moreover, the book is in many respects a good primer on the kinds of competitor intelligence problems that often confound the strategic planning of a small company's larger competitors. That itself may be a useful source of competitor intelligence.[6]

SCOPE AND PLAN OF THE BOOK

As is evident from the table of contents, this book represents the collaborative effort of analysts, managers, and executives involved in various aspects of competitor intelligence. Whether they are servicing corporations as consultants, bankers, and suppliers, or employed by them in various planning positions, the contributors' professional responsibilities require a sound knowledge of competitor strategies and an understanding of the sources and techniques used to develop the intelligence that illuminates those strategies.

The book is organized to provide easy access to the wide range of competitor intelligence topics covered in the text. Written by and for those engaged in the intriguing study of business competitors, the book is designed to be used as an analytical reference handbook on competitor intelligence methods of organization, collection, and analysis. From their broad business and intelligence backgrounds the authors have drawn many practical observations and "lessons learned" that analysts, managers, and senior executives will find particularly relevant to their professional tasks and strategic concerns.

The chapters are grouped into four parts:

1. *Competitor Intelligence/Strategic Planning.* This is the analytical core of the book and addresses the crucial interrelationship between intelligence and planning in corporate decision making.
2. *Special Applications.* As a group, these three chapters illustrate the application of competitor intelligence in different strategic environments—commodity, consumer, and international.
3. *Sources and Types of Competitor Intelligence.* In this section, major functional categories and associated sources of competitor intelligence—marketing, finance, economics, media, and technological—are discussed in detail by seasoned practitioners. They represent both the analytical disciplines and the service institutions that can be fruitfully used to obtain a wide range of relevant competitor intelligence.

4. *Special Issues.* The last section gives the reader a basic introduction to four intelligence issues that confront and often confound both consumers and producers of competitor intelligence:

   How can managers collect and use competitor intelligence without going to jail?
   How should competitor risk be evaluated in foreign areas where the basic rules are radically different?
   What factors should be considered in hiring an outside competitor intelligence agent to collect and/or analyze competitor data?
   How should competitor intelligence be used to develop acquisition and divestment candidates?

While there is a natural order in moving sequentially through the book's four parts, much value can be derived from approaching the chapters according to topical or analytical interest. The choice should be dictated by the reader's needs. That is why the book is structured in a modular fashion with distinct and independent components.

Readers currently involved in an ongoing, established competitor intelligence program may find it useful to focus their attention on the specific categories of functional intelligence discussed in Part 3. Those who are versed in strategic planning but new to the "mysteries" of intelligence will want to begin their reading with Chapters 1 through 4, which provide an overview of the relationship between strategic planning and competitor intelligence. Executives who are troubled by the sinister aura of espionage evoked by the idea of competitor intelligence-gathering may find Chapters 2 and 14 particularly instructive. Analysts who must transform oceans of competitor data into digestable financial and planning reports will gain a number of valuable tips from Chapter 5 and Part 3 (particularly Chapter 10 on financial intelligence, Chapter 11 on economic intelligence, and Chapter 13 on R&D or technical intelligence). Those who are confronted with the difficult task of tracking foreign competitors will probably begin their readings with a review of Chapter 8. Marketing and planning managers who are trying to organize an intelligence data base for their company's industries will find appropriate intelligence approaches outlined in Chapters 6, 7, and 9.

To facilitate those readers who may want to track a more narrow intelligence topic—for example, competitor manufacturing costs, competitor financial ratio analysis, published sources of competitor data, or corporate culture—a detailed index covering key concepts, subjects, and techniques has been compiled.

As is frequently the case in contributed books, the separate chapters reflect the diverse writing styles, professional education, and business experiences of their individual authors. However disconcerting this approach may be, the editors believe the reader is best served by an organizational design that captures the diverse techniques of the rapidly evolving but still novel business concept of competitor intelligence. The editors wish to thank the contributing authors, whose reflections and writings on their particular areas of expertise in competitor intelligence made this book possible.

WILLIAM L. SAMMON
MARK A. KURLAND
ROBERT SPITALNIC

Carmel, New York
Chappaqua, New York
New York, New York
March 1984

[1]Jean A. Briggs, "White Paper Drenched in Red Ink," *Forbes,* April 12, 1983 pp. 134–36.

[2]Claire Makin, "Ranking Corporate Reputations," *Fortune,* January 10, 1983, pp. 34–44.

[3]"Survival in the Basic Industries," *Business Week,* April 26, 1982, pp. 80 and 84.

[4]Michael Porter, *Competitive Strategy: Techniques for Analyzing Industries and Competitors,* New York, Free Press, 1980; Peter Carroll, "The Link Between Performance and Strategy," *The Journal of Business Strategy,* vol. 2, no 4 (Spring 1982); D. B. Montgomery and C. E. Weinberg, "Towards Strategic Intelligence Systems," *Journal of Marketing,* Fall 1979.

[5]Michael Hergert, "Has Financial Leverage Gone Too Far," *Planning Review,* May 1983, pp. 43–44.

[6]See Robert Hershey, "Commercial Intelligence on a Shoe String," *Harvard Business Review,* September–October 1980, pp. 1–5, for an excellent overview of competitor intelligence techniques practiced by small companies

Contents

PART III SOURCES AND TYPES OF COMPETITOR INTELLIGENCE

PART IV SPECIAL ISSUES

I

Competitor Intelligence/Strategic Planning

1

Competitor Intelligence: The Sine Qua Non of Corporate Strategic Planning

JAMES R. GARDNER

Dr. Gardner is Director-Corporate Planning for Pfizer, the pharmaceutical multinational. His primary responsibilities involve insuring that the plans of Pfizer's various operating divisions reflect corporate strategic decisions and guidance. Areas of special project involvement include new product development, acquisitions, facilities planning, and strategic organization.

Before joining Pfizer in 1977, Dr. Gardner completed 11 years of active duty in the U.S. Army as a combat infantry commander; Senior Aide-de-Camp of the Military District of Washington, D.C.; Special Assistant to the Army Chief of Staff; Staff Assistant to the U.S. Attorney General (Department of Justice); and faculty member at West Point, where he taught economics, politics, and management. A graduate of the Army Ranger School and the Command and General Staff College, he has received over 20 military decorations for service and achievement. As a Lieutenant Colonel in the Army Reserve, he holds a post as a Visiting Professor of Public Policy at West Point.

In addition to an M.B.A. in Finance, Dr. Gardner holds a B.S. in Engineering from the U.S. Military Academy and both an M.B.A. in International Affairs and a Ph.D. in Public Administration from Princeton. He is a coauthor of *American National Security: Policy and Process*, and serves as a Director of the New York Chapter of the North American Society for Corporate Planning.

THE METHODOLOGY EXPLOSION

During the past two decades, strategic planning has blossomed as a discipline and as a function. Both the "primacy" and "pervasiveness" of planning have been recognized.[1] Increasingly, corporate leadership has come to view strategic planning as being (in the words of George Steiner) "inextricably interwoven in the entire fabric of management" rather than "something separate and distinct."[2] Confronted by a world of accelerating complexity, change, and uncertainty, executives have embraced planning as a means of charting and maintaining corporate direction. Within most major corporations, the strategic planning function has become firmly entrenched, playing a pivotal role in what Peter Drucker has described as the prime task of top management:

> thinking through the mission of the business, that is, of asking the question what is our business and what should it be? . . . [leading to] the setting of objectives, the development of strategies and plans, and the making of today's decisions for tomorrow's results.[3]

Concurrent with this functional blossoming of strategic planning has been an explosion in methods and "tools" for analysis and decision-making. To a degree, such was inevitable, given the structure and logic demanded by formalized planning. After all, strategic planning encourages viewing "a company as a system . . . [thereby permitting] top management . . . to look at the enterprise as a whole . . . rather than deal with each separate part alone."[4] It emphasizes the setting of specific objectives and the systematic evaluation of future opportunities and potential problems. Planning highlights the need for identifying strategic issues and measuring performance, both qualitatively and quantitatively. And it advocates a rational planning framework, one linked to other essential functions and with mechanisms for constructive feedback. In short, strategic planning, by its very nature, stimulates a demand for "higher order" analytical methods, ones with which to sort order out of chaos.

This recent explosion in strategic planning "technologies" has been broadly based, with roots in the academic community and the public sector as well as in business. However, credit for the vigor with which these methods burst forth and for the eagerness with which they were embraced rests with a handful of aggressive management consulting firms. Armed with what one *critic* has termed a "sweet collection of surefire concepts . . . that promised an easy win,"[5] they found a ready audience in corporate America. After all, when one is confronted with a task as complex as directing the energies of a large corporation, it's hard to resist simple yet powerful concepts that seem to penetrate to the heart of the business and put it all in focus. Especially attractive were the concepts of strategic business units (SBUs), learning curves, and their intellectual derivatives, the growth/share matrix and the company position/industry attractiveness matrix.

The first of these concepts—strategic business units—evolved from General Electric's experiences during the 1960s, a time when that company achieved rapid sales growth but little increase in earnings per share. Better strategic control over operations was deemed the problem, and with assistance from McKinsey & Co., GE created "strategic business units" in order to achieve that goal. By definition, each SBU had its own unique and identifiable products and markets—a self-contained "pea," if you will, within the corporate "pod." In theory, each SBU would develop its own strategies, based upon its own capabilities, needs, and perceptive insights. The corporation, in turn, would allocate resources based upon how each SBU contributed to overall corporate objectives.

The second concept—the experience curve—was spawned by the Boston Consulting Group, and is an extension of the old "learning curve" idea. In general, the concept linked declining unit costs to accumulated volume experience in producing a standardized product. It maintained that the company that grows the fastest will accumulate "experience" the most rapidly, and, as a result, will achieve cost advantages over its competitors. In turn, these cost advantages will permit the company to expand its market share even further, setting the stage for more "experience" and even lower unit costs. The obvious implication is that a market-share leader has inherent leverage to expand or defend that position, a fact that smaller competitors and potential entrants neglect only at their own risk.

Having defined, with the SBU, a logical focal point for business strategy development, and with the experience curve linking growth and market share, it was only a short hop in logic to "business gridding" and "business portfolio management." Simply stated, the assumption underlying "business gridding" is that the current strategic position of any business should be a principal determinant of *future* strategies. The grid assists in gauging relative position by relating two distinct factors—the attractiveness of the industry and the competitive strength of the company. Of the several versions in use, the two most popular have been the Boston Consulting Group's "2×2" matrix, and the "3×3" matrix created by McKinsey and General Electric.[6]

The BCG matrix (Figure 1.1) uses industry growth rate as a surrogate for industry attractiveness, and market share as a surrogate for competitive strength. The various quadrants intrinsically suggest different strategies for businesses positioned within each:

Star: Maintain or increase strength, exploiting inherent market leverage.

Cash cow: Slow growth minimizes investment needs; use business to generate cash for investment.

Wildcat: Coordinate investment and business strategies to transform to a "star."

Dog: No future, exit from the business.

The McKinsey/General Electric matrix (Figure 1.2) uses industry attractiveness and company strength for its axes, rather than their proxies, growth rate and market share. Attractiveness and strength can be rated as high, medium, or low. The factors used to define each parameter can be tailored to individual businesses. Such tailoring gives

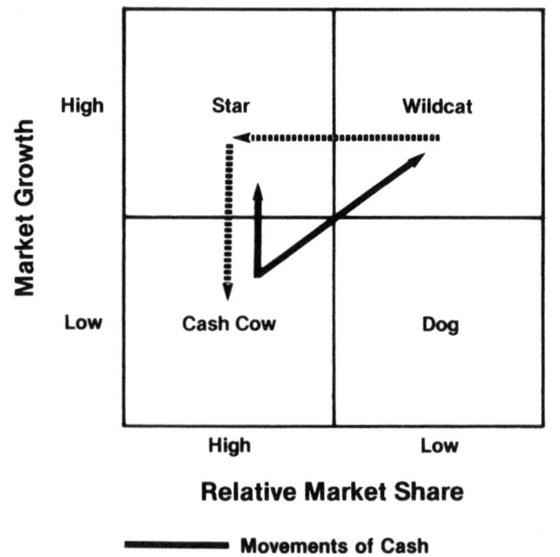

Figure 1.1 2 × 2 Matrix (Boston Consulting Group)

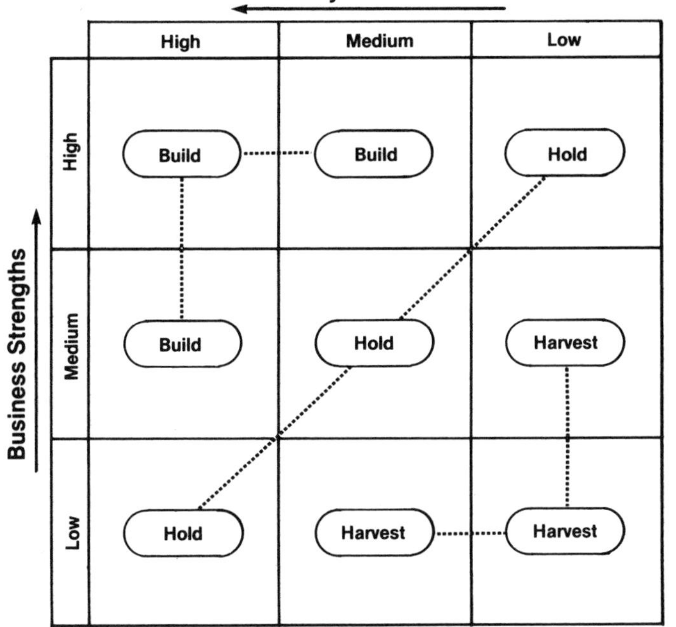

Figure 1.2 3 × 3 Matrix (McKinsey/General Electric)

the matrix both expanded flexibility and greater prescriptive power. Once again, each compartment of the matrix suggests differing strategic thrusts for businesses falling therein—for example, "build," "hold," "harvest."

Using these matrices, individual companies were better able to chart and steer their own courses. Larger, more diversified corporations were better able to more effectively manage their "portfolio" of businesses—balancing and maximizing cash flows, identifying candidates for divestment, and customizing compensation and incentive programs.

The contribution of these concepts (and their many derivatives) to the art and science of corporate planning was profound. To the mass of helpful but loosely integrated ideas that before had constituted strategic planning theory, these concepts imparted structure and logical rigor. They stimulated companies to think strategically, to a depth and with a breadth not common before. And the concepts brought a sense of clarity and understanding to the discussion of strategic alternatives, often rendering difficult strategic decisions, and their communication, easier.

THINKING COMPETITIVELY: ESSENTIAL FOR THINKING STRATEGICALLY

Another important impact of these methods was that they demanded that businesses begin to think of strategy in a *competitive* context. The use of either matrix, for example, forced corporations (and their component companies) to probe the nature and dimensions of both their own strengths and the attractiveness of their industry.

In assessing their strengths, companies had to identify those key factors that constituted, in their industry, the difference between success and failure. Moreover, they had to gauge how well their capabilities stacked up compared to their competitors. Company strengths become viewed not as absolute but relative. Detailed review was demanded of those individual factors contributing to strength—share, product quality, costs, distribution, patent protection, and so on—and of their interrelationships. Competitive position was seen as perishable, requiring constant maintenance and defense.

As they wrestled with the question of industry attractiveness, companies were forced to get a grip on the competitive dynamics of their industry as well as its quantitative characteristics. Market size, profitability, and relative costs had to be measured and weighed. In addition, increased (and largely unaccustomed) attention had to be focused on issues of industry structure, competitive leverage, relative company capabilities, and potential competitor initiatives. The acknowledged goal was a timely and thorough definition of opportunities, threats, and critical issues. Opportunities, it was recognized, were spawned by the interplay of the market and its competitive participants. These opportunities belonged to companies quick enough to recognize and seize them. Some threats might conceivably arise that would jeopardize all industry participants. But, increasingly, threats were perceived as the result of a competitor being first to seize an opportunity. Critical issues, long restricted to matters of action, came to include matters of position. Increasingly, critical issues were framed in terms of strategic matrix positions instead of near-term tactical concerns.

As corporations injected these competitive perspectives into their planning processes, they experienced a quantum increase in the effectiveness of their direction-setting and decision-making. No longer were they just making and meeting budgets nor were they simply attempting to predict and plan for the future. Instead, they were for the first time beginning to truly "think strategically".

This linkage between thinking competitively and thinking strategically has been spotlighted in the now-classic article on the evolution of strategic planning, written by three members of McKinsey & Company in 1978. They noted that:

> Formal strategic planning appears to be evolving through similar phases of development, although at widely varying rates of progress, in most large business organizations around the world. . . . The evolution of formal planning can be segmented into four fairly clear, sequential phases.[7]

According to this schema (Figure 1.3), the first of these evolutionary stages is financial planning in which the focus is functional and the

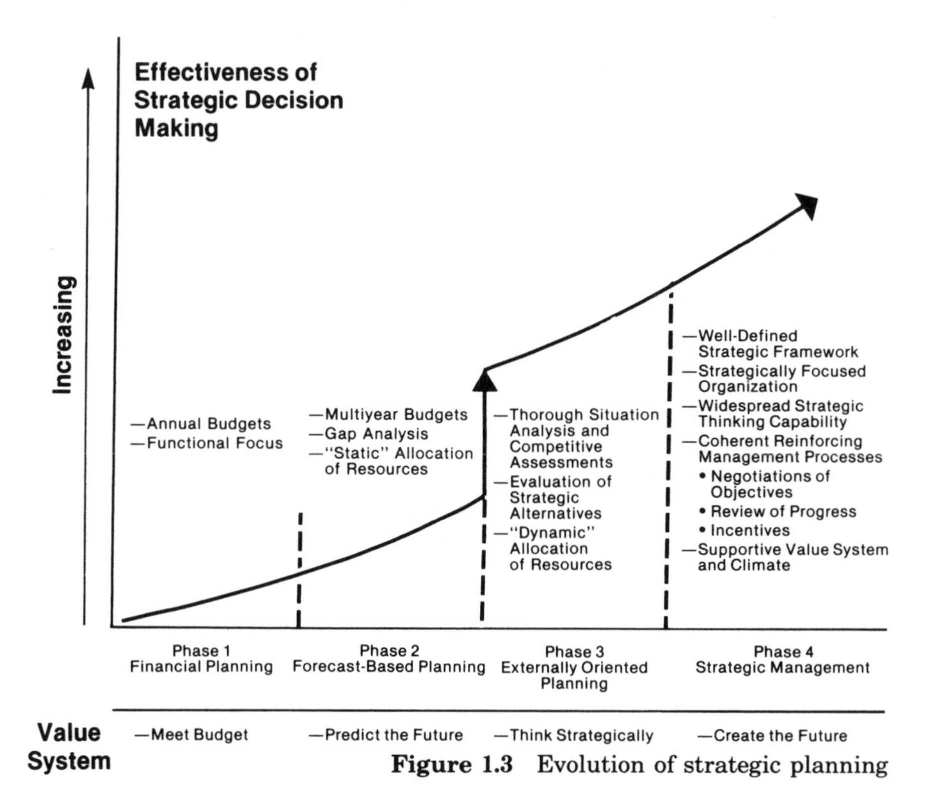

Figure 1.3 Evolution of strategic planning

process narrowly budgetary in nature. Specific financial targets are established for the year and guidelines are set for permissible expenses and capital consumption. Results are periodically reviewed, stressing performance against budget; corollary management activities—training, personnel evaluations, and compensation—echo this annual cycle. Strategy, in this phase, is usually implicit in form and intuitive in source, as opposed to being the product of a formal system.

Phase 2 was described as forecast-based planning, characterized by efforts to extrapolate the future, by multiyear budgets, and by a relatively static approach to resource allocation. Companies evolve to this stage as their increasing complexity exceeds the capabilities of an implicit strategy. Greater use is made of forecasting methods such as trend analysis, regression, and simulations. Management begins to systematically grapple with key issues identified via the planning process: trade-offs among competing objectives, the relative effectiveness of various operating programs, the comparative productivity of component businesses. Portfolio analysis emerges as a technique but (to use McKinsey's terms) is "static" and "deterministic." The perceived purpose of business gridding is to describe *current* positions and their appropriate strategies rather than suggest options for changing those positions. The matrix is seen as being descriptive of strategy rather than as a starting point for strategy development.

During its passage through phases 1 and 2, a company—so the theory goes—should experience a steadily increasing effectiveness in its strategic decision making. However, the advance to phase 3, externally oriented planning, involves a quantum jump forward in planning and management capabilities and signals the beginning of thinking strategically. And the key to achieving this breakthrough in effectiveness is *thinking competitively.*

Planning in phase 3 begins with an analysis of the business environment and the competitive situation. Strategies are competitive in tone, designed to exploit unique company strengths or to exploit opportunities posed by the confluence of market conditions and competitors' weaknesses. Plans are neither static nor sterile; instead, they are dynamic and creative. As Gluck et al. note:

> The Phase 3 planner looks for opportunities to "shift the dot" of a business on a portfolio matrix into a more attractive sector, either by creating new capabilities that will improve his company's ability to satisfy the most important prerequisites for success within a market, or by changing the customer's buying criteria to correspond to his own strengths.[8]

The final phase in the McKinsey evolutionary schema is strategic management, characterized by the merging of strategic planning and management into a single process distinguished not by "the sophistication of . . . planning techniques, but rather the care and thoroughness with which strategic planning is linked to operational decision making."[9] Companies attaining this level of development possess a well-understood and workable strategic planning framework, separate from but coupled with a strategically focused organizational structure. As a result, new initiatives are seldom strangled by organizational considerations; worthwhile ideas can be readily converted into systematically managed action programs. Strategic thinking is widespread within the company, nurtured by deliberate training and position rotations. Incentive systems are formulated to reward strategic contributions; the formal aspects of this forward-looking management process are reinforced by a supportive value system and corporate climate. Phase 4 companies, normatively speaking, think and act as a coherent strategic entity and as such possess the unique potential to influence their future *before* it unfolds.

Few American business organizations can claim to be strategically managed. However, most major corporations can validly claim to be strategically thinking to some degree, and therefore are positioned somewhere within McKinsey's phase 3. Recent research has indicated that by 1981 roughly half of the Fortune 1000 industries were actively using some version of the business portfolio matrix as part of their regular planning process.[10]

LOOKING BACK . . . AND AHEAD

One way to visualize the past decade's developments in corporate strategic planning is to think in terms of a general "input-output" system model. Such a model portrays a process (one having component methods, procedures, and technologies) that transforms specific inputs ("raw materials") into outputs ("products"). The characteristics and quality of the output are determined by two factors: (1) the nature of the process methodology, and (2) the quality of the inputs and the degree to which they meet the requirements and maximize the potential of the process. If one thinks of the corporate strategic planning process in this way, data about self, competitors, and the business environment constitute the inputs. The outputs, obviously, are the strategic concepts, objectives, and plans developed via the planning process.

Within this model, a jump to a higher-order system (as measured by effectiveness) usually occurs as the result of new technologies that make better use of the existing inputs. However, it is important to note that step-wise increases in effectiveness may also result from better quality inputs and/or improved utilization of the process outputs. During the past decade, the evolution of strategic planning concepts and practice have been driven by improvements in planning methods and technologies. It was the analytical tools and the competitive awareness they stimulated that propelled most major corporations out of the "stone age" of budgets and long-range forecasting into the current era of "externally oriented planning."

However, a major reappraisal is currently underway within the field of corporate planning, a reappraisal that is questioning the very planning technologies that provided the impetus for the transformations of the past decade. Looking ahead, it appears highly probable that progress towards strategic management will *not* come from improved planning technologies—that is, from a wave of "second generation" matrices. Instead, as depicted by Figure 1.4, that next plateau of effectiveness will be reached through improvements in the inputs to the

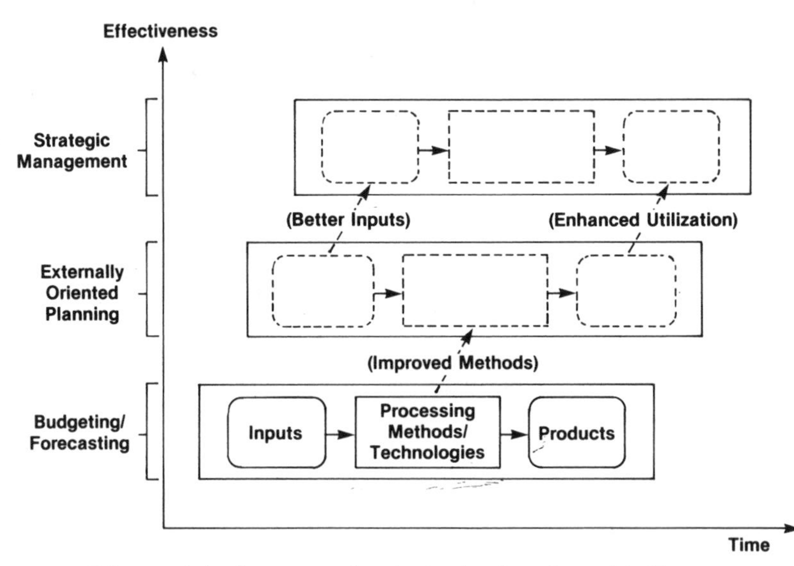

Figure 1.4 Increases in strategic planning effectiveness

planning process and by enhanced utilization ("implementation") of the plans that result.

For competitor intelligence, the implications are clear. In the evolution to externally oriented planning, competitor intelligence was a vital ingredient, stimulated by the matrix approach and its requirements to assess company strength and industry attractiveness. Inherent in the ongoing reappraisal is recognition of the fact that competitor intelligence is the *sine qua non* of strategic management as well.

THE PATH TO STRATEGIC MANAGEMENT

Some observers have attributed the apparent disenchantment with the matrix-based approach to corporate planning to nothing more than the novelty wearing off. Others have suggested that, as use and understanding of the techniques grew, so did an awareness of their intrinsic limitations. In the case of the Boston Consulting Group's 2 × 2 matrix, the use of growth and market share as criteria has been criticized and the matrix's preoccupation with balancing cash flows has been questioned. Other observers have cited changing economic conditions as contributing to the reappraisal. Suited to the "go-go" years of the early 1970s, the matrix approach—in their view—has been far less relevant for some businesses in the years since then:

> If your portfolio has no businesses that have significant growth, you'd better forget about the matrix and learn to manage for efficiency and return.[11]

Undoubtedly each of these factors has contributed in some degree to the waning popularity of the matrix "planning technologies." But by stepping back a bit and viewing the scene in a broader perspective, another explanation can be seen.

The future holds unsettling prospects for many American companies, given the increasing dimensions of global competition and the structural alteration of entire industries by new technologies. No corporation can assume itself to be insulated from these forces or from their effects upon its component businesses and markets. It is imperative that threats and opportunities be perceived far enough in advance so that resources can be mobilized to counter or capitalize on them, as the case may be.

A phase 3 corporation doing externally oriented planning has already attained substantial effectiveness in its planning processes. A staff and framework exist for the definition of objectives, the identification of opportunities and perils, and the allocation of resources. Critical corporate issues are regularly surfaced and analyzed. Some attention, by necessity, is given to the position and capabilities of competitors. Component businesses are evaluated in terms of their resource demands and their contribution to the whole. Performance shortfalls and portfolio gaps are spotlighted and remedial plans developed. General management takes an active, not passive, role in the planning effort.

However, for the business environment of the future, thinking strategically may not be enough. Only by managing strategically can a corporation reasonably assure its continued competitive viability, growth, and profitability. And it is being recognized that the next step in the evolution of corporate planning requires more than the matrix-based methodologies, by themselves, can offer. As so aptly put by one prominent corporate planner:

> Never has the need for planning and a better understanding of the futurity of current decisions been greater. Seldom has the penalty for the wrong decision been so severe. Seldom has there been a need for more intellectual value added in planning and less sterile methodology.[12]

For a corporation to begin to manage strategically, strategic planning and management must be welded into a single process. In addition, constructive and complementary changes must take place in other areas as well: organization, personnel policies, corporate culture and style. The process by which this transformation occurs and the final result will be different for every corporation, reflecting the unique needs and heritage of each. However, clearly evident in the behavior and decision-making of any strategically managed company must be four characteristics (Figure 1.5):

1. Widespread strategic thinking, reflecting and based upon an intimate knowledge of the business environment.
2. A pragmatic emphasis on strategy implementation as opposed to strategy development.
3. A supportive corporate organization and style.
4. An acknowledgement of the essential role of *competitive intelligence,* both as an input to the strategic thinking process and as a prerequisite for effective implementation.

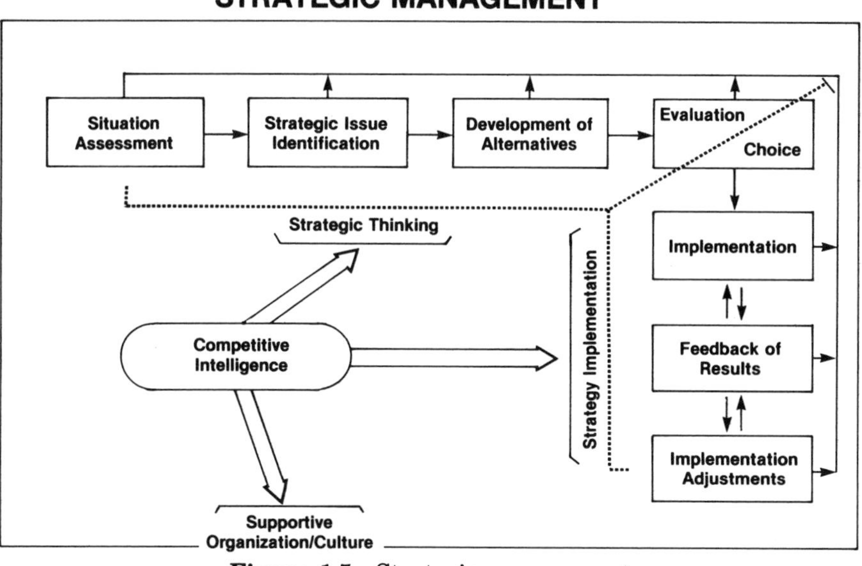

Figure 1.5 Strategic management

Strategic management's emphasis upon strategic thinking and effective strategy execution gives it a striking resemblance to another "game," chess. In that classic pastime, a similar premium is placed upon integrating insightful thought and timely, effective maneuver:

> A series of smart moves without some broader strategy will not finally win the game against a capable competition, and a grand design without a series of moves to achieve it remains but a twinkle in the loser's eye.[13]

Clearly, the degree of success experienced in either game is largely a function of how well one understands one's position relative to the competition and acts upon that knowledge.

COMPETITIVE INTELLIGENCE: ESSENTIAL FOR STRATEGIC MANAGEMENT

As indicated by Figure 1.5, competitive intelligence has a pervasive impact upon the strategic management process and is a prime determinant of the quality of both its inputs and outputs. The expanded scope and effectiveness that distinguishes strategic management from externally oriented planning reflects the contributions of competitive intelligence to:

1. The development and evaluation of strategic issues and alternatives.
2. The selection and implementation of key strategies.
3. The recognition of the need for and the design of mid-course implementation adjustments.
4. The nurturing of a supportive corporate organization and culture.

To the first two of these areas, competitive intelligence contributes in much the same way it does in externally oriented planning. Any differences are largely of degree; in strategic management the intelligence requirements are more stringent (both in quantity and quality) and the impact of intelligence is consequently greater.

The process of identifying and evaluating strategic issues and alternatives begins with a situation assessment or audit. The goal of this assessment is to provide operating management with the best possible understanding of itself and its competitive environment. In doing so, the corporation's own purposes and goals are first reaffirmed or clarified. Principal competitors are profiled, emphasizing their relative strengths and weaknesses, capabilities, and apparent intentions. In turn, these profiles and the dynamics of the market define the specific threats and opportunities with which the corporation must cope. Alternative strategies are proposed, with relentless attention given to the question: "Where and what do we want to be in the future?" Selection from among the various alternatives is based upon one principal criterion: the ability of each strategy to constructively alter the competitive situation, thereby magnifying the comparative advantage of the corporation. Management then moves aggressively to make its view of the future a reality, shaping rather than reacting to its environment. In sum, the total process is systematic, comprehensive, and integrated. Issues and alternatives are evaluated and strategies implemented through a judicious blending of competitive intelligence, strategic thought, and purposeful action.

The third area—mid-course implementation adjustments—demands advanced competitive intelligence capabilities, intimately linked to operations. Otherwise, any adjustments made might be neither timely nor effective. Defining and embarking upon a given strategic direction is one thing. Being able to monitor the impacts of that strategy and to fine-tune it while it unfolds is another. What is required is a repetitive "act-assess-react" capability, one with a short enough cycle time so that it is not—to use the cliche—"overtaken by events." An inefficient act-assess-react capability causes an organization to respond after the fact. Inaccurate or insensitive assessments compound the problem by making corrective actions not only tardy but off-target as well.

The reality is that only a strategically managed corporation can hope to exercise "real-time" control over strategy implementation. That level of effectiveness in implementation lies beyond the grasp of organizations practicing externally oriented planning. Being able to forge effective responses to unexpected opportunities on a continuing and systematic basis is the hallmark of a strategically managed company. That capability, in turn, is a function of its competitive intelligence system and how well operational management is conditioned to react to the stream of insights and information.

The role of competitive intelligence in nurturing a supportive organizational climate—the fourth area—is less obvious than its role in the first three areas, but is no less substantial or important.

Among the prerequisites for the success of any management system are internal acceptance and commitment. Coping with externally generated problems is difficult enough without additional distractions caused by internal conflict. Major contributors to a climate of harmony and teamwork are two factors: (1) a sense of shared purpose, based upon mission understanding and unfettered internal communications, and (2) a sense of shared accomplishment reinforced by repeated interaction. Unfortunately, in a large corporation functional boundaries and the decentralization of responsibilities tend to restrict communications and interactions. A fully functional competitive intelligence system assists in countering both of those centrifugal tendencies. The process of defining intelligence needs, collecting data, and disseminating information creates active and multiple channels of communications, both laterally between functions and horizontally between operating levels. Interactions become more frequent, increasing both the sense of organizational unity and the prospects for serendipitous insights that translate into commercial advantages.

Through its contributions to each of these four areas, competitive intelligence insures the vigor, within a strategically managed company, of each of the three mechanisms involved in the formulation and execution of effective strategy:

1. Systematic, comprehensive planning/implementation.
2. Effective responses to unexpected opportunities and problems.
3. Creative, entrepreneurial insights.

By doing so (Figure 1.6), competitive intelligence provides the essential underpinning for the crucial output of strategic management:

> an integrated set of actions aimed at increasing the long term well-being and strength of an enterprise relative to its competitors.[14]

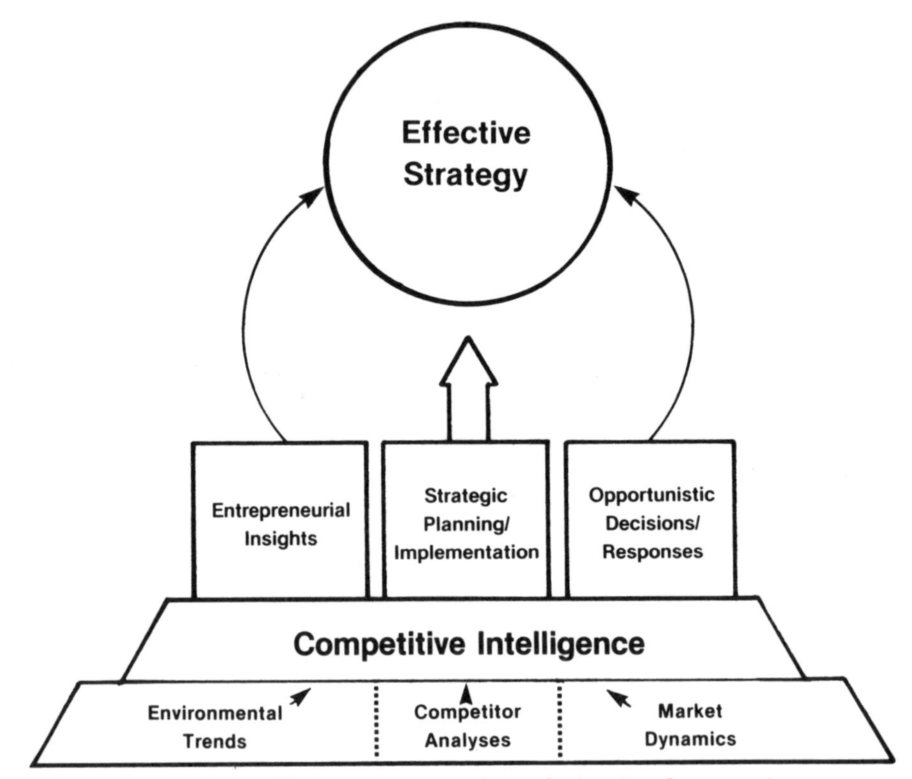

Figure 1.6 Effective strategy formulation/implementation

CONCLUSION

The focus of this chapter has been the relevance of competitive intelligence to corporate strategic planning and its evolution, both past and future. The chapter's title was its thesis: that competitive intelligence is the *sine qua non* of effective planning. In the military, it has long been recognized that:

> intelligence . . . and . . . operations are interdependent. . . . The degree of success achieved by any unit in accomplishing its mission will be directly affected by the intelligence which it develops and uses, and the manner in which it is used.[15]

Sun Tzu, writing in the 4th century BC, emphasized that meticulous planning, based upon sound intelligence, was the key to victory in war:

> Know the enemy and know yourself; in a hundred battles you will never be in peril. When you are ignorant of the enemy but know yourself, your chances of winning or losing are equal. If ignorant both of your enemy and of yourself, you are certain in every battle to be in peril.[16]

Modern military doctrine continues to emphasize "understand the enemy and the battlefield"[17] as fundamental to offense and defense. Intelligence is seen as a prerequisite for winning and is deemed a responsibility of all levels of command. Moreover, it is demanded that intelligence must be systematized, event-oriented, timely, and completely integrated with operations, with its focus being enemy capabilities, intentions, and probable actions.

The primacy of intelligence within the military reflects a very basic reality—in their "business," the competition is direct, the stakes are very high, and comparative advantage becomes critical to the outcome of any battle. Modern technology, by speeding up the pace of warfare and its lethality, has accentuated the need for quality intelligence and has put a premium on informed action.

It is, of course, a similar escalation in competition that is fueling the growing interest of American business in competitive intelligence. As you continue in this book, you might well ponder this sage and recent advice:

> By the modern rules of business, you must take business away from the competition to survive.
>
> In previous decades when most markets were expanding, many companies could sustain sales growth merely by maintaining constant mar-

ket share. But the 1980s are different. Many markets exhibit no growth, or are declining.

With softer markets comes intensified competition, companies eagerly eyeing each others' sales volume and customers to ensure their survival. *The law of the jungle has resurfaced, and those companies which do not anticipate and effectively plan for increasingly tough competition will become legitimate prey in the marketplace*[18] [Emphasis added.]

---

[1]"Primacy" and "pervasiveness" were terms used by Kootnz and O'Donnell to define, in part, the essential nature of planning. Harold Koontz and Cyril O'Donnell, *Management: A Systems and Contingency Analysis of Managerial Functions,* New York, McGraw-Hill, pp. 131–32.

[2]George Steiner, *Strategic Planning: What Every Manager Must Know,* New York, Free Press, 1979, p. 3.

[3]Peter F. Drucker, *Management: Tasks, Responsibilities, Practices,* New York, Harper & Row, 1974, p. 611.

[4]Steiner, p. 38.

[5]Walter Kiechel III, "Corporate Strategists Under Fire," *Fortune,* December 27, 1982, p. 34.

[6]The matrix representations (Figures 1.1 and 1.2) are adapted from Albert A. Fried, "Budgeting and the Strategic Planning Process," in H.W. Allen Sweeney and Robert Rachlin, *Handbook of Budgeting,* New York, Wiley, 1981, pp. 33, 45.

[7]Frederick W. Gluck, Stephen P. Kaufman, and A. Steven Walleck, "The Evolution of Strategic Management," Staff Paper, McKinsey & Company, October 1978, p. 3 (later published as: "Strategic Management for Competitive Advantage," *Harvard Business Review,* July–August 1980).

[8]Gluck et al., p. 11.

[9]Gluck et al., pp. 13–14.

[10]Kiechel, p. 36.

[11]Juergen Ladendorf (Norton Simon, Inc.), quoted by Walter Kiechel III, "Oh Where, Oh Where Has My Little Dog Gone? Or My Cash Cow? Or My Star?", *Fortune,* November 2, 1981, p. 149.

[12]James F. Lyons (United Technologies Corporation), "Strategic Management and Strategic Planning in the 1980s," in Kenneth J. Albert, ed., *The Strategic Management Handbook,* New York, McGraw-Hill, 1983, pp. 3–4.

[13]Boris Yavitz and William H. Newman, *Strategy In Action: The Execution, Politics, and Payoff of Business Planning,* New York, Free Press, 1982, p. 7.

[14]Gluck et al., p. 7.

[15]U.S. Army Field Manual 30–5 (October 1973), "Combat Intelligence," p. 2–13.

[16]Sun Tzu, in Samuel Griffith, ed., *Sun Tzu: The Art of War,* p. 37.

[17]U.S. Army Field Manual 100–5 (July 1976), "Operations," pp. 4–3, 5–2.

[18]Ian Gordon, "Competitive Intelligence: A Key To Marketplace Survival," *Industrial Marketing,* November 1982, p. 69.

2

Strategic Intelligence: An Analytical Resource for Decision Makers

WILLIAM L. SAMMON

William Sammon is in the Corporate Strategic Planning Department at Pfizer. His primary area of responsibility involves corporate planning issues and the analysis of corporate and business division competitors. From 1979 to 1982 he was with International Paper, where he helped develop a senior-level competitor intelligence program. His last position was manager of competitive analysis in International Paper's corporate planning department.

Mr. Sammon served on active duty in the U.S. Army from 1968 to 1979. A specialist in strategic and counter intelligence, he served in a number of field and staff assignments as a military intelligence officer in Vietnam and Washington, D.C. In his last assignment, from 1975–79, Mr. Sammon served as Assistant Professor of Public Policy and International Relations in the Department of Social Sciences, USMA, West Point. A Major in the Army Reserve, he holds a post as Visiting Professor of International Politics at West Point.

Mr. Sammon earned his B.A. in Political Science at Boston College, an M.A. in Social Sciences at the University of Chicago, and an M.B.A. in Finance at the University of Long Island.

This chapter introduces the concept of "intelligence" as a practical method to overcome a critical information shortfall in contemporary business strategies. To improve the strategic planning process by the addition of competitor analysis, relevant competitor intelligence is required. Competitor intelligence is presented as an organized and evaluated strategic information resource that supports detailed, systematic analyses of competitors' position, performance, and strategic threat.

Intelligence has long been valued and practiced by resourceful military and political leaders. For many, it has been the handmaiden of their strategic plans. To illustrate the historical use of intelligence as a strategic analytical resource, its development and application will be briefly traced through a number of classic military, political, and commercial examples.

The operational pressure cooker in which most general managers find themselves encourages a decision-making style that is direct, action-oriented, and focused on the most visible factors in the immediate competitive environment—for example, price moves by competitors, government regulatory decisions, customer purchase patterns, and competitor capacity investments. This essentially reactive and improvisational operating style usually results in intuitive, incremental decisions made with only a fragmentary base of knowledge about the complex external business environment.

From the broadest environmental scanning of global issues, to the detailed analysis of a competitor firm's strategic strengths and weaknesses, external information topics cover an extremely wide spectrum. Their complexity and scope is daunting. That is often why managers give the subject so little attention despite its potential significance. As Peter Drucker pointed out more than 20 years ago, "information overload" can have a particularly debilitating effect on a company's long-range planning capability:

> One way to summarize what is new and different in the process of entrepreneurial decision-making is in terms of information. The amount, diversity, and ambiguity of the information that is beating in on the decision-maker have all been increasing so much that the built-in experience reaction that a good manager has cannot handle it. He breaks down; and his breakdown will take either of the two forms known to any experimental psychologists. One is withdrawal from reality, i.e., "I know what I know and I only go by it; the rest is quite irrelevant and I won't even look at it." Or there is a feeling that the universe has become completely irrational so that one decision is as good as the other,

resulting in paralysis. We see both in executives who have to make decisions today. Neither is likely to result in rational or in successful decisions.[1]

The flow of competitive information within a corporation is often discontinuous and haphazard because the data is usually required on an ad hoc basis. For example, a firm considering a new plant might need comparative data on competing facilities in the immediate geographic region; a proposed acquisition may require an extensive background file on the target company; the launch of a new product line is normally preceded by exhaustive market research on customer attitudes towards competitor and/or substitute products; pricing decisions are rarely made without detailed field reports on competitor moves; the timing of a bond issue is normally based on a detailed analysis and projection of interest rates; R&D projects are often designed to exploit a known limitation in a competitor's product.

Those firms which do recognize the strategic value of competitive information on their external environment generally get that data in a remarkably casual and uncoordinated fashion. The rigorous disciplines that management brings to the organization, transmittal, and scrutiny of information about their company's internal operations (e.g., financial trends, product profitability, organizational structure, R&D programs, capital projects, facility plans) are noticeably lacking in the collection and review of available information about the external competitive environment.

One of the most crucial, but often least understood elements in a company's external environment is its competitors' strategies. Professor Michael E. Porter, author of the bestseller, *Competitive Strategy* (Free Press, New York, 1980), suggests why this analytical myopia is so widespread in business planning.

Planning Review: You talk about more consideration of competitor strategies than companies have ever done. How many companies out of 100 have ever thought about their competitors' strategies?

Michael E. Porter: I'd say the number of companies that have thought about strategy—at least that have uttered those words certainly among the larger companies, is a non-trivial percentage, about 50 percent or 60 percent. Out of

	100 companies, the number of companies that pushed the analysis of their competitors beyond the superficial level—thought systematically about the evolution of their industry and what's driving it—is close to zero. I can think of a few examples, but not many.
Planning Review:	What are the most common flaws of strategic planning systems? What is it that managers overlook most of the time?
Michael E. Porter:	I'd say one of the things would be they don't examine their competitors in any depth. They make a list of their strengths and weaknesses but don't really understand the motivations and their competitors' likely behavior. I see very few examples where that is done well.[2]

Yet few companies have tried to resolve this dilemma by either applying basic management principles to the gathering of competitive data or formalizing the function as a specialized service. There is some evidence that suggests that larger companies place greater organizational emphasis on the value of competitive information, and therefore are more inclined to devote the staff and funds necessary for its management. One of the few longitudinal surveys that measured executive attitudes on the importance of organized competitive information was made by the *Harvard Business Review* in 1959 and 1973.

It is interesting that the only discernable trend was a sizable increase in the percentage of respondents who said their company used sporadic reporting on an as-needed basis to gather competitor information.[3] This suggests that although the perceived need for systematic competitive information has increased, for the most part management continues to collect it in the customary informal, ad hoc, uncoordinated manner.

INTELLIGENCE—A SYSTEMATIC APPROACH TO COMPETITIVE INFORMATION

To resolve this problem by improving the management of competitive information tasks, a few corporations have begun to borrow and adapt intelligence techniques long used by the government and the military.

The basic theme of this book is that these borrowings, adaptations, and modifications of political and military intelligence methods by business firms is a natural extension of the corporate strategic planning process and a practical way to overcome one of its current analytical shortcomings.

Information is the medium of exchange in government. Thus it is not surprising that the concept of intelligence as a staff activity and a method of analysis is most fully developed in the political sector. Among the major powers, intelligence has become an elaborately developed organizational resource, serving political and military leaders with a steady stream of sophisticated analyses.

With some minor modifications, the time-tested, highly practical methods and procedures of governmental intelligence are easily adapted to the decision-making routines of most companies. Like political and military institutions, corporations are essentially complex organizations with definable strategic goals, the achievement of which is highly dependent upon a thorough understanding of the external environment—particularly the capabilities, behavior, and objectives of strategic peers, be they foreign nations, enemy armies, or business competitors.

INTELLIGENCE—ITS DEVELOPMENT AND USES

In one form or another the gathering of intelligence on opponents has been an integral part of most political, military, and commercial organizations throughout history. One of the first recognized efforts to delineate the principles of intelligence in statecraft was a perceptive, very reflective series of essays on *The Art of War* by a fourth century BC Chinese military theorist named Sun Tzu. Although Sun Tzu grandly overstates the efficacy of espionage,[4] he explains very clearly the value of intelligence to decision makers:

> Now the reason the enlightened prince and the wise general conquer the enemy whenever they move and their achievements surpass those of ordinary men is foreknowledge. What is called "foreknowledge" cannot be elicited from spirits, nor from goals, nor by analogy with past events nor from calculations [so much for econometrics]. It must be obtained from men who know the enemy situation.[5]

In the same manner that opportunity favors the prepared mind, so does "foreknowledge" favor and perhaps arm those with a talent for getting and then maintaining the initiative in competitive situations.

For example, in athletic competitions the coaches with the most wins are often those with the best scouts and the largest library of training films on opponent teams.

One of the most awesome strategic triumphs in military history was the Mongol's stunning invasion and conquest of Asia and Eastern Europe in the thirteenth century. The Mongols' unprecedented tactics and strategy masterfully combined concentrated firepower, maneuver, unity of command, economy of force, security, simplicity, mobility, and surprise into a military force of overwhelming organizational effectiveness.[6] The devastating style of warfare developed by the Mongols was also based on a remarkably coordinated system of operational intelligence that foreshadowed by 700 years the "blitzkreig" strategies of the 20th century. Under the leadership of illiterate military geniuses like Genghis Khan and his lieutenant, Subedei, the Mongols routinely swept opposing armies three and four times their size from the field of battle. According to Professor H. H. Ransom, a leading authority on contemporary intelligence organizations:

> The pattern of history suggests that aggressive, expansionist societies have the best organized intelligence systems. Foreknowledge is of primary importance to those who would seize the initiative in international affairs. It has been of equal importance to nations on the defensive, but often neglected by them.[7]

While it may seem bizzare to suggest that managers in the contemporary corporate world can learn something significant from the operational methods of thirteenth-century nomadic warriors, there is an even more valuable insight to be gleaned from the Mongols' application of intelligence to the planning and execution of strategy. As the following excerpt from the *Encyclopedia of Military History* points out, the rapid communication of enemy intelligence throughout their armies helped Mongol commanders to maintain both central control of their striking force and maximum local initiative by subgroups, thus overcoming the classic operational paradox which confronts leaders of all complex organizations:

> An essential element of Mongol planning was its intelligence system. Operations plans were always based on thorough study and evaluation of amazingly complete and accurate information. The Mongol intelligence network spread throughout the world; its thoroughness excelled all others of the Middle Ages. Spies generally operated under the guise of merchants or traders. Once the intelligence had been evaluated, lines

> of operation were decided upon in advance for the entire campaign and touman were assigned to follow these lines, each with its own objective. Nevertheless, the widest latitude was given to each subordinate commander in accomplishing the specific objective assigned to him. Prior to a general engagement a touman [largest independent unit] commander was at liberty to maneuver and to meet the enemy at his discretion, and was required only to maintain general conformance with the over-all plan. Orders and the exchange of combat intelligence information passed rapidly between the Khan's headquarters and his subordinate units by swift mounted couriers. Thus Genghis, to an extent rarely matched in history was able to assure complete unity of command at all levels and yet retain close personal control over the most extensive operations.[8]

This then is the larger organizational value of a coordinated intelligence system. Not only does it provide valuable foreknowledge about competitor actions, but it is also a communication and control mechanism managers can use to mobilize and direct their organization's resources in a more efficient manner.

INTELLIGENCE IN THE WEST

Europeans did not begin to approach the Eastern world's sophisticated use of intelligence until the late Renaissance, when nation-states began to replace the loosely organized feudal order. The more developed political systems of the period were the mercantile city-states of Italy and North Central Europe. Their practice of sending diplomats to foreign states to represent their political interests reflected a growing need for regular channels of communication, particularly those of an economic nature. In a haphazard way many of the early diplomats began to collect, codify, and pass "secret information" back to their political superiors. The Venetians were particularly adept at developing codes and ciphers to communicate sensitive political and economic information.

Another small but influential maritime power that also became a master in the use of diplomatic intelligence was England. Sir Frances Walsingham, Queen Elizabeth's Secretary of State, is generally credited with developing one of the most extensive and successful political intelligence systems of the period. While his methods of collecting information depended heavily on the use of spies (who reported not only on the activities of foreign diplomats but also on the veracity of dispatches from English ambassadors), Walsingham is also known for the highly analytical way in which he organized and carefully interpreted the field reports of his "secret service." Evidence of Walsingham's systematic methods are reflected in an operational plan he drew up in 1587 to orchestrate the collection of information by English agents on the developing Spanish Armada which constituted a serious strategic threat to England. Entitled the "Plot for Intelligence Out of Spain," this remarkable document identifies the key sources of information and then lays out an involved network of agents to gather it.[9] Walsingham's collection plan gave England's political and military leaders extensive details and valuable foreknowledge about the Spanish Armada's capabilities and intentions. This intelligence contributed to the decisive defeat of the Armada the following year.

During the seventeenth century, France's Cardinal Richelieu, and Oliver Cromwell's Secretary of State, John Thurbe, developed elaborate networks of secret agents to supplement their aggressive diplomacy. Thurbe's and Richelieu's intelligence networks lacked, however, the systematic organization and emphasis on analysis that distinguished Walsingham's operations. Two of the leading commercial nations of the period, the Kingdom of Sweden and the Dutch Republic, also developed relatively sophisticated intelligence systems based upon extensive and accurate reporting by diplomats and secret agents. As the former chief of the CIA, Allen Dulles, notes in his survey of the history of intelligence, the Swedish and Dutch systems "illustrate how relatively small countries can make up for many power deficiencies with superior intelligence combined with technical and organizational ingenuity."[10]

THE FUGGERS AND THE ROTHSCHILDS—EARLY COMMERCIAL INTELLIGENCE

While the incipient development of political intelligence systems in the West is usually attributed to the growing sophistication of international diplomacy, another force at work was the rapid growth of international commerce. At roughly the same time that Western political systems were consolidating into geographically defined nation-states, commerce was expanding outwards far beyond the narrow geographical confines of the Medieval guilds and the merchant city states. Mercantilism and its latter offspring, capitalism, gave an economic form to the new expansionary dynamics that transformed European commerce into a powerful international force. The European transformation of world politics in the post-Medieval period was thus due in large measure to the Europeans' ability to ride and in some ways shape a rising tide of international commerce.[11]

The emergence of international trading houses, joint ventures, and holding companies to exploit the wealth of the New World, coupled with the rise of international banking as a legitimate institution serving the financial needs of Europe's political and economic elite, created a powerful need for accurate information about distant places, persons, and institutions. These commercial trends gave rise to a nonpolitical form of intelligence that paralleled and in some ways exceeded the quality of the spy-based diplomatic intelligence favored by European statesmen.

One of Europe's first international banking houses was founded in the late fourteenth century by the south German House of Fugger. After amassing a large fortune in textile manufacturing, the Fuggers quickly acquired one of the largest and most lucrative holdings in silver, copper, and iron mining in Central Europe. They achieved this powerful economic base by providing capital to their Hapsburg patrons in return for special economic mining monopolies. Under Emperor Charles V, the Fuggers (who supported his election as Holy Roman Emperor in 1519 with a loan of 500,000 florins) became the private bankers of the powerful Hapsburg Court, a position they skillfully used to consolidate their preeminence in international finance. While the Fuggers's formative role in developing Europe's first modern system of international banking is generally known, their equally influential role in developing one of modern Europe's first forms of commercial intelligence is not. To keep the numerous branches of their far-flung operations current on important matters, the Fuggers of Augsburg developed one of the first "manuscript newsletters." Filled with columns of political and commercial information that would influence the bank's important financial decisions, it was a private commercial intelligence report that equaled and probably exceeded the scope and accuracy of comparable diplomatic intelligence reports. Available to selected outsiders, particularly those with important political connections, the Fugger newletters were widely imitated by other, emerging international trading houses, and to some extent became the prototypes of public newspapers.[12]

A later example of the systematic collection and rapid transmittal of highly reliable commercial intelligence is also associated with one of Europe's great merchant banking houses, the Rothschilds. The "five brothers" conducted the bank's transactions jointly from the five branches set up across Europe to coordinate the growth of the House of Rothschild. As the preeminent bankers to Europe's political elite in the late eighteenth and early nineteenth centuries, the Rothschilds developed an informal but highly efficient network of commercial and political intelligence equalled by few governments of the period. Nathan Rothschild established the bank's London branch in 1804 and adroitly used the family's financial connections and extensive intelligence to prop up both British trade and Wellington's troops during the darkest days of the Napoleonic Wars.[13]

The Rothschilds were also instrumental in providing timely financial assistance to Britain's Continental allies. This complex aspect of Britain's economic war against Napoleon required thorough intelligence from the continent. Nathan Rothschild seems to have been the ablest of financial geniuses, and became the favorite intermediary of the British government in its financial relations with foreign powers; it was he or his agents who transmitted from England to Austria and Prussia the subsidies that enabled them to fight Napoleon. As Allen Dulles points out in his retelling of a famous anecdote about the Rothschilds, Nathan also knew how to use the family's unparalleled "inside information" to advance the bank's commercial interests:

> In promoting their employers' financial interests from headquarters in Frankfurt-am-Main, London, Paris, Vienna and Naples, Rothschild agents were often able to gain vital intelligence before governments did. In 1815, while Europe awaited news of the Battle of Waterloo, Nathan Rothschild in London already knew that the British had been victorious. In order to make a financial killing, he then depressed the market by selling British Government securities; those who watched his every move in the market did likewise, concluding that Waterloo had been lost by the British and their allies. At the proper moment he bought back in at the low, and when the news was finally generally known, the value of government securities naturally soared.[14]

PRUSSIA AND NAPOLEON: MILITARIZED INTELLIGENCE

One of the reasons governments occasionally turned to businessmen like the Rothschilds for commercial and political intelligence was the narrowing focus of the intelligence collected by political ministries. During the eighteenth and nineteenth centuries governmental intelligence became fixed on two subjects: the strength of foreign armies and the activities of secret political agents. For all essential purposes, the major theme of governmental intelligence became military intelligence and its minor theme was internal security. Intelligence, which had been the useful handmaiden of the broad-gauged diplomats and political leaders of the sixteenth and seventeenth centuries, gradually became the special preserve of the professional soldier and the secret police.

Prussia's soldier-king, Frederick the Great (1712–86), was one of the first European leaders to create a specialized staff to collect and analyze foreign military intelligence. Surrounded and often isolated by the large standing armies of hostile nations like France, Austria, and Russia, it is not surprising that the Prussian leader placed such a high priority on the military aspects of intelligence. The key intelligence tasks were an accurate assessment of the enemy's order of battle, the degree of assistance expected from an enemy's allies, and topographic details of the region in which the next campaign would be waged. Like Sun Tzu, Frederick relied primarily on spies to collect the field information his military officers would turn into usable intelligence.

Napoleon never appreciated the value of the nonmilitary strategic intelligence that the Rothschilds mastered, and thus his empire was vulnerable to it. Ever the decisive commander of action and one of history's most brilliant tacticians, Napoleon was also an innovative strategist. But the intelligence he sought reflected his focus on the devastating tactical stroke. The extensive intelligence he factored into his war plans came from two traditional, narrowly focused, but reasonably efficient sources: spies and cavalry reconnaissance. As the destruction of his enemies armies was the prime objective of his tactics and strategy, that of course was the subject of his intelligence, often to the exclusion of vital nonmilitary issues. Napoleon was a master at developing detailed order of battle intelligence, that is, data on the identification of enemy units, estimates of their strength, desposition of units, details about their command structure, analytical profiles of the enemy commander, and details about personnel, units, and equipment.

The efficient French espionage system run by General Savary collected everything from rumors about enemy movements to foreign newspapers and secret dispatches when possible. From his hard-riding cavalry patrols that were constantly screening and reconnoitering the enemy's field forces, Napoleon received a steady stream of intelligence reports on enemy movements and dispositions. A preliminary review and synthesis of the enemy information flowing in from the cavalry reconnaissance was carried out by Napoleon's Chief of Staff, Marshal

Berthier, who "evaluated it, gleaned the useful from the useless and passed it on, along with a sampling of whatever other information had become available".[15] Then Napoleon himself went to work. David Chandler describes Napoleon's intelligence method:

> First of all the Emperor would accumulate as much information about the forces facing him from captured newspapers, deserters and most especially from the indication brought in by his probing cavalry patrols. From the data thus provided, he would carefully plot the known despositions of his foes on the map, and then select the place where their respective Army boundaries converged. This was the "hinge" or "joint" of the enemy's strategic dispositions, and as such was vulnerable to attack. This point would be selected by Napoleon for his initial *blitzkreig* attack carried as often as not in full strength. Shielded by the cavalry screen, the French army would perform a crash concentration and fall like a thunderbolt on the handful of troops defending the central point. Invariably the initial onslaught would be successful. Immediately after Napoleon had massed his army at this newly captured point, he was master of the "central position"—that is to say, he had successfully interposed his concentrated army between the forces of his enemies, who, ideally, would have staggered back under the impact of the surprise blow in such a way as to increase the distance between their respective armies. This would inevitably mean that the foe would have to operate on "exterior lines" (i.e., have greater distances to march from one flank to the other) while the better-positioned French would have a shorter distance to travel to reach either enemy.[16]

CLAUSEWITZ ON INTELLIGENCE

After Napoleon's demise, the Prussians carried the Corsican's obsession with battle intelligence to a much higher degree of organization and systematization. Whereas Frederick The Great was primarily concerned with its collection, Karl Von Clausewitz (1780–1831) fretted over its interpretation by the harried commander. He feared that an avalanche of conflicting reports—the majority of which, he claimed, are usually false—would immobilize the commander, thus undermining the will to act.

Karl Von Clausewitz was a minor Prussian general who served his country in a number of Napoleonic campaigns. He was a competent officer whose military career was not exceptional. However, like his celebrated countryman, Frederick the Great, Clausewitz did have a formative influence on the strategic thinking of the Prussian military establishment that emerged from the Napoleonic ruins. The radical reforms instituted in the Prussian army during the Napoleonic period and further developed throughout the remainder of the nineteenth century are significant to the West because they introduced the organizational forms and professional standards that have since become (with some salutary modifications) the hallmarks of the twentieth century's professional military. Clausewitz's influence is due largely to his writings, in which he systematically sought to understand and explain the nature of war, politics, and the concept that connects them—strategy. In his seminal work *On War* (1832), Clausewitz repeatedly stresses the "friction" of war, the large and small obstacles that are usually unforeseen and that make the execution of strategy a very chancy thing. Friction greatly multiplies the inherent uncertainty that confronts all strategists and makes a mockery of those plans predicated on the precise orchestration of organizations and material. War's inevitable friction and uncertainty can never be eliminated, Clausewitz advises, but the successful commander can overcome these obstacles primarily through an intuition born of seasoned professional experience coupled with a strong personal will to win. Clausewitz thus has little to say about the collection of intelligence, but rather emphasizes the problem the strategists or commander faces in interpreting it:

> Imperfect knowledge of the situation is another cause for suspension of military action. No commander has accurate knowledge of any position but his own; his adversary's is known to him only through uncertain reports. Through mistakes in his judgment of these reports, a commander can believe that the initiative lies with his opponent when it really lies with himself.[17]

As Clausewitz saw it, the commander ultimately had to rely on his own experience and judgment when interpreting the conflicting intelligence reports generated by his staff. In short, it was up to each commander to make the final interpretation of the reported intelligence:

> War is the province of uncertainty. A fine and penetrating intellect is thus required to feel out the truth with instinctive judgment. . . . A great

> part of the information in war is contradictory, a still greater part is false, and by far the greatest part is somewhat doubtful. This requires that an officer possess a certain power of discrimination, which only knowledge of men and things and good judgment can give. The law of probability must be his guide. This is difficult even in the pre-war plans, which are made in the study and outside the actual sphere of war. It is enormously more difficult when, in the turmoil of war, one report follows hard upon another. It is fortunate if these reports, in contradicting each other, produce a sort of balance and thus demand further examination.[18]

Had Frederick and his military caste been less ignorant and contemptuous of the rising middle classes, perhaps they would have appreciated the vantage points available to international merchants like the Rothschilds, and thus incorporated information from commercial circles into their government's foreign intelligence. However, the Prussian's militarized approach to foreign intelligence became the dominant model for both the organization and analysis of political intelligence, particularly on the continent, where the forces of nationalism brought forth a kaleidoscope of complex political alliances and military plans.

In terms of sheer activity governmental intelligence was practiced on an unprecedented scale in the nineteenth and early twentieth centuries by most European powers. However, the narrow military focus of the typical state intelligence service of the period caused other equally important political subjects such as economic growth, domestic politics, cultural values, and diplomatic relations, to be dangerously deemphazised in both the collection and interpretation of foreign intelligence. Ironically the larger the intelligence bureaucracies grew, the more obsessed they became with matters military, and thus contributed to the poltical myopia of their governments' leaders:

> Intelligence bureaus blossomed in Europe, and their heavy investment in espionage efforts provoked great counterintelligence activity. By the eve of World War I, Europe was covered by a complex network of espionage and counterintelligence. Much of this was military rather than political intelligence activity. Most European nations developed a single military intelligence agency, which became the principle foreign intelligence arm. Even so, the available evidence suggests that the leaders of the Great Powers entered the war with inefficient intelligence bureaus. Not a single strategic action in war was decisively influenced by any of the military espionage services.[19]

CONTEMPORARY GOVERNMENTAL INTELLIGENCE—A BROADER ANALYTICAL FOCUS

If the intelligence services of the European political powers were ineffectual and narrowly focused in 1914, by 1939, on the eve of another World War, they had become the prototypes of the powerful information collection and analysis organizations that exist today. Although both the Allies and the Axis experienced significant intelligence failures during World War II (with those of the Axis being far more serious), the highly sophisticated, broad-based intelligence agencies that served the military and political leaders of both sides were relatively efficient, large-scale bureaucracies capable of collecting and integrating a wide range of technical, scientific, military, economic, cultural, and political data. The rapid growth and success of these new intelligence forces precipitated an equally unprecedented expansion and development of counterintelligence services. These were "defensive" intelligence *security* departments whose job it was to counter the efforts by hostile powers to use offensive intelligence to collect various types of sensitive information (a large portion of which was secret) about the target country's capabilities, resources, and plans.

Contrary to popular images, it was not the spy who raised the concept and organization of political intelligence to a new level of success and sophistication in World War II. It was rather the path-breaking work of the remarkably talented and complex analytical sections that made the difference between the antique and the contemporary style of governmental intelligence. Intelligence that had, until World War II, been synonymous with the narrow focus and romantic tradition of the espionage agent, furtively seeking that critical item of clandestine information upon which the war would turn (and of course never did in reality), now became an unparalleled information resource produced by legions of analysts covering the full spectrum of political, economic, scientific, military, and cultural knowledge.

In the United States, a new staff organization, the Office of Strategic Services (OSS), was created in 1942 to coordinate the nation's strategic intelligence efforts. Its charter was restrictive and while the OSS became a vital intelligence agency in the war effort it did not have responsibility for the vast operational and tactical intelligence staffs that served the military forces. Nor did it become involved in domestic counterintelligence—the special preserve of the FBI. What is most significant about the OSS, aside from the fact that it became the organizational nucleus for its postwar successor, the Central Intelligence Agency, is the important organizational role it played in first fostering and then developing new methods of research and analysis that greatly expanded the scope and utility of strategic intelligence to the nation's war planning.[20]

In his excellent analysis of the development of the contemporary U.S. "Intelligence Establishment," Professor Harry Howe Ransom sums up the OSS's most significant but least recognized contribution in World War II:

> The popular heroes of the wartime OSS—those who play the major roles in motion pictures and in television scripts about OSS—are the secret agents who worked behind enemy lines, or the secret operatives whose function was essentially sabotage or counterespionage. But perhaps the most significant work was done by those unheralded college professors, lawyers and others who worked tirelessly in the research units, in the analysis of economic objectives, and in other operational analysis and technical groups within OSS. These groups contributed much information on which successful wartime operations were based, and developed techniques useful to contemporary intelligence research and analysis. Probably these analysts played a more significant role than the estimated 1,600 Americans who were infiltrated by OSS behind enemy-held territory. . . .
>
> The primary point to be made about the impact of OSS government intelligence is that it brought recognition that scholars and the best scholarly technique have a fundamental role in uncovering facts required for material decision.[21]

CONCLUSION

In World War II intelligence came of age. As we have seen, the strategic focus changed dramatically. All crucial aspects of the strategic environment—economic as well as military, sociological, political, geographic, and cultural, the technology of weaponry and the technology of mass production—all these and more came under close systematic research and analysis by intelligence specialists and generalists. The tools of their trade were an inquisitive instinct, an appetite for obscure kinds of information, an extensive but well-thumbed set of files, an ability to read between the lines, a critical and reflective intellect, and an aptitude for making reasoned guesses about large subjects from a limited base of knowledge. Political and military strategy was not always better because of this new "analytical" form of intelligence, but strategy became impossible without it.

For the world, the strategic environment and the ponderous but powerful military and political organizations that intelligence served had become too complex. A new form of intelligence—broader in focus and far more analytical in content—emerged. It included but went beyond espionage, and in so doing, made the office-bound analyst an influential player in policy circles. These new intelligence bureaucracies can never guarantee superior strategy, but if properly used,[22] they at least increase the probability of *informed* strategies.

In the 1950s, the business world discovered the concept of strategy; in the 1960s, some corporations experimented with strategic planning; by the 1970s, most large corporations were actively involved in it in one fashion or another; and by the 1980s, many were wondering why it worked so poorly. Part of the answer may be that strategy without intelligence has become a contradiction in terms. Like their military and political counterparts, business organizations have belatedly discovered the practical value of intelligence to their strategies in an increasingly complex and competitive world where the margin for error is fast disappearing. However, some managers and executives continue to confuse intelligence with espionage, and that is the subject of the following chapter.

---

[1]Peter F. Drucker, "Long-Range Planning: Challenge to Management," *Management Science,* April 1959, pp. 242–44.

[2]M.W. Pennington and S. M. Cohen, "Michael E. Porter Speaks on Strategy," *Planning Review,* January 1982, pp. 8–11, reprinted with permission. Published by Robert J. Allio & Associates, Inc. for the North American Society for Corporate Planning, copyright 1982.

[3]Jerry L. Wall, "Probing Opinions: A Survey of Executives' Attitudes, Practices, and Ethics vis-á-vis Espionage and Other Forms of Information Gathering," *Harvard Business Review,* November–December, 1974, pp. 23–25.

[4]Espionage does not equal intelligence, as will be explained further on, espionage is the surreptious/illegal collection of information, usually by secret agents, i.e., spies.

[5]Samuel B. Griffith translator, *Sun Tzu: The Art of War,* New York, Oxford University Press, 1963, p. 143.

[6]James Chambers, *The Devil's Horsemen: The Mongol Invasion of Europe,* New York, Atheneum, 1979.

[7]Harry Howe Ransom, *The Intelligence Establishment,* Cambridge, Massachusetts, Harvard University Press, 1970, p. 49.

[8]R. E. Dupuy and T. W. Dupuy, *The Encyclopedia of Military History,* New York, Harper and Row, 1970, p. 343.

[9]Richard Deacon, *A History of the British Secret Service, New York, Taplinger, 1969, p. 20.*

[10]Allen W. Dulles, *The Craft of Intelligence,* New York, New American Library, 1965, p. 21.

[11]William H. McNeil, *The Rise of the West,* Chicago, University of Chicago Press, 1963.

[12]George Unwin and Phillip Unwin, "The History of Publishing," in *Encyclopedia Britannica,* Macropedia vol. 15, 1976, p. 236.

[13]Georges Lefebvre, *Napoleon, From Tilsit to Waterloo,* New York, Columbia University Press, 1969, p. 132; Will and Ariel Durant, *The Story of Civilization: Part XI—The Age of Napoleon,* New York, Simon & Schuster, 1975, p. 361.

[14]Dulles, p. 24.

[15]Albert Nofi, "Napoleon at War," *Strategy and Tactics,* May, 1972, p. 10.

[16]David Chandler, *The Campaigns of Napoleon,* New York, Macmillan, 1966, p. 170.

[17]Karl Von Clausewitz, *War, Politics, and Power: Selections from 'On War' and 'I Believe and Profess,'* translated and edited by E. M. Collins, Chicago, Henry Regnery, 1962, p. 77.

[18]Von Clausewitz, p. 117, 128–129.

[19]Harry Howe Ransom, "Intelligence Political and Military," *International Encyclopedia of the Social Sciences,* vol. 7, 1964, MacMillan, pp. 415–21.

[20]Roger Hilsman, Jr. *Strategic Intelligence and National Defense,* Glencoe, Illinois, Free Press, 1958, p. 211.

[21]Harry Howe Ransom, *The Intelligence Establishment,* Cambridge, Massachusetts, Harvard University Press, 1977, p. 73.

[22]A complex policy issue in its own right; see Ransom, *The Intelligence Establishment,* and Hilsman, *Strategic Intelligence and National Defense.*

3

Competitor Intelligence or Industrial Espionage?

WILLIAM L. SAMMON

Biographical data for this chapter author appear on page 21.

It is vital that the distinction between intelligence as a systematic way to collect, analyze, and disseminate strategic information about one's opponents, and intelligence as espionage—the clandestine collection of secret or proprietary information—be clearly understood. For although espionage is one element, albeit a secondary one, of governmental intelligence methods, it cannot (as the reader will see in Chapter 14) be a legal part of any American corporation's competitor intelligence programs. Therefore, what is useful and most transferable to the planning and decision-making system of contemporary corporations are the organizational principles, the *overt* collection techniques, the analytical methods, and the dissemination formats that are the institutional core of the modern state's strategic intelligence agencies.

INTELLIGENCE AND ESPIONAGE

Aside from the legal prohibition, there is a sound practical and analytical reason why corporate managers should make certain that clandestine methods are excluded from their companies' intelligence systems. Espionage is far too romantic and costly for the minimal return it makes. Because of its glamorous and sinister psychological appeal, espionage can easily grab the favorable attention of some unscrupulous managers and corporate decision-makers, thereby diverting attention and resources from the prosaic but ultimately more critical work of overt intelligence collection and analysis. One of the U.S. Navy's senior intelligence analysts in World War II, Captain Ellis M. Zacharias, summed up the nature of this peculiar dilemma that confronts all intelligence organizations. In peacetime, he said, the Navy derived its information from three types of sources in these proportions:

95 percent from public sources.
4 percent through semipublic sources.
1 percent or less from secret sources.

Zacharias, a seasoned professional, put clandestine intelligence in its proper place when he wrote "There is very little these confidential agents can tell that is not accessible to an alert analyst who knows what he is looking for and knows how to find it in open sources".[1]

INDUSTRIAL ESPIONAGE: THE IBM–HITACHI CASE

In recent years the American business community has rediscovered the old specter of industrial espionage, which many have wrongly concluded is the same thing as business intelligence and a new phenomenon. The startling arrest and indictment of executives from Mitsubishi and Hitachi (two leading Japanese electronics corporations) by the FBI in July 1982 on the accusation—supported by videotape evidence—that they had conspired to steal and transport to Japan trade secrets belonging to IBM, was a dramatic reminder of the ever-present threat of industrial espionage.[2]

The high drama of these and other prominent industrial espionage cases obscures the more significant intelligence successes achieved by Japanese and other foreign corporations (and a few American ones) through the systematic harvesting of legal, overt competitor information programs. As *Business Week* noted in a December 1981 article on Japanese industry, a number of large Japanese firms have developed some of the more sophisticated commercial intelligence programs in the modern business world:

The Business Intelligence Beehive

Japan's phenomenally rapid progress in high technology is due in no small measure to highly effective intelligence gathering. The Japanese are so much more proficient than Americans at collecting business intelligence that some U.S. executives are convinced there must be a CIA-type organization behind it all, probably Japan's Ministry of International Trade & Industry (MITI).

"It's very similar to the way the CIA is set up," asserts John D. Shea, president of Technology Analysis Group Inc. (TAG), a San Jose (Calif.) company that does technology forecasting for the Defense Dept. and major corporations. "The Japanese have people gathering data and sending the data back to a central clearing operation run by MITI and Jetro." Jetro—the Japan External Trade Organization—is a MITI subsidiary with 80 offices around the world, including nine in the U.S.; it was established in 1958 to promote trade and now concentrates on increasing imports into Japan.

'An Anthill.' More and more U.S. businessmen are coming to view such indictments as oversimplistic reactions, however. The plain fact is that the Japanese are doing a superb job of market research and technology tracking. Instead of resenting Japan's success, the U.S. would be better advised, they contend, to improve its own operations.

"The Japanese have a much better intelligence-gathering operation than Jetro," says Paul H. Aron, executive vice-president of Daiwa Securities America Inc. "It's a company called Mitsubishi—and Mitsui and Sumitomo and Marubeni." The Pan Am Building in New York is "an anthill of intelligence activity," according to an American who visits it often. Mitsubishi International Corp., for example, occupies two floors and has a small army of people screening technical magazines and contacting companies for brochures and other materials. "The firms do their own microfilming and a lot of preliminary indexing," he notes, "then definitive indexing is done back in Japan."

A computer company executive who lived in Tokyo reports that after contact with a foreigner, "all Japanese go through debriefing sessions. The information they've gathered is put down" and analyzed. Interesting data are then published and circulated freely among companies, often grouped with digests of related articles in U.S. technical magazines or reports on technical conferences. "They've made a science of it," he sums up.

The Payoff. For example, executives of U.S. high-tech companies figure that intelligence gleanings made major contributions to the VLSI program. That $280 million, four-year project, coordinated by MITI and funded with $140 million of government money, was designed to raise Japan at least to a par with the U.S. in very large-scale integrated (VLSI) circuits, the next generation of semiconductors. "Our estimate," says Shea of TAG, "is that intelligence operations provided at least 35% to 40% of the base-line data on which they were able to extrapolate and achieve what they did" by 1979. Other estimates range up to twice that level.

In the next stage—applying VLSI techniques to produce a so-called fifth-generation computer by 1990—Shea believes that "information from the West very definitely will support [the program] on a grand scale." To implement VLSI hardware, he explains, "the driving factor will be software," an area in which Japan clearly lags behind the U.S.

Closing the software gap is now the main thrust of Japan's activities in Silicon Valley, says Shea. "For three years they've been staffing listening posts here with software engineers and hiring American software guys." Shea figures that Japanese companies have deployed 1,500 software experts in the U.S., supported by a collective budget of $25 million to $30 million a year.

Except for rare cases of outright bribery, none of these practices is illegal or even unethical. What really piques U.S. executives is the pronounced imbalance in the flow of information: The U.S. is just not doing its homework in Japan. One rough index of the scope of the Japanese presence in the U.S.: In the Justice Dept. report on registered foreign agents, Japanese agents fill 44 pages. In contrast, the lists of British

> and West German agents run 23 and 17 pages. "By comparison," laments Aron of Daiwa Securities, "American industrial intelligence in Japan is nothing."[3]

The systematic surveillance of published information coupled with the aggressive collection of competitor data through extensive field interviews, reverse engineering of products, facility site inspections, and the careful development of customer and supplier contacts, have given Japanese firms a number of intelligence coups in Silicon Valley—the Dodge City of high-tech commercial intelligence. But as the IBM trade secrets case indicates, the Japanese firms' enormous appetite for technical and product-related competitor information has led some companies to use information-collection techniques that border on and occasionally drift into the illegal realm of industrial espionage. Although the resort to such illegal measures—bribery, "special consultant fees" to a competitor's ex-employees for inside information, and the hiring of third parties to obtain a competitor's proprietary data—may reflect the extraordinarily high value placed on the desired intelligence, covert collection methods risk the reputation of the companies that use them. They also work to undermine the legal, overt intelligence programs that are the major sources of usable competitor information. For when an industrial espionage attempt is brought to court and publicized, it sends shock waves through the targeted companies, heightens management's security fears, and usually closes off valuable overt sources of competitor information.

According to a 1978 *Fortune* article that profiled Japanese corporations' intelligence activities in Silicon Valley, "liaison offices" are set up to collect and analyze publicly available information about American electronics firms. However, as their collection methods became more aggressive, these liaison offices begin to draw unfavorable attention, raising accusations of industrial espionage and triggering lawsuits.

> The liaison offices are thinly disguised listening posts staffed by experts including designers of semiconductor circuits, who engage in a complex intelligence gathering effort as thoroughly organized as a military operation. A lot of the information gathering, of course, is above board, such as attending conferences, courses and exhibits. The liaison offices also commission technical and market studies from local data houses.
>
> But some activities of the liaison offices enrage U.S. executives in the semiconductor industry. For example, the liaison men cultivate secret personal contacts within local companies. . . .

> The liaison offices track executives and engineers between jobs as assiduously as intelligence agents watch the movements of an adversary's military personnel. The Japanese have quite a pool to choose from because semiconductor-company employees have a habit of keeping on the move. Job turnovers in the valley run about 15 to 20% a year, according to industry estimates, and as a result, trade secrets don't stay secret very long.
>
> Once they spot a knowledgeable individual the Japanese tempt him with offers of generous consulting fees. For short-term "consultations," which are really attempts to pump dry a source of knowledge about the company he has worked for, the Japanese pay $500 a day. For longer "consultations," the fees have gone as high as $60,000 to a single person.[4]

The *Fortune* article goes on to note that the Japanese firms that staff and fund these listening posts are "anxious to maintain the appearance of legality" even while their more zealous agents are pressing the law to and in some instances beyond its limits. Not surprisingly, the initial defense advanced by Hitachi when their employees were arrested by the FBI in June 1982 for illegally acquiring IBM trade secrets, was that they were unwittingly misled by the consulting firm hired to collect industry information. Shortly after the arrests, the director of Hitachi's computer division, Mr. Hatano, told the press that his firm was simply buying information about the industry, as all companies routinely do. And that although Hitachi engineers had never confirmed the sources of their information, he said, "We have blindly trusted that the supplier obtained the information legally. Now we think we have been silly."[5]

According to the FBI affidavit, their undercover agents posing as electronics-industry technology consultants repeatedly warned the Hitachi representatives that the IBM data Hitachi wanted could not be obtained through legal means. When pressed by reporters on this point, Hatano said that "none of [Hitachi's] employees really thought the information was coming from an illegal source. . . . The people they were dealing with were supposed to be respectable."[6] Hatano also claimed that the Hitachi employees believed that the consultants' warnings about having to use illegal clandestine techniques to collect the IBM data were just a standard ruse used by many consultants in the industry to jack up their fees.

It was an interesting but not a completely persuasive explanation. Companies that hire consulting firms to collect information and/or carry out market research on competitors can safeguard themselves against the illegal espionage methods these consultants may employ by inserting a clause in their contract which reads as follows:

> The undersigned in agreeing to serve Company X as a private research firm for the purposes of collecting industry, market product, and/or competitor-related information, certifies and affirms that all information collected and passed on to Company X has been obtained legally and is publicly available nonproprietary information.

The absence of a contract including such a clause is at best irresponsible and at worst an indirect encouragement of illegal information-gathering. Given the inherently sensitive nature of all competitor intelligence activities, when a firm hires a consultant to collect competitor-related data, "gentlemen's agreements" that assume the use only of legal, overt collection methods are disingenuous.

On September 16, 1982, IBM sued Hitachi, its American partner—National Advanced Systems, the computer subsidiary of National Semiconductor Corporation—and 16 individuals for damages arising out of the alleged theft of its trade secrets and for violation of the Racketeer Influenced and Corrupt Organizations Act.[7] Many of those named in the civil suit were facing federal charges of industrial espionage based on the FBI investigation and arrests announced the previous June.

IBM, which is extremely aggressive in defending its proprietary information despite the costly and risky litigation this usually involves, said the suit was initiated because it was unable to reach a satisfactory out-of-court settlement with Hitachi and National Semiconductor. Executives of National Semiconductor denounced IBM's action, claiming that IBM was not truly interested in trying to negotiate a settlement before filing its lawsuit. The president of National Semiconductor saw an ulterior motive in IBM's eagerness to drag the case into Federal Court. "I.B.M.," he said, "must feel it's been less able to hold its own (in the market) over the past few years and is now attempting to use its obvious legal strength to remedy that."[8]

In the suit, filed in San Francisco in U.S. Federal Court, IBM requested that:

- A court order be issued prohibiting the defendants from using any of the confidential IBM material they were alleged to have stolen.
- IBM be awarded an unspecified amount of damages from the defendants and that the amount be trebled.
- The defendants be assessed punitive damages by the court.
- The defendants be required to pay IBM's legal fees.
- A special master be appointed by the court to enforce its decision.[9]

In its statement to the court, IBM explained that in August, 1981 its own security investigation confirmed a suspicion that Hitachi had obtained confidential IBM documents (later identified in the course of the undercover FBI operation as ten secret design manuals for IBM's largest computer models).

IBM first learned of Hitachi's possible espionage from Palyn Associates, a market research consulting firm staffed by former IBM employees. Since the early 1970s, Hitachi had been one of Palyn's major clients. In the summer of 1981, Hitachi's representative, Kenji Hayashi, turned down Palyn's latest study of IBM's new 3081 computers, explaining that his company already had internal IBM documents (workbooks and manuals) detailing the material reviewed in Palyn's new research report. Much to the amazement of Palyn's management, Hayashi then sent the research firm a confidential telex in which he offered to buy any additional IBM 3081 technical manuals Palyn could obtain.[10]

Suspecting that Hitachi had illegally obtained confidential IBM data, Palyn Associates tipped off IBM's management. IBM quickly mounted a masterfully orchestrated counterintelligence operation to learn more about Hayashi's activities and the secret IBM documents he reportedly had. Once IBM security officials verified the extent of their company's intelligence loss, IBM's attorneys took the allegations of Hitachi's industrial espionage to the FBI.

Coincidently, in early 1981, the FBI had initiated a special counterintelligence operation to gather information on Soviet bloc industrial espionage activities in the Silicon Valley area. U.S. technology has, of course, always been a high-priority target for Soviet intelligence. California, with its concentration of high-tech electronics and defense-aerospace industries, is a magnet for Soviet agents—overt and covert. Of the 52 diplomats in the USSR's large San Francisco Consulate, 30 are thought to be officers of the KGB, the Soviet espionage service.[11]

IBM was not only aware of the FBI's PENGEM operation (Penetration of the Gray Electronics Market), but had been actively assisting the FBI by training their agents in the business practices of the computer industry and providing cover stories (including badges and credentials) for them.[12] The FBI added the Hitachi case to PENGEM and a joint FBI–IBM operation that ultimately lasted eight months was set up to sting Hitachi.

As the FBI–IBM undercover sting operation revealed, advanced information on IBM's new technology has significant market value—so significant that some competitors, like Hitachi, were prepared to use illegal espionage methods to get critical technical intelligence at an early stage. A surreptitious recording made by the FBI of a January 20, 1982 meeting between Hitachi executives—Kenji Hayashi and Isao Ohnishi—and their "research consultants," Callahan (an IBM security officer), and Garretson, the senior FBI agent, reveals the economic rationale for espionage in the intensely competitive computer business. This unedited excerpt from the FBI's investigation transcript was submitted as evidence against Hitachi by the federal prosecutor:[13]

RICHARD A. CALLAHAN: Well, if you buy this program, you buy the program from IBM. Do they give you the microfiche?

ISAO OHNISHI: Yes, they give each customers.

ALAN J. GARRETSON: Yes, yes.

CALLAHAN: I see . . .

OHNISHI: When it's released.

CALLAHAN: O.K.

OHNISHI: Actually released. The IBM sells actually this itself . . .

CALLAHAN: The question comes to mind of course why don't you wait until they ship it and then buy the product.

OHNISHI: Well, we want to get this earlier because we need the information early, early enough to catch up with IBM.

CALLAHAN: Oh, I see, but it . . .

GARRETSON: They want it before it's released.

CALLAHAN: Yeah, I understand that, but if it's all the work you would have to do when you've got bits and pieces of information, could you possibly have the whole, ah, programming copy? When, you, does your, your software work exactly the same as IBM's?

OHNISHI: No, not exactly the same, but ah, we have very similar software system so we want to know what the IBM's doing.

CALLAHAN: So, if you get the IBM system early, you can copy that and make it part of yours, I see.

OHNISHI: Um-huh, that's right.

CALLAHAN: And if you bought, and if you wait until you buy it then you still have to do all of that other work to convert it into your software . . . (unintelligible)

GARRETSON and KENJI HAYASHI: (unintelligible)

OHNISHI: For example, if we can get one year earlier than general release, we can deliver our product one year earlier than it . . .

CALLAHAN: Yeah, but do you copy it line for line, or you just copy . . .

OHNISHI: We just look at this product and what they are doing and we apply it to our product.

CALLAHAN: I see the, but, so, if you took, if you wait until, if you wait until it's shipped and then buy it, you would still have to convert it into your own.

OHNISHI: Yes, that's right.

CALLAHAN: And you would have to pay them a royalty too, I suppose, when you bought it.

OHNISHI: Um-hum.

In June, 1982, Raymond Cadet, a National Semiconductor technical analyst, and his boss, Barry Saffaie, a product planning manager at NAS, were indicted by the Federal Government as accomplices in the Hitachi espionage case. In the course of their counterintelligence investigation, the FBI learned that when Cadet resigned from IBM to work for a Washington, D.C. area computer firm in November, 1980, he took 10 confidential IBM design manuals for the new 308X line of computers. Altogether, there were 27 design workbooks for the 308X computers. According to a March, 1983 *Fortune* article that provided additional details on the FBI–IBM sting operation, the IBM notebooks carried a special warning stating that the material contained therein was proprietary, and that their dissemination within IBM was restricted on a need-to-know basis. Each page was emblazoned with a red overprint—DO NOT REPRODUCE.[14] When he left IBM's employment, Cadet signed a standard company document stating that he would not take any confidential IBM material on his departure.

Apparently, Saffaie hired Cadet in June, 1981 because of his experience working on IBM's new 308X models, not because he had confidential IBM technical manuals in his possession. But soon thereafter, the ten workbooks were turned over to Saffaie, copies were made and then passed on to National Semiconductor's business partner—Hitachi. It was the 17 other volumes of 308X series workbooks that Hayashi had originally asked Payln Associates to try and get, thus initiating the curious chain of events that ended in his arrest and conviction for industrial espionage.

According to the FBI affidavit supporting the indictments against Hitachi and the others, the technical materials the Japanese company was seeking would have enabled a competitor to close the technology gap that IBM dramatically widened with the 1981–82 introduction of its new 3081 computer. The shopping list Hayashi gave to "Glenmar Associates," the FBI front firm, included:

Design information for the IBM 3081 computer.
Components of the 3081.
Tapes containing source microcode and test and maintenance programs for the 3081.
Design information for the IBM 3033 computer.
Design information for the IBM 3380 disk storage unit.
Components of the 3380.
Documents containing maintenance information for the 3380.
Automated logic diagrams for the 3380 and the IBM 3380 storage control unit.
Tapes containing source code for the MVS/SP
Version 2 operating systems program.[15]

In August, 1982, shortly before the IBM civil suit was filed, Raymond Cadet's attorney stated that four of NAS's top executives knew about and had access to the documents that Saffaie and Cadet allegedly acquired from IBM and passed on to Hitachi.[16] In preparing their defense of Cadet and Saffaie against the federal indictment for industrial espionage, the defense attorneys obtained a discovery court order against the FBI. The documents requested by the defense dealt with the extent and nature of the IBM–FBI relationship in the sting operation. The defense attorneys claimed that these documents would support the defendants' countercharge of entrapment and anticompetitive practices against IBM.

In October, 1982, the Justice Department refused to comply with the federal court's discovery order on the grounds that giving defense attorneys access to the material in question would be physically inconvenient by reason of bulk, would disclose much that was irrelevant, and could further endanger trade secrets. Because of this refusal by the Justice Department to comply with the discovery order, the federal court dismissed all indictments against Saffaie and Cadet. However, this action did not affect the criminal charges against Hitachi.[17]

The following month IBM, National Advanced Systems, and Hitachi reached a tentative out-of-court settlement on IBM's pending civil suit. In return for its "secret documents," IBM agreed to suspend temporarily all civil proceedings against the two firms.

Hitachi's Plea

In February, 1983, Hitachi surprised some followers of the case when it suddenly pleaded guilty to the federal charges of conspiring to transport stolen IBM trade secrets. A spokesman for Hitachi, Vice President Keisuke Arai, said that the guilty plea reflected his company's "greatest respect" for the U.S. legal system. He then went on to say that Hitachi got into this difficulty because it "lacked prudence in information-gathering activities in a foreign country, especially in understanding differences between Japan and other countries in history, culture and the legal system." In another statement accompanying its guilty plea, Hitachi said it "will take the lessons of this case in complete sincerity . . . and make this case a springboard for our development as a truly international enterprise."[18] Hitachi's penalty for its lack of prudence in competitive information gathering activities was as modest as its explanation of those activities. Two of its employees who figured prominently in the FBI investigation were fined $10,000 and $4000, placed on probation, and prohibited from representing Hitachi in the United States. The corporation was fined $10,000.

Hitachi's surprise plea to the Federal charges strengthened IBM's position in the civil case. However, National Semiconductor and Hitachi continued to claim that IBM masterminded the undercover sting operation in order to disrupt its competitors and that the FBI illegally allowed IBM to play too active a role.

IBM and Hitachi agreed to a negotiated settlement of the American company's civil suit in October 1983. While the monetary payments were minimal—Hitachi agreed to reimburse IBM for its litigation and investigational costs—the other conditions seemed designed to add further proof to the accuracy of IBM's complaint. Hitachi agreed to:

Return all proprietary material stolen from IBM.

Not use any IBM secrets it obtained.

Disclose the names, addresses, and business connections of all individuals who sold and/or *offered* to sell confidential IBM material.[19]

The latter condition is rather unusual and will no doubt give many "IBM watchers" good reason to reconsider their intelligence methods and/or increase their legal budgets. IBM's suit against National Semiconductor is still pending.

CLANDESTINE INTELLIGENCE—THE HIGH-TECH CONNECTION

The resort to clandestine intelligence (espionage) usually reflects a firm's inability to collect the desired competitive information through legal, overt means and/or the pressures of a severe time constraint. There is little reliable survey information about incidences or trends in clandestine intelligence. Whether the NAS Hitachi/Mitsubishi cases are the tip of a growing iceberg or simply a dramatic but atypical event in competitor intelligence activities, is very much open to speculation. One of the few systematic efforts to analyze the relative role of clandestine collection methods in commercial competitive information gathering were the *1959 and 1974 Harvard Business Review* surveys cited previously.[20] In his 1974 update, Jerry L. Wall, a reserve officer in military intelligence and a member of the American Society for Industrial Security, reached the conclusion based on the study's survey of executive attitudes and beliefs that industrial espionage was probably becoming more prevalent. He stated:

> Executives in general believe espionage has increased over the past ten years and as a result, many are taking more precautionary measures to protect their business secrets. Further evidence of this belief is an increase in tightening of company security, and justification of it in the level of interest in all types of competitive information.
>
> Although I found no evidence of an increased level of espionage activities in the study, a subsequent check with nonrespondents shows the study responses may be slightly conservative. I feel somewhat confident on this basis, that there has been an increase in espionage activity, although perhaps not a tremendous one. A part of my justification for this view is the belief that "good" spies do not get caught.[21]

According to executives from industrial security firms like Pinkerton's, Burns International Security Services, and the Wackenhut Corporation, this general tendency not to wash a company's dirty linen in public can cause unsuspecting managers to underestimate the character of the industrial espionage threat. Herchell Britton, an executive vice president at Burns, has stated that not only is industrial espionage a thriving, "booming" business, but it is also a highly organized one:

> The United States is in an unprecedented contest to protect its technological lead from the Soviet bloc, China, and even some of its more

> competitive trading partners, such as Japan, France, and West Germany. Few Americans are aware that there are special industrial espionage schools where one can learn state-of-the-art skills in this highly lucrative and criminal profession. Japan and Switzerland are each said to have a major secret school. It is quite apparent from the number of Soviet agents scattered all over the world that the K.G.B. has a training school and that most European Communist countries, notably East Germany, have sophisticated training institutions.[22]

Security consultants, of course, have both an expert and a biased view of industrial espionage trends. But if the perceived value of organized competitive information in business planning is increasing, as appears to be the case, then perhaps it is reasonable to conclude that the dark underside of competitor intelligence—industrial espionage—is also on the rise. When Jerry Wall asked executives in his 1974 survey what factors they thought were contributing to the rise in industrial espionage, he received the replies summarized in Table 3.1.

Intense competition certainly contributes to industrial espionage. However, another factor is usually the trigger—technical secrets. Industrial espionage seems to be more prevalent in high-technology industries such as electronics, specialty chemicals, aerospace, and drugs because the rapid pace of technological change adds a highly volatile element to the competitive mix. Proprietary know-how and critical technical secrets usually separate the leaders from the laggards in

TABLE 3.1. FACTORS CONTRIBUTING TO INCREASE IN INDUSTRIAL ESPIONAGE (PERCENTAGES)

	1973	1959
Tougher competition	62	53
Decline of ethical standards	55	77
Survival of company threatened	41	*
Self-defense	37	38
Higher executive stake in company success	28	7
Other	7	3

*Not provided as an alternative in 1959. Note: Sums to more than 100 percent because of multiple responses.[23]

those industries. In a high-tech industry, a firm that loses its technical edge can rarely compensate with superior marketing programs or operating efficiences. It was principally this dilemma that caused Hitachi to extend its competitor intelligence dragnet into the twilight realm of illegal industrial espionage. As the Hitachi case illustrates, the usual focus of industrial espionage is very specific, product-related technological information—a secret blueprint, a proprietary chemical formula, a confidential production process. Sophisticated technology is thus a natural magnet for sophisticated espionage.

How much of a deterrent to industrial espionage the IBM/Hitachi case and the FBI's new sting tactics will be is not clear. Certainly the novel aspects of the case and the wide publicity it has generated will alert a larger segment of the business community to the dangers and new risks inherent in industrial espionage. On a more positive note, these and other industrial espionage cases may have a beneficial effect if they draw the attention of more managers to a recognition of the increasing importance that many of their counterparts are placing on competitor intelligence programs. For dramatic accounts of illegal espionage usually reveal aspects of a larger if more mundane story, the increasingly widespread commitment of foreign and domestic corporations to a sustained, systematic competitor intelligence program that relies primarily upon overt, legal methods to collect the raw information that teams of trained analysts can convert into actionable intelligence.

A company whose priority is industrial espionage may be able to use clandestine intelligence to steal transitory technical secrets from a competitor. But to fully *understand* a competitor and successfully compete against it in a strategic sense, a far more encompassing, analytical form of competitor intelligence is required. To this larger purpose of competitor intelligence, industrial espionage can ultimately make only a meager contribution.

DEFLECTING COMPETITORS' INTELLIGENCE EFFORTS

Before passing on to a discussion of the analytical methods and strategic uses of this larger form of competitor intelligence, a final point about clandestine intelligence is worth noting. Those firms like IBM that have been stung by industrial espionage incidents often become very wise in the ways of intelligence—clandestine and overt, defensive and offensive. The more knowledgeable management becomes about both the strategic threat and practical value of competitor intelligence, the more successful it also becomes at both collecting competitor information and defending against legal and illegal competitor intelligence programs.

The Japanese, who assiduously collect and carefully analyze the reams of competitor information available on most American corporations, know full well the intelligence value of a friendly plant tour—whether it be that of a supplier, customer, competitor, or partner. As the U.S. electronic firms in Silicon Valley discovered much to their chagrin, the Japanese are quite as expert in protecting their company's information as they are in collecting that of their competitors.

> Not too many years ago, the Japanese were as welcome on plant tours as any other customers. Now all they are permitted to see are the interior of conference rooms. Such a turnabout is long overdue. For years, the security-conscious Japanese have seldom allowed executives of U.S. companies inside their plants. "I've been in Japan about fourteen times and never saw a semiconductor plant," say National Semiconductor's Kramme. "I've called, having been given an invitation as a return favor for having shown my factory to them. When I'd ask to see the operations, they would say, 'The operations manager is out today and we've a number of matters to discuss. Oh, our time is all gone.' 'Ooh, ooh, and ooh, and all I would see is a lot of conference rooms."[24]

In industries where marketing and technology consultants are frequently used to collect competitor information, there is a heightened sensitivity to the fact that from an intelligence viewpoint consultants can be a two-edged sword. Their industry-wide contacts, familiarity with diverse sources of information, and analytical detachment often give consultants a perspective on competitors that is very insightful. Most consultants respect the confidentiality agreements that are a routine aspect of their assignments and take pains to collect industry information in an above-board fashion. There are exceptions, however—consultants whose aggressive attempts to collect information border on the illegal.

The open nature of most American corporations can make their employees vulnerable to the advances of unscrupulous consultants—particularly when management is indifferent or unaware of this espionage threat. Those who have been stung by consultant leaks, however, are taking a more active role in safeguarding their company's information resources.

A recent convert to defensive counterintelligence procedures, is Wang Laboratories, a leading innovator and manufacturer in word processing technology. For years this young and rapidly growing company opened its plants in Lowell, Massachusetts to suppliers, customers, and other interested parties. Tours were conducted as a matter of goodwill and to demonstrate the progressive manufacturing operations and advanced product technology that had given Wang a leading edge in the emerging office automation markets. However, the accidental discovery of the intelligence pieced together by a Japanese "study group" that toured Wang's manufacturing facilities dramatically introduced Wang officials to the firm's intelligence vulnerabilities and ended the practice of visitor tours.[25]

ESPIONAGE AND INTELLIGENCE—THE LOWELL CASE

While industrial espionage should not be condoned, neither should it be confused with methods of collecting strategic information on competitors that are legal, if perhaps aggressive. The Japanese study team that deftly used its tour of the Wang facilities to collect detailed intelligence on their host's products and manufacturing technology, might be accused of overly sharp, if not unethical business conduct. But lest American managers, stung by the Japanese's shrewd collection and use of competitor intelligence, be too quick to condemn the "underhanded tactics" of their Asian competitors, they ought to reflect briefly on their own commercial heritage.

In an ironic way the intelligence methods employed by the Japanese study team in its tour of Wang's Lowell, Massachusetts plant paid tribute to the memory of the Yankee entrepreneur who was a founder of America's textile manufacturing industry and for whom the city of Lowell is named.

Francis Cabot Lowell, one of early nineteenth century Boston's leading shipping merchants, came from two of New England's most distinguished families. A member of the city's most influential social and political circles, he was also a visionary entrepreneur, an adventurous risk taker, and a master of industrial intelligence.

Lowell's contemporaries and competitors, Almy and Brown, the Rhode Island merchants, were the first to succeed in replicating Britain's revolutionary industrial machinery in technologically backward America. With the aid of emigrant mechanics like the young Englishman Samuel Slater, New England merchants like Almy and Brown began to build small cotton mills with machinery that was illegally copied from British patents.[26] Lowell, on the other hand, not only copied Britain's advanced manufacturing technology, but he significantly increased its productivity with larger-scale factories organized around more efficient, less labor-intensive production methods.

Lowell guided a team of Boston mechanics who successfully reproduced the sophisticated cotton-weaving machinery that was Britain's technological pride. But Lowell's personal intelligence on British manufacturing methods gave him more than their technical designs—for he had also observed the organizational weakness of the English mills he visited.

Lowell realized something that few British mill owners understood: the layout or "industrial design" of their factories did not match the sophisticated machinery they housed. In his pioneer factory at Waltham, Massachusetts, Lowell used the competitor intelligence he brought back from Britain to duplicate his competitors' technology and then to improve its productivity through better equipment organization and factory layout. In Britain, the components of the manufacturing process were still organized along traditional craft lines; weaving, dyeing, and finishing were accomplished at different locations, often by totally separate establishments. The technological advances of the industrial revolution had enabled British mill owners to *mechanize* the *key components* of the manufacturing process. But with cheap, plentiful labor available they saw no need to change the *structure* of the manufacturing *process*. Smug in the arrogance of their unquestioned technological superiority, the British were obsessed with safeguarding their technological advantages. They expected foreign competitors like the New England merchants would try to copy their new machines and thus were on guard against that particular threat. Through their complex embargo and patent laws, they may have delayed the introduction of Britain's new industrial technology into the United States by 20 years or so.[27]

But British manufacturers were not alive to the larger, more significant competitive threat embodied in Lowell's Waltham factory—the innovative adaptation of new technology to radically different organizational and production methods.

Lowell died in 1817 but his business partners, known as the Boston Associates, continued his path-breaking experiment. With the expressed intent of building a new, larger-scale complex that would embody all of Lowell's innovative factory designs but would at the same time avoid recreating the social misery of those dismal industrial slums in the English Midlands that Lowell and his colleagues had found so depressing, the Boston Associates acquired 400 acres of sparsely populated farmland along the Merrimack River 20 miles north of the Waltham factory. An intricate series of canals were dug to harness the waterpower of the fast-flowing river to the new textile mills that followed Lowell's original plan.

The new mill site was appropriately named "Lowell." Like his Waltham factory, Lowell's city was a large and instant success. The cotton textile industry in America grew at the remarkable annual rate of 16 percent between 1815 and 1833. By 1840, the new industrial city of Lowell was Massachusett's second-largest city and America's most successful and largest manufacturing complex.

JAPANESE COMPETITOR INTELLIGENCE—THE CORE STRENGTH

The parallels between Lowell's phenomenal success and that of many contemporary Japanese companies is striking. The shrewd managers who pilot Japan's premier firm,—Toyota, Sony, Matsushita, Honda, Suzuki—are an inquisitive, outward looking lot. Traders at heart, many of the founders of these firms are like Lowell, risk-takers who minimize the uncertainty inherent in their business ventures with detailed intelligence on their competitors and the other factors that create and reflect the ever-changing turbulence that passes for industrial trends.

For example, Eliji Toyoda, the current chairman of Toyota Motor Corporation, was sent to the United States in 1950 by his uncle, Sakichi Toyoda, the firm's founder. His mission was to learn all he could about Detroit's manufacturing methods, the most productive and sophisticated automobile assembly operations in the world—at the time. Toyota, which had been making a small number of automobiles for the domestic Japanese market since 1937, was embarking on a new strategy to become a world-class producer of quality, inexpensive cars. Competitor intelligence was a first step.

For over a month, pen and paper in hand, Eliji Toyoda toured America's auto plants. Chrysler, Studebaker, General Motors, Ford—he went methodically to one plant after another, observing the machines, the lines, the workers, and the management that made the best cars in the world. At each plant Toyoda closely watched the manufacturing operations in action to see what worked and what didn't. And he took copious notes that became the core of the competitor intelligence Toyota was slowly building.[28]

Thirty-three years later the student became the teacher when Detroit's premier manufacturer, General Motors, signed a joint-venture agreement with Toyota to produce subcompacts in a California GM plant that had been closed in part because the company was steadily losing market share to Toyota and other Japanese auto manufacturers who, by 1982, had siphoned off a stunning 23 percent of Detroit's huge domestic market. Many industry observers interpreted the unprecedented Toyota–GM deal as another painful acknowledgement by Detroit of Japan's superior expertise in the new technique of automobile manufacture. The joint venture was also viewed as a special intelligence opportunity for the besieged American auto manufacturers now driven to collecting competitor intelligence the hard way, via a costly and potentially embarrassing joint venture:

> So structured, the deal is testimony to Toyota's superiority in manufacturing efficiency. Its plant design, tooling, materials handling, inventory control and labor practices enable the Japanese company to produce and ship a small car to the United States for $1,500 to $2,000 less than American companies can make a comparable model, according to various studies. "I'm convinced that G.M.'s main reason for getting involved with Toyota on this joint venture is to see how Toyota runs a factory," said James C. Abegglen, Vice President of the Boston Consulting Group's Tokyo office.[29]

This interpretation was reflected in the exceptionally candid statements of GM's management. According to Robert C. Stempel, vice president of the important Chevrolet division, GM entered the joint venture in an effort to learn the details of Japanese automobile manufacturing methods and to see if they could be adapted to Detroit's assembly lines:

> "We've been working hard for 18 months on our Cavalier, and we've only taken $125 out of it. We need thousands, and it will have to come from a whole new way of doing things.[30]

Among the other things that GM may learn from Toyota is that detailed, systematic competitor intelligence is the handmaiden of their business strategies. Like Francis Cabot Lowell, the executives of Toyota and other premier Japanese companies make a major, continuing effort to closely observe their competitor's methods, organization, management, products, and technologies.

This broad-focused intelligence gives them a special vantage point. As Lowell did, managers like Eliji Toyoda develop a strategic perspective that affords them an understanding not only of their competitors' technology and products, but more importantly a valuable insight into their competitors' behavior, assumptions, and conceptual blindspots. Lowell, with no manufacturing experience, but something far more important—a critical, reflective intellect—observed what his British competitors did not: shortfalls in their manufacturing system that could be converted into innovative approaches that promised higher productivity.

As the above examples suggest, the ultimate value of competitor intelligence is that it helps managers focus on the strategic fundamentals that determine the dynamic interactions of their firm's competitive situation. Effective corporate strategy requires an assessment of the external competitive environment that gets to the heart of matters and is not diverted by the myriad surface events that are often dramatic but frequently irrelevant to the main issues and trends strategy should address. When it is done thoroughly, systematically, and coherently, competitor intelligence becomes an analytical prism that refracts the external stream of competitor information into its constituent elements. In this way, intelligence reveals the structural and behavioral patterns that influence a competitor's strategic choices and actions. When a firm's intelligence resources are mobilized and coordinated to support its strategic planning, the firm's managers are then in a position "to see into" rather than merely "look at" their competitors. The following chapters outline an organizational framework and an analytical approach that managers can use to do just that.

---

[1]Captain Ellis M. Zacharis, USN, *Secret Mission: The Story of an Intelligence Officer,* Putnam, New York, 1946, pp. 117–18.

[2]"Mitsubishi Electric, Four Employees Indicted on Charges of Conspiring to Steal IBM Data," *Wall Street Journal,* July 20, 1982; David B. Tinnin, "How IBM Stung Hitachi: Espionage," *Fortune,* March 7, 1983, pp. 50–56.

[3]"The Business Intelligence Beehive," *Business Week,* December 14, 1981, p. 52. Reprinted by special permission, (C) 1981 by McGraw-Hill, Inc.

[4]Gene Bylinsky, "The Japanese Spies in Silicon Valley," *Fortune* February 27, 1978, pp. 74–79. Time, Inc. All rights reserved.

[5]"Mitsubishi Qualifies Its Denial in IBM Stolen Data Case," *New York Times,* June 25, 1982, p. D3.

[6]"Japan's High-Tech Spies," *Newsweek,* July 5, 1982, pp. 53–55.

[7]"IBM Files Suit Charging Theft of Trade Secrets," *Wall Street Journal,* September 15, 1982.

[8]"Throwing the Book at Industrial Spies," *Business Week,* October 4, 1982, pp. 84–85.

[9]"IBM Files Suit Charging Theft of Trade Secrets," *Wall Street Journal,* September 15, 1982.

[10]Tinnin, "How IBM Stung Hitachi," p. 52.

[11]"Corporate Cloak and Dagger," *Time,* August 30, 1982, pp. 62–65.

[12]Tinnin, "How IBM Stung Hitachi," p. 52.

[13]"Transcript Excerpt," reprinted in *The New York Times,* May 13, 1983, p. D3.

[14]Tinnin, "How IBM Stung Hitachi," p. 51.

[15]"America Posts Bail as Details Unfold in IBM Theft Case," *The New York Times,* June 25, 1982.

[16]"Trade Secrets, National Advanced Systems," *MIS Week,* August 25, 1982.

[17]"Trade Secrets Case Dismissed," *Electronics News,* October 4, 1982, p. 20.

[18]"Concern for Future Led to Hitachi Plea," Associated Press story reported in *The Reporter Dispatch,* February 10, 1983, p. 6.

[19]"Hitachi Ltd. and I.B.M. Settle Case," *New York Times,* October 7, 1983, p. D1.

[20]Edward E. Furash, "Problems in Review: Industrial Espionage," *Harvard Business Review,* November–December, 1959; Jerry L. Wall, "What the Competition is Doing: Your Need to Know," *Harvard Business Review,* November–December, 1974. Reprinted by permission of the *Harvard Business Review* from "What the Competition is Doing: Your Need to Know," by Jerry L. Wall (November–December, 1974). Copyright© 1974 by the President and Fellows of Harvard College; all rights reserved.

[21]Wall, "What the Competition is Doing: Your Need to Know," pp. 23–24.

[22]Herchel Britton, "The Industrial-Spy Peril," *The New York Times,* June 30, 1981. By The New York Times Company. Reprinted by permission.

[23]Wall, "What the Competition is Doing: Your Need to to Know," p. 106.

[24]Gene Bylinsky, "The Japanese Spies in Silicon Valley," *Fortune,* February 27, 1978, p. 78. Time, Inc. All rights reserved.

[25]Paul Richter, "Most Everyone Plays 'I Spy' in Silicon Valley," *Los Angeles Times,* July 11, 1982.

[26]Daniel T. Boorstein, *The Americans: The National Experience,* New York, Random House, 1965, pp. 26–27.

[27]Boorstein, *The Americans,* p. 25.

[28]"Toyota Chairman Back in U.S. for G.M. Venture," *The New York Times,* February 22, 1983.

[29]"The Aging of Japan's Auto Industry," *The New York Times,* February 20, 1983. By The New York Times Company. Reprinted by permission.

[30]John Holusha, "Strategy in Ventury of G.M. and Toyota," *The New York Times,* February 28, 1983. By The New York Times Company. Reprinted by permission.

4

Competitor Intelligence: An Organizational Framework for Business

WILLIAM L. SAMMON

Biographical data for this chapter author appear on page 21.

This chapter outlines an organizational structure for managing and coordinating the competitor intelligence function in a corporation. Chapter 5 discusses an analytical method for obtaining competitor information and converting the raw data collected into usable intelligence that effectively supports the strategic planning process. Together, these two chapters cover the core organizational and analytical issues a company confronts when it sets out to marry competitor intelligence to business strategy.

As noted in Chapter 3, competitor intelligence is broader in scope and more benign in purpose than industrial espionage. The objective of competitor intelligence is not to steal a competitor's trade secrets or other proprietary property, but rather to gather in a systematic, overt (i.e., legal) manner a wide range of information that when collated and analyzed provides a fuller understanding of a competitor firm's structure, culture, behavior, capabilities, and weaknesses.

CORPORATE INTELLIGENCE GATHERING: INFORMAL AND DISAGGREGATED

Despite the fact that companies are engaged in a continuous, dynamic struggle with inter- and intra-industry competitors for market share, customers, profits, capital, and a wide range of resources, few companies study their competitors as closely as they study internal manufacturing variances or new product proposals. The complex information systems of the modern corporation are primarily designed to monitor internal operations and to facilitate management's control and allocation of organizational resources. When management tries to add a competitive perspective to the company's strategic planning process, it often discovers that its knowledge of key competitors is extremely incomplete, widely scattered throughout the corporation, and generally not coordinated. What is perhaps even more frustrating is that the available internal assessments and opinions about competitors are frequently in conflict, unsubstantiated by facts, and often based on assumptions and intuitive hunches that are partially right, partially wrong, and usually out of date. As the following parable suggests, partial perspectives—no matter how accurate in their separate details—rarely add up to an adequate collective strategic picture.

The Parable of Collective Wisdom[1]

Beyond the desert was a city in which all were blind. The king and his entourage arrived to camp nearby, bringing with them a mighty elephant.

The populous was eager to see the elephant, and from among this blind community, some ran like fools to find it. As they did not know even the form or shape of the elephant, they groped sightlessly, gathering information by touching some part of it. Each thought that he knew something, because he could feel a part.

When they returned to their fellow citizens, eager groups clustered around them. Anxious to learn the truth from those who were themselves astray, they asked about the form and shape of the elephant; they listened to all they were told.

The man whose hand had reached an ear was asked about the elephant's nature. He said, "It is a large, rough thing, wide and broad, like a rug."

And the one who had felt the trunk said, "I have the facts about it. It is like a straight and hollow pipe, awful and destructive."

The one who had felt its feet and legs said, "It is mighty and firm, like a pillar."

Each had felt one part out of many. Each had perceived it wrongly. No mind knew all: knowledge is not the companion of the blind. . . .

Faced with this perceptual dilemma and recognizing the growing need for more complete information, management in a number of companies have begun to set up programs to organize and coordinate their company's intelligence resources. The task of developing and monitoring competitor intelligence activities frequently begins as an ancillary research effort in the company's marketing, planning, or technical staffs because these groups must periodically review various aspects of the external competitive environment in order to accomplish their primary functions. Moreover, these staff groups tend to have a strong research, analytical orientation, which facilitates the systematic collection and analysis of competitive data. It is often the case that competitor intelligence is being collected in some systematic manner at both the corporate and business-unit level, particularly in those companies with a decentralized organizational structure. As they collect competitor data and prepare their departmental reports that may profile one aspect of competitor activity—for example, regional market strength, debt payout ratio, licensing programs, product promotional campaigns, or business development activities—these groups may tap into each other's competitor data bases and an informal network that collects and shares competitor information emerges within the corporation.

Although an informal intelligence network does generate some useful competitor intelligence, it rarely surfaces the most critical *strategic* competitor intelligence. As Michael Porter points out, an informal intelligence system diffuses responsibility, and valuable competitor data may simply be lost:

> Compiling the data for a sophisticated competitor analysis probably requires more than just hard work. To be effective, there is the need for an organized mechanism—some sort of competitive intelligence system—to insure that the process is efficient. The elements of a competitor intelligence system can vary according to the particular firm's needs, based on its industry, its staff capability, and its management's interests and talents. . . .
>
> One observes a variety of alternative ways firms organize to perform these [intelligence] functions in practice. They range from a competitor analysis group that is part of the planning department and performs all the functions (perhaps drawing on others in the organization for collecting field data) to a competitor intelligence coordinator who performs the compiling, cataloging and communication functions; to a system in which a strategist does it all informally. All too often however, no one is made responsible for the competitor analysis at all. There seems to be no single correct way to collect competitor data, but it is clear that someone must take an active interest or much useful information will be lost. Top management can do a lot to stimulate the effort by requiring sophisticated profiles of competitors as part of the planning process. As a minimum, some managers with responsibility to serve as a focal point for competitor intelligence gathering seems to be necessary.[2]

Figure 4.1 depicts the informal competitor intelligence system that exists in most large corporations. Scattered throughout the company's four business units (A,B,C, and D) and its corporate staff functions (public relations, marketing, planning, manufacturing, and so on) are various "pools" of competitor information. The meaning that the managers in the business units and staff groups extract from these competitor information pools is highly selective and invariably biased by their professional orientation and organizational needs. The manufacturing vice-president who tracks a competitor's capacity investment announcements may overstate the potential threat inherent in the capacity additions because he or she does not realize that competitor

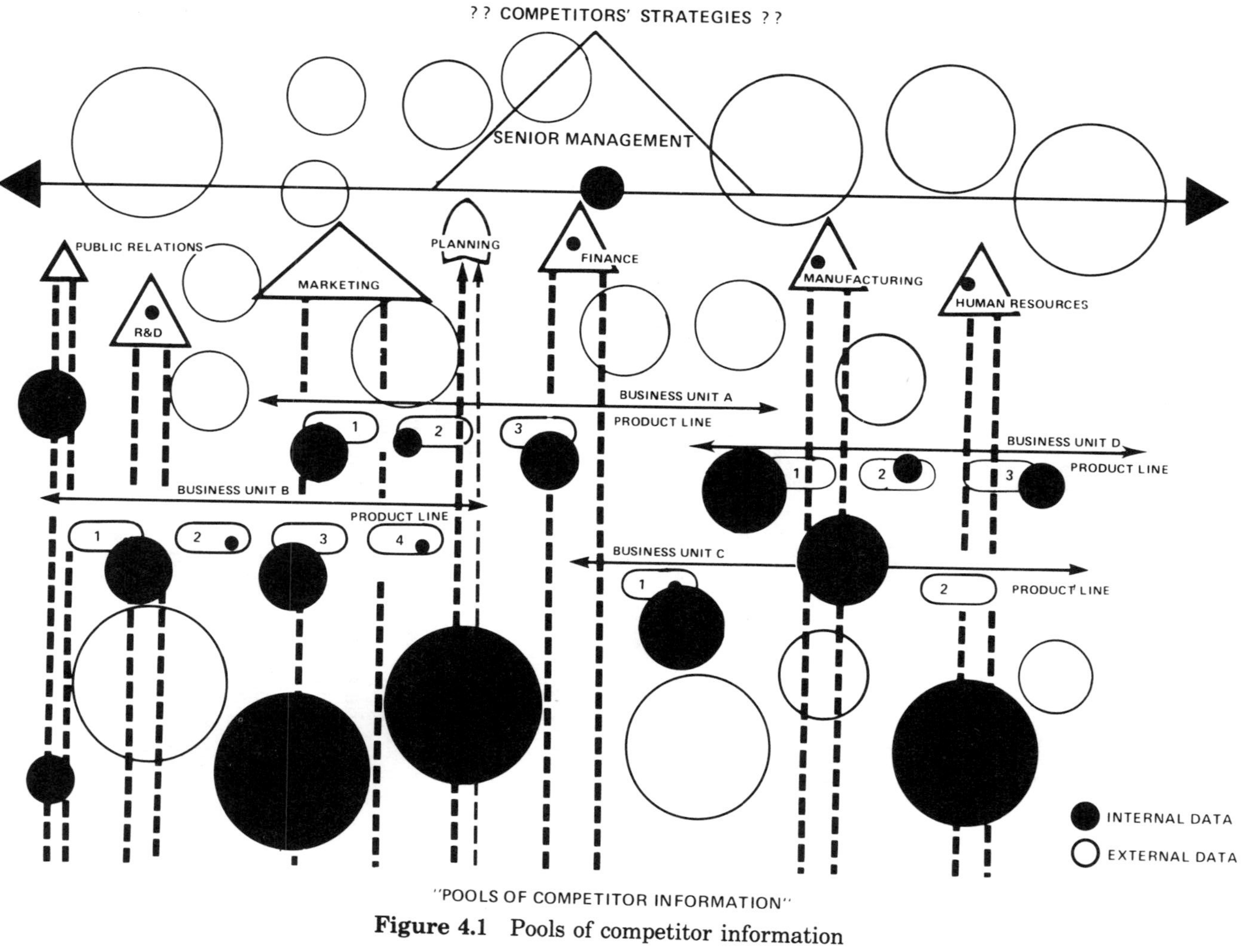

Figure 4.1 Pools of competitor information

X lacks the cash flow to carry through these plans. If the finance staff has run a series of sensitivity profiles on competitor X, it may realize that rising interest payments will probably compel the competitor's management to delay or perhaps cancel key capital projects. The marketing staff in business unit B may be certain that their industrial adhesives are technically superior to those of competitor X, yet be unaware of new patents competitor X has filed on a radically new adhesive that business unit B's corporate R&D staff views as a technological breakthrough. In the course of labor negotiations, the corporate industrial relations staff may learn that the national union is planning to strike competitor Y's plants in the Southeast. However, this information which business unit A could use in its campaign to take market share from competitor Y on the East Coast regional market is not passed on.

Of course some competitor intelligence is communicated across business units and between corporate staff and the business divisions. However, if competitor intelligence relies on informal channels, the communications will be partial, the data incomplete, and the understanding of competitors' strategies will continue to be half-formed.

THE MISINFORMATION SYNDROME

In one respect an informal competitor intelligence system may be more damaging than none at all. For in an informal system those groups with access to a limited source of competitor information that provides only a partial perspective on competitor plans and actions may be able to use that "intelligence" in a manipulative manner to advance vested interests at the expense of the company's larger needs. For example, business units have been known to overstate the character of investments being made by direct competitors in order to justify a larger allocation of corporate resources to their division, so that they may "defend" established markets against the well-advertised competitor threat. Alternatively, business units and/or staff groups that have access to business intelligence that indicates the competitor's performance is superior to their own may be understandably reluctant to communicate the potential significance of this intelligence to senior management. On the dubious premise that the competitive situation will improve in the long term—as long as corporate management doesn't realize how adverse the near-term situation is—subordinate managers have been known to overstate their divisions' competitive strength while conveniently ignoring evidence of a competitor's growing superiority.

Competitor intelligence deals with a highly controversial subject—the strategic position and operating performance of business opponents. In the complex organizations that characterize most large corporations, information does not always travel well, and negative information about competitors is sometimes suppressed or manipulated to protect subordinate vested interests within the company. Thus, while an increasing number of staff and line groups may be collecting disparate kinds of information about competitors, the strategic value of this potentially rich data is not realized by the corporation as a whole. Information that reaches management in bits and pieces is often communicated haphazardly in a piecemeal, disaggregated fashion by those who have it. The net result is a debilitating strategic intelligence situation in which senior management is intermittently showered with selective items of competitor data that, in their unorganized form, frequently distort rather than clarify the true features of the competitive environment confronting the corporation.

In this miasma of partial data, misinformation, and conventional thinking about competitors, it is not surprising that confusion often results and critical strategic decisions are often made in a perceptual vacuum. The distorted perceptions about competitors' strategies that are the inevitable fruit of an informal, competitor intelligence system, ultimately brings home to senior corporate executives the bitter truth of the old axiom and first principle of intelligence: "It isn't the things you don't know that hurt you; its the things you do know that aren't so."

CURRENT STATUS OF CORPORATE COMPETITOR INTELLIGENCE

The few surveys that have examined the ways in which corporations gather, analyze, and communicate competitior information generally reach the same conclusions.

There is a growing consensus among managers that more competitor information is needed to support marketing and planning programs.

To monitor their competitors, managers rely on their own division's resources, and most competitor information is gleaned from two primary sources:

Published data such as trade press articles, formal market research studies, and financial reports.

Personal contacts within the company, such as sales personnel and analysts, and outside the company, such as consultants and customers.

Most managers recognize the limited range of the competitor data they are able to obtain with their own organizational and personal resources.

Managers generally believe that there is a significant amount of useful competitor information in other parts of their company and in other external sources, but they have neither the time nor the resources to tap these data pools.

Given the growing importance of competitor information to their operations and the difficulties they encounter in getting it, most managers believe there is a need within their companies for a more formal, organized system of collecting, organizing, and communicating legally available competitor data.[3]

The 1974 Wall survey in the *Harvard Business Review* of corporate competitive information gathering, although almost ten years old, is still one of the most complete analyses of practices and attitudes on this subject. A central question in the survey was:

> Do you think your company should have a more systematic method of gathering, processing, analyzing, and reporting information about competitors?

The responses of the corporate managers and executives who took part in the survey (Table 4.1) indicate a growing recognition of the need for a more formal corporate competitor intelligence program.

In commenting on the shifting patterns in the response to this question, Wall noted that although an increasing percentage of managers acknowledge the need for a formally managed system of corporate competitor information, the survey data showed that;

> There have been no detectable major shifts toward more formal regular reporting since 1959: In other words, there is a great deal of difference between what executives want and what they are likely to get.[5]

The 1981 Information Data Search (IDS) survey of a representative sample of Fortune 500 planners suggested that although planners

TABLE 4.1. NEED FOR A CORPORATE COMPETITOR INTELLIGENCE PROGRAM

	1973	1959
Definitely	37%	57% (Yes)
Probably	35%	
Uncertain	6%	
Probably Not	18%	
Definitely Not	4%	43% (No)

frequently collected competitor data, "In many cases, information collected by one of these divisional planning units remains within that unit, and is not circulated to other operating divisions within the company. *25% of the planners polled said they gather intelligence only for their own divisions.*"[6]

Although the 1982 IDS survey that attempted to evaluate corporate intelligence gathering was based on a statistically insignificant sample of Fortune 500 marketing and planning executives, the picture of corporate competitor information-gathering techniques that it depicts rings true and reflects the findings in the more extensive Wall surveys as well as the anecdotal evidence found in the business press and academic journals:[7]

> The marketing and planning executives who participated in this survey were somewhat aware of the intelligence sources available to them outside of their organization.
>
> They can quickly compile a basic list of research sources, but often cannot go beyond the commonly known reference books and credit agencies.
>
> Their roster of experts is also limited. Time after time, they call on the same group of experts, rarely appearing to go outside their established network of contacts.
>
> On the corporate level, organizations have made few strides towards constructing an internal intelligence network. Lack of cooperation and unity of purpose further compounds the organization's ability to retain internal intelligence. Much internally collected competitor information is slipping through the cracks not reaching the executive who needs it. In the case of companies with foreign sales offices, these offices rarely respond to the intelligence needs of the parent company.[8]

ORGANIZING A CORPORATE COMPETITOR INTELLIGENCE SYSTEM

A higher quality of timely competitor intelligence is possible when the corporation's intelligence resources are identified and centrally coordinated. The probing competitor analyses that are essential to a strategic understanding of a rapidly changing competitive environment cut across and involve all the major line divisions and staff functions in a corporation—domestic businesses, foreign businesses, sales, marketing, manufacturing, R & D, purchasing, finance, personnel, government affairs, public relations, and planning. By identifying, developing, and communicating the competitor information relevant to each, and then molding those disparate information resources into a coherent, relevant intelligence picture of key corporate and business-unit competitors, a far more comprehensive, forward-looking, and dynamic view of the changing competitive situation emerges. With a solid base of competitor data that is continually updated to maintain its currency, senior executives and general managers—the corporation's key decision-makers—will be in a much stronger position to:

Understand and anticipate competitor moves.
Ask the right strategic questions.
Take the most effective actions for the long term.

The most significant value of a coordinated intelligence system is not that it gins up a greater volume of competitor information, but rather that it sifts a wider range of competitor data available to external and internal sources. By organizing, collating, and refining a larger body of competitor information, the intelligence most relevant to the company's strategic situation can be extracted and converted into a valuable analytical resource for key decision-makers. However, if the focus is not on competitive strategy and the intelligence needs of key decision-makers, administrative and organizational improvements of the company's intelligence resources will simply increase the bottom-up flow of raw competitor information. At best, this will waste valuable resources; at worst it will flood the company's information networks with an undigestible volume of competitor data that simply adds more "noise" to the din and confusion that surrounds managers and executives groping for an effective strategy.

If it is oriented toward competitors' strategies and organized to tap a broad range of intelligence sources rapidly and efficiently, a corporate intelligence system can improve the company's strategic planning process. Such a "top-down" coordinated system can mobilize the extensive competitor data and sources scattered throughout the company's many "information pools," screen out the secondary undergrowth of misinformation, and link this streamlined corporate information network with external competitor data sources to produce a continuous flow of strategic competitor intelligence that is reliable and relevant. As Figure 4.2 suggests, an organized corporate intelligence system acts like an interlinked radar grid that constantly monitors competitor activity, filters the raw information picked up by external and internal sources, processes it for strategic significance, and efficiently communicates actionable intelligence to those who need it.

CORPORATE PLANNING: A FOCAL POINT FOR STRATEGIC INTELLIGENCE

Given the broad scope and strategic purpose of a corporate competitor intelligence system, a logical way to organize it is to establish a small corporate-level staff element to serve as a focal point for the coordination, guidance, and communication of competitor intelligence. The analysis of competitor intelligence involves the methods and techniques of the market researcher and the financial analyst. Like the market researcher, the intelligence analyst is a close observer of customer and competitor behavior, who must understand and evaluate R & D efforts, pricing and promotional tactics, market segmentation strategies, production and distribution resources, product mix, and other market-related factors that reflect and influence a competitor's strategy.

The financial element of competitor analysis is also substantial. Like the security analyst who follows stocks and the business analyst who reviews operating plans, the competitor intelligence analysts must be able to use the quantitative language of finance to chart and probe a competitor's anatomy. Because they need to dissect and understand a competitor's financial situation at both the corporate and business-segment/product-line level, the competitor intelligence analysts must be equally at home with the techniques of portfolio analysis and standard cost accounting.

Because competitor analysis/intelligence draws so heavily on the substantive disciplines and analytical methods of the market researcher and the financial analyst, a case can be made that the com-

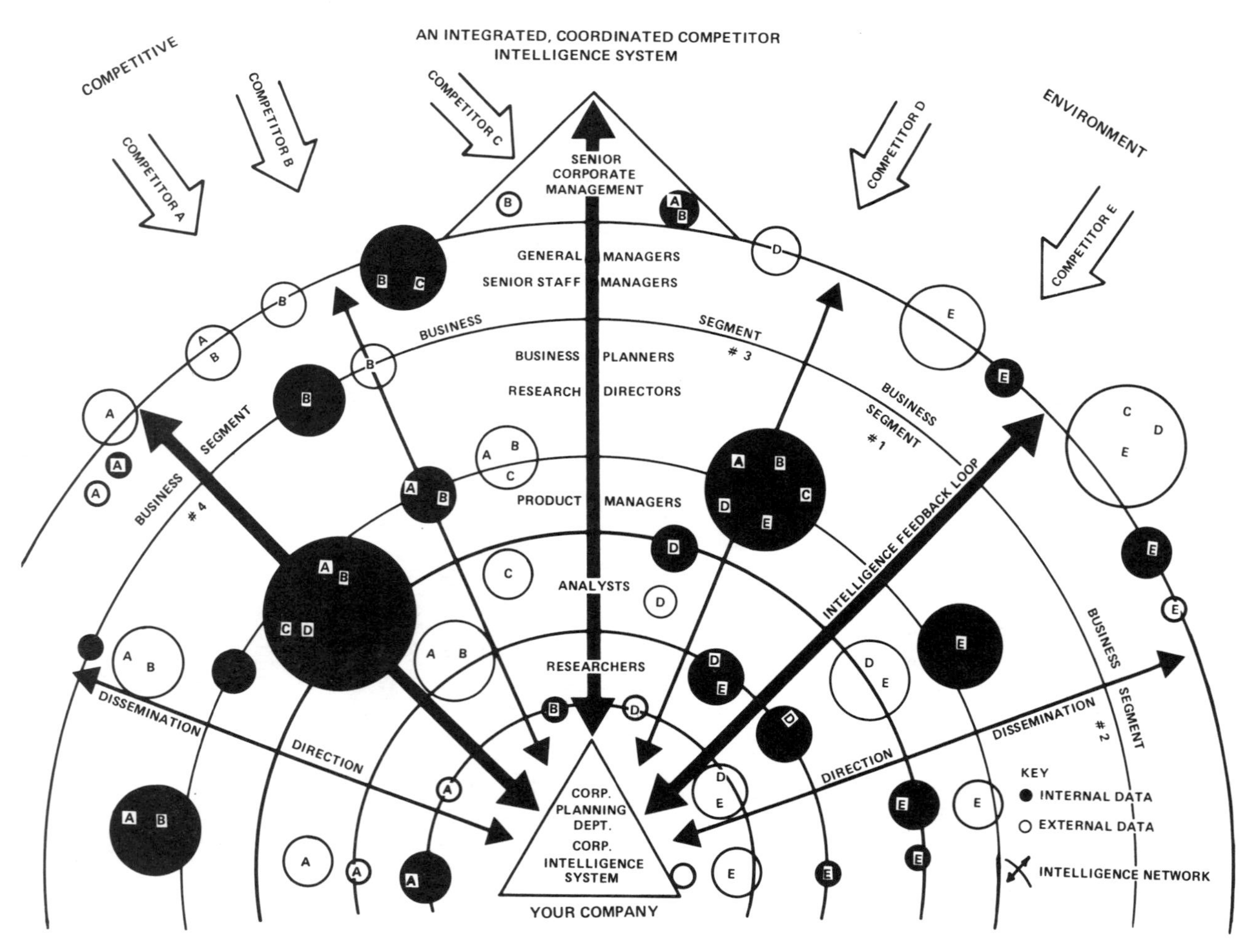

Figure 4.2 An integrated, coordinated competitor intelligence system

petitor intelligence function should be lodged either in the corporate marketing or the corporate financial staff. However, this overlooks two fundamental features of competitor intelligence. Its analytical approach is integrative and synergistic, while its ultimate focus is competitor strategy. A stronger case can therefore be made that competitor intelligence is closer in style and purpose to the somewhat broader methods, concerns, and issues of the strategic planning function at both the business unit and the corporate level.

THE MILITARY ANALOGUE: G2, THE INTELLIGENCE STAFF

In the military, which has been in the strategic planning business a long time, the G2—the intelligence staff—was an outgrowth of the G3 planning/operations staff. The concept of a military staff that provides the commander with detailed administrative and analytic support is a relatively recent feature of military organizations. A by-product of the Napoleonic Wars, the general staff concept was formalized in the Prussian military system, and by 1900 had been adopted by the military in most Western nations. While the general staff concept was often feared and denigrated for its association with Prussian militarism, it was an important vehicle for professionalism and an efficient way to structure and coordinate the more sophisticated analytical staff resources needed by a modern commander to run increasingly complex military organizations.[9]

The primary purpose of the general staff was to assist the commander in making war plans and coordinating the operational commitment of line units. This was the task of the G3, and the central importance of this function made him the de facto senior staff officer. G1 was the staff section responsible for personnel issues, and G4 handled logistics. As the planning and operations functions increased in complexity and sophistication, more attention was paid to the formal analysis of the enemy's plans and operations. First as a distinct but subordinate G3 function, and then as a separate general staff function, the military intelligence staff emerged. The G2 became the commander's analytical resource and advisor on the enemy.

The primary task of the G2 is to collect sufficient information on the enemy's situation so that a reasonably accurate analysis can be made of the enemy's capabilities, vulnerabilities, plans, and most probable courses of actions. The G2 is also responsible for evaluating the "area of operations" to determine the environmental influence of weather and terrain on both the enemy and friendly forces. The operational plans drawn up by the G3 to implement the commander's strategy are often issued in the form of operational orders. In the U.S. Army, the standard format for these operational plans/orders is the "five-paragraph field order." Elegant in its simplicity, it covers the key operational elements the commander must consider in developing his strategic plans. The "body" reads as follows:

Operation Order/Plan Format[10]

	Responsible Staff
1. Situation	
a. Enemy forces	G2
b. Friendly forces	G3
c. Attachments and detachments	G3
d. Assumptions (used only in operations plan)	G2/G3
2. Mission	
A clear, concise statement of the specified and implied operational tasks the military unit will accomplish in order to implement the commander's strategy.	G3
3. Execution	
a. The commander's concept of the operation explains how the organization's resources will be employed using "fire" and "maneuver" to accomplish the mission.	G3
b. Coordinating instructions define special constraints and establish tasking requirements between staff and line units.	G1, G2, G3, and G4
4. Administration and Logistics	G1 and G4
5. Command and Signal	
Covers the location of the command operations center and special communications instructions.	G3

As is evident, the operational plan begins with the G2's concise summary of the enemy's forces—their composition, size, strength, disposition, capabilities, vulnerabilities, effects of the area of operations (the immediate environment—weather and terrain) on them, and the enemy's probable courses of action. The last element—the enemy's probable course of action—is the most difficult to assess because it requires the greatest degree of judgment and interpretation. Essentially it requires the intelligence staff officer to outline the enemy's strategy and then discern the enemy's near-term objectives in light of the G2's understanding of the enemy's long-term strategic goals and customary mode of operation.

Designing an operational plan is an extremely difficult analytical task fraught with uncertainty. Strategies are general plans for achieving important long-term goals. Details and circumstances change, and so must the plans and intentions of successful commanders and executives. Thus, however clear and complete the G2's understanding of the enemy's strategy, the implementation of a strategy is an ongoing, fluid action subject to the changes induced by accident, luck, and calculated adjustments.

Therefore, although the G2's estimate of the enemy situation includes a very important statement about enemy intentions, that statement is at best a guarded estimate of enemy actions, couched in terms of probabilities. No seasoned G2 would confuse intelligence analysis with black magic and don the wizard's cap to proclaim what the enemy *will* do. No one, including the enemy commander, knows that. There are too many variables involved and the calculus is beyond human comprehension. In lieu of certainty, the experienced intelligence officer provides a carefully researched and clearly reasoned "estimate."

What is most striking about the military's approach to strategy is how interdependent the analytical and operational relationship is between planning and intelligence. No G3 would put together an operational order or strategic plan for a commander that did not include current estimates of both the environmental and enemy situations. In the military, strategic planning, by definition, requires and presumes a supporting intelligence function.

STRATEGIC INTELLIGENCE ESTIMATES: MILITARY VERSUS BUSINESS

The contemporary business corporation has adopted many of the forms and techniques of the military general staff. It has also, with middling success, tried to emulate the military's approach to strategic planning. And yet, with a few notable exceptions, corporations have shown little interest in or appreciation of the military's emphasis on the supporting intelligence function. As suggested in the previous chapter, this ignorance of and indifference to the analytical value of intelligence is due to a number of factors, not the least of which is the naive confusion in some quarters of intelligence analysis with industrial espionage. But if executives hope to improve the generally low quality of strategic planning that afflicts most corporations today—if they expect to revive the concept of corporate planning from the moribund paper drill into which it has often degenerated—they should examine with greater care the inner workings of the military general staff from whence the notion of strategic planning comes.

Compared to the military's analytical approach, strategic plans in most large corporations are formulated with comparatively little systematic intelligence on the "enemy"—that is, competitors. The "intelligence" that exists and is used to frame strategic plans is largely concerned with macroeconomic variables and/or marketing data. These are necessary intelligence subjects, but insufficient for a full understanding of the total strategic environment. Macroeconomic and market intelligence are analogous to the military's "area of operations" intelligence. They give the CEO and/or general manager a good sense of what the weather (macroeconomic variables) and the terrain (market details) will be like. Although terrain and weather are always constraints and often obstacles that any sound military strategy must take into consideration, they are usually subjects of secondary importance to intelligence on the enemy's forces, capabilities, and intentions. The former has an indirect effect on the commander's strategic plans; the latter has a far more direct and immediate effect. One of the reasons why business strategy is developed with such a limited intelligence perspective is that intelligence about the macroeconomic and market environments deals largely with the non-controversial issue of relative *strategic position,* whereas systematic intelligence about competitors' capabilities, vulnerabilities, and intentions raises the potentially troublesome subject of relative *strategic performance.* From a military perspective, then, business strategy is a curious phenomenon formulated by executives and planners who, given the odd imbalance in their strategic intelligence estimates, are apparently far more concerned with the effects of weather (macroeconomics) and terrain (market dimensions) on their plans than the potential impact of the enemy/competitors (see Table 4.2).

CORPORATE INTELLIGENCE STAFF ELEMENT: ORGANIZATIONAL ROLE

The basic role of a corporate intelligence staff is to serve as a focal point and coordination mechanism for the following:

TABLE 4.2. THE STRATEGIC INTELLIGENCE ESTIMATE

Military		Business	
Topic	Analytical Methods	Topic	Analytical Methods
The area of operations		The area of operations	
Weather	Meteorology	General economic environment	Macroeconomic analysis
Terrain	Geography	Markets/industry sectors	Market research industry analysis
Enemy situation	Military intelligence analysis	Competitive situation	Competitive analysis
Enemy capabilities	Military intelligence analysis	Competitive capabilities	Competitive analysis

As they develop strategic plans both the military and the business planner must evaluate the strategic environment. In the military roughly two-thirds of the strategic intelligence estimate focuses on the enemy's situation and capabilities; in the business world analysis of the "area of operations" (macroeconomics and markets) is stressed and only a marginal effort is made to evaluate competitors' situation and capabilities.

Initial development of a company-wide competitor intelligence program.

Training of business unit and staff personnel in intelligence methods.

Identification and organization of the company's internal sources of competitor information.

Identification of and liaison with external sources of competitor information—for example, public agencies, competitive data search firms, and market/financial research firms.

Liaison with corporate counsel on all relevant intelligence issues.

Development and maintenance of a competitor intelligence data base on the corporation's strategic peers (domestic and foreign corporations that are direct or indirect competitors in the company's major markets and industries).

Preparation and presentation of corporate and business level strategic intelligence analyses on key competitors.

Dissemination of special competitor intelligence (e.g., technical, financial, customer, legal) between business groups.

Development of competitor intelligence research and resources for internal corporate committees and task forces.

Because the tasks and the organization of a corporate strategic intelligence system are novel—and in some respects alien—concepts to most American companies, there is relatively little public information available on how to structure, operate, and integrate competitor-oriented business intelligence into the corporate planning process. Set up as an extra staffer in the planning department, or attached as an afterthought to the finance staff, the middle-level analyst or manager who is given the pioneering job of iniating a corporate-wide or a business-unit level strategic intelligence/competitor analysis program has an oversized analytical mandate, a fishing license to collect competitor information, but usually no road map and few if any company precedents or business experiences to fall back on. The laundry list of corporate roles and functions suggested above is easy to ennumerate, but difficult to realize because of the bureaucratic inertia in all large complex organizations, the novelty of the strategic intelligence function in most companies, and the hard political fact that competitor intelligence—once it gets up to speed—deals with a highly sensitive category of information. As the authors of a 1979 study that surveyed strategic intelligence systems in over 30 companies concluded:

> The construction of a viable strategic intelligence system is exceedingly complex because of the unstructured nature of strategic decisions, the difficulty of separating out important and relevant information from the vast amounts of data accessible to the manager, and the reliance of managers on personal information sources. As would be expected, in most of the companies interviewed, tactical information systems were better articulated than strategic ones. On the other hand, a number of companies have developed effective means of learning about their environments and, most importantly, have implemented strategic decision systems which allow them to capitalize on opportunities and to defend themselves against threats.[11]

CORPORATE INTELLIGENCE STAFF: INTRA-COMPANY RELATIONSHIPS

While the organization of a corporate level staff element to guide the strategic intelligence program and develop the competitor intelligence data base is important, the relationship of this intelligence section to other business units and staff groups is crucial to the overall success of a corporate-wide competitor intelligence system. Without access to and the support of key staff and business group managers, a corporate level intelligence staff will not be able to tap the company's valuable internal sources of competitor information. Nor will it be able to act as the company's switchboard for the rapid transmittal of critical competitor intelligence across business units and staff functions. Without a broad range of input, the competitor intelligence staff can easily become a passive reference and research arm of corporate or business unit planning that produces excessively detailed competitor reports derived from publicly available secondary sources. Whatever the marginal value of such intelligence reports, they do not begin to equal in richness, depth, or strategic value the ongoing intelligence output of an integrated, active, company-wide competitor intelligence system that connects all key operating and staff groups with an interactive feedback loop that efficiently disseminates relevant competitor intelligence, whatever its origin.

There are very practical reasons why some managers may resist any systematic corporate effort to tap competitor information and sources in their divisions. It is customary for a manager, particularly a business unit line manager, to be evaluated against budget; it is unusual and potentially more troublesome, however, to have one's performance compared and contrasted with that of major competitors.

Comparative information about competitor performance is the flip side of all competitive intelligence. For those managers who are struggling unsuccessfully to defend market share against aggressive, innovative competitors, the light shed on their dilemma by a rigorous competitor analysis may come at a high price. Better to attribute the division's trouble to the capraciousness of a difficult (but abstract) "market" or the inherent limitations of one's relative strategic "position" within the industry than to the superior strategy and performance of immediate competitors.

As Peter J. Carroll trenchantly observes, in most corporations strategic planning staffers are not encouraged to examine issues of comparative competitive performance as they apply to business-unit strategies. The *median profitability* of a business such as industrial chemicals may be 28 percent pre-tax ROE versus 32 percent for newspaper publishing. This, as Carroll explains, is the "positional component" of strategy. It reflects the inherent structural characteristics of the business and the effect of macroeconomic forces (e.g., end-use demand growth, basic supply/demand balance, and government regulation).[12] If strategy is defined only in "positional" terms, one can conclude that newspaper publishing is an inherently better business than industrial chemical manufacturing. However, if one conducts a careful comparative analysis of industrial chemical competitors, it soon becomes obvious that there is a wide variation in the profitability levels of the competing firms, with some achieving a pre-tax ROE well above the 32 percent median enjoyed by the newspaper publishers. The *profitability variations* within a business/industry reflect the "performance component" of strategy. Carroll ascribes the variations in relative strategic performance to two factors of unequal influence.

The microeconomics of a business (e.g., distribution cost per unit, R & D costs, production run length, sales coverage, and variable manufacturing costs) are the underlying "economic imperatives" that determine the sources of comparative strategic advantage in a business. They have the largest influence on a company's competitive strategic performance.

The secondary factor is operational efficiency within the firm—running a tighter ship with a leaner, more diligent crew. Ironically, but perhaps understandably, managers usually focus their time, energy, and resources on efforts to improve their businesses' operational efficiency. Perhaps that is because it requires less imagination to concentrate one's efforts on running an existing operation faster with more diligence and greater administrative control than it does to step back and carefully study in detail the more complex, abstract relationships that structure the microeconomic factors that determine the sources of comparative advantage within a business. To put it another way, many line managers define operational success as working harder, not smarter. They are rather like those nineteenth century Lancashire mill owners who tried to improve output by running the spinning jennys faster and maintaining tighter control of the work force. Unlike those British managers, Francis Cabot Lowell thought long and hard about the microeconomic factors—economies of scale, the interrelationship of manufacturing steps, factory design—that could, if properly identified and shrewdly exploited, significantly improve the comparative advantage of the textile mill he was planning to build in Waltham.

If a company's competitor intelligence program is effectively organized and given guidance by management, it will collect data on:

1. The *positional elements* of a competitor's strategy—the macroeconomic business environment.
2. The two *performance elements* of a competitor's strategy: operational efficiency (how well the business is run internally), and differences in management's understanding and exploitation of the microeconomic sources of comparative advantage.

The collection and analysis of data on a competitor's strategic position is relatively straightforward and routinely done by most companies. Although it is an essential intelligence task, it is neither a difficult nor controversial one. As Carroll defines it, the information required to accomplish this phase of the competitor intelligence profile would include[13]:

Market Definition.
- Market size and growth.
- Product segments.
- Customer segments.
- Market structure and product flow.
- Nature of demand.
- Other competitors and their positioning.

External Macroeconomic actors.
- Demand-related factors (e.g., radical substitution, government regulation).

Production-related factors (e.g., resource availability, technology).
Competitive factors (e.g., irrational or massive competitors).
Financial factors (e.g., interest rates, capital availability).
Political factors (e.g., country risk).

But when the analytical focus shifts to the detailed evaluation of those business factors that determine a competitor's strategic performance—its operational efficiency and microeconomic sources of comparative advantage—the competitor intelligence task becomes extremely difficult and potentially controversial. On their own, few corporate-level intelligence staffers have either the business experience, extensive information sources, or intuitive grasp of the complex interplay of a business' microeconomic factors to effectively identify and evaluate the performance aspect of a competitor's strategy. An experienced line or staff manager with a seasoned understanding of the fixed (structural) and variable (responsive) factors that can be manipulated to achieve a comparative strategic advantage over the competition in a particular business must be actively involved in this phase of the competitor intelligence effort.

To illustrate, an analyst who is preparing a strategic intelligence assessment of a competitor in the forest products industry knows that competitor X's strategic performance will be influenced by its ability to exploit a source of comparative advantage such as distribution cost per unit shipped, or a secure raw material source such as timber. But to completely evaluate and collect adequate data on these "intelligence factors", the analyst needs the assistance of a seasoned operator who has a "feel" for the nuances of paper-mill freight practices and the complex distinctions between sources, costs, and characteristics of different fiber alternatives—roundwood versus chipped, Southern yellow pine versus Douglas fir, fee timber versus leased. The intelligence analyst can help the general manager to see more clearly the analytical link between the comparative performance of business opponents and their competitive strategy; the general manager, in turn, can focus the intelligence program on the most critical microeconomic factors in the business and improve the collection of competitor data by identifying the most useful, reliable information sources. Over the long run, the development of this critical intelligence partnership between the planning/intelligence staff and the line managers will:

Foster the growth of a corporate intelligence program that effectively covers the full spectrum—positional and performance—of competitors' strategy.

Tie the corporate level strategic intelligence effort into the operational concerns and information sources of the business units.

Help business-unit line managers increase their understanding of the key sources of comparative advantage that competitors may manipulate to achieve superior strategic performance.

Facilitate the efficient use of limited intelligence resources by targeting the collection and analysis effort on the most relevant measures of competitor strategy.

Enable both business units and the corporation to improve their relative competitive performance by exploiting new or changing sources of comparative advantage before the competition does.

However, as Carroll reminds us, there are a number of complex reasons why the strategic (and thus the intelligence) agenda of most companies is focused on the more benign "positional" strategic issues and avoids the controversial but equally vital issues of strategic "performance":

Role of the Strategic Planning Departments
Planning has a unique political problem. The positional component of strategy requires a good market definition and an analysis of external factors. The performance component of strategy requires a fundamental analysis of the underlying functional areas, and a competitive analysis which will then reveal the company's relative standing in terms relevant to strategy. As a staff department, planning can sell the first but not the second component. The line areas typically will not permit an explicit discussion of the economics of a business.

Functional Specialization
The functional specialization which exists in almost all companies helps to insure that many important economic relationships which exist across functional lines are either not recognized at all nor seen in proper perspective. Again, the integrative role required should be fulfilled by a strategy department.

Anti-intellectualism
A great many companies perceive analysis and inquiry in a suspicious light. Pressure to get the job done, the failure of business education, bad experiences—these may all contribute to this attitude. . . .

Lack of a General Concept
. . . the lack of a general concept that there is or could be a performance strategy which would yield superior financial performance. Most people implicitly believe that all companies in a business receive the "margin" for that business. Small deviations are acknowledged but attributed to differences of execution, of persistent diligence. In fact, performance

varies enormously, reflecting not only differences of execution, but also differences with respect to the sources of comparative advantage in a business.

No Framework for Analysis
Where the existence of sources of comparative advantage is recognized in principle, the lack of framework for analysis inhibits their explicit development. Line managers, under these circumstances, are assumed to incorporate their collective intuition somehow into the strategy development process. The political difficulties of the strategic planning department in encouraging such explicit analysis reinforce the tendency to rely on "intuitive incorporation".[14]

DIVISIONAL COMPETITOR INTELLIGENCE LIAISON REPS

To link the strategic planning department's intelligence staff to other parts of the corporation with an ongoing need for competitor intelligence to a point of contact should be designated in each critical staff and line unit. These individuals would serve as the intelligence liaison between the divisions and the corporate planning department. For most, the "intelligence" task would be a secondary responsibility. Working with, but not for, the corporate intelligence staff on an exception basis, they would coordinate the collection of competitor information within their unit, maintain an appropriate but division-specific competitor data base, serve as a communications channel on intelligence issues, and guide the corporate intelligence staff's efforts to optimize the division's intelligence resources with minimum disruption to ongoing operations. Formally trained in the methods of competitor analysis and schooled in the basic techniques of business intelligence, these "intelligence liaison reps" would help insure the smooth functioning of a company-wide competitor intelligence network, while at the same time developing the intelligence resources and serving the intelligence needs of their division. In view of the sensitivity of competitor intelligence, the divisional intelligence liaison rep should probably be a senior departmental manager who reports directly to the executive in charge of the division. Business units with their own planning staffs will probably make the senior planning manager the unit's intelligence rep; otherwise, a senior marketing or financial manager is a logical choice.

Where the corporation has foreign operations and/or subsidiaries, an international intelligence liaison rep should be established as a point of contact. Where possible, personnel permitting, each country should have a designated representative to handle competitor intelligence requests from corporate and business staffs that need information about competitors with headquarters and/or operations in that country. Adequate business intelligence on international competitors is usually one of the most serious intelligence gaps in corporations. At great expense, outside consultants are often hired to collect international competitor intelligence despite the fact that their office in country X (if they have one) has inferior contacts and less in-country experience than the nationals of country X that staff and run the corporation's own operations. Again, this illustrates the ironic fact that most companies have internal competitor intelligence resources that are inherently superior to external sources, but are often overlooked and underutilized. Besides providing raw data and finished intelligence on foreign competitors, the country intelligence representatives are in an excellent position to advise the corporation on the best methods of and sources for collecting foreign competitor intelligence.

As will be discussed in more detail in subsequent chapters, competitor intelligence-gathering varies substantially from country to country. In Canada and Europe, for example—where antitrust laws are less restrictive than those in the United States—trade associations may publish detailed competitor data and competitors may routinely share operational details that would land a business executive in jail in the United States.

Alternatively, competitor intelligence might be far more difficult to collect because of different cultural and political customs. In Japan, for example, an employed or retired business executive who discusses corporate operations with outsiders—be they market researchers or investment analysts—runs a grave risk of social banishment. With their strong sense of company loyalty, deference to senior leaders, and sensitivity to the practical value of commercial intelligence, Japanese businessmen make difficult intelligence targets. As a result, available competitor data is, by Western standards, very limited in Japan. The company and industry reports put out by the country's leading investment brokerage firms—e.g., Nomura, Daiwa, and Yamiachi—are improving, but they do not approach the details common in U.S. security analysis reports.

Because Japanese banks are the major source of capital funds and hold such a large position in many firms, they represent one of the most thorough and accurate sources of both quantitative and qualitative company information. Few Japanese banks, however, will make this valuable competitor intelligence available to outsiders, and contract research of a competitive nature is virtually unknown. The Mitsubishi Group, one the country's largest industrial-financial organizations, publishes some of Japan's most informative company and industry reports, although the orientation is heavily financial. Another useful source of quantitative data is the Ministry of Finance reports that publicly owned forms file on an annual basis. Many subsidiaries of large firms must also file Ministry of Finance reports that provide unusually specific details on sources of supply and manufacturing cost inputs as well as production data, sales, and earnings.

But in Japan, the most valuable and practical source of information is usually a senior, experienced business executive with the social and professional credentials needed to access the leading business circles. Such an individual is able to tap the important information lodes within the banking industry in addition to picking up the more informal qualitative data that circulates, albeit in a highly circumscribed fashion, in important business and professional circles.

An American analyzing West German competitors will find that the assistance of a European well-versed in the subtleties of German accounting is crucial to an accurate understanding of the voluminous numbers that march across the public financial statements of these firms. As a *Forbes* article on Germany's large chemical companies points out, the analytical significance of financial terms varies considerably across national boundaries and can easily mislead the uninitiated:

> Profits. It is here that the U.S. and German chemical industries really part company. In the U.S., for example, Union Carbide has something of a reputation as a sluggish performer. Yet Carbide earned, net, 6 cents on the sales dollar last year [1979]; BASF reported only 2 cents on the sales dollar. So, where are the profits that Seefelder [BASF Chairman] talks about? They are there, but less visible than in the U.S. You can put it this way: Germans understate profits. Or, you can put it another: Americans overstate *real* profits. In either case, the quality of earnings is much higher in Germany. Unlike U.S. firms, the Germans reduce rather than inflate reported profits. Frequently, their assets are depreciated at up to twice the common rate permitted here. Then there are the special reserves companies can charge against income under German law. These can range from future pension payments, to the extra costs a company expects to pay for its raw materials during inflationary times. . . .

> In Germany, pension plans must be fully funded, but that's no real hardship. This reserve reduces earnings—and taxes—but the company still gets full use of the funds, paying the annual pension liability out of current earningss. There is no ERISA there. In effect, those German pension reserves amount to a huge low interest loan, often running into billions of marks.[15]

While over time an American-based analyst will probably become familiar with these and other intricacies of German financial reports, time is usually a major constraint in gathering competitor intelligence. Therefore, the country intelligence rep is in a better position to provide the most accurate interpretation of the required data in the shortest period of time. From the rep's vantage point and intuitive cultural knowledge, the analytical traps can be avoided that will inevitably confuse and confound the analyst who foolishly tries to interpret foreign competitive information from afar.

CONCLUSION

To improve the strategic planning process, intelligence must be organized and managed, not left to half measures and chance. Despite the increased awareness of the strategic value of continuous and systematic competitor intelligence, relatively few companies have identified the internal organization aspects of their competitor intelligence gap. There are extensive governmental and military intelligence organizations that corporations could draw on selectively to meet their intelligence organizational needs. But executives in most corporations are still focused on the issue of what function competitor intelligence will serve. Until that policy issue is resolved, the complicated and potentially controversial issues raised by the specter of a "corporate intelligence organization" will not be addressed.

Yet the policy and the organizational aspects of intelligence are uniquely intertwined. A reservoir of valuable competitor information lies within most companies waiting to be systematically tapped by a lean, loosely structured, corporate-wide intelligence network. The mobilization of that underutilized strategic resource will position the company to collect and use a more relevant range of external competitor data not usually fed into the corporate planning system. Thus, the issue of competitor intelligence comes down—as most significant problems do in complex institutions—to the organizational aspects.

How the collection, coordination, and dissemination of competitor intelligence will be organized within a corporation is the difficult part. Once this structural problem is addressed, if not resolved, the "intelligence process" will have the stable foundation it needs. Chapter 5 will explore the analytical techniques that drive this intelligence process.

A final caution. Competitor intelligence is organizational dynamite in most corporations. To be successful, it requires the operation of an internal information network that focuses on the raw data of the most dynamic and psychologically interesting aspect of a company's strategic environment—its competitors. Yet, as suggested in earlier chapters, competitor intelligence may also become both a corporate analytical resource for sharper strategies, and an information vehicle that fosters more effective lateral intelligence between widely scattered business units operating in disparate markets, industries, and countries. This lateral intelligence should enable business units in large corporations to respond more rapidly and more successfully to the strategic threats posed by indirect competitors. In this respect, then, a carefully crafted competitor intelligence organization may significantly improve both the strategic cohesion of operating units and the strategic decision-making process of the entire corporation.

---

[1]From the Dervish Tales of Idries Shah, *Planning Review,* January, 1982, p. 47. Published by Robert J. Allio and Associates, Inc. for the North American Society for Corporate Planning.

[2]Michael Porter, *Competitive Strategy,* New York, Free Press, a division of Macmillan, 1980, p. 72.

[3]Wall, "What the Competition Is Doing—Your Need to Know," p.23; Information Data Search, Inc., "Fortune 500 Planners and Their Commercial Intelligence Need," Cambridge, Mass., 1981, and "Corporate Intelligence Gathering," Cambridge, Mass., 1982; Robert H. Solomon, "Industrial Intelligence: Does Your Company Need It?" *Industrial Marketing,* May, 1978, pp. 24–26.

[4]Wall, p. 30.

[5]Ibid.

[6]IDS, 1981, p. 4.

[7]See F. T. Pearee, "Business Intelligence Systems—The Need For Development and Integration," *Industrial Marketing Management,* June 1976, pp. 115–138; and D. I. Cleland and W. R. King, "Competitive Business Intelligence Systems," *Business Horizons,* December 1975, pp. 19–28.

[8]IDS, 1982.

[9]Samuel P. Huntington, *The Soldier and the State,* New York, Random House, 1957, pp. 50–52.

[10]U.S. Army Infantry School, *Operations and Training Handbook,* Fort Benning, Georgia, 1968, p. 5–2.

[11]David Montgomery and Charles Weinberg, "Toward Strategic Intelligence Systems," *The Journal of Marketing,* Vol. 43 (Fall, 1979).

[12]Peter J. Carroll, "The Link Between Performance and Strategy," *The Journal of Business Strategy,* Spring, 1982, pp. 5–9.

[13]Carroll, "The Link Between Performance and Strategy," p. 10.

[14]Peter J. Carroll, *The Journal of Business Strategy,* Volume 2, No. 4, Spring, 1982.

[15]Paul Gibson, "How the Germans Dominate the World Chemical Industry," *Forbes,* October 13, 1980, p. 159.

5

Competitor Intelligence: An Analytical Approach

WILLIAM L. SAMMON

Biographical data for this chapter author appear on page 21.

Once an organizational structure has been tentatively established within the company to carry out the corporation's competitor intelligence program, analytical procedures for collecting competitor information and processing it into usable intelligence can be adapted to the corporation's needs.

INFORMATION AND INTELLIGENCE

A basic but often misunderstood principle is that intelligence $\neq$ information. Information is the raw material of the intelligence process. It is unevaluated, unanalyzed data derived from every possible source of information—financial statements, trade show gossip, union newsletters, marketplace rumors, product brochures, executive speeches, and so on. The bits and pieces of competitor information that flow by in a constant stream may be true or false, relevant or irrelevant, confirmed or unconfirmed, positive or negative, deceptive or insightful. In its undigested state, this voluminous competitor information, 90 percent of which is publicly available, may be vaguely interesting and occasionally intriguing, but however glittering it is essentially an unusable and potentially dangerous resource.

Within this disorganized, confused stream of competitor information there is, however, a pattern of knowledge that if pieced together and analyzed can be very revealing and strategically significant. *Intelligence is the analytical process that transforms disaggregated competitor data into relevant, accurate, and usable strategic knowledge about competitors' position, performance, capabilities, and intentions.* With this intelligence—this knowledge about competitors' strategy—the uncertainty that confronts executives who make strategic decisions is reduced, and the probability of making the right decision is increased. The clear connection of intelligence to strategic planning is seen in this classic definition of intelligence drawn from the *Dictionary of United States Military Terms for Joint Usage*:

> Intelligence—The product resulting from the collection, evaluation, integration and interpretation of all available information which concerns one or more aspects of foreign nations or of areas of operations and which is immediately or potentially significant to planning.[1]

Strategies represent the most fundamental policy decisions that senior management must make. Intelligence influences, but does not exclusively determine, the informational component of strategic policy in which fundamental corporate "objectives" are defined, and a long-term plan is developed to achieve those "strategic objectives" through the effective utilization of corporate resources, the strategic "means" available to management. Obviously, the information resources management draws on in developing the corporation's strategy will profoundly influence both the choice of strategic objectives and the selection of corporate resources used to implement the chosen strategy and achieve the desired strategic objectives.

As a formally analyzed type of evaluated information, strategic competitor intelligence can be a valuable source of environmental information but is never the only source, and is always subject to interpretation by the decision-maker for whom it is developed. Those involved in the production of intelligence need to remember this in order to keep their work in perspective. In the production of environmental information and the formulation of strategic decisions, the role of strategic intelligence is *supplemental,* not determinative. Even in governmental circles where the use of formal intelligence estimates is a long-established part of the policy process, decision-makers do not base their actions solely on the information developed by their sophisticated intelligence systems:

> The body of information offered under the label of strategic or national intelligence to governmental leaders as they ponder national security policy issues is merely one element in the intellectual process by which responsible officials reach a decision or make a policy. Certainly, the intelligence ingredient in this process must compete with other factors to be considered, and other "pictures in the mind" of the decision maker. These include not only his receptivity to, and faith in the accuracy of, the proffered intelligence estimate, but also his own assumptions, biases, perceptions, and knowledge from other sources and from experience. In a sense, the official intelligence estimate must compete also with the sometimes unconscious evaluations made by the decision maker from his reading of *The Washington Post* or *The New York Times.* Undeniably, such influential newspapers are a major intelligence source for decision makers.[2]

In corporations where formal strategic intelligence is still a rudimentary concept, management's perception of the environmental situation will continue to be largely derived from an intuitive understanding of the strategic forces at play. If strategic competitor intelligence is presented to senior managers as a supplemental resource that needs to be interpreted by them in light of their intuitive understanding of the strategic situation, the concept of intelligence as an analytical resource will not be oversold and it will probably be less threatening to the decision-makers who would use it.

THE INTELLIGENCE CYCLE

One of the more useful analytical concepts for identifying the components of the intelligence process and understanding their complex interrelationships is the notion of the intelligence cycle. In military and governmental intelligence agencies, the intelligence cycle is one of the most traditional analytical concepts, and has frequently been used to differentiate the process of intelligence into discrete organizational activities. The basic elements or phases of the intelligence cycle are shown in Figure 5.1. In recent years, the concept of the intelligence cycle has crossed over into the business literature and been modified by a number of authors to fit the competitor intelligence needs of the strategic planning process. (See Figure 5.2).

In this extremely detailed and informative schematic, Michael Porter, the author of *Competitive Strategy,* a seminal work in the strategic planning/competitor analysis literature, provides a series of practical "options" that can be used to operationalize a number of the intelligence system's functions. That, of course, is the core of the organizational problem that confronts managers trying to set up a corporate-wide competitor intelligence system—developing practical and effective procedures to implement the phases or steps of the intelligence cycle. Figure 5.3, the military's expanded version of the intelligence cycle, clearly delineates the four phases of the intelligence cycle and highlights the key elements of each.

PHASE 1: DIRECTING THE INTELLIGENCE EFFORT

The first phase of the intelligence cycle—collection planning or intelligence direction—is the most critical and yet frequently the most ignored. It is often the case that when a competitor intelligence program is first authorized in a company, collecting information—the second phase in the cycle—looms up as the major problem. At conferences and seminars on competitor intelligence the overwhelming number of questions from the floor focus on what appears to be the

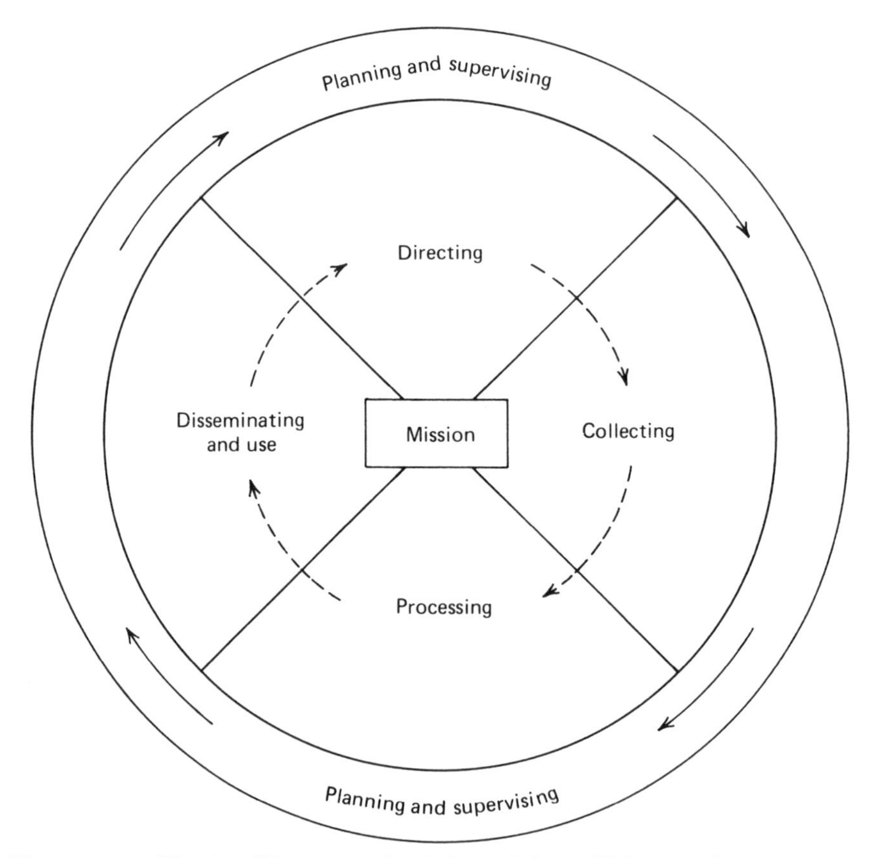

Figure 5.1 The intelligence cycle. Adapted from FM 30-5, *Combat Intelligence,* Headquarters Department of the Army, G.P.O., Washington, D.C., 1973, pp. 2–14.

most troublesome issue: How is information on competitors gathered? What are the best sources? Where does one go to get data on private companies, divisions of large firms, or foreign corporations?

But after the competitor intelligence program is set up and in operation, it soon becomes evident that collecting relevant information and finding useful sources is not nearly as large a problem as it was thought to be. In fact, the opposite is usually the case. The managers and analysts trying to run the intelligence program can quickly find themselves and their system overwhelmed by a cornucopia of competitor information. At this point those involved in the program belatedly recognize that the fundamental intelligence problem is not collecting information, but rather *what* to collect and for *what purpose.*

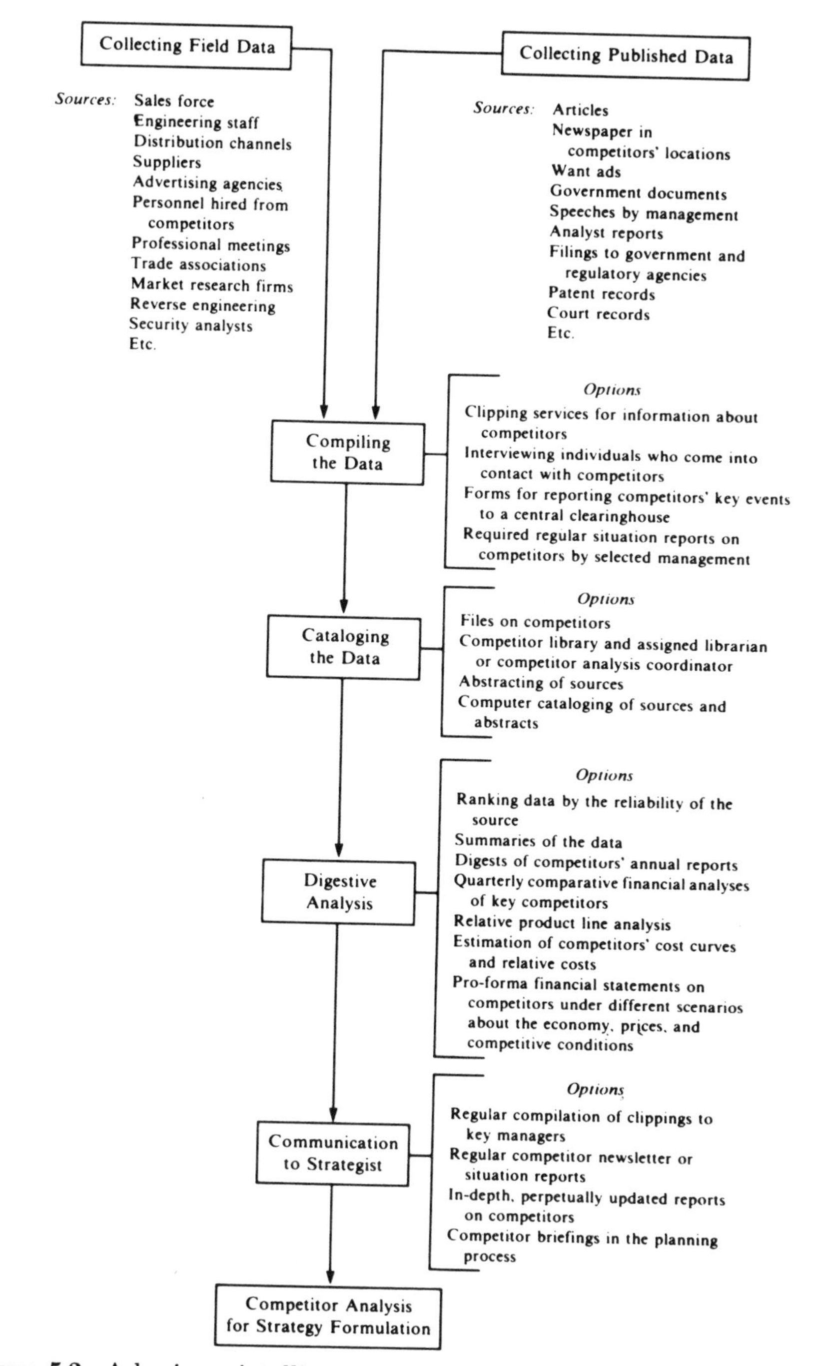

Figure 5.2 A business intelligence system. From Michael E. Porter, *Competitor Strategy,* Free Press New York, 1980, Figure 3.4, p. 73.

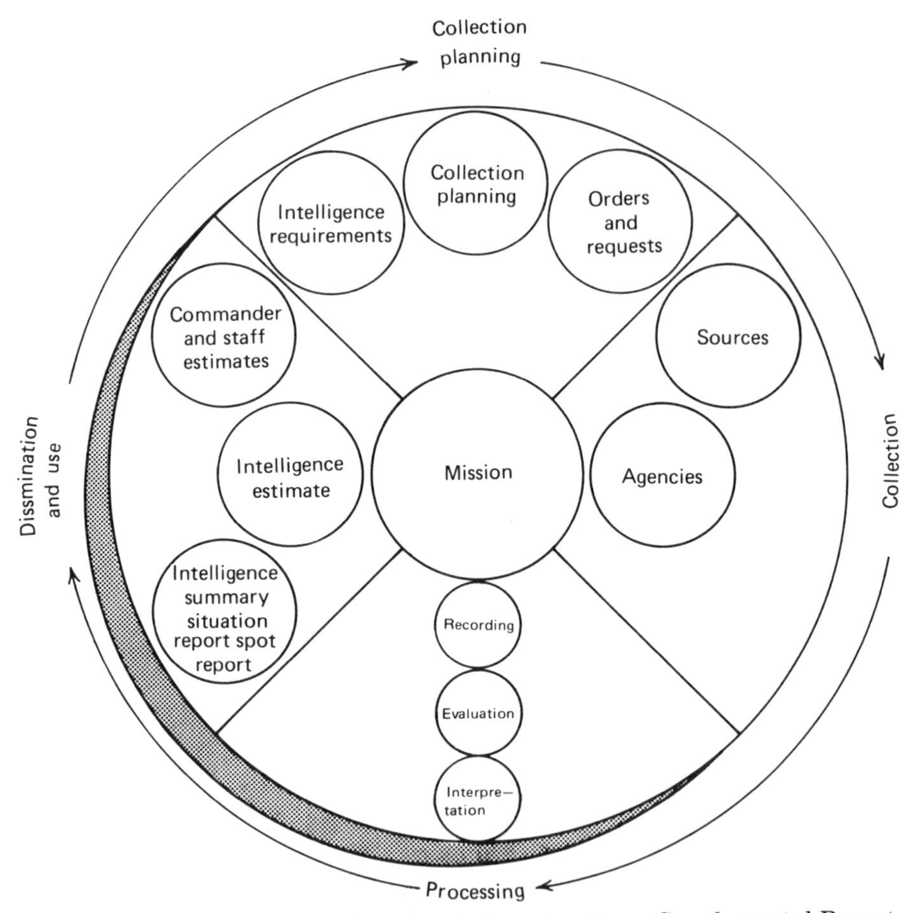

Figure 5.3 Intelligence cycle, expanded version. From Supplemental Report 67510 (D/NRI) *Intelligence Orientation,* U.S. Army Intelligence School, June 1968, p. 8.

If the company's competitor intelligence needs are not first carefully defined and then rank-ordered according to senior management's guidance, competitor information will be collected in an aimless, unsystematic fashion. Intelligence priorities will be set by those who produce it rather than those who use it—the key decision-makers. If collection takes precedence over direction, senior management is probably uninvolved in the intelligence program, or worse, involved in a pro forma manner only. In the long run an intelligence program that fails to get senior management actively involved in the direction phase of the cycle will find that its intelligence products have little strategic value and less and less organizational relevance.

From a strategic perspective, management will usually need intelligence for two general purposes: environmental scanning and competitor analysis. The major elements in each are outlined below.

- I. Environmental scanning
    - a. Macroeconomic analysis
    - b. Market research/industry analysis
    - c. Public issue analysis (social, governmental, cultural)
- II. Competitor analysis
    - a. Current strategy and long-term goals
        - 1. Strategic position
            - a. Historical development
            - b. Corporate culture
        - 2. Strategic performance
            - a. Financial
            - b. Operational
            - c. Sources of comparative advantage
        - 3. Organizational and functional capabilities and vulnerabilities
        - 4. Business segments portfolio
        - 5. Management characteristics
    - b. Future strategy and long-term goals
    - c. Strategic net assessment
        - 1. Probable moves and reactions
        - 2. Threat posed to your company
        - 3. Opportunity open to your company

Intelligence Requirements for Competitor Analysis

Although some regard competitor analysis as a subcomponent of environmental scanning, it is probably advisable to identify it as a separate and distinct analytical effort to insure that it is given the strategic priority and management attention it requires. Too often the study of competitors will be subsumed in market research or industry analyses, and only an incomplete and very partial view of competitors' strategies will emerge. The potential influence of competitors on a company's fortunes is too significant to be indirectly addressed as a side issue of market/industry analyses.

The detailed competitor intelligence requirements will, of course, vary over time and between companies. However, the fundamental strategic issue that should be in the forefront of senior management's competitor intelligence requirement is the basic question: What is the competitor's strategy, and how does that strategy threaten our current and/or desired strategic position and goals? The major elements of a full competitor analysis that addresses all the major aspects of this key strategic question are outlined above. The items in IIA, IIB, and IIC can easily be converted into distinct and specific intelligence requirements on the competitors that senior management wants covered.

If these intelligence requirements are satisfied, planning analysts at the corporate and business-unit level should have sufficient intelligence to complete the full-scale, multidimensional competitor analyses that are an essential part of the strategic planning process. The strategic intelligence components of the competitor analysis framework outlined above are fairly inclusive and would require an extensive collection and analysis effort. Often, however, a limited or partial competitor analysis will suffice.

There are many different approaches to strategic competitor analysis, but if the analytical orientation is strategic, for the most part they tend to be variations on the basic competitor analysis framework delineated above. Some of the more prominent and useful analytical frameworks for structuring competitor analyses were discussed in Chapter 1. The well-known growth/share matrix, which defines a firm's competitive business strength in terms of relative market share and uses total market growth as a relative comparative measure of industry attractiveness, is a widely used framework for competitor analysis. It is, however, of limited value because of its simplicity and questionable objectivity. There are, of course, many other factors besides market growth and market share that influence and reflect a competitor's strategy. Michael Porter's analytical framework (see Figure 5.4) for competitor analysis is far more ambitious and complex in scope and design, but ultimately more practical.

One of the strong virtues of Porter's approach to competitor analysis is the emphasis he wisely places on the need to understand a competitor's assumptions about itself and the industry in which it competes. Too often managers incorrectly assume that counterparts in competing firms are driven by the same set of variables and view the world from a similar perspective. Understanding a competitor's as-

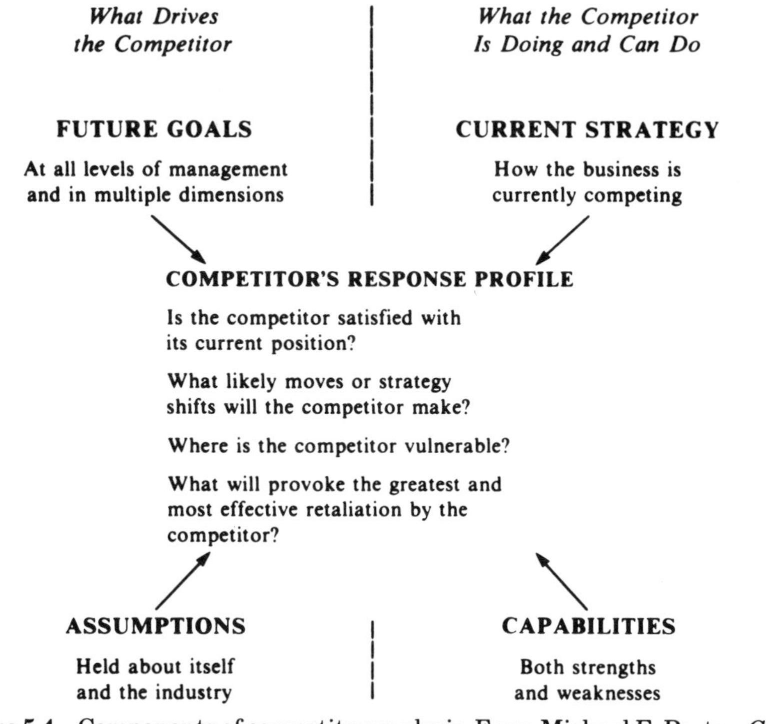

Figure 5.4 Components of competitor analysis. From Michael E. Porter, *Competitive Strategy,* Free Press, New York, 1980, Figure 3.1, p. 49. Reprinted with permission of the Macmillan Publishing Company.

sumptions is one of the most challenging intelligence tasks because it requires an insightful evaluation of a competitor's value system, organizational culture, and historical pattern of behavior. It is a qualitative kind of competitor intelligence that is very rare in most corporations, where the strategic focus tends to be on the quantifiable facts that detail a competitor's observable business strengths and weaknesses.

Unless the managers who coordinate the collection of competitor information and the analysts who interpret it in terms of its potential strategic significance are fully cognizant of their own company's strategic plans and goals, their intelligence work will be done in a vacuum. That is another reason why the relationship between senior executives—the consumers of intelligence—and the planning analysts and managers who produce the intelligence, must be relatively close.

The relationship between decision-makers and their intelligence staffs has long been one of the most troublesome aspects of the intelligence cycle in government quarters. Corporations that would develop an intelligence system need to carefully consider the inherent organizational difficulties that can easily disrupt the direction phase of the intelligence cycle. In his seminal study of the organization and activity of strategic political intelligence, Sherman Kent succinctly summarizes the nature of this crucial problem:

> There is no phase of the intelligence business which is more important than the proper relationship between intelligence itself and the people who use its product. Oddly enough, this relationship, which one would expect to establish itself automatically, does not do this. It is established as a result of a great deal of persistent conscious effort, and is likely to disappear when the effort is relaxed.
>
> Proper relationships between intelligence producers and consumers is one of the utmost delicacy. Intelligence must be close enough to policy, plans, and operations to have the greatest amount of guidance, and must not be so close that it loses its objectivity and integrity of judgment. . .
>
> The need for guidance is evident, for if the intelligence staff is sealed off from the world in which action is planned and carried out, the knowledge which it produces will not fill the bill. . . . Its job is to see that the doers are generally well-informed; its job is to stand behind them with the book opened at the right page, to call their attention to the stubborn fact that they may be neglecting, and—at their request—to analyze alternative courses without indicating choice. Intelligence cannot serve if it does not know the doers' mind; it cannot serve if it has not their confidence; it cannot serve unless it can have the kind of guidance any professional man must have from his client.[3]

If management of the competitor intelligence function is assigned to the strategic planning staffs, while responsibility for establishing and rank-ordering competitor intelligence requirements rests with senior management, a corporation can minimize the lack of "intelligence direction" to which Kent refers.

Although senior management should be actively involved in setting intelligence requirements and priorities, a serious problem arises if the orientation of senior management to competitive issues is not strategic. If that is the case, they may restrict their intelligence requirements to secondary tactical, operational, and/or marketing targets. Unfortunately, the evidence suggests many executives are more interested in competitor data that deals with secondary operational issues they are most familiar with such as competitor pricing, than with broader-focused intelligence that delineates a competitor's strategy. For example, the 1982 IDS Corporate Intelligence Gathering survey found that "Product line income, marketing strategy and production costs were the most sought-after competitor data," but "executives seemed least interested in knowing about a competitor's human resources or management policies."[4] As discussed in the previous chapter, for some executives in high-tech industries, strategic intelligence is reduced to technical intelligence.

Although his data was collected in 1974 when the concept of strategic planning was still a novelty to many executives, Jerry Wall's *Harvard Business Review* survey on managers' attitudes toward competitor information suggested that strategic intelligence subjects were gradually increasing in relative importance (particularly in large corporations), but were still viewed as of secondary importance to details about competitor's pricing (see Figure 5.5). In commenting on the implications of this data, Wall concluded that executives seemed less interested in how their competitors handled internal operations and were more interested in their competitors plans for dealing with an increasingly uncertain strategic environment:

> As the exhibit indicates, the level of interest has increased for *all* categories of information, and certain shifts in their relative values have occurred since 1959. Next, considering the uncertain environment that executives face today, it is not surprising to note that the importance of both expansion and competitive plans has increased markedly, while that of both research and development and manufacturing processes has declined. This could mean that, at least for the present, executives are more concerned with how competitors plan to cope with uncertainty than with how they operate internally.[5]

In setting the competitor intelligence requirements, if senior management lowers its sights and focuses the intelligence effort on secondary, non-strategic issues, only time, diplomacy and the educational value of competitor intelligence can be used to gradually redirect the intelligence program to a more valuable strategic orientation. As Montgomery and Weinberg concluded in their survey of corporate strategic intelligence systems:

> For a strategic intelligence system to be useful, a company must have a real commitment to strategic planning. Otherwise, the planning process, if carried out at all, becomes only an exercise and managers appear to put limited effort into gathering and communicating accurate, relevant intelligence.[6]

Exhibit II
Kind of information respondents feel management needs to know about competitors

Kind of information	1973 rank	Percent of all respondents	1959 rank	Percent of all respondents	Industries most interested (by percent of respondents)		Companies most interested (by percent of respondents)	
Pricing	1	79%	1	67%	Retail or wholesale trade	91	Under 1,000 employees	80%
					Manufacturing industrial goods	88		
					Manufacturing consumer goods	82		
Expansion plans	2	54	7	20	Retail or wholesale trade	70	10,000 or more employees	64
					Education, social services	62		
					Transportation, public utility	61		
Competitive plans	3	52	8	18	Transportation, public utility	75	20,000 or more employees	62
					Advertising, media, publishing	70		
					Banking, investment, insurance	61		
Promotional strategy	4	49	2	41	Advertising, media, publishing	79	1 – 49 employees	54
					Retail or wholesale trade	69	10,000 or more employees	52
					Transportation, public utility	61		
Cost data	5	47	6	24	Defense or space industry	59	20,000 or more employees	53
					Construction, mining, oil	56		
					Manufacturing industrial goods	54		
Sales statistics	6	46	4	27	Retail or wholesale trade	63	10,000 or more employees	55
					Advertising, media, publishing	61		
					Manufacturing industrial goods	56		

R&D	7	41	3	36	Defense or space industry	72	500 or more employees	48
					Manufacturing consumer goods	52		
					Manufacturing industrial goods	52		
Product styling	8	31	9	18	Manufacturing consumer goods	53	10,000 or more employees	34
					Advertising, media, publishing	52		
Manufacturing processes	9	30	5	25	Manufacturing consumer goods	54	10,000 or more employees	40
					Manufacturing industrial goods	45		
					Government	44		
Patents and infringements	10	22	11	5	Manufacturing industrial goods	38	20,000 or more employees	34
					Manufacturing consumer goods	30		
Financing	11	20	10	6	Construction, mining, oil	34	20,000 or more employees	26
					Transportation, public utility	30		
Executive compensation	12	20	12	2	Education, social services	39	Under 250 employees	23
					Banking, investment, insurance	38		

Figure 5.5 Kind of information respondents feel management needs to know about competitors. Reprinted by permission of the *Harvard Business Review.* From "What the Competition Is Doing: Your Need to Know" by Jerry L. Wall (November/December 1974.

Strategic Competitor Mapping

One useful technique for orienting senior management on relevant *strategic* competitor intelligence requirements is a graphical picture of competitors that combines elements of the "strategic group map" with an analytical matrix that depicts competitors' financial performance. The strategic group map is a useful tool for graphically depicting the major qualitative variables or potential sources of comparative advantage that characterize the strategic competitive combinations and conditions within an industry. Michael Porter develops the concept of Strategic Groups at length in his recent book, *Competitive Strategy* (for a full understanding the reader is referred to Chapter 7, Structural Analysis Within Industries).[7]

Having first identified a business unit's or a corporation's major competitors, its "strategic peers," the analyst then groups them according to one or more significant strategic qualitative variables—for example, size, degree of vertical integration, business portfolio or product line mix, geographical focus, manufacturing costs position, distribution channels, and so on. As Porter notes, the best strategic variables to use "are those that *determine the key mobility barriers* in the industry."[8] In defining the intra-industry strategic groups, it is also preferable to use two strategic variables that are independent of each other.

Based on their relationship to these key strategic variables, major competitors are then classified in one of the industry's major "strategic groups." Size and product mix are two of the most familiar strategic differences between competitors, and it is often useful to employ these qualitative variables to initially categorize and dimension competitors.

One of the problems with strategic group maps is that they are a highly qualitative and abstract analytical tool. Initially they will be more palatible to senior management if they are combined with a quantitative frame of reference that provides a comparative picture of competitors' financial performance. It is a rare executive who is not intrigued by a well-researched and organized graphic map that provides a dual qualitative and quantitative perspective on competitors' strategic position and financial performance. After all, the ultimate payoff of a superior competitive strategy should be a *superior long-term* financial performance.

The quantitative dimension of competitors' relative strategic position and performance can be shown graphically by using the classic duPont Matrix. The financial quantitative frame of reference is established by the duPont Financial Ratio Analysis Formula: operating margin × asset turnover = return on assets (ROA). A simple but extremely informative matrix can be structured around this formula, as shown in Figure 5.6. ROA can be increased by moving up the X axis (increasing margin) and/or moving up the Y axis (raising asset turnover).

For example, competitor 2 and competitor 1 have the same profitability at 30 percent ROA, but they got there using very different strategies. Competitor 2's business has a comparatively low operating margin and high turnover; competitor 1's business is probably more

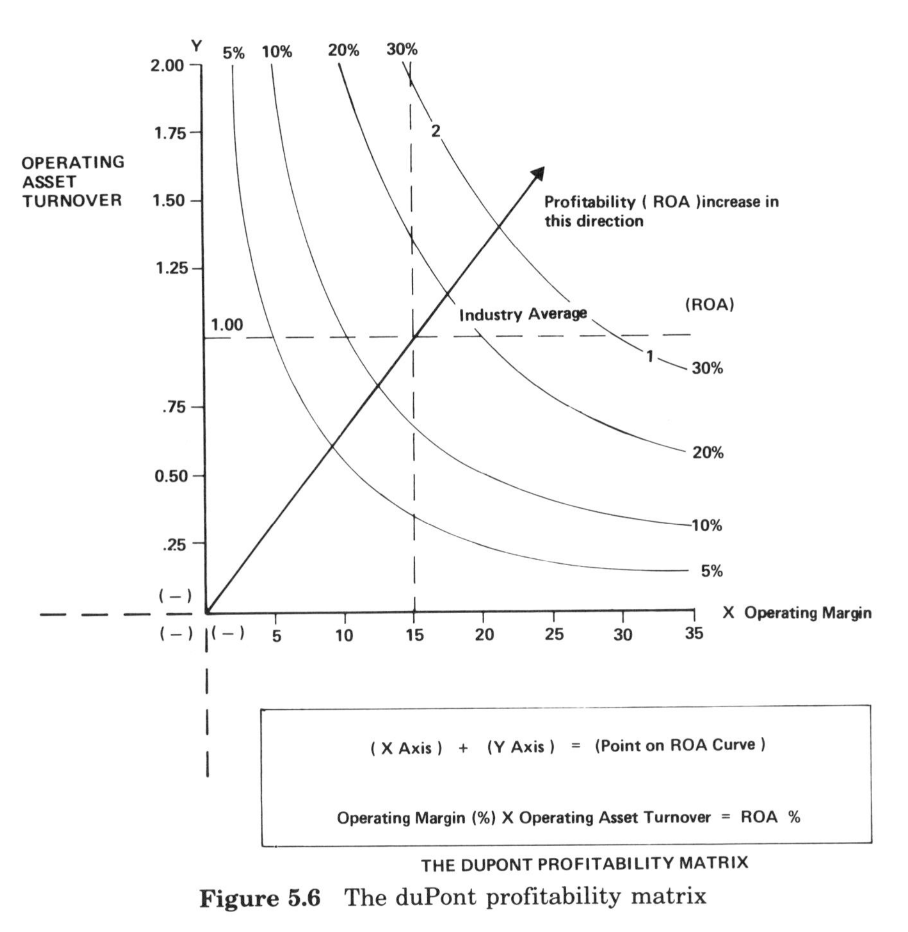

Figure 5.6 The duPont profitability matrix

capital-intensive because the margin is much higher than the turnover. Competitor 2 could be a dealer who sells a high volume of economical Fords, while competitor 1 could be a dealer who sells a small number of premium-priced Cadillacs. The duPont Profitability Matrix can be used to chart a competitor's movement over time and/or show a competitor's comparative position. This versatile matrix draws attention to the underlying relationships between strategic variables and financial performance—it does not explain them. Only detailed competitor intelligence can do that.

In the example illustrated in Figures 5.7 through 5.10, sixteen major competitors in the forest products industry have been analytically arrayed according to the following strategic dimensions:

Quantitative	*Qualitative*
4-year operating profitability: profits/assets	Product mix (wood, paper, or balanced)
4-year operating margin: profits/sales	Comparative size based on sales
4-year operating turnover: sales/assets	

In the forest products industry, the major commodity manufacturers tend to have a product line oriented to solid wood products (lumber, plywood, logs), paper products (linerboard, newsprint, printing paper), or a product mix that is almost equally weighted (in terms of sales) in wood and paper product lines. Initially, the product mix variable is used to define three qualitatively distinct strategic groups—wood, paper, and balanced. Although the three strategic groups are artificial entities, the financials (sales, profits, assets) of their constituent companies are totaled to get a representative set of financial ratios for the strategic group. All ratios are based on four or five years of data in order to minimize quantitative distortions due to cyclicalty. The strategic groups like the individual companies are sized with circles that are proportional to their relative four-year sales average.

Similarly, the competitors within each group are positioned along the axis of the duPont Matrix and located according to their four-year ROA percentage. They are also comparatively sized according to their four-year sales average.

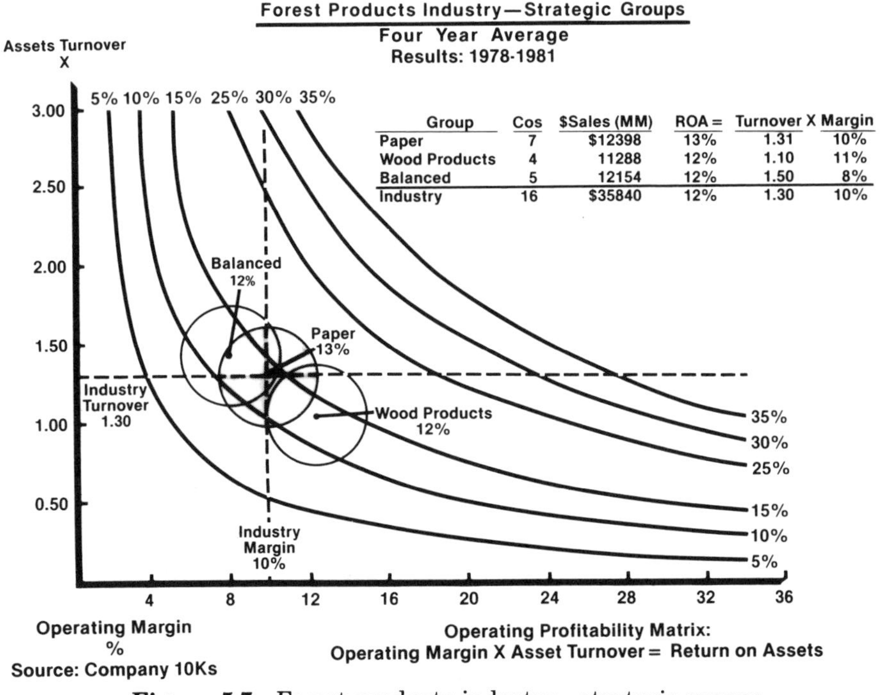

Group	Cos	$Sales (MM)	ROA =	Turnover X	Margin
Paper	7	$12398	13%	1.31	10%
Wood Products	4	11288	12%	1.10	11%
Balanced	5	12154	12%	1.50	8%
Industry	16	$35840	12%	1.30	10%

Figure 5.7 Forest products industry—strategic groups

The contribution of this "Strategic Group–duPont Profitability Matrix" to the competitor intelligence program is strictly heuristic. In no way does it constitute an adequate analytical framework for the full strategic competitor analyses outlined previously. Although it can be a useful component of those conceptual frameworks, its major value is its utility as an analytical device that provides a straightforward, easily graphed comparative perspective on the strategic position and competitive financial performance of a company's or business unit's strategic peers. With luck it may raise a few eyebrows and keep senior management's intelligence priorities focused on strategic rather than tactical/operational issues. For example, a brief perusal of the "Strategic Group–duPont Profitability Matrices" suggests the following strategic issues:

The paper strategic group enjoys the highest ROA—13 percent—of the three groups despite the fact that it includes one of the industry's largest but least profitable competitors. Does a product mix oriented

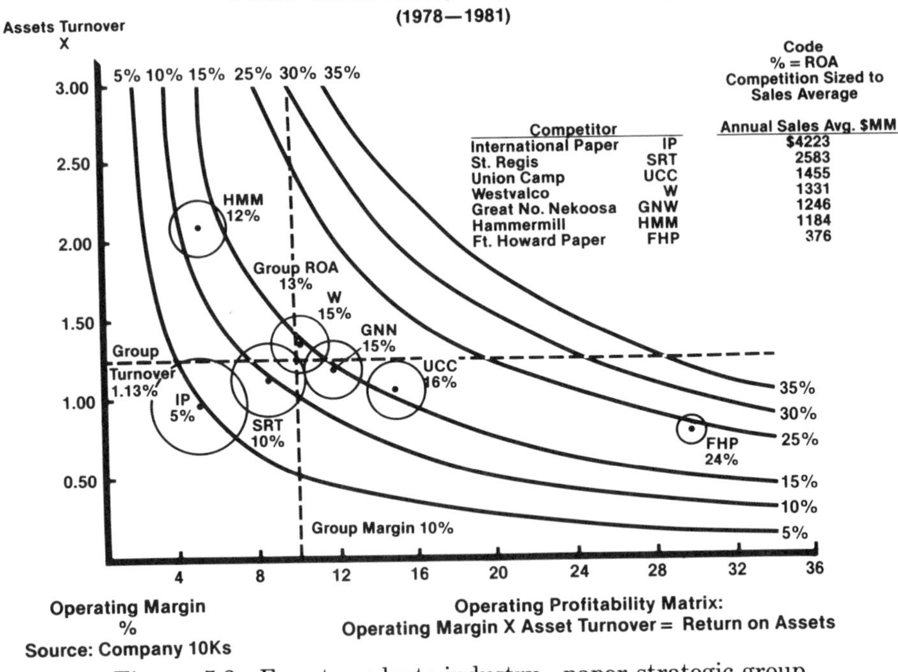

Figure 5.8 Forest products industry—paper strategic group

towards paper lines confer a strategic advantage in the current economic environment?

In the wood products group, large competitors have achieved a financial performance markedly superior to the group's smaller competitors. The reverse is the case in the paper group, where size seems to be a strategic disadvantage. Why?

With one or two notable exceptions, the balanced strategic group has the weakest mix of competitors in the industry. In their attempt to straddle both the wood and paper sectors, have they ended up with half measure-strategies and suffered a financial penalty as a consequence?

What explains the exceptional outlying performance of Ft. Howard Paper, one of the industry's smallest competitors, yet its most profitable by far?

Three competitors—Hammermill (paper group), Mead (balanced group), and Crown Zellerbach (balanced group)—have asset turnover ratios far above the industry norm of 1.30. This suggests that they have a product line and/or at least one business segment that is not capital intensive—unusual in a "smokestack" basic manufacturing industry like forest products. What are these segments or product lines and, in terms of ROA, is this an effective strategic option for increasing overall profitability while reducing the capital intensity of a company's business portfolio?[9]

Once senior management has defined its competitor intelligence requirements and established its priorities, the next step in the direction phase is to convert them into a competitor information collection plan that will be used to guide the second phase of the intelligence cycle—collection.

Intelligence Requirements: Essential Elements of Information

In the military the analytical link between the commander's intelligence requirements and the collection effort are the EEIs—"essential elements of information." EEIs are defined as:

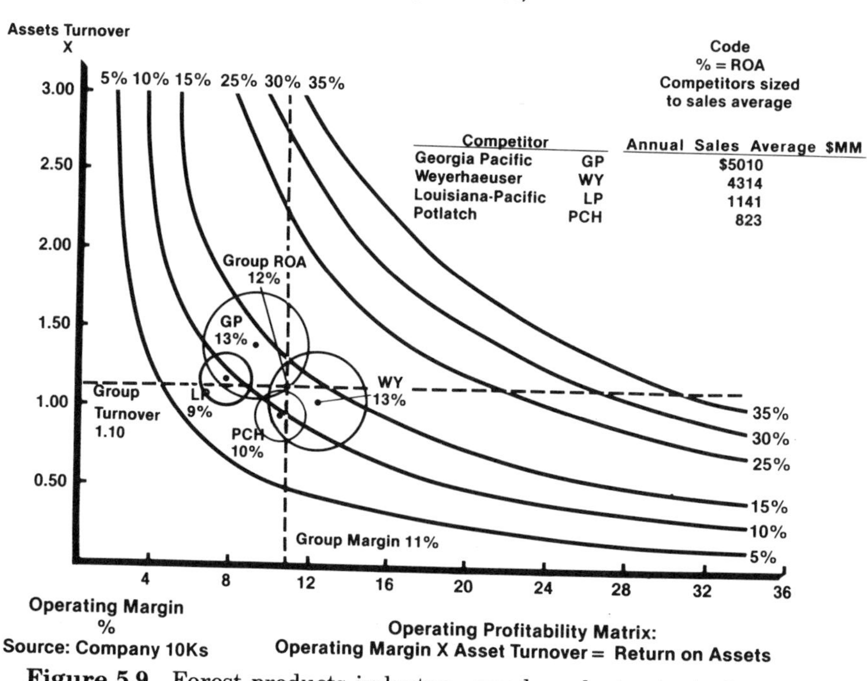

Figure 5.9 Forest products industry—wood products strategic group

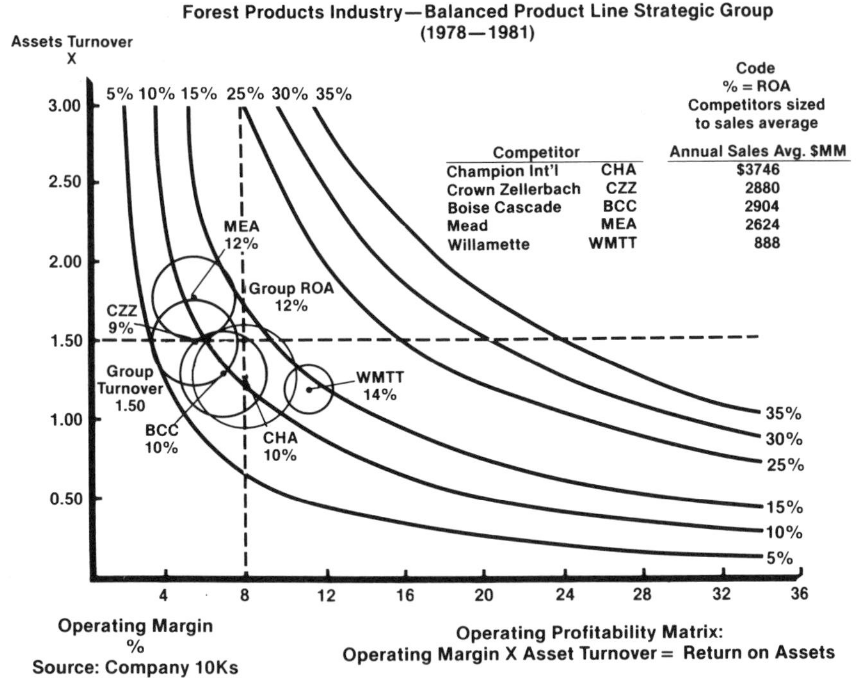

Figure 5.10 Forest products industry—balanced product line strategic group

> the critical items of information regarding the enemy and the environment needed by the commander by a particular time to relate with other available information and intelligence to assist him in reaching a logical decision. The decision involves the mission of the command and the choice of courses of action to accomplish the mission. Any enemy capability or characteristic of the area of operation which is a governing factor in the choice of courses of action will be an EEI. . . . Care must be exercised to limit EEIs to only those critical items of information.[10]

The inclination to collect everything about a competitor must be resisted. Focus is required both to control the collection of information and to use intelligence resources in the most cost-effective manner. EEIs boil down competitor intelligence requirements into a set of priorities. The EEIs should reflect the relevant analytical framework used to evaluate competitors for the strategic questions at issue. Those strategic concerns may be broad—for example, what are the mobility barriers that new competitors must overcome to enter our industry?—or very specific—which competitors have the strongest R & D capabilities and in what product areas are they now concentrating their resources?

If management's intelligence requirements are defined in terms of an agreed-upon competitor analysis framework, converting intelligence requirements to specific EEIs will be simplified.

Examples of intelligence requirements and the EEIs that can be developed from them are suggested below.

1. If the intelligence requirement is to "Develop a brief strategic profile of competitor X," the EEIs might be defined as:

Company X Profile Outline

I. Background/history
   Major events, acquisitions, divestitures, mergers
   Overseas investments
   Industry reputation
   Corporate culture: past, present, continuity
II. Business/product mix
   Five-year segment analysis: sales/profits/investments
   Major products: market share/market growth
III. Major corporate objectives/strategies
IV. Recent trends/business developments
V. Financial analysis: 5-year comparison with industry/business norms
   Sales growth
   Profit growth
   Return on assets
   Asset turnover
   Operating margin
   Net margin
   Return on equity
   Debt ratio
VI. Strategic assessment
   Strengths/weaknesses: functional and operational
   Strategic direction/management assumptions
   Expected performance/responsive capability
   Implications to company Z and company Y (your company)

2. If the intelligence requirement is to evaluate the competitive strength and potential of company Z's Industrial Chemical Division, EEIs might be framed as specific questions:

I. *Business Activity*
What is the division's sales of each product?
What is the percent breakdown of each product by type?
What are the major features of each product?
What are the key components?
How is the product used? What markets are served?

II. *Marketing*
What has been the division's strategy? How successful is it?
Distribution channels used?
Terms of sale and credit policies?
Market share by product line?
Geographic regions served and concentrations in each?
Size, competence, and organization of sales force?
Technical service provided?

III. *Financial Record*
Is this division more or less profitable than the company's other businesses?
Does this segment use more capital than it generates?
How does the financial performance of the segment compare with industry norms?
 Growth (sales, profits, assets)?
 ROA?
 ROS (operating margins)?
 Asset turnover?
What are the major cost issues in this division?
What are the key sources of profits?

IV. *Manufacturing*
Character and productivity of manufacturing process?
Size, capacity, operating rates of major facilities?
Plant locations?
Capital investments?
Overseas sourcing?
Relationship to marketing staff?

V. *Competition*
Number and size of rivals?
Comparative market share and growth prospects?
Strategic position and performance?
Comparative financial statistics?

VI. *Management Competence*
Age, length of service, depth?
Dominant professional background—e.g., marketing, technical, financial?
Company reputation; industry reputation?
Organizational and functional ability?
Recruitment sources; advancement paths?
Flexibility and adaptability?

3. If the intelligence requirement is to evaluate the strategic significance of a competitor's announcement of a $100-million capital investment at a key manufacturing facility, the EEIs could be defined this way:

What is the configuration (production components layout) of this facility?
In terms of scale and manufacturing cost, what is its comparative competitive position?
Which key elements of production equipment are subscale?
What are the major reasons for the announced investment?
  What identified production "bottlenecks" will it address?
  How will it affect total and variable manufacturing costs?
  How will customers view this investment?
In what way does this facility improvement/expansion further the competitor's corporate and/or product line strategies?
What is the competitive significance of this investment to our strategic position?

Defining the Intelligence Spectrum

Decision-makers and analysts alike must be careful not to define the strategic issues and their competitors too narrowly. Because the strategic threat posed by direct competitors (companies that provide the same service or manufacture similar products) is obvious and information about them plentiful—particularly from internal sources—there is a natural tendency to restrict competitor intelligence requirements to the most visible domestic competitors. Often, however, it is the indirect competitor (supplier of substitute services or products) or the foreign competitor that represents the most dangerous strategic threat. Less visible strategic peers are more difficult to evaluate because their management may be operating by alien strategic values (geographical diversification into politically stable foreign markets rather than high-profit margins or increased market share), or because the sources of comparative advantage that determine their strategic performance are radically different (R & D capabilities are critical to ethical pharmaceutical manufacturers, whereas distribution networks are more vital to manufacturers of generic drugs). The more "distant" and/or "different" the competitor, the greater the probability of an intelligence gap and the more complicated the definition of intelligence requirements and specific EEIs.

To minimize the dangers of this "intelligence myopia," competitor intelligence requirements should be developed in consideration of the full competitive spectrum—near-term, intermediate, and potential. A useful framework for covering this aspect of the direction phase is the model long used by the military to demarcate operational/intelligence boundaries. As shown in Figure 5.11, the three zones covering the competitive spectrum are:

Intelligence Zone	Strategic Significance	Illustration
Areas of *Influence*	Industry, market segments firm is concentrated in	Network broadcasting
Contiguous (immediate)	Close or indirect competitors	Motion picture industry
Areas of *Interest*	Longer-term competitive threats or opportunities	Video tape cassettes

The applicability of this military paradigm to business strategy was first suggested by Montgomery and Weinberg in their pioneering article, "Towards Strategic Intelligence Systems." In that article, the authors cited the example of a company that successfully used over-

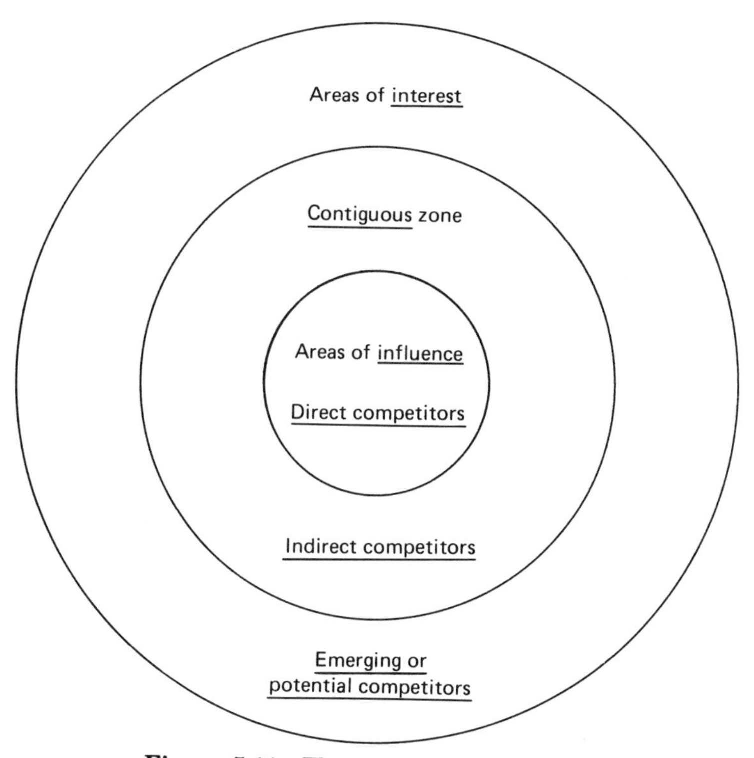

Figure 5.11 The competitive spectrum

the-horizon intelligence to identify and respond to a distant strategic threat, and thus minimized the competitive danger it represented:

> Many companies fail to utilize available opportunities because of their exclusive concentration on their areas of influence and consequent lack of attention to their immediate zone and areas of interest. As an example of this kind of opportunity, Gillette noted that Bic, which had been a formidable competitor in the disposable lighter market, had pioneered disposable razors in Europe in 1975. When Gillette learned that Bic had introduced the disposable razor in Canada in early 1976, it became clear that a major potential competitor was drawing near to the U.S. market. In response, Gillette rushed its *Good News* disposable razor into production and on the the national market in early 1976. Bic followed with U.S. test markets in mid-1976, but Gillette had apparently already paved the way for its dominance of this market. It is clear that by paying attention to its immediate zone and area of interest, Gillette was able to capitalize on an opportunity it would have lost had it only focused on its domestic markets.[11]

Intelligence Indicators

Having established specific EEIs oriented to the full competitive spectrum and management's strategic plans and competitor intelligence needs, the next step in the collection plan is to identify "indicators" that will tip off the analyst to the answers to the EEIs. Some EEIs, such as a company's corporate sales or its major product lines, can be collected directly and require little or no interpretation. Others, however—particularly those relating to strategic intentions—can only be answered by a careful monitoring and interpretation of competitor activity or statements that indirectly suggest the answer to EEIs. For example, if one of the key EEIs is to determine what product lines or business segments a competitor will withdraw from, a close between-the-lines reading of company publications and management speeches may suggest what businesses are least important by the order in which they're addressed or the amount of copy devoted to them. Alternatively, if a company restates its segment accounting and retroactively upgrades the profitability of a lagging business division, this may indicate that management is "dressing up" the division prior to divesting it at a good premium.

If one of the EEIs is to determine a competitor's R & D priorities, a close perusal of its hiring activities may reveal the scientific and technical expertise the company is building up to support emerging R & D projects. Both want-ads and employment search firms may be screened for these indicators.

Shifts in competitor manufacturing costs are one of the most common, but often difficult, EEIs to answer, but a close reading of key indicators like energy mix and use patterns, staffing, capital equipment purchases, facility plant investments, and a broad range of environmental and land use filings may, when viewed in conjunction with each other, indicate (albeit indirectly) both the direction and the magnitude of manufacturing cost changes.

If a competitor that has traditionally serviced its foreign markets through exports and local distributors acquires a half-interest in a foreign manufacturing facility, and then quietly cancels its long-standing relationship with independent distributors in that country, these actions may be viewed as important indicators that partially answer the EEI "What is company X's international strategy for product line Y?"

Although intelligence indicators are vital to an understanding of the more complex intelligence requirements, they are only suggestive and usually subject to multiple interpretations. For example, the competitor that restated its segment financials may have been addressing an internal allocation issue that was unfairly penalyzing a key division senior management was anxious to develop. The competitor who suddenly switches to overseas sourcing of a product line may simply be protecting an existing market share in a foreign country by reacting to political pressures in that country to source locally. Indicators may reflect very different competitor strategies and actions. Therefore, they should be read with care and caution by a *seasoned* analyst. The most revealing indicators are based on the known operating characteristics of the competitor and the main sources of comparative advantage in the industry(s) in which that competitor is found. In defining and interpreting indicators, intelligence analysts must draw upon both their knowledge of the firm being tracked and the competitive dynamics of that firm's industry and markets. Obviously, it takes experience to build such a complex knowledge base.

PHASE 2: COLLECTION

The next step in collection planning is to choose the relevant mix of *information sources* and *collection agencies* (indigenous and contracted to the company) that can provide the raw (unevaluated) competitor information required.

The useful distinction between "sources" and "collectors" of competitor information is frequently overlooked, resulting in confusion, unwarranted duplication of effort, and a waste of time and money. In governmental intelligence circles a source is defined as a person (e.g., a competitor's customer), a thing (e.g., a product), or a system (e.g., a distribution/supply network) from which information is originally obtained. An agency is defined as any individual (a company saleperson) or organization (corporate intelligence search firm) that can access a source to collect information. Although a source may also be a collector (e.g., a security analyst), for purposes of managing the collection efforts the distinction between the two should be maintained.

Company Intelligence Audit

As noted previously, one of the most fruitful but often underutilized sources and collectors of competitor information are the company's own employees and existing files. Before these extensive company pools of competitor information and collection resources can be used in an organized manner, they must be identified, cataloged, and evaluated. As a minimum, this will require an internal company-wide "intelligence audit" of the existing information base on competitors and the potential company collectors. This is a time consuming and tedious task, but it is one of the most cost-effective actions an intelligence staff can take.

The company intelligence audit can be as simple as a brief telephone survey of key departments and personnel, a review of personnel files with Human Resources managers to identify company employees who have worked for the competition, and a manual or preferably a computer scan of existing company data bases to identify potential pockets of competitor information. Alternatively, a more formal intelligence audit may be launched to insure a complete combing of the company's intelligence resources. This obviously takes more staff, time, and money. It also may generate strong resistance from managers and departments reluctant to identify their data bases and sources of competitor information. However the overall, long-term value of the corporation of identifying, organizing, and mobilizing its indigenous intelligence resources justifies the administrative and organizational costs of an extensive audit. If subordinate staff and divisional managers are assured that they will receive more extensive, timely, and relevant competitor information as a consequence of the intelligence audit, they may be more inclined to cooperate.

Although there are many ways to run an intelligence audit, it should be coordinated by the corporate planning department's intelligence staff with the "field work" done by the "intelligence reps" identified at each key staff and line group. Those who need a format for an intelligence audit should consider the excellent intelligence audit/survey developed by the Corporate Intelligence Group of Information Data Search, Inc. of Cambridge, Massachusetts.[12] To maintain currency, the intelligence audit should be updated on an annual basis. Once the intelligence audit is analyzed, identified company sources and collectors of competitor information can be easily rank-ordered and classified according to specific intelligence concerns and needs.

Internal Company Data Bases

Computers and electronic communications have ushered in the world of automated data bases. They now provide users with a remarkably rapid access to a wide range of secondary, and in come cases primary, information sources. Publicly available commercial data bases such as Lexis, Lockheed, and Compustat have valuable uses and are discussed in subsequent chapters. But all publicly available data bases—financial and text—have many drawbacks. The primary limitations are:

1. They are developed and maintained by someone else, whose priorities and definitions (key code structures) may not meet a company's intelligence needs.
2. They are available to anybody for a price.

An invaluable complement to commercial data bases is a proprietary competitor intelligence data base developed within and maintained by a company's own personnel. No individual can possibly screen the voluminous secondary and primary data available on competitors. Nor can a sweep of commercial data bases turn up the raw competitor data that may be most relevant to competitor analyses. However, a network of individuals scattered throughout the corporation has the expertise, the access, and hopefully the interest to monitor their professional sectors for the relevant items of competitor data that come their way. Based on aptitude, experience, and position, company individuals at the analyst and managerial level could be asked to serve as "intelligence stringers" for the company's competitor intelligence data base. They would screen the usual trade periodicals, professional newsletters, departmental reports, and other secondary and primary printed information that routinely crosses their desks. To avoid duplication of effort, the sources screened by each would be centrally coordinated.

An identified item would be collected and filed by the responsible stringer. Examples of such items include a credit report on a competitor who supplies the company, a trade press story on a competitor plant, a presentation by a competitor's CEO to a regional group of security analysts, a local newspaper article on a competitor's workforce, a technical paper by a competitor scientist, a district sales manager's summary of new marketing initatives by competitors, and a profile on a competitor's overseas subsidiary in a foreign business journal. Each stringer would maintain a separate competitor information file on an automated or manual system. A brief "input data base record" would then be completed on the more significant items of information. The input record should be terse as it is simply an index reference that will be coded and added to the company's computerized data base. A simple input record would include no more than the following:

Originator's code.
Competitor code.
Subject code (engineering, management, R & D, financial, etc.).
Date code.
Source code (trade press, trade show, investment banker, technical service rep, etc.).
Author (by name if available).
Quantity code (1–10 indicating extent of information).
Qualitative code (1–20 indicating originator's overall evaluation of information's probable value).

As these input cards are sent or called into the central data base manager, they would be quickly added to the proprietary competitor data base with a minimum of effort. The central data base source index can easily be cross-referenced to organize what is essentially a master index of the company's widespread internal sources of competitor information. By accessing the central competitor data base index, a manager or intelligence analyst could get a quick read on the extent and probable quality of various categories of competitor information within the company. Moreover, they would also be quickly directed to the company's major professional source on the particular competitor topic in question. That alone may be the most valuable aspect of such a proprietary competitor data base source index.

Outside Competitor Information

After a company's internal competitor information resources are organized, outside sources of information should be analyzed. There are basically two types of outside sources of competitor information: (1) those external to the competitor, and (2) internal competitor sources. Many of these will be discussed and evaluated in subsequent chapters. A basic list of each contains the following:

External Sources	*Internal Sources*
Regulatory groups	Memoranda
Company unions	Staff meetings

External Sources

Federal agencies
State government
Town clerks
Realtors
Voter registries
Trade groups
Banks
Stock analysts
Consultants
Advertising agencies
Universities
Newspapers and magazines
Distributors
Suppliers
Retailers
Wholesalers
Consumers
Consumer groups
Newsclipping agencies
Consulates
Foreign trade groups
Conferences
Trade shows
Government reports
Congressional studies

Internal Sources

Public relations
Press releases
Company directory
R & D
Production
Marketing
Advertising
Sales force
Customer service
Factory representatives
Internal consultants
Purchasing department
Engineering staff
Employees
Accounting
Strategic planning
Company unions
Company newsletters
Plant and operations
Design

Both categories should be screened to determine which can be accessed through a company's own collection agencies in a convenient, legal, and ethical manner. Competitor press releases and financial statements, for example, can be easily collected by the corporate legal or communications staff; relevant government reports and filings can probably be acquired through the legal department or by company lobbyists at the state and national level; the investor relations staff can get security analyst reports; and so on. Only after it is decided that company collection agencies are unsuitable for the job should outside collection agencies be contracted to fill in the gaps.

Two major reasons for using outside consultants, market researchers, and intelligence search firms (see Chapter 16) are to prevent the competition from learning about a company's collection plan strategy and to approach "unfriendly" sources of information.

Outside sources of information may or may not be "friendly." In commercial intelligence the following factors are useful in determining the character of these sources:[13]

Potential customer.
Industry ties.
Personal stake.
Detached, noncompetitive.
Government.
Reporting function.
Consumer.

A friendly source might be characterized this way:

Stance	*Motivation*	*Relationship*
Friendly	Nonthreatening, impartial	Trade group
		University research center
		Government agency
	Noncompetitive	Competitor's distributor
		Competitor's consumers
		Regulatory agency
		Unions
	Potential business transaction	Your customer
		Your supplier
		Your distributor
		Your retailer
		Your consultant

An unfriendly source might be characterized this way:

Stance	*Motivation*	*Relationship*
Unfriendly	Industry ties	Accounting Agencies
		Law firms

Stance	*Motivation*	*Relationship*
		Professional associations
		Consultants
		Investment bankers
		Local governments
	Personal Stake	Competitors' employees, active and retired
		"Captive" suppliers/distributers
		Purchasing agents
		Advertising agencies

As a general rule of thumb, contract collection agencies should be usd to approach outside sources of information that are potentially "unfriendly." As explained in Chapter 16, contract intelligence gatherers can tap potentially hostile sources of information in a manner that is effective, legal, timely, and protective of the client's identity. It may be as important to conceal one's interest in a competitor's activity as it is to collect information on that activity.

A common method of tasking indigenous and contract collection agencies is to draft a brief intelligence collection plan that delineates intelligence requirements and then lists those sources of information that each will be assigned to collect.

In dividing the collection effort among different agencies, four criteria should be applied:

1. *Capability.* Is the identified agency physically able to collect the specific item of information in an economical, timely, and legal manner?
2. *Suitability.* Given the character and resources available to the collection agency, is the collection task compatible with its primary role and function?
3. *Multiplicity.* When possible, more than one collection agency should be tasked to cover each relevant source of information. This assures full coverage of the source and safeguards against the lapses of any single collector.
4. *Balance.* Are the most suitable agencies being used to satisfy the intelligence requirements without either overloading or creating too much of a dependency on any single agency (e.g., the most familiar may not be the most relevant)? Intelligence analysts must not become overly enamored of any single collection agency and yet, as noted previously, planners and managers

tend to overuse the most convenient, accessible, and familiar sources and collectors of competitor information.

Managing the mechanics of the collection phase is a continuous process. The intelligence manager must constantly review the information gained against the established requirements, eliminate those that have been satisfied, add new requirements, pick up and develop new leads of inquiry that may not have been in the original requirements but are strategically relevant, and redirect the collection effort to assure active control of both the collection plan and the agencies developing the desired information.

Evaluation Ratings

For years, military and governmental intelligence organizations have used a convenient and practical shorthand evaluation rating scheme that adds considerable value to the management of the collection phase. As shown in Table 5.1, the raw information funneled into the analytical staff sections is "graded" in terms of the probable *accuracy of the information* and the *reliability of the source of the information.*

Both company and contract collection agencies should be asked to include this evaluation rating on all competitor information forwarded. These ratings will not only facilitate the processing of the raw information into usable intelligence, but they will assist the intelligence managers in developing a qualitative profile of potential sources of competitor information. Over time these "source profiles" will be quite useful in drawing up future collection plans.

PHASE 3: PROCESSING INFORMATION INTO INTELLIGENCE

The third phase of the intelligence cycle is the critical state where the raw data of competitor information is recorded, evaluated, interpreted, and transformed into usable intelligence. In this step, the analyst is king and drudge. Every relevant piece of collected information must be critically assessed and then fitted into a larger, more meaningful whole before the collected information can be upgraded to the category of competitor intelligence. The nature of the intelligence work at this stage is the intellectual activity of sifting diverse, often conflicting strands of competitor information to find the meaningful stra-

TABLE 5.1. EVALUATION RATINGS

Reliability of Source of Information	Accuracy of Information
A — Completely reliable	1 — Confirmed by other sources
B — Usually reliable	2 — Probably true
C — Fairly reliable	3 — Possibly true
D — Not usually reliable	4 — Doubtfully true
E — Unreliable	5 — Improbable
F — Reliability cannot be judged	6 — Truth cannot be judged

tegic pattern within the stream of available data. William J. Donovan, who created and then led the OSS in World War II, summed up the essence of this task. Intelligence work is, he said, mostly a matter of "pulling together myriad facts, making a pattern of them, and drawing inferences from that pattern."[14]

Recording Competitor Information

Often the most time-consuming aspect of this phase of the intelligence cycle is the tedious but necessary task of recording the raw information as it is collected. As noted above, an evaulation rating of the reliability of the source and the accuracy of the data helps the analyst track the relative value of the raw information. In addition, a corporate data base index is a useful resource that keeps the collected competitor data decentralized by function, but readily accessible when needed by the analyst.

If the "intelligence stringer" system is used, much of the recording chores can be delegated to those most familiar with the sources and collection agencies from which the competitor information is drawn. Raw data, like fire, is a good servant, but a difficult master. The analyst who must record everything he or she analyzes will spend 80 percent of the time recording, cataloging, and filing, and a bare 20 percent at the primary task of analyzing, reviewing, and piecing together disparate sources of information to get the intelligence required.

Where possible, the collected data should be accumulated, recorded, and aggregated at the lowest level in the corporation. This will free up the limited analytical talent at the mid and senior organizational levels to concentrate their resources on the crucial work of analysis.

Although the full records of the raw information collected should always be available at the level or department that receives it, the further up it goes in the corporation, the more synthesized and collated it should be. If it is done well, recording will reduce the collected raw information into a written digest or summary form of graphical representation. Recording should also catalog or group the collected information into relevant areas of competitor interest. Ideally, the recorded data should be in a form that enables the analyst to scan it quickly and glean the most significant intelligence it contains. For example, if part of the collection effort is directed towards a compilation of data on a competitor's manufacturing capabilities, the manufacturing and/or engineering staff that collects the data will probably want to record it in a summary format that clearly displays both the relevant qualitative and quantitative data (see Figure 5.12).

Competitor financial information is often the easiest data to upgrade through a creative recording format. In Figure 5.13 four years of financial data on the corporate and business segment performance of a health care industry competitor have been accumulated and aggregated into a Four-Year Average duPont Profitability Matrix. With a little extra recording, a time dimension can be added and performance *trends* can be tracked on a yearly basis as shown in Figures 5.14 and 5.15. This gives a better sense of the financial dynamics that characterize reported business segments. Similar financial recording techniques can be used to chart the comparative record of multiple competitors (see Figure 5.16). Although the analytical interpretation of the strategic intelligence that can be developed from these financial charts is beyond the scope of the chapter, it should be evident that this kind of summarized recording data is more valuable to the planning/intelligence analyst than a simple, unorganized tabular series of raw financial figures.

Information recording should be done in a creative but economical fashion that helps the analyst focus on the *pattern of competitor activity* rather than the *surface details.* To put it another way, strategic analysis and thus competitor intelligence that supports it is concerned with direction, not decimal points.

Evaluation

Although an initial evaluation of the collected information has previously been made by the collection agencies, at the third phase of the intelligence cycle a separate evaluation oriented on the substantive

Mill	Total Pulp (TPD)*		Total Paper/Board (TPD)*		Original Age	Date Rebuilt	Former	Paper Machine Former Width	Trim	Speed	TPD	Product
#1	Ground-wood	250	Ctd/Unctd. Grdwd.	500	(Not In Use)		#4 Fourdrinier	150"	140"	1100	80	Unctd. Grdwd.
	Mkt. Pulp	?	Spec				#5 Fourdrinier	150"	140"	1150	115	Ctd. Printing
	Secondary Fiber	?					#6 Fourdrinier	165"	154"	1600	125	Ctd. Printing
							#7 Cylinder	74"	64"	200	15	Specialties
							#9 Fourdrinier	165"	154"	1450	143	Ctd. Printing
#2	Unb. Kraft	810	Fine Papers	50	1912		#1 Fourdrinier	136"	124"	1400	35	Tissue
	Magnefite	440	Tissue	290	1912		#2 Harper	115"	105"	1100	25	Tissue
		1250	Industrial	760	1915		#3 Fourdrinier	137"	126"	875	40	Tissue
				1100	1907		#4 Fourdrinier	126"	114"	1100	75	Kraft Wrap
					1948		#5 Fourdrinier	155"	138"	1440	100	Bl. Sul. Wrap
					1930		#6 Fourdrinier	138"	126"	1650	140	Unb. Kraft Wrap
					1930		#7 Fourdrinier	138"	126"	1950	85	Bl/Unb. Kraft
					1936		#8 Fourdrinier	87"	75"	815	40	Bl. Sul. Wrap
					1940		#9 Fourdrinier	137"	126"	2000	45	Tissue
					1930		#10 Yankee	133"	126"	875	110	Kraft Wrap
					1930		#11 Yankee	176"	165"	2024	85	Tissue
					1932		#12 Yankee	111"	104"	400	45	Bl/Unb. Kraft
					1948		#14 Yankee	100"	91"	3500	40	Tissue
					1960		#15 Fourdrinier	155"	138"	1550	140	Bl/Unb. Spec.
					1962		#16 Fourdrinier	138"	126"	2000	150	Kraft Wrap
#3	Ground-wood	510	Newsprint	445	1922		#1 Fourdrinier	167"	155"	1500	82	Newsprint
					1923		#2 Fourdrinier	165"	155"	2000	110	Newsprint
					1925		#3 Fourdrinier	242"	226"	2550	272	Newsprint
#4	Unb. Kraft	445	Kraft Wrapping Linerboard Boxboard	420			#1 Fourdrinier	134"	114"	450	100	Linerboard
							#2 Fourdrinier	252"	235"	1750	310	Kft. Bag/Wrap
#5	TMP	375	Newsprint	750	1952		#1 Fourdrinier	286"	274"	3000	NA	
	Gdwd	310	Unb. Kraftbag	120	1957		#2 Fourdrinier	264"	248"	3000	NA	
	Unb. Kraft	390	Linerboard	140	1966		#3 Fourdrinier	184"	162"	1800	NA	
	Bl. Kraft	740	Bl. Mkt Pulp	800	1963		#4 Pulp Board	198"	192"	500	NA	
		1815		1810								

*Estimated capacity

Figure 5.12 Company X primary manufacturing facilities, 1981

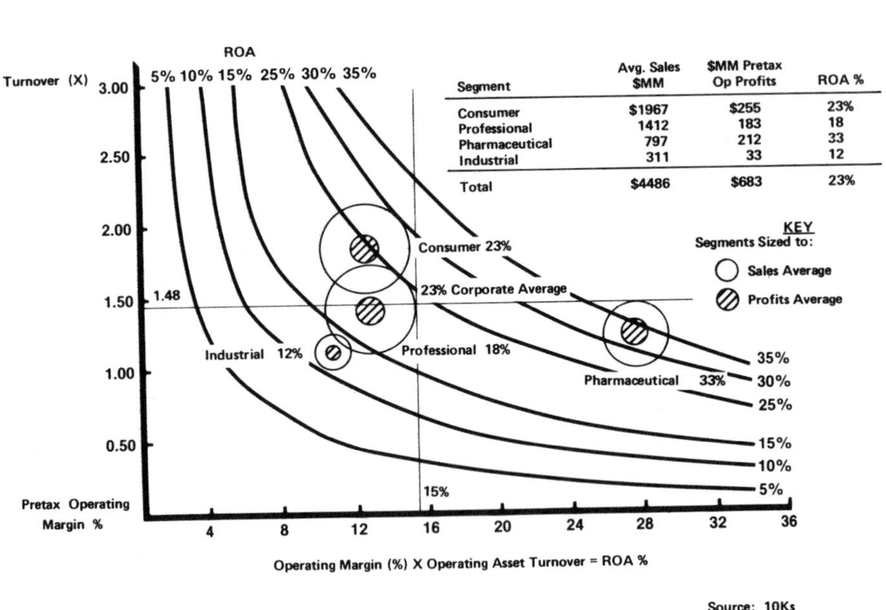

Figure 5.13 Johnson & Johnson business segment financial performance trend—4-year average (1978–81)

merits of the information should be accomplished. This evaluation can take the form of a simple but critical question: "In light of our existing understanding of this competitor, its track record, customary mode of operation, and perceived strategy, how significant is this information?" When the analyst is in doubt, more than one individual familiar with the competitor and particularly the substantive issue the information addresses should evaluate the data to determine its strategic import. The comments of these "experts" are invaluable in assisting the intelligence analyst in the arduous task of separating out the critical from the secondary.

Interpretation

The core of the processing phase is interpretation—the high art of analysis. The intellectual question is straightforward—What does it all mean? But answering that question requires judgment, a careful

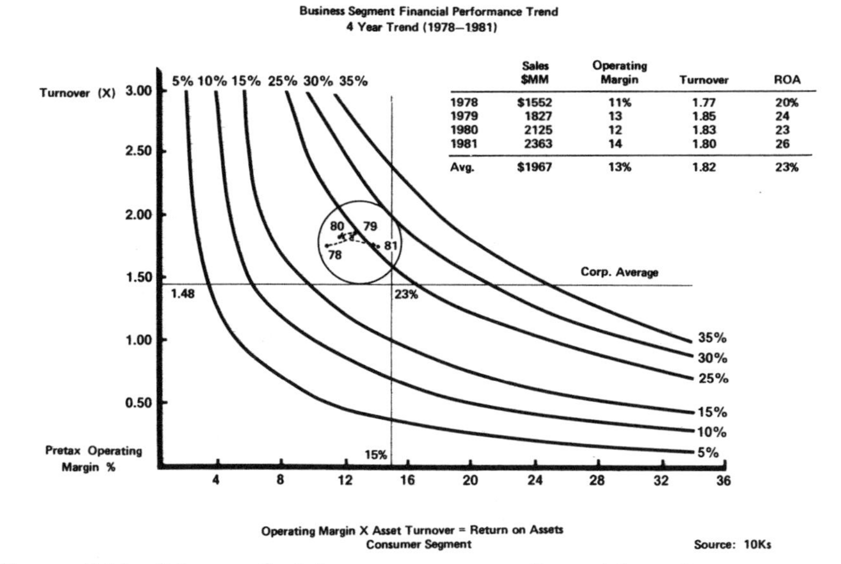

Figure 5.14 Johnson & Johnson consumer—financial performance trend (1978–81)

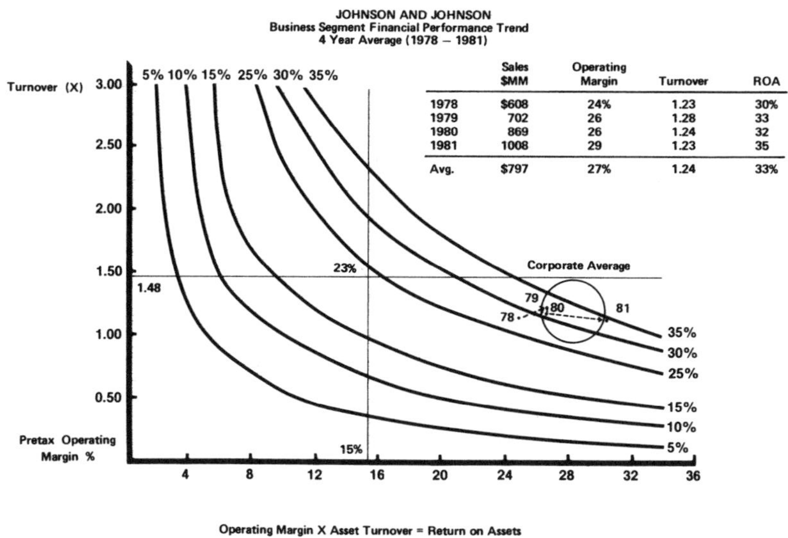

Figure 5.15 Johnson & Johnson pharmaceuticals—financial performance trend (1978–81)

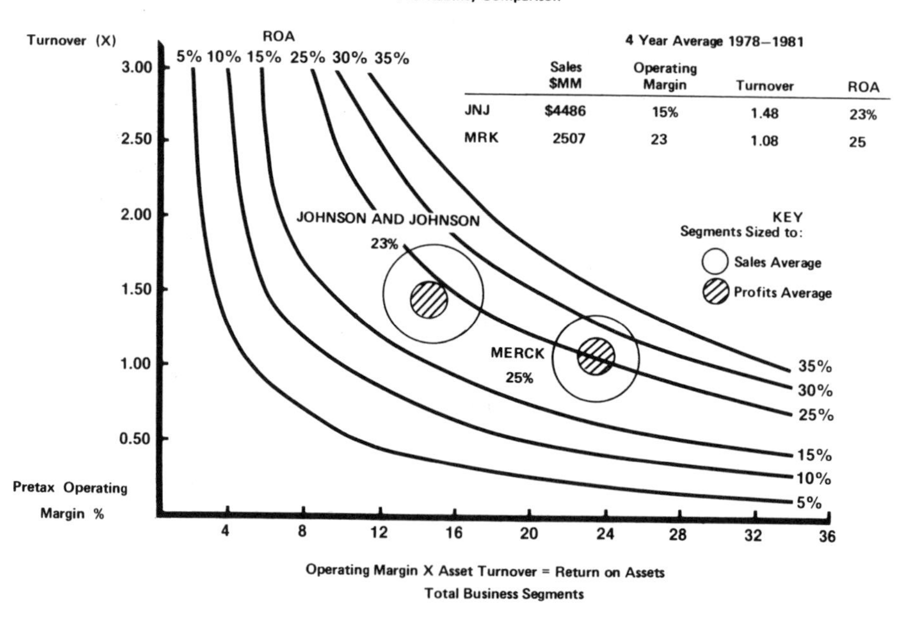

Figure 5.16 Two health-care-industry competitors: profitability comparison

appreciation of details, and above all, perspective. The sifting and sorting of evaluated information also requires a clear understanding of the following points:

Strategic objectives of the decision-maker—the intelligence consumer.

Character of the established intelligence requirements.

Macro forces affecting the competitor.

Operating characteristics of the competitor.

Main sources of comparative advantage in the industries and markets in which the competitor moves.

Primarily through the mental processes of integration—the combination of isolated but relevant elements with other information—a logical hypothesis about a competitor's strategic objectives, intentions, or potential is formed. To the extent practicable, the analyst must try to understand the perspective, values, and pressures that influence the behavior and form the strategic goals of the competitor's management.

The hypothesis the intelligence analyst develops must then be tested and refined against new information and indicators of competitor actions and plans. Gradually, a valid, verifiable analytical profile of the competitor will emerge. Although it is never complete nor totally accurate, this kind of interpretative analysis will produce a systematically organized and integrated body of knowledge from which reasonable deductions about a competitor's probable courses of action, operational character, and strategic objectives can be derived. Allen Dulles, former CIA Director, succinctly describes the intellectual challenge that confronts the intelligence analyst:

> For it is the patient analyst who arranges, ponders, tries out alternate hypotheses and draws conclusions. What he is bringing to the task is the substantive background, the imagination and originality of the sound and careful scholar.
>
> The analyst has sometimes been described as the man who takes forty-nine documents and from them produces a fiftieth. He does not do this by combining all the others, condensing and summarizing them, but by comparing them for their similarities and contradictions and shaking them down until he has sorted out what is probably true and significant, what is probably true but insignificant, and what is doubtful. He is, in a sense, finding out from the mass of unanalyzed information at hand what we really know with some surety and what its value is, and what we don't know.[15]

Most pieces of information and shards of evidence that pass the collector's screen have relevance. But very few if any are the "essential key" that answers the intelligence requirement—particularly when the focus is as broad and ambiguous as competitor strategies. For strategies are based on plans, aspirations, and often vain hopes. They are subject to many dislocations. This underlying uncertainty must always be in the forefront of the analyst's mind.

It is useful to think of interpretation as the slow crafting of a mosaic, the gradual piecing together of a thousand bits of data that utlimately reveal the fundamental pattern of the whole assemblage. Intelligence analysis is the building up, the layering, the overlapping, the careful collating of disparate forms and types of competitor information into a coherent pattern of meaning that elicits the intellectual sensation of "Aha, so that's what it means!" rather than the intellectual jolt of "Eureka! I've found it!"

However, some pieces of data glitter more than others, and may too easily delight the imagination of the analyst. From an intellectual or psychological perspective, some items of information may be too stimulating. Caught off guard, having lost his or her detachment, the analyst may overestimate their intelligence value. The glittering data that mesmerizes may do so because it confirms a deep-seated value judgment held by the analyst, or comes from a highly valued collection agency, or is the kind of information the analyst is most comfortable with due to academic background or professional training. The analyst must check his or her conclusions with others to safeguard the intelligence product from these subtle perceptual distortions. Therefore, the processing of information is best approached as a team rather than a solitary effort of analysis.

PHASE 4: DISSEMINATION AND USE

The final phase of the intelligence cycle is the communication of the intelligence produced to decision-makers who need it to formulate their plans and inform their decisions. In this phase, the intelligence product is passed on, disseminated to consumers in many formats. The best, most complete and accurate intelligence is simply a costly academic exercise if it does not reach the user in time for appropriate review and/or action.

Occasionally, the depth, completeness, and accuracy of the intelligence product must be sacrificed because the competitive situation forces a strategic decision before all the intelligence requirements can be met. However, a limited amount of *timely* intelligence is always more valuable than a full-dress competitor intelligence report that is ready only after the competitor has won the contract or acquired the business.

A practical way to structure the dissemination and use of competitor intelligence is to develop an integrated set of intelligence reports or briefs that cover four generic categories of intelligence (see Figure 5.17). Rank-ordered by operational and strategic value, they are:

- Net estimates of competitor strategies.
- Periodic reports on competitor activity and trends.

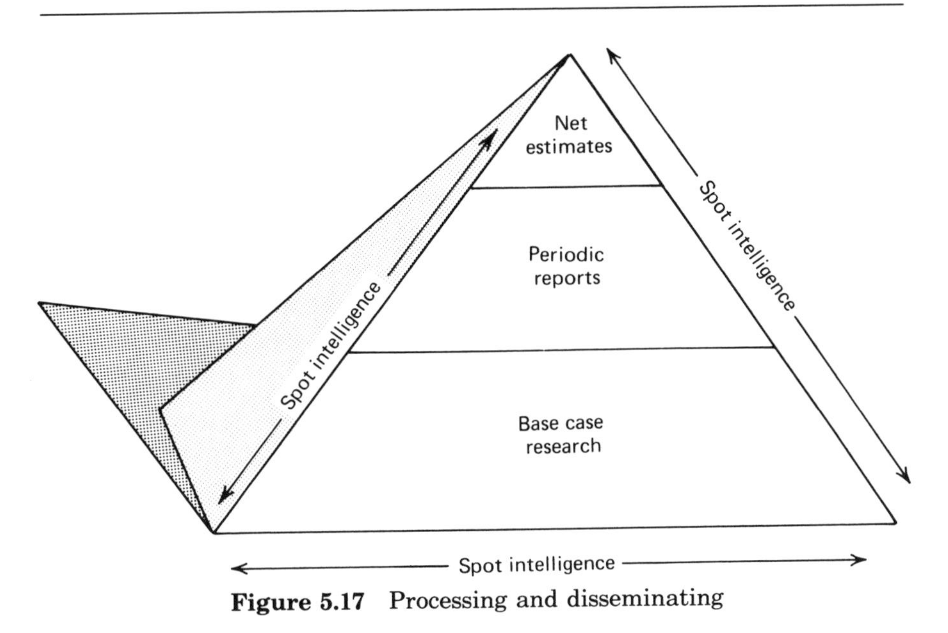

Figure 5.17 Processing and disseminating

3. Base case intelligence research on competitors.
4. Spot intelligence items of interest.

In most corporations these formats can be used to communicate competitor intelligence at both the business-unit and corporate level. The analytical scheme is the same at both levels; only the definition of strategic peers and the scope of the intelligence requirements will vary. Presumably, there will usually be a larger element of short-term "operational" intelligence required at the business-unit level, and a greater emphasis placed on general strategic competitor intelligence at the corporate level. Although boundaries will overlap, the competitor intelligence developed at both levels should be complementary from a total corporate perspective. Coordination and cooperation between the "intelligence producers" at both levels is essential to avoid unnecessary duplication of effort and to insure that the competitor intelligence produced is based on a common frame of reference. These dissemination formats can help develop that intelligence relationship and frame of reference. But whatever the dissemination formats used at the business-unit or corporate level, the primary objective is to edit the finished intelligence into a suitable form that quickly reveals the key items of interest it contains to the consumers who requested it.

Spot Intelligence

Spot intelligence is the bane of all intelligence systems: the odd request from senior management about a narrow topic of interest concerning the competitor that must be answered yesterday. As indicated in Table 5.2, it is the short-order cook's version of intelligence. It meets a secondary reference need and, although generally viewed as a minor nuisance to the producers of intelligence, is often overly appreciated by consumers.

The danger is that the company's entire competitor intelligence program can be reduced to this discontinuous, unstructured, reactive form of "reference intelligence."

Base Case Intelligence

Base case intelligence (Table 5.3) is the exhaustive, never-completed, competitor intelligence case study. It should cover all aspects of a competitor's organization, its business units, functional divisions, and the full range of identified capabilities, strengths, and weaknesses.

It is the "research core" of the intelligence pyramid, and is best viewed as the working intelligence file on a competitor that details

TABLE 5.2. SPOT INTELLIGENCE

Scope and Type
- Specific topic
- User request
- Descriptive/responsive
- Short deadline

Purpose
- Satisfy ad hoc intelligence needs
- Fill in minor information gaps
- Quick dissemination of secondary information

Level
- Any

Audience
- User-defined

Format
- Telephonic
- Short memo

TABLE 5.3. BASE CASE INTELLIGENCE

Scope and Type
- Broad
- Background
- Strategic/operational
- Descriptive/analytical

Purpose
- Outline competitor's organization, performance, strengths, vulnerability, and strategic direction

Level
- Strategic/operational

Audience
- Planning, marketing, and financial analysts

Format
- Working file (automated)
- Detailed research report
- Limited distribution

the past, outlines the present, and suggests the future. A time-consuming descriptive and analytical compendium of the essential intelligence on hand about a given competitor, it must be constantly updated, pruned, and changed.

A simple but practical analytical outline for a base case intelligence file, whether it be a formalized and lengthy report or only a set of working files, is suggested in Table 5.4.

TABLE 5.4. BASE CASE INTELLIGENCE FILE

Strategic Background

1. Overall competitive position within core industry
   - General reputation
   - Management reputation
   - Major qualitative strengths
   - Major qualitative weaknesses
2. Comparative financial performance (last five years)
   - Profitability trend vs industry averages (sales margin, asset turnover, return on operating assets)

(Continued)

TABLE 5.4. (Continued)

Key growth rates (sales S&A, cost of goods, R&D, profit margins, etc.)
Capital structure, earnings pattern, and stock performance

3. Business portfolio analysis/investment strategy
   Product mix by segment
   Distribution of operating assets by segment
   Comparative analysis of segment financial performance
      Sales and profitability trends
      Funds deployment trends (funds used/funds generated)
4. Geographic balance
   Domestic versus international
   Foreign subsidiaries
5. Corporate culture and history
   Historical perspective—growth pattern/development milestones
   Core organizational values and business mission/vision
   Managerial/operational style

Corporate Strategy

1. Announced objectives and strategies
2. Inferred goals—domestic and international
3. Past strategies—consistency/continuity
4. Short term—long-term constraints and tradeoffs
5. Competitors' reaction
6. Planning and implementation capabilities
7. Capital investment program
8. Acquisition and divestment pattern
9. Relative emphasis on growth through acquisitions versus interval development

---

Business-Unit Strategies

1.	Segment #1	Products/market share rank/demand assumptions
2.	Segment #2	Capabilities, goals, actions
3.	Segment #3	Relationship to corporate strategy
4.	Segment #4	

Joint Ventures

1. Type and purpose
2. Trends

TABLE 5.4 (Continued)

Functional Analyses

1. Sales and marketing
   - Key products, market share, commitment
   - Product quality, customer reputation
   - Pattern of product introductions
   - Pricing tactics
   - Distribution
   - Sales force caliber/reputation compensation
   - Market research capability
   - Technical service
   - Major accounts/key customers
   - Marketing image—overall, by key businesses and/or products
2. Manufacturing and operations
   - Production thrust/orientation
   - Competitive cost position (geographic and by major product lines)
   - Facility profiles
     - a. Location, capacities, bottlenecks
     - b. Production mix
     - c. Capacity utilization trends
   - Expenditure patterns
   - Capacity expansions/reductions
   - Raw materials
   - Supply relationships
   - Quality control
   - Union issues
   - Regulatory concerns
3. Research and development
   - Technological focus, priorities, and innovativeness
   - R&D mix
   - Track record and reputation of research labs and staff
   - Key product development projects
   - Corporate financial support (levels and trends)
   - Strategic priority
   - Major patents and proprietary areas
   - Security issues

(Continued)

TABLE 5.4 (Continued)

4. Financial
    - Overall financial management ability
    - Credit ratings, borrowing capacity
    - Lender relationships
    - Business growth and development funding strategies
5. Organizational
    - Senior management control/decision-making process
    - Corporate structure
        - Line operations/supporting staff
        - Business units/product lines
        - Global/country teams
        - Centralization/decentralization
    - Congruence with corporate values
    - Informal structure and sources of influence
        - Dominant functions
        - Strongest business units
    - Human resources/personnel strategies
    - Employee talent, morale, turnover, productivity
6. Legal/governmental ssues

Management

1. Overall reputation and accomplishment
    - Background, experience, functional orientation
    - Flexibility/adaptability
2. CEO profile
    - Abilities, tenure, reputation
    - Succession
3. Other key decision-makers
    - Dominant role models
    - Sources of influence
    - Value consensus
4. Depth and continuity
5. Outside board of directors

Strategic Net Assessment

1. Capabilities/weaknesses recap
    - Best at / Worst at — operations and functions

TABLE 5.4 (Continued)

Trends, capacity for change and/or growth
2. Evaluation of perceived strategy
   Management commitment
   Coherence and consistency (compatible goals)
   Congruence with managements' assumptions, industry trends, business unit strategies, and stated corporate goals
   Financial ability
   Match between company capabilities and strategic objectives
   Timing and implementation problems
   Probability of success (expected performance)
3. Probable competitive reactions and company response
4. Strategic implications (for your company)
   Threats
   Opportunities
   New issues

Periodic Intelligence

Periodic competitor intelligence (Table 5.5) serves a monitoring and reporting function. Produced on a quarterly or semiannual basis, the periodic format provides a quick summarized update on current competitor activity. It is a useful vehicle for organizing and structuring the routine stream of competitor data flowing into the company. As such, it is also a valuable recording format that constitutes the first aggregation and collation of competitor information into a preliminary intelligence form.

A hybrid between an intelligence newsletter and a scorecard on competitor activity, its short length and highly descriptive contents usually make it a "good read." It thus can serve a useful ancillary purpose as a widely distributed communication vehicle that helps keep the company's dispersed intelligence "liaison reps" and "stringers" in tune with the ever-shifting tides of competitor information.The periodic format can also be used to communicate EEIs (usually of a secondary order) across the company.

The other major purpose the periodic report serves is to update base case intelligence. While the unending requirement to meet the constant deadlines of periodic intelligence reports may seem onerous, it does act as a salutory administrative discipline. For it requires some

TABLE 5.5. PERIODIC COMPETITOR INTELLIGENCE

Scope and Type
  Focused on key indicators
  Communicates essential elements of information (EEIs)
  Descriptive/reportorial
Purpose
  Monitor and track competitor activities and trends
  Identify new EEIs and indicators
  Provide quick summary of comparative performance
  Updates base case intelligence
  Provide common frame of reference on competitors
Level
  Operational/strategic
Audience
  Senior management, line management, analysts
Format
  Written report in brief summary format
  Maximum use of matrices, tables, and graphics
  Minimal analysis
  Wide distribution

intelligence staffers to keep a constant eye on the activity of important competitors, and to relate that information back to a broader intelligence perspective in order that the trend patterns can be closely monitored and relevant indicators quickly identified.

As a periodic summary briefing or report, this kind of intelligence format must be tightly organized and aggressively edited. Maximum use should be made of bulletin-like information summaries. Where possible, graphical charts should be used to display competitor financial data. Comparison against industry financial norms is a commonly used trend chart format.

Strategic Net Estimates

At once the most critical and the most difficult intelligence to develop, strategic net estimates (Table 5.6) are a final totalling-up of a competitor's:

Strengths and weaknesses.

Known capabilities and identified vulnerabilities.

TABLE 5.6. STRATEGIC NET ESTIMATES

Scope and Type
- Broad synthesis
- Action oriented
- Strategic
- Reasoned extrapolation

Purpose
- Delineate competitor's strategy—means and objectives
- Profile strategic assets and vulnerabilities
- Assess strategic threats and opportunities
- Provide comparative framework for competitive analysis
- Outline competitor's self-appraisal of its position, performance, and potential
- Forecast competitor's probable and alternate courses of action

Level
- Strategic

Audience
- Senior management

Format
- Component of strategic plans
- Specialized briefing and/or written report profiling competitors's strategies
- Limited distribution

Operational objectives.
Strategic position and competitive performance.
Strategic goals.
Most probable courses of action and reaction.

The net estimate should address the ultimate strategic intelligence questions:

Is this competitor a strategic threat to our current strategic position?
Does this competitor have the resources to disrupt our strategy?
Will this competitor view our planned move in situation X as a serious strategic threat? If so, what will the competitor's response be?

Do the actions or inactions of this competitor represent a strategic opportunity for us? In what way can we exploit this competitive opportunity?

An estimate is, after all is said and done, a shrewd guess. It is, however, a *reasoned* guess, a reasonable extrapolation of the competitor's future actions derived from an interpretative but systematic knowledge of existing facts about that competitor. A well-organized, clearly delineated strategic net estimate should give senior management the crucial intelligence needed to compare their strategic resources and goals with those of key competitors. The strategic insights derived from this vital comparative knowledge should help management choose the course of action that is most favorable to their company and that minimizes the strategic threat posed by competitors.

As the strategic net estimate is the distillation of the most vital competitor intelligence produced, it should be disseminated in a clear but simple form. It must not be lost in dense copy or waylaid in obscure appendices.

Like a pithy executive summary, the strategic net estimate should be up front to insure it gets the recognition it requires. Clear, concise, and brief, it should communicate its intelligence in a comparative format that effectively contrasts a competitor's vulnerabilities, capabilities, courses of action, and probable intentions against the company's. Another reason for brevity is the necessity of keeping the strategic net estimate current.

Any briefing that touches at length on competitor activity should start with a succinct strategic net estimate on the relevant competitors. On a semiannual or at the very least an annual basis, competitor strategic net estimates should be included as an integral part of the corporate and business-unit strategic and operating plans. Strategic net estimate intelligence should also be included as a routine item in major functional studies and plans, such as marketing campaigns or R & D plans. A yearly benchmark report that updates and collates all strategic net estimates developed by the business-unit and corporate staffs should be prepared and briefed as part of the annual planning cycle.

CONCLUSION

This chapter has covered the basic outline of the functions and operations that intelligence involves. As is evident, the bulk of intelligence work revolves around the analysis, not the theft of information. Many of the intelligence tasks are routine and far from dramatic—collecting disparate pieces of scattered information, recording it on files and charts and graphs, and communicating it in summaries or briefings. But it is a challenging and complex responsibility nevertheless. Although it may not involve the stimulating stress and sinister charm that gives espionage its romantic appeal, the operational task of organizing and managing an efficient competitor intelligence program, large or small, corporate-level or business-unit, requires an unusual mix of talents, not the least of which is a clear understanding of the consumer's needs and a thorough grasp of the strengths and limitations of the intelligence product produced.

---

[1]*Dictionary of United States Military Terms for Joint Usage,* Washington, D. C., Departments of the Army, Navy, and Air Force, May 1955, p. 53.

[2]Harry Howe Ransom, *The Intelligence Establishment,* Cambridge, Massachusetts, Harvard University Press, 1970, p. 9.

[3]Sherman Kent, *Strategic Intelligence for American World Policy,* Princeton University Press, 1971, pp. 180–2. Kent was a senior professor of history at Yale University when he was recruited in 1941 to serve in an important post in the Research and Analysis Branch of the new OSS. He later served in the State Department and retired in 1968 as Director of the CIA's Office of National Estimates. In 1948, after his World War II service, he published *Strategic Intelligence for American World Policy,* which drew on his intelligence experience in the OSS's analytical and policy divisions. The book was one of the first systematic analyses of the organizational, substantive, and methodological elements of strategic political intelligence. It is a classic in its field.

[4]Information Data Search, Inc., *Corporate Intelligence Gathering: A Survey,* Cambridge, Massachusetts, 1982.

[5]Jerry Wall, "Probing Opinions: What the Competition Is Doing: Your Need to Know," *Harvard Business Review,* November–December, 1974, p. 23.

[6]David Montgomery and Charles Weinberg, "Toward Strategic Intelligence Systems," *The Journal of Marketing,* Vol. 43 (Fall 1979), p. 52.

[7]Michael Porter, *Competitive Strategy,* New York, Free Press, 1980, pp. 126–155.

[8]Ibid., p. 152.

[9]More detailed intelligence on these competitors will show that their "high" turnover ratio is largely due to their captive distribution businesses. Whether such businesses are a profitable way to offset the inherent capital intensitivity of a commodity forest product's manufacturer is a subject of much debate in the industry.

[10]U.S. Army FM 30-5, "Combat Intelligence," pp. 3–5.

[11]Montgomery and Weinberg, pp. 44–45.

[12]This format developed by Leonard Fuld, Managing Director of Information Data Search, combines the features of both an information and a diagnostic audit. It has been used by a number of companies as the first step in developing a competitor intelligence system (see chapter 16).

[13]"Competitor Intelligence Seminar," *The Corporate Intelligence Group,* Cambridge, Massachusetts, Information Data Search, Inc., 1982, pp. 13–50.

[14]Quoted in Harry Howe Ransom, *The Intelligence Establishment,* Cambridge, Massachusetts, Harvard University Press, 1970, p. 33.

[15]Allen Dulles, *The Craft of Intelligence,* New York, New American Library, 1965 p. 149.

II

Special Applications of Competitor Intelligence

6

Competitor Intelligence in a Commodity Business

MARK KURLAND

Mark Kurland is currently with Mabon, Nugent & Company in their Investment Research Department, where he follows forest products, paper, and packaging companies. He is also involved in corporate finance activities.

Mr. Kurland was formerly in the Corporate Planning Department at International Paper Company with primary responsibilities for strategic planning and corporate development. Prior to joining International Paper in 1979, he was with International Playtex as manager of financial marketing for their Family Products Division. From 1974 to 1976, he was with Pfizer's Leeming Pacquin Consumer Products Division as a financial analyst in their manufacturing facility. He also was in the controller's department of Manufacturers Hanover Trust.

Mr. Kurland holds an M.B.A. in finance from Bernard Baruch College and a B.S. in Economics from Hofstra University.

THE NATURE OF THE COMPETITIVE PROCESS

Competitive analysis, whether it relates to a consumer product or a commodity product, is an important and vital component of strategy development. Many companies tend to develop plans primarily on the basis of their own internal situation, with only a cursory glance at their competitive environment. Their strategic plan tends to be in response to their own perceived problems, inadequacies, or goals, rather than in response to the demands of the competitive environment. Too often, businesses fail because planners fail to recognize that their company's success or failure is largely determined by the actions and reactions of its competitors rather than by its own initiative.

The competitive process should be viewed as dynamic and not static. For example, the manufacturing cost position relative to competitors is not as meaningful as understanding the motivation, commitment, and future plans of one's competitors, and the direction their cost position will follow over time. A competitor might have a low-cost position today, but if new capacity is coming on stream with larger or faster-producing machines, it is only a matter of time before the current low-cost producer will suffer margin erosion or obsolesence at the hands of the newer capacity.

Economic theory uses the concepts of equilibrium and disequilibrium to explain the fundamental nature of the competitive process. Many of these basic principles can be used to explain the nature of the competitive process within industry. The equilibrium theory simply states that a disturbance in the way a company interacts with its competition upsets the nature of the previous equilibrium. A competitor may change price, consumers may cut back spending, substitute materials may be developed, or technology may alter the traditional cost structure. As a result, counter reactions from competitors will take place until a new, different equilibrium is established.

The analogy of marbles in a fishbowl is very appropriate in this context. Marbles rolling in a fishbowl are in a kind of fragile equilibrium, touching each other and dependent on each other for equilibrium and stability. If one were to shake the bowl, the equilibrium would be disturbed, but once the outside shock subsided a new equilibrium would be established. Although this may sound like a lot of theoretical mumbo-jumbo, it contains a basic precept that relates to industry. The position of each individual marble in the bowl is a function of the position of every other marble in the bowl. In short, the competitive position of an individual firm is not only a function of its own decisions, but also of the decisions of all its competitors.

An important aspect of competitive analysis is understanding success criteria for one's own industry. What are the factors in gaining a competitive advantage—technology, logistics, manufacturing efficiency, and so on? Ultimately, the purpose of competitive analysis is to use that knowledge to one's own benefit.

CHARACTERISTICS OF COMMODITY COMPANIES

Competitive analysis, whether it is used for an industrial/commodity environment or for a nondurable consumer packaged goods product, utilizes the same fundamental precepts. However, because the nature of the competitive process and the success criteria are at opposite ends of the spectrum, the analytic process is somewhat ifferent.

Commodity companies typically have slower growth curves, which correspond more closely to GNP than to a derived demand typical in consumer product companies. Slow growth means more competition for market share. With companies unable to maintain historical growth rates merely by holding market share competitive, attention turns inward towards attacking the share of others. Increased competition for market share requires a fundamental reorientation about how competitors behave. Understanding your competitor's pricing/cost structure becomes important to internal strategy development.

Commodity products are very similar in nature to each other and lack product-differentiating characteristics. A paper, chemical, or steel product is very similar in nature whether it is manufactured by company A, B, or C. Conversely, a breakfast cereal or a perfume have demonstrably differentiated characteristics that set one product off from another. Product differentiation, as is the case with a perfume, creates layers of insulation against competitive warfare. A product that is differentiated from a competitor's product has the hope of generating a perceived need and thus can generate demand without necessarily displacing or competing directly with a competitor. A commodity product, on the other hand, that lacks differentiation characteristics has to rely on price, service, and reliability to make inroads into the marketplace.

Commodity products tend to have high fixed costs. Commodity manufacturing requires large investments in plant and equipment to produce a product that is cost-competitive with the existing competitive infrastructure. As a result, competitive success is largely determined by the cost structure of the industry, with the low-cost competitors having a decided advantage over the high-cost competitors. Longevity in the marketplace and profitability are functions of one's cost relationship to the competition. Advertising and marketing strategies that are so important where product differentiation exists are quite unimportant for commodity businesses.

COMPETITIVE SUCCESS

One of the most critical decisions that a company producing a commodity product can make is when to invest in plant and equipment. Capacity expansion is measured both in terms of the amount of capital involved and the complexity of the decision-making problem. It is probably the central aspect of strategy development for a commodity-type business. This is because capacity additions usually take years to complete, from the time the idea is first conceived until the resources are committed and the product is actually being manufactured. The firm is also committing resources based upon expectations of future demand and competitive behavior. Capacity expansions thus involve all the classic problems of oligopoly in which firms are mutually dependent upon one another's actions and investments.[1]

The strategic issue in capacity expansion is how to add capacity to further the objectives of the firm while avoiding industry overcapacity. Such objectives are usually centered around improving one's competitive position and increasing market share and profitability.

Undercapacity is usually not a problem because it attracts new investment. Overbuilding has historically been a problem adversely affecting many industries—paper, lumber, shipping, iron ore, and aluminum.

The capacity decision is predicated both on economic conditions and on competitors' actions. Predicting competitor behavior is a difficult and dynamic process, because what a competitor does will influence others, particularly if that competitor is an industry leader.

The next step in the analysis is adding competitors' capacity to yield total industry capacity and individual market shares. If forecasted demand is perceived to be strong, the capacity-expansion process becomes one of preempting competition. In most industries, firms signal in the marketplace or through the trade press that they are contemplating an expansion, in the hope of detering others from investing in the same geographical region.

The problem occurs when too many firms try to preempt each other, resulting in excess capacity because firms misread one another's intentions and misjudge their relative strengths and staying power. Overbuilding is most prevalant in commodity type businesses for three reasons:

1. The cyclical nature of many commodity businesses leads to overcapacity in downturns and undercapacity in upturns.
2. Additionally, firms are too optimistic in bull markets and, thus add too much capacity, causing heavy losses during downturns.
3. Because manufacturing costs are so important in commodity businesses, new capacity additions tend to be only world-scale facilities.

A good example of this is the oil tanker shipping industry, where new supertankers are many times the size of older vessels. The capacity of a supertanker ordered in the early 1970s far exceeded the market demand. Similar examples exist in the steel and aluminum industries, which have suffered because of excess capacity due to overly optimistic forecasts during boom years.

In many commodity industries, a "topping-out" problem exists in adding industry capacity and personnel. As the industry adjusts to slower growth, the rate of capacity addition must slow down or overcapacity will occur. Many industries are also affected by exogenous factors that impinge growth. Such factors are typically product displacements because of product substitution, technological changes, or simply lower-priced imports. Thus, a firm is confronted with the need to monitor competitors' capacity additions closely and to time its additions. A firm must also monitor technological advancements that might dramatically affect the demand for its products. For example, the need to produce lighter automobiles in order to reduce gasoline consumption has resulted in technological advancements in engineered plastics, which are now substituting for steel in automobiles. This is one factor that could change the nature of demand for prefabricated steel. There are many other examples of technology or innovation in another industry affecting the demand/supply balance of an existing established industry. The office of the future and the checkless society could have enormous ramifications for a basic commodity industry, paper.

The key point of capacity expansion is that rapid growth will no longer quickly cover mistakes by eliminating excess capacity. Furthermore, as larger and larger increments of capacity are required to be competitive, the more difficult the topping-out problem. Firms must understand both the size and scope of their competitors' capacity increments, as well as monitor and understand technological change and innovation that could result in product substitution and/or displacement. Such changes fundamentally alter the way firms have been doing business for the last 20 to 30 years.

COMPETITIVE SUCCESS THROUGH COMPARATIVE ADVANTAGE

As previously mentioned, the nature of competition is a dynamic one where competitors interact on many levels. The reason participants in a business exhibit differences in financial performance is reflected in the different degrees to which they have been able to exploit a range of important microeconomic advantages that govern their business. These advantages are termed "sources of comparative advantage." Simply stated, a competitive advantage is a factor or numerous factors that permit one competitor to offer products or services more effectively than competitors.[2]

The notion of competitive advantage suggests the opportunity for sustained profitability over competitors. There are a number of areas in which sources of competitive advantage can be found:

Organizational—may have effects on the execution of strategies.

Geography—may dictate access to raw materials and markets.

Cost—is probably the most crucial element of comparative advantage in commodity-type industries. Cost is important in pricing and determining the inherent profitability of a company.

Integration—may permit scale and economic advantages.

Service and product quality, since most commodity products are undifferentiated, better service, and "perceived" or real quality differences can be a big asset.

For many commodity products, having a low delivered cost postition relative to the competition is a crucial element of comparative advantage. A delivered cost position is made up of two components: manufacturing costs and proximity to markets. Manufacturing cost is usually dictated by scale. This relationship is one of the best-known of all economic phenomena. Although the degree of the relationship varies from business to business, most commodity industries have their cost curve governed by scale of operation. The second important relationship has to do with the distribution cost per unit. It is usually true that the distribution cost is proportional to distance shipped. The relationship need not be linear, as there are a variety of components of cost, including mode of transportation, loading and unloading, and the relationship of value of product to weight and density. However, for almost all commodity products, the shipping costs represent a significant proportion of the final delivered cost of the product. As a result, the competitiveness of a particular manufacturer may be highly dependent on geography.

COMPARATIVE IMPLICATIONS OF THE COST CURVE

The traditional model of commodity businesses indicates that they are usually decreasing-cost businesses. New facilities, which involve new processes and technologies, are typically more productive than existing plants. It follows that competitors who aggressively invest in new facilities as well as keep their existing facilities modern will achieve and maintain a favorable cost position. In a commodity business, a favorable cost position translates into high market share, high profitability, and a key position with respect to price determination.

To apply cost concepts it is important to have reasonably accurate information about competitors' costs. Any firm without this information will be unable to assess either its present competitive position or the probable effects of new capacity investments.

The cost curve concept, conceptually, is easy to understand. The only caution is that it is only as good as the quality of the inputs that go into its composition. Figure 6.1 displays a cost curve for a typical commodity industry. On the horizontal axis, units of production for each manufacturing facility are plotted. Company A represents a manufacturing facility that has the capacity to produce 100 widgets, while facility B has the capacity to produce 80 widgets. The vertical axis represents the manufacturing costs required to produce a specific number of units. It could be one unit or one thousand units. The unit of measure depends upon how a particular industry determines a unit or product.

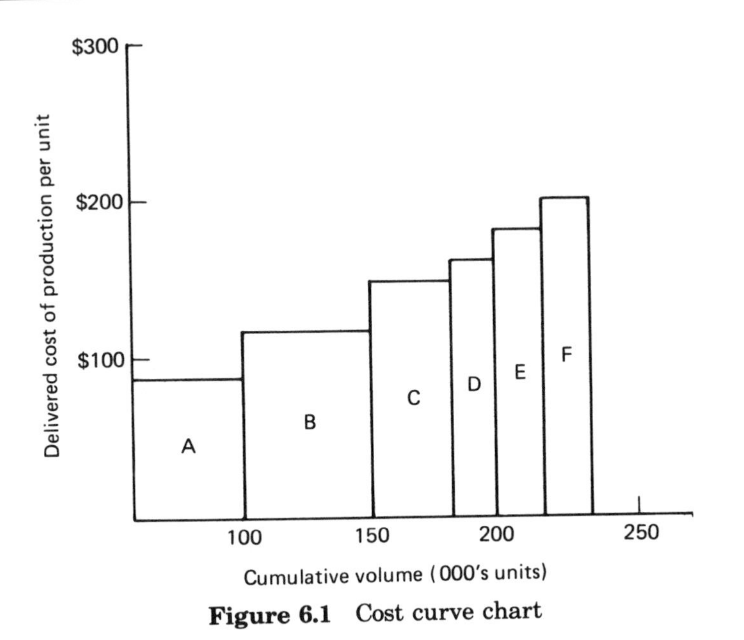

Figure 6.1 Cost curve chart

By displaying all competitors in this manner, a visual cost curve displaying all competitors can be used as a valuable strategic tool. The size and shape of the cost curve provides insights into both the macroeconomic nature of the industry and the relative strength of individual companies. For example, in an industry that has a gradually sloping cost curve (see Figure 6.2), there is very little difference between the low- and high-cost producer. This suggests that the industry is uniform in its capital investment structure. This is typical of an industry that has invested heavily in large plants and scale equipment. Thus it is difficult for a competitor to gain a cost advantage over another competitor. The steel industry and fertilizer industry are good examples of this type of cost-curve configuration.

Industries with this type of cost curve also tend to be highly competitive, low-margined, and capital-intensive. Prices tend to reflect the cost of the marginal producer. As long as the marginal or high-cost producer can cover production costs, it will remain in business. Once prices drop below the cost of production, it no longer makes sense to be in business. Therefore, in industries where there is little difference between competitors[1] cost structures, there is little opportunity for prices to be far in excess of costs. Because of this tight cost relationship between competitors, the successful companies generate most of their sales within close proximity of their manufacturing facilities. For prod-

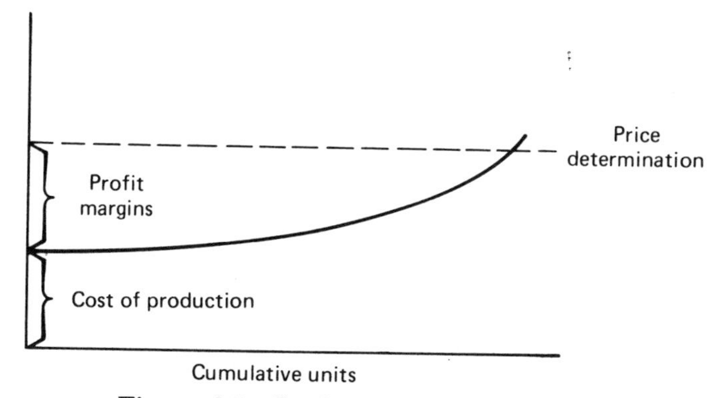

Figure 6.2 Gradually sloping cost curve

ucts with low value-to-weight ratios, shipping costs represent a significant proportion of the ultimate delivered cost of the product. As a result, the competitiveness of a particular manufacturer may be dependent on the proximity to customers.

The salt business demonstrates these principles. Most of the larger salt producers have similar costs of production. Salt has a low value-to-weight ratio, so that transportation costs are a significant portion of total costs. From a strategy perspective, each manufacturer should strive to control the market around the production facility right out to the point where the delivered cost per pound equals a competitor's total delivered cost coming in another direction. This principle also offers opportunities for companies to segment their business geographically.

Conversely, for industries that have steeper sloping cost curves (see Figure 6.3), there is a greater disparity between the marginal or high-cost producer and the low-cost producer. Manufacturers at the low end of the cost curve are protected by the price umbrella set by the high-cost producer. As a result, margins and the ability to make a superior profit are greater. Industries that have a proprietary production process, or are more specialized in nature, tend to have this type of supply curve.

THE IMPORTANCE OF MARKET SHARE

One of the basic principles of business, particularly a commodity business, is that high market share correlates with high investment returns. This principle of business strategy has recently become widely

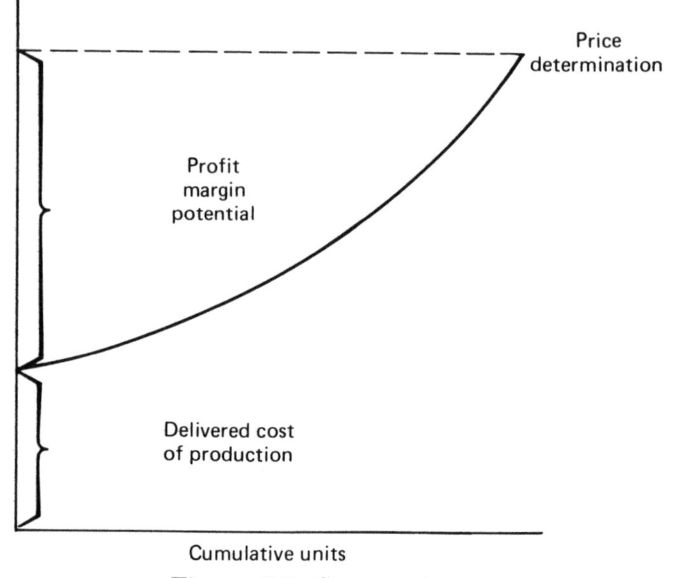

Figure 6.3 Steep cost curve

accepted, since it was first offered by General Electric, the Boston Consulting Group, and Pims.

One of the biggest supporters of the importance of market share is the Boston Consulting Group's Bruce Henderson. His analysis hinges on the "law" of experiences, wherein the number of hours required to complete a task bears an inverse relationship to the number of times the task is performed. Stated another way, the BCG law argues that the company with the highest market share will have the lowest cost because of superior learning opportunities. The law goes on to say that "costs of value added to a product decline approximately 20 to 30 percent in real terms each time the accumulated experience is doubled." A learning curve is generally plotted with total units produced on the horizontal axis, and the direct labor costs per unit on the vertical axis. An 80 percent learning curve is shown in Figure 6.4. The 80 percent refers to the fact that every time total production doubles, direct labor costs per unit decrease 20 percent. For example, the direct labor cost of the 200th unit of production is about 80 percent of the labor cost of the 100th unit. Although the experience curve is simple in concept, it is relatively complex in practice, and its effective use is very much more an art than a science.

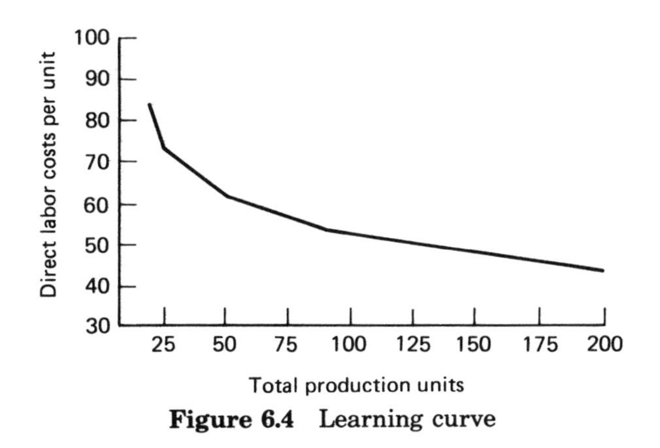

Figure 6.4 Learning curve

The experience curve/market share approach seems to have merit in industries that are growing and can benefit from increasing the scale of the manufacturing operation, or where the costs of the dominant producer are declining at a rapid rate. If competitor's costs decrease at a slower rate, either because they are not pursuing cost reductions as aggressively as the leader or because they are growing at a slower rate than the leader, then profits will eventually disappear.

Experience seems to be most significant in businesses involving a high labor content performing intricate tasks or a complex assembly operation. Electronic components are good examples of the experience curve used strategically. Sony, Texas Instruments, and Emerson Electric have invested in capacity to build large-scale volumes in the development of products, often by pricing in anticipation of future cost declines as they move down the experience curve. If costs decline rapidly with experience in an industry, then getting a head start and building a large market share can be a source of competitive advantage. Market share, in these circumstances, could be a key success factor.

An important corollary of the learning curve is the need to think in relative terms. For example, although it is admirable for a business to reduce its real costs of production over time, it is not important if the competition is moving at a faster pace. The only thing that matters is whether the business improves its cost position relative to competition. Viewed another way, comparing one's current performance to that a year earlier is a flawed way of thinking about how successfully a business is being managed. Acceptable performance must be gauged in terms of gaining ground on the competitors, not on oneself.

The cost curve/market share approach is somewhat flawed in industries defined as mature. Since well over half of all U.S. industry is described as mature, and projected GNP growth rates do not indicate much of a significant change, this encompasses many industries.[3]

In industries where demand is inelastic and growth is slowed, it becomes increasingly difficult to add volume strictly for the sake of increasing share. Adding volume in such markets can only be accomplished by price cutting and reducing margins. Doing so will result in low-cost manufacturing, but could also lead to a plant full of unprofitable business. Certainly the fertilizer, steel, and paper industries have suffered from time to time because of untimely capital additions. DuPont's experience in nylon is a good case in point. After years of reducing nylon prices to gain a large market share, DuPont found itself up against a wall when it tried to raise prices to increase profitability. Nylon end users showed themselves ready to switch to substitute products rather than pay higher nylon prices.[4]

Even in a few fast-growing industries like electronics, overly intensive market-share competition can lead to deteriorating profits for the entire industry. Nowhere is this more true than in the semiconductor field.

In reality there are many low-market-share companies that reap superior returns. However, many of these companies that are competing in basic commodity businesses with subscale equipment tend to move to more specialized segments or noncommodity segments of the business in order to survive. Many commodity industries have large segments that require large-scale, fast-running equipment to be successful. However, within these same industries there are usually more specialized subsegments that require either a more rigorous manufacturing process or differentiated product performance characteristics, setting them apart from the commodity segment of the business. Manufacturing scale and market share for these specialty subsegments are not as important as the commodity side of the business. In fact, smaller machines might be desired because of the flexibility they offer. The paper industry demonstrates this point quite well. There are numerous market segments in the commercial printing arena that require more rigorous paper specifications than the basic commodity printing papers. Such markets can best be served by producers with smaller slower-moving machines. As a result, the products produced on these machines can command a higher price to compensate for the lack of scale.

Thus it is difficult to compare the performance of companies within the industry without the first understanding the business segments within which they compete. Further, market share cannot be viewed in a total sense, but has to be broken down into its subsegment components in order to capture their relevance. There are many examples of companies that have small overall industry market shares but have high subsegment market shares and consistantly outperform the "industry leaders." For example, Kaiser Steel and Inland Steel, with smaller overall market shares than the national giants, consistently outperform Bethelem and U.S. Steel. James River and Pentair, which have relatively small shares of the paper business, consistently outperform the Weyerhaeusers and International Paper Companies of the world. Thus, having a large market share in a particular industry is not the sole criterion for superior performance. Market share has to be viewed in the context of the barriers separating the basic commodity product from its specialty subsegments, the macroeconomic factor affecting the growth of the various segments, and the level of competition within each segment. Market share alone is too simplistic a concept to evolve a meaningful strategy. At best, it is merely one weapon among many that strategists should keep in the arsenal.

Some of the factors that should be considered in evaluating competitive strengths and weaknesses are the following, which were identified by McKinsey & Company, the management consulting firm:

Market size (domestic/global).
Market growth (domestic/global).
Price trend.
Captive market.
Cyclicality.
Concentration.
Competitive characteristics.
Top group strength.
Replacement threats.
Market leader's profit trend.
Sociopolitical and economic environment.
Labor situation.
Legal issues.

Technology position.
Inflation vulnerability.

STRENGTHS AND WEAKNESSES

Most companies do not take a realistic view of themselves in the context of their competition. Too often, companies fall victim to the belief that they are better than the competition. Most managers delude themselves with self-praise and do not perform the necessary analysis to ascertain which firms are the superior competitors, and more importantly, what are the reasons for their superior performance. Identifying current competitive advantage begins with assessing the financial and market performance of the competition and then evaluating the strengths and weaknesses that account for a superior or inferior performance. Critical factors that should be reviewed are:

Cost position of competitors.
Pricing tactics.
Organizational differences.
Level of technology.
Degree of integration (could be advantage or disadvantage).
Industry segmentation.
Ability to serve markets.
Financial ability to maintain or enlarge the business.
Perception of customers concerning the strengths and weaknesses of competitor.

The evaluation of strengths/weaknesses and the principles of comparative advantages should always be viewed in a dynamic sense. A current advantage could dissipate quickly, particularly if the state of the art in manufacturing changes, or if technology creates a new or superior product that is either better or performs the same function more economically. Assessing future changes by competitors is vitally important in determining future strategic moves. Again, the key to gaining success is to be in a better relative competitive position rather than to improve in an absolute sense. The success of a firm's business strategy is dependent upon the actions and reactions of the competitors rather than the firm's own initiatives.

THREAT OF ENTRY

New entrants into an industry creates new capacity. This capacity causes intense competition for market share, which frequently reduces the profitability for the incumbents. The decision of whether or not to enter a new market largely depends upon the anticipated rewards. The new firm has to assess the potential profits against the expected costs of entry. The costs of entry into an industry can be broken into two basic areas. The first is the initial capital requirements to build and purchase plant, equipment, inventory, and start-up expenses. The second area is less tangible and less predictable. This is the cost of competitive advantage retaliation. Most incumbents will not simply stand by and watch their market share erode. Instead, there is usually a period of price discounting or promotion/advertising to protect one's turf. The more commodity-oriented an industry is, the more likely it is to experience the former rather than the latter. From a competitive vantage point, it behooves a new firm to gather intelligence information about prior new entries, so as to be prepared for the retaliations.

Unlike the consumer goods business, once a new commodity entrant has committed investment capital it is unlikely that the firm will be dissuaded because of temporary price and margin erosion. That is because the fixed investment required to enter most commodity industries is huge compared to the fixed costs to enter many consumer goods businesses. Therefore, if a new entrant exits a new market after having already committed capital, it stands to lose considerable sums of money as well as credibility with the board of directors. In the consumer goods field, in contrast, fixed capital is certainly a large part of the cost of entering a market but often the advertising and promotion costs are the biggest. Advertising and promotion costs are generally more variable in nature because they can be retracted if plans are changed.

As previously discussed, one of the major entry hurdles faced by a new commodity competitor is the economics of scale of the existing competitors. Scale economics deter entry because they force the new firm to either come in with expensive large-scale equipment or face an initial cost disadvantage.[15] Scale economies are present not only in manufacturing but could also be present in research and development, and in marketing and distribution.

For example, manufacturing economies are important for mineral extraction, paper and aluminum production, but marketing and service are key barriers for the office products and mainframe computer industry. Xerox created a major comparative advantage in copiers when it chose to rent copiers rather than sell them outright, which greatly increased the working-capital requirements. Each component of cost for a particular industry should be examined separately to determine which economies of scale are important and the extent to which they will influence the outcome of the business.

Scale economies and barriers to entry may also relate to vertical and/or horizontal integration. A company may be able to achieve significant economic advantages over its competition if its product costs can be shared by other products that can either be made on the same equipment or assembled in a similar fashion. Consider, for example, a company that manufactures plastic components that go into calculators, pens, watches, television sets, and other products assembled by another division of a firm. If its economies of production extend beyond calculator manufacturing, it will reap economies in calculator manufacturing that exceed those competitors who manufacture only for use in radios. Thus, horizontal integration can either create an entry barrier if other producers are integrated, or make it more difficult to enter a market.

The benefits of horizontal integration of diversification are not limited only to the costs of manufacturing. The benefits of horizontal integration can be particularly great in sharing marketing and distribution expenses. For example, a chemical company that sells only resins would be at a disadvantage over one that sells a multitude of products. The multiproduct manufacturer would reap economic advantage in freight costs, billing expenses, selling expenses (if the same customers buys more than one product), and handling expenses.

Vertical integration can also generate similar scale advantages over horizontal integration, and thus create additional barriers to entry. Also, nonintegrated firms face possible foreclosure of inputs on markets for its product if most firms are integrated. Take, for example, paper company A, which is vertically integrated into making its own pulp. A new entrant that has made an investment in paper-producing machinery, but lacks the financial resources to invest in a pulp mill, might be at a disadvantage producing similar products to those made by the integrated producer. This would be particularly true during tight paper markets when pulp prices are high. In this situation, the nonintegrated producer would have to seek out those paper markets served only by nonintegrated paper producers in order to effectively compete.

This is where understanding the market segments in an industry becomes important. As is usually the case, the nonintegrated producer or the producer with smaller-scale equipment has to seek out a smaller, more specialized niche in the market in order to survive.

A similar advantage can accrue to a company whose manufacturing process results in a by-product. The entrant that cannot capture and sell the by-product will be at a disadvantage over the existing competitors that can sell the by-product.

SUMMARY

The process of competitive analysis is dynamic, constantly changing as new capacity comes on stream and old capacity exits. The technique for doing competitive analysis requires diligence in gathering and interpreting data information.

In most commodity-type businesses the focal point of doing the analysis hinges on a few simple strategic concepts:

Assess the position of each competitor in terms of delivered cost position, financial capabilities, marketing and service capabilities, product quality, and so on. Where are the sources of competitive advantage of each firm?

Estimate the direction in which each competitor is going over a period of time. This involves assessing their past actions and interpreting their intentions and capabilities. Are they increasing or decreasing their commitment to a particular business segment? Are they conveying an expansionary or contractionary posture to their customers?

Assess any new potential sources of competition that might evolve either from internal diversification efforts or through acquisition. What effect could this new source of competition have on the industry and one's own position?

The application of this type of competitive surveillance usually results in a critical self-evaluation of the position of one's own firm. Systematically going through each step in the gathering and interpreting of information allows for a more substantial and realistic view of a firm and its competitors. Pinpointing the leading competitors is normally not as difficult as identifying the primary sources of comparative advantage. The key message is that in order to make sound strategic decisions either at the corporate or business level, it is imperative that there be a deep-seated understanding of the external competitive environment. Further, the strategic decisions that are made should focus on exploiting the limitations of the competition rather than going against the strengths of the industry leaders.

---

[1] Michael E. Porter, *Competitive Strategy,* New York, Free Press, 1980, p. 327.

[2] Ian MacMillan, "Seizing Competitive Initiative," *Journal of Business,* Spring 1982.

[3] "Management Practice, Market Share and ROI: A Popular Delusion,"Main, Jackson & Garfield, Inc., Fall 1978, p. 3.

[4] Walter Kiechel, "The Decline of the Experience Curve," *Fortune,* October 5, 1981, p. 23.

[5] Michael E. Porter, "Industry Structure and Competitive Strategy Key to Profitability, *Financial Analysts Journal,* July–August 1980, p. 32.

7

Competitor Intelligence in Consumer Industries

MARK KURLAND

Biographical data for this chapter author appear on page 147

ROLE OF COMPETITOR INTELLIGENCE IN CONSUMER INDUSTRIES

Competitor intelligence, whether it is for a commodity of a consumer-related product, aims to provide not only an in-depth understanding of the industry but also a picture of competitors in relation to one another and to the overall business environment. Industry structure has a strong influence in determining the competitive rules of the game, as well as the strategies potentially available to a firm. Although the goals of intelligence are the same for both a commodity business and a consumer products business, the functions of the two industries differ greatly and therefore require different tools to prosper.

In simpler terms, a competitive advantage is dependent upon fulfilling a market need more effectively than a competitor can. A company must provide an equivalent product at a lower price, a better product at an equal price, or another value combination—such as a better marketing or distribution system—that will benefit the consumer. In a competitive environment, it is the relative position of a company compared to its competitors that is paramount.

Because competitive position is so important to the success of a firm, it is imperative that competitor analysis be given a central role in strategy development. Competitor analysis concerns itself with understanding the components of comparative advantage over time. These advantages include such factors as cost position, market share, brand loyalty, proprietary technology, superior distribution, and superior organizational strengths. Once these factors can be determined and analyzed for each competitor, inferences can be made about competitors' strategic alternatives and most likely strategies. Keep in mind that strategies are competitors' attempts to influence relative position in their favor. Since one's own strategy is designed for the future as well as for the present, it is necessary to take into account any possible changes in a competitor's strategies in order to formulate one's own strategy.

DIFFERENCES BETWEEN CONSUMER BUSINESS AND COMMODITY BUSINESS

Although the basic elements used in assessing competitors are roughly the same for consumer product firms and commodity firms, there are a few essential precepts that require a different type of analysis. The fundamental differences in a consumer-related business is that the growth potential is less confining than for a commodity business and the profit potential differs. Commodity industries like fertilizers, steel, and paper offer predictable returns based on the products' supply/demand balance and the cost structure of the competition. Success for these products is measured in terms of profitability and market share is primarily a function of being able to deliver a product to the market at the lowest cost. The ability to deliver a low-cost product usually requires a high degree of capital intensity to gain manufacturing economies of scale cost reductions in production and distribution.

In comparison, consumer products such as foods, cosmetics, toys, and the like could offer the potential for much faster growth and higher returns if marketed and priced accordingly. However, consumer products tend to have shorter life cycles than commodity products. Therefore, it is important to manage the product or business for profit optimization over its life cycle. This usually entails adjusting the levels of spending for advertising, promotion, and merchandising. At a product's inception, heavy advertising and promotion dollars will probably be required to gain a presence in the marketplace and an awareness among consumers. As the product matures and loyalties among competing brands are more established, managing for profit maximization usually dictates a reduction in advertising and promotion spending. In order to set realistic goals about a product's life cycle, an assessment and understanding of the life cycle of similar products or brand categories provides valuable insights into expectation of one's own product.

The supply and demand for consumer products is not as important as it is for commodity products. There is an unlimited supply for most consumer products and demand is created through marketing, advertising, and creating a real or perceived need for the product. The elements of brand loyalty and brand awareness are also crucial for consumer products, but play only a minor role for commodity products. Brand loyalty—or the propensity to buy a certain brand—is a key factor in the strategy development for many consumer packaged goods. That is why many consumer firms share existing brand names with new products. The cost of creating a brand name need then be borne only once.

Consumer product companies establish brand loyalty and brand awareness through advertising and promoting. Advertising is the vehicle for conveying a message to the consumer about the characteristics that differentiate one's product from the rest of the pack. Sales promotion attempts to gain trial and stimulate repeat purchases for a product. Although sales promotion and advertising are more complicated and have motives and benefits other than those just mentioned, it is safe to say that they are tools that stimulate demand through identifying perceived and real differentiated product characteristics.

Commodity products, whether they are manufactured by A, B, or C, are very similar in nature and have very a similar utilitarian value to the end user. As a result, the benefits from advertising and promoting are minimal. Most commodity producers spend very little on advertising and promotion, and instead concentrate on cost improvement programs and more expedient and effective ways to distribute their products. Unlike the commodity business, merchandising also plays an important role in the consumer products business. There is a positive relationship between shelf space and sales in a given store. There is also the important secondary relationship connecting the value of the shelf space with its location and its height relative to eye level.[1] Relationships of this type that lead to sources of competitive advantage are fundamental to the structure of the consumer product's competitive environment. Competitive market share information is often used as a tool in bargaining for shelf space in a given store. An astute consumer product's salesman will use competitive share information to influence a grocery store clerk to increase shelf space in a company's favor.

The consumer products business also differs from a commodity business in the way in which profits are determined. In a commodity business, relative cost position is the primary criterion in generating profits. Being the low-cost producer is important because the customer is not willing to pay a higher price for what is basically an undifferentiated product. As a result, superior margins are afforded the low-cost producer. Although cost position has some significance in the consumer business, it is not nearly as important as market share, distribution, and perceived product differentiation, for which a consumer is willing to pay a higher price.

Entry barriers are also quite different between a commodity product and a consumer product. Entry into a commodity business is facilitated by the capital investment and the relationship between supply and demand. The entry barriers in the consumer business are largely determined by advertising and promotion costs, the levels of which are usually predicated upon the promotion and advertising spending of the existing competitive brands.

INGREDIENTS FOR SUCCESS

In its simplest terms, for a product to be successful it has to be perceived by the consumer as being different and better than another similiar product. The differentiated product position is usually obtained by winning customer preference and loyalty by effectively communicating product differences through advertising, promotion, and distribution. Success in gaining a differentiated product position typically leads to faster growth, higher prices, and superior operating margins. It also helps either to have a product that is demonstrably different from a competitor's product or, at the very least, an advertising strategy that conveys a "perceived" quality or performance superiority.

A good example is the cosmetics industry. Max Factor may produce cosmetics in its factories, but it sells glamour, sex appeal, and hope to the consumer. What is important is not so much what Max Factor puts into its compact, but the ideas it puts inside the consumer's head through appealing packaging and effective advertising. Elements that are related to gaining customer acceptance include the following:

Testimonials from influential people in your product category (e.g., doctors, dentists).
Favorable mention in the public media.
Word of mouth support.
Brand awareness.
Brand loyalty.

Key factors to gain market penetration include the following:

Effective trade and consumer promotions.
Effective and efficient advertising.
Extensive distribution.
Brand Trial.
Preferred shelf and display space.
Cooperative advertising and in-store featuring.

THE VALUE OF COMPETITOR INTELLIGENCE

Knowledge of how companies compete in the marketplace is paramount to developing any business or product strategy. The most significant elements of any business or marketing plan take into account the capabilities of competitors as well as information about the market's potential. Once the forces affecting competition in a product category have been diagnosed, a company is in a position to evaluate its strengths and weaknesses relative to the competition. The crucial questions to be addressed are: Where does the product stand against substitute products and technologies? Against the sources of entry barriers? In coping with rivalry from established competitors?

In addressing these questions of competitive positioning, competitor analysis first has to deal with market definition, which encompasses market size and growth, market segmentation, number of competitors, distribution channels, competitive shares, and competitive financial strength and weaknesses. Once this type of basic data is gathered and analyzed, positions of comparative advantage can be ranked.

Competitor strategy development arises from an appraisal of one's strengths and weaknesses. It then focuses on developing offensive and/or defensive actions in order to strengthen a company's position. An offensive strategy can take the form of an aggressive sampling campaign in order to increase brand awareness and usage, with the aim of increasing market share. A defensive strategy might be to drop price to temporarily dissuade a new competitive threat. In either case, knowledge of a competitor's capabilities and marketing plans is a positive step towards exploiting change by choosing appropriate strategies.

PRODUCT INTRODUCTIONS IN A COMPETITIVE ENVIRONMENT

The consumer packaged-goods industry is characterized by the existence of firms that produce products that are close substitutes for one another. The truly new product representing an entirely new departure in concept that creates a new market, is a rarity. Instead, most new product entries tend to be line extensions or offshoots of existing brands. Clairol typifies a company that has been quite successful in bringing new products to market in this fashion. The hair-care category, where Clairol has a strong name, has many competitive products, each claiming to have certain performance characteristics that set them apart from the rest of the pack. In a category that is infiltrated with so many different brands, it is increasingly more difficult for an entirely new brand to gain enough of a market share to maintain its credibility in the marketplace. However, an established brand with a strong presence in the marketplace does not face quite the same uphill battle of establishing credibility with the retailer and, ultimately, with the consumer. The key point is that the expense of establishing a brand identity need only be borne once. The brand name may then be used for other products of the company.

The firm with a new product must convince the retailer to give it space on the fiercely competitive supermarket shelf. Promotions are expensive, whether they are trade promotions such as discounts and cooperative advertising rebates, or consumer promotions such as cents-off coupons. The more competitive the category, the more difficult it is for a new brand to gain a foothold in the marketplace. For example, in the highly competitive toothpaste category, unless a firm is a nationally known consumer package goods company it is unlikely that the product could get distribution among nationally known retailers. Their shelf space is already cluttered with long-standing toothpaste brands and they would see little reason to carry a new brand, particularly a brand that did not have an identity as a toothpaste.

Assessing the competitive distribution channels is also vital to launching a new product. To the extent that logical distribution channels for one's product are already being served sufficiently by competition, as is the case in the toothpaste example, a new firm might seek other channels that are not as costly to enter. Jhirmack, which competes in the hair care products market, found the traditional distribution channels into food and drug stores cost-prohibitive. Jhirmack simply did not have the financial strength to promote and advertise with the major existing marketers. Instead, Jhirmack found a new way to get into the market via beauty salons. In fact, they were so successful in penetrating the market in this fashion that they were able to establish an identity and quality image with the consumer. This eventually led to a licensing agreement with a nationally known consumer packaged-goods firm, who was able to successfully gain distribution in food and drug stores.

Conversely, a firm that has an established track record and a well-developed distribution channel for one product category might find it easier to gain distribution in a new product. Gillette, with strong distribution channels for razors and blades, found lower costs of entry for disposable lighters than did many other firms.

Competitive entrance barriers for a particular category provides valuable insight into understanding the cost of competitive warfare. Advertising and promotion levels for competitive brands can be gathered through trade publications, advertising agencies, sales personnel, and market research. Too often, new products are launched without enough advertising and promotion, and are doomed to failure. If there are four or five products in a particular category, and each brand is spending ten to fifteen million dollars in advertising and promotion, the chances of competing successfully with a one or two million dollar spending budget are pretty small. The same analogy holds true for existing competitive brands. If brands A and B have been spending at a given level for a number of years and then A gradually increases the spending level without B being aware of this change, the effects on B's market share can be devastating. Therefore, gathering competitor intelligence is not a one-time exercise, but a dynamic one to ensure that the competition is not gaining an unfair advantage.

One must also recognize that increasing the level of advertising and promotion spending is not always the most prudent and advisable strategy. There are times, particularly in the mature phase of a product's life cycle, when reducing spending dollars might be the most logical and profitable strategy. Even under this scenario, competitor intelligence might prove beneficial. If the competition has reduced dollars on advertising with no appreciable loss in market share, you might be able to do the same.

COMPETITIVE RIVALRY

Competitive rivalry takes many shapes and forms. In some situations, it can be compared to warfare or a hotly contested sporting event. The clearest examples of head-to-head rivalry exist when a new brand is being introduced against existing brands. Frequently, competitors who are already established in an area where a new product is being test marketed double their advertising levels and/or offer unusually large consumer and retail promotions in an effort to undermine the test market results of the new competitor. Their purpose is to either delay the launch of the product or force the test results—namely, low market share—to be so poor that the product launch is either postponed pending a new test market or cancelled.

In 1979, when Procter & Gamble was test marketing Rely tampons in Rochester, New York, an existing tampon producer analyzed the Rely product in its research lab and determined that Procter & Gamble had a potentially consumer desired product. Fearing that the Rely product would be successfully launched at the expense of existing brands, it was time to go on the defense to protect their existing brand franchise. The established competitor's strategy was to impair Proctor & Gamble's test-market results. This was accomplished by promoting and advertising heavily in Rochester. The strategy paid off, as Rely failed to gain enough share points to justify a national launch. In the interim, the aggressive defensive strategy paid off, as the company was able to advertise aggressively and gain valuable share points from the existing competitors prior to Rely's market entry.

If a company is fortunate enough to "own a market" and reap high returns, it is very likely that competition is around the corner. There are just too many well-capitalized consumer packaging firms looking for profitable, underexposed niches. These large firms are willing to pay the entrance fee to get into the market as long as they have a differentiated product that stands a chance of gaining a reasonable market share.

One company that established a brand category that eventually attracted a tremendous amount of competition is Minnitonka. Minnitonka's liquid soap product burst open a new category in the highly competitive billion-dollar soap market, through a novel and convenient way to dispense soap. The product caught on immediately with the consumer. Total sales shot up from $25 million to $73 million in one year, and the company's stock went from $8 to $18 a share in the same year. The problem was that Minnitonka's only product was liquid soap. There was nothing proprietary about the product and thus it could easily be duplicated. Although Minnitonka expected to and got some competition from the heavy hitters like Procter & Gamble and Jergens, it did not anticipate the 50 brands of liquid soap that soon appeared on the market. This resulted in the temporary curtailment of Minnitonka's growth and profits.[2]

It has been demonstrated that product differentiation, awareness, and loyalty are usually the traits of the market leader, and as such create barriers to entry. Sometimes, however, the market leader can get lackadaisical and open up the door to an aggressive new competitor. Tampax Inc. created the first feminine tampon product that served a need not being satisfied by existing products. By being the first product of its kind in the marketplace, it was able to command a high degree of brand loyalty, to the point where Tampax became almost the generic name for tampons. Although Tampax prospered, it was in a vulnerable strategic position. Management at Tampax became complacement and did not have a contingency plan to ward off competitive threats. International Playtex introduced a tampon product in the early 1970s with a few minor changes that offered a perceived advantage to the user. The success of the Playtex product was predicated on their advertising and promotion strategy. Playtex was the first tampon product to gain approval to advertise on national TV. The advertising strategy took the dormant Tampax by surpise, with the result that Playtex was able to bite off over a 30 percent market share in a relatively short period of time.

The lesson to be learned from the tampon example is that competition is always lurking around the corner, and a contingency strategy should be in place to counter any new product entry.

Some companies protect their franchise by conveying a strong message that a competitive new product entry will be an expensive proposition. Procter and Gamble's disposable diaper—Pampers—is illustrative of a brand with unusually high awareness and loyalty. Procter & Gamble promotes and advertises heavily to support Pampers. This conveys a strong message to potential competitors: if you want a piece of the disposable diaper market you had better be prepared to commit substantial funds to advertising and promotion, and run the risk of heavy losses in the first few years of the product's launch. Very few companies have the financial muscle to tackle a product that is supported so strongly by a company such as Procter & Gamble. Recently, Johnson & Johnson had to scrap its attempt to enter the diaper market because of the financial strain on the company. Product differentiation and loyalty are perhaps the most important entry barriers in baby products, over-the-counter drugs, and cosmetics. If you can somehow persuade anybody looking at your business that it's going to be an expensive and bloody battle, they might not be so anxious to do battle.

COMPETITIVE RIVALRY AND ITS IMPLICATIONS

Some forms of competition—notably price competition—are highly unstable and are likely to leave the entire industry worse off from the standpoint of profitability. When firms pursue short-sighted goals, price wars are almost inevitable and tend to spread and harm all the players. When Procter & Gamble began moving Folgers coffee brand East in 1971, General Food's Maxwell House brand responded vigorously to the competitive onslaught. The head-to-head battle brought with it a wave of deep trade discounts, price cutting, couponing, and advertising. It cost Maxwell House its status as the nation's leading brand and made Folgers number one, but it cost Procter & Gamble millions in introductory losses. It drove smaller competitors to the Federal Trade Commission with complaints, accusing General Foods of predatory pricing and unfair competition. While the case may yet be reviewed by the full Federal Trade Commission, the preliminary decision signals that marketers who pull out aggressive promotional weapons to defend their turf from invaders have little to fear from federal antitrusters, nor can smaller companies expect much comfort when they find themselves squeezed in a price war.[3]

The inevitable consequence of pricing competition results in profit losses by both large and small competitors. The competitive struggle involves winners and losers, but price wars usually hurt everyone.

Advertising battles, on the other hand, may well expand demand or enhance the level of product differentiation in the industry to the benefit of all firms. The advertising rivalry currently being waged in the light beer market by Phillip Morris, Anheuser Busch, and Schlitz has served to increase the total size of the beer market by expanding the population of potential beer drinkers, while at the same time creating a whole new brand category.

RIVALRY AMONG GENERICS

Another potential threat to most consumer packaged-goods firms is pressure from substitute or generic products. A generic product is simply a product very similar to a brand product but usually selling at a substantial price discount because very little money is spent on promoting and advertising to build brand identity. Generic brands are sometimes manufactured by a branded consumer packaged goods firm under a supermarket label, or may be manufactured by a contract packager. Generic products are quite prevalent these days, particularly among food and health and beauty items. Substitutes, or generic brands, tend to have a damaging effect on the competitive structure of an industry by placing a ceiling on the prices firms can charge.[4] The more attractive the price performance alternative offered by the substitute, the firmer the lid is placed on industry profits. A good example of this is the tissue market, where almost every major food chain has an in-house toilet, facial, and napkin product that competes at a lower price than the nationally branded products.

WHAT CAN BE LEARNED FROM COMPETITIVE ACTIONS

In order to be successful in today's marketplace, a company must be competitor-oriented. It should look for weak points in a competitor's strategy and then launch market attacks against those weak points. In the consumer products environment, marketing costs probably vary more from firm to firm than production costs. Also, they are not always monitored as carefully as they should be. Similarly, a competitor's product is not always evaluated and understood. Although companies spend many dollars in market research evaluating consumers' likes and dislikes about their own product, usually not much effort goes into understanding a competitor's products. The benefits from a clear understanding of a competitor's product could prove vital to a product's success.

Procter & Gamble's Pringle product was a snack food formulated and designed around market research. It appeared that the firm had a winner that would encroach on Frito Lay and Wise. Frito Lay and Wise invested in market research to determine what the consumer disliked about Pringles. The answer was taste and lack of natural ingredients. Frito Lay and Wise then produced a flavor and natural ingredient campaign that eventually proved to be Pringle's undoing in the marketplace.

The lesson to be learned from this is the value of knowing the strengths and weaknesses of your competitor's products. If your product is superior in taste, color, performance, shape, ease of handling, or any other way that demonstrates its superiority—make "noise" about its benefits.

One of the most difficult chores in marketing, if not *the* most difficult, is the product turnaround. This is especially true when a brand has lost much of its distribution. Tic Tac, the imported candy sensation of the early 1970s, saw its stature eroded by domestic competition and was finally shot down by another import before the end of the 1970s.

The original concept for Tic Tac was developed 15 years ago. Tic Tac was able to get up to 12 percent of the hard candy and mint category in a few short years. For years, the field was dominated by the multiflavored Life Savers and Warner Lambert's Certs. Serious competition began for Tic Tac when Warner Lambert copied Tic Tac's clear plastic packaging for its Dynamints. Then, along came sugar-free Velamints from a German Company, Ragold. That was almost the death blow, as the new brand cut into the breath-conscious and weight-conscious adult market. Tic Tac's market share dropped to 2 percent.

Once again, the factor that turned it around for Tic Tac was market research concerning their product vis-a-vis the competition. Their research showed that there was a common misconception that sugar-free meant calorie free. Since Tic Tac had the lowest amount of calories of the competitive products and Americans were very calorie conscious, Tic Tac changed its advertising campaign. Tic Tac's advertising campaign was a comparative ad that named the primary competition. The ad said that a single small Tic Tac has less calories than the larger Breathsavers, Trident, or Velamints—"Tic Tac, the 1 1/2 calorie breath mint." Market share for Tic Tac has since increased to 6 percent and is rising. Again, the concept that turned the brand around was the competitive communication that highlighted the difference between calorie-free versus sugar free.[5]

In some cases, understanding the physical characteristics of a competitor's product might provide some understanding of its success. After 113 years of offering Tabasco brand pepper sauce in only a 2-ounce size, Mellhenny began introducing a 5-ounce size. Why? Market research showed that competitive products did 93 percent of their sales in 4-ounce bottles or larger. Mellhenny's new 5-ounce size did so well that it increased sales of the 2-ounce size.

THINGS TO LOOK FOR WHEN DOING COMPETITIVE INTELLIGENCE

There are innumerable things to look at and research when evaluating the competition. Among those that should help assess the strength of the competition are the following:

Buy competitor's products, tear them down, and evaluate them.

Require field sales personnel to provide feedback on activities of customers, suppliers, distributors, and competitors. The sales force is usually a good source of competitive information that is largely underutilized.

Assign key officers to spend several days a year talking to customers.

Evaluate competitors, promotions, and advertising to determine the thrust and intensity of their marketing endeavors.

Become familiar with the kinds of competitor information available under the Freedom of Information Act by asking your department managers to compile a list of reports your company is required to submit to the Federal government.

Market research firms can provide a wealth of information about publicly held companies—patents, labor contracts, research and development activities, biographical information on company executives, plans for new plants and plant expansions.

Literature searches of relevant trade magazines should also prove beneficial.

SUMMARY

This chapter has pointed out a number of examples of how a better understanding of a competitor's actions and strategies can cause a change in the market planning of one's own product. The big question, however, is how does a firm gain knowledge about the competitive structure of a particular category and, more specifically, a competitive product within a category? The primary tool for gaining this knowledge base is market research. Chapter 9 will explore the "whys" and "hows" of market research and demonstrate its importance in conducting competitor intelligence. First, however, we want to broaden our topic by taking a look at international competition.

---

[1]"Competitive Analysis," *Hayes/Hill Report,* April 1981, vol. 14, p. 4.

[2]"Minnetonka Slip-Slidin' Away," *Forbes,* February 15, 1982, p. 100.

[3]Richard L. Gordon, "FTC Judge OK's GF Defense vs. Folger," *Advertising Age,* February 8, 1982, p. 6.

[4]Michael E. Porter, "Industry Structure and Competitive Strategy: Keys to Profitability," *Financial Analysts Journal,* July–August 1980, p. 8.

[5]Philip H. Dougherty, "Tic Tac's Turnaround", *The New York Times,* April 19, 1982, p. 57.

8

International Competition

ROBERT S. REITZES

Dr. Reitzes is currently Director of International Public Affairs for the Monsanto Company and a part-time instructor in International Economics at Washington University in St. Louis. He is a member of the Chemical Manufacturer's Association's International Trade Committee and served on the staff for the U.S. – Japanese Economic Advisory Committee. He was Manager of International Economic Analysis at Monsanto and International Paper and an International Economist at the duPont Company. He received a Ph.D. from Georgetown University in 1972 and a B.A. from the University of Delaware in 1966.

THE CHALLENGE OF INTERNATIONAL COMPETITION

The lowering of tariff and non-tariff barriers, the emphasis on economies-of-scale and state of the art technology and research, and the development of high speed transportation and communications have contributed significantly to the growth of international competition since the end of World War II. Products and markets once dominated by American firms are now either controlled by or shared with foreign companies. During the postwar period several American companies failed to recognize the emerging pattern of international competition, and as a consequence were forced out of business or lost a sizable share of their domestic and/or international markets.

An example of this oversight occurred to the Singer Corporation's Friden Calculator Division. The failure of Friden, a leading American producer of calculators during the 1960s, to recognize or adjust to its Japanese and also U.S. competitors contributed to large losses and to its ultimate withdrawal from the business. During the mid-1960s, Friden helped to revolutionize the calculator market by introducing a high-speed electronic calculator based on the developments of the new semiconductor technology. This calculator was sold at a premium to the old-style, noisy, and relatively slow "rotary-type" calculators—even though the cost of production was comparable.

Friden enjoyed a strong position in the marketplace, and its management believed it would be able to maintain its market share. However, several Japanese companies (Sharp and Casio) and Texas Instruments were able to copy and improve on the technology, and developed a new strategy to gain market leadership. These companies miniaturized, cut prices, and mass-produced the electronic calculator, displacing Friden and eventually forcing Singer to withdraw from the market.

The lessons inherent in the Friden experience have also been taught to several other American companies during the last 25 years. In 1960, the United States accounted for more than one-fourth of the manufactured exports among the industrial nations, while supplying 98 percent of its domestic market. Since then, the United States has lost market share both at home and abroad even in those sectors in which this country has had a comparative advantage. The aircraft industry, for example, which has a positive trade balance, has lost part of its world market share—dropping from a 66 percent share in the 1960s to between 55 percent and 60 percent currently. This industry is under attack from the European Airbus and a Japanese consortium. The

U.S. textile machinery fabricators have also been adversely impacted by international competition. Today, the United States share of world exports of textile machinery is less than 7 percent compared to more than 15 percent in the 1960s. Meanwhile, American manufacturers only supply between 50 percent and 60 percent of the domestic market for textile machinery, while in the 1960s they supplied over 90 percent of the market.

The international and domestic position of the American metal-working machinery industry has been undercut by its German competitors. In the early 1960s, each country had about one-third of world export sales; but today, German firms hold about a 40 percent share compared to a 20 percent share for the United States. The American metal-working industry's domestic share has also dropped to 70 percent from 93 percent in the same period.

Foreign competition has been particularly tough in the consumer electronics, steel, and auto industries. In 1960, U.S. manufacturers of consumer electronics supplied over 95 percent of the domestic radios, television sets, and the like. But today, imports control half of the market. Two out of three television sets purchased in the United States are assembled by Japanese companies either in the United States or abroad.

The loss of competitiveness of the American auto industry and the dramatic growth of Japanese sales both at home and in foreign countries has had a significant impact on the economies of both nations. The Japanese auto manufacturers have replaced the United States as the world's largest motor vehicle producer and account for approximately 23 percent of the cars sold in the United States. (Table 8.1 graphically shows the loss that the British and American auto producers have incurred during the last 20 years and the gains that Japan and other emerging auto producers have achieved.) Japan's success is due, in part, to the U.S. auto producers' failure to comprehend the challenge posed by the Japanese—the ability to satisfy the growing desire of Americans for simple, efficient, and modestly priced transportation. Part of the loss of U.S. industrial world market share can be attributed to shifting demand patterns and maturing product life cycles, lower cost labor abroad, rapid development and growth of foreign economies, and the transfer of new technology by U.S. multinational companies to their foreign subsidiaries or to licensees. The decline in U.S. competitiveness has resulted from poor planning and a lack of understanding by top U.S. corporate management of the changing world marketplace and of their foreign competition; and an

TABLE 8.1. TRENDS IN WORLD VEHICLE PRODUCTION (PERCENT OF TOTAL).

	1960	1970	1980
United States	48	28	22
Japan	3	18	24
France	8	9	10
Germany	13	13	12
Italy	4	6	5
England	11	7	3
USSR	3	3	6
Other	10	16	18

Source: Motor Vehicle Manufacturers Association.

unwillingness of labor, at times, to scale down its demands to meet foreign competition. However, several U.S. companies such as Procter & Gamble, General Electric, IBM, and Monsanto have recognized the importance of international markets in competition and have been able to develop successful strategies to maintain their leading position in various world markets.

The need to comprehend and develop world market strategies is now clearly recognized by most U.S. corporations as well as foreign-based enterprises. Large multinational companies are continually studying the development of markets, new industrial innovations, and the strategies of their competition. Corporate management has become acquainted with the competitive thrusts of its foreign and domestic competition. The major U.S. chemical companies, for example, are quite knowledgeable concerning the goals and objectives of their German, Japanese, and English competitors. To be competitive or dominant in domestic and international markets and avert a decline in competitiveness, companies must develop a strong research and internal communication organization capable of analyzing and disseminating international competitor information. The most important factors to review are:

International and domestic market-share information—indicates the size of the current market, past growth trends, and possible clues to future growth of markets.

Manufacturing costs and capacity increases—aids in the understanding of competitors[1] cost structures, which is essential to remain competitive and necessary to make future investment decisions (not only for commodity-type products but also for differentiated products such as autos and televisions).

Financial strength of competitors—enables corporations to understand competitors[1] ability to invest or reinvest and will verify cost information.

International and domestic economic conditions (including wage rates, currency movements, and economic growth patterns)—can determine or affect significantly the competitiveness of a firm.

Technological developments—can give firm or firms competitive advantage.

Special incentives in each country (such as special tax advantages or government subsidies)—can provide a foreign firm with a significant competitive edge.

A brief review of the competitive situation of the world kraftlinerboard industry and the European synthetic fiber market during the 1970s will illustrate how international competitor information is gathered and how this information is assembled to develop corporate strategies and responses. Such information and analyses are also the basis for determining offshore investment opportunities, joint venture approaches in foreign countries, and marketing plans both at home and abroad. The importance of currency movement, unit labor costs, and special incentives provided by various countries will also be discussed.

WORLD KRAFTLINERBOARD MARKETS

Supply and Demand

The most important building block in developing an international corporate strategy (offensive and defensive) is to assess the size of the world market and identify the major producers (by region and company). Kraftlinerboard[1] is used primarily for the packaging of industrial or fruit products and is consumed worldwide. Another product, testlinerboard,[2] competes directly with kraftlinerboard and is produced primarily in Japan and urope.

Although the major U.S. paper companies[3] appear to dominate the domestic and foreign markets, the importance of these international markets (16 percent of sales of the U.S. industry were accounted for by export sales in 1980) and the strong competition from Sweden in Europe forces these companies to thoroughly analyze the major factors governing the world kraftlinerboard market. As Table 8.2 shows, the United States is a leading producer, consumer, and exporter of kraftlinerboard. However, Scandinavia exports most of its production to Europe and accounted for over 29 percent of world export sales in 1980. The table also indicates that exports are evenly divided between the industrial and developing countries.

In determining future marketing-investment strategies, U.S. companies have to make the following assessments:

What are the factors determining growth in consumption in various markets?

Will U.S. producers gain, lose, or maintain their world market share?

Will other competitive products undermine kraftlinerboard sales?

Will macroeconomic conditions support continued growth?

To gain a better understanding of the current trends in the marketplace, it is important to understand more about the consumption patterns in the various parts of the world. The consumption pattern for kraftlinerboard in Western Europe and Japan (see Table 8.3) indicates that demand was relatively flat between 1973 and 1980, reflecting weak economic growth, sharp increases in the real price of kraftlinerboard, increased competition from lower-cost testlinerboard and plastics, and an end to the substitution of linerboard for wood and metal packaging.

Historic data in other parts of the world are sketchy, but demand for linerboard grew relatively quickly in the developing countries. Packaging needs will be strongest in those developing countries that are large exporters (linerboard is used primarily for the packaging of exports) especially from the newly industrialized countries (Taiwan, Hong Kong, Singapore, Brazil, Mexico, and South Korea) and the exporters of tropical fruits and other food products. Because of the lack of products to export, the poorer regions of the world will remain marginal consumers of kraftlinerboard. Based on modest economic growth forecasts, end-use analysis, and an analysis of the testlinerboard and plastics industries, it is likely that growth of kraftlinerboard consumption in the industrial and newly industrialized countries during the next decade will be modest and that the major consumers will continue to be the primary markets.

TABLE 8.2. WORLD SUPPLY–DEMAND OF KRAFTLINERBOARD IN 1980 (000 METRIC TONS). (APPARENT CONSUMPTION – PRODUCTION = BALANCE)

	Apparent Consumption	Production	Balance[1]
Total	19,588	19,550	38
Developed	16,885	18,528	−1,643
North America	12,365	14,929	−2,564
United States	11,546	13,814	−2,268
Canada	819	1,115	−296
Western Europe	2,900	2,005	895
Western Europe (except Scandinavia)	2,620	650	1,970
Scandinavia	280	1,355	−1,075
Japan	1,535	1,459	76
Australia/New Zealand	85	135	−50
Developing	2,703	1,022	1,681
Latin America	1,071	582	489
Mexico	284	255	29
Brazil	235	235	00
Other	552	92	460
Asia	1,172	290	882
Nics[2]	376	240	136
China	372	00	372
Other Asia[3]	306	50	256
Near East	118	00	118
Africa	400	150	250
South Africa	159	130	29
Other[4]	241	20	221
Soviet Bloc[5]	60	00	60

[1]Negative number equals country's exports and positive number is equivalent to imports.
[2]Includes Taiwan, Singapore, Hong Kong, and South Korea.
[3]Mostly Asian countries (Indonesia, Thailand, Philippines, and Malaysia).
[4]Mostly Nigeria, Egypt, Ivory Coast, Kenya, and Lageria.
[5]Soviet Bloc includes only imports from OECD countries.
Source: OECD, UN (FAO), American Paper Institute.

TABLE 8.3. APPARENT CONSUMPTION OF KRAFTLINERBOARD BY REGION OF THE WORLD, 1974–80 (0000 METRIC TONS)

	1973	1977	1980	CAR[1] 1980/78 (%)
Total	16,293	16,098	19,588	2.7
Developed	14,943	14,685	16,885	1.7
North America	10,683	10,704	12,365	2.1
Western Europe	2,759	2,600	2,900	0.2
Japan	1,416	1,296	1,535	1.1
Australia/New Zealand	85	85	85	00
Developing	1,290	1,353	2,643	10.8
Latin America	390	403	1,071	15.5
Asia	500	600	1,172	12.9
Africa	300	350	400	4.2
Soviet Bloc[2]	60	60	60	—

[1]Compound annual growth rate.
[2]Only imports from OECD.
Source: OECD, UN (FAO), American Paper Institute, author's estimates.

Cost/Productivity

Once the size of the market has been assessed, a firm must then determine the cost and production factors that can provide a comparative advantage to a region or a firm. The key determinants of cost in kraftlinerboard are: wood (raw materials), unit labor costs, energy, machine speeds (efficiency), and currency rates. In 1981, the United States enjoyed a superior cost position relative to Scandinavia, Canada, and the emerging new forest products regions such as Brazil. American wood costs were cheaper because the United States enjoyed a longer growing season, its plantations were more efficiently managed and integrated with the paper companies, and the cost of hauling wood was less expensive. Brazil's softwood (wood used in kraftlinerboard) forests at present are too small, and its infrastructure (roads, electricity, housing, and so on) are inadequate to support several world-scale kraftlinerboard facilities.

U.S. energy costs, although approaching world levels, are still relatively low compared to Europe, reflecting cheaper coal and natural gas prices. The American unit labor costs are also lower than Scandinavia due to more up-to-date facilities. Furthermore, interest rates for Brazil and Mexico are approximately 250 basis points higher than in the United States. According to studies published by the Japanese Paper Association, Japanese kraftlinerboard costs are approximately twice as high as its American competitors.

The comparative cost estimates, however, were based on 1981 currency parity rates—at that time the Swedish krona was valued at $0.20; it has since depreciated to $0.136 (December 1982). The sharp appreciation in the value of the U.S. dollar has greatly reduced the U.S. international competitive advantage in kraftlinerboard, especially compared to Sweden. Based on current information, U.S. producers will have to be extremely aggressive to maintain their market share in Europe and in some other parts of the world. However, it is unlikely that during the next ten years U.S producers will face a serious challenge from foreign manufacturers. The U.S. producers enjoy a relative cost advantage compared to Scandinavia, and a swing in currency rates in the opposite direction coupled with higher inflation rates in Europe will significantly undercut Scandinavia's competitiveness. The relative lack of softwood forests in Brazil and the need to conserve foreign currency will constrain the growth of the forest products industry in both Mexico and Brazil.

Financial Situation and Future Strategies

A brief review of the financial strength of the American corporations compared to the Scandinavian companies also verifies America's competitive advantage. The Swedish pulp and paper companies barely broke even in 1980 compared to about an 8 percent profit margin for the American companies. The Japanese and Scandinavian paper producers also recognize the inherent advantage of the U.S. kraftlinerboard manufacturers. Therefore, companies in these countries are investing their resources in higher value-added paper products (printing and writing papers, in which they are more competitive and receive a higher rate of return). The U.S. companies are extremely cautious regarding capital investment in the kraftlinerboard industry. At present, the operating rates are well below optimal capacity utilization rates and the economic outlook for the United States as well as the major foreign economies is for only modest economic growth during the next two years. In addition, the price for building a world-scale plant is $550 million, and with the high real interest rates companies can ill afford to make a mistake.

EUROPEAN SYNTHETIC FIBER PRODUCERS

The decline in the international competitiveness and profitability of the European synthetic fiber industry occurred rapidly and was due to the confluence of several factors. During the latter half of the 1970s Western European industry operating rates averaged approximately 66 percent, and operating income losses between 1975 and 1978 for six of the major textile producers in Europe were estimated to be over $2 billion (see Table 8.4). The dramatic change in the fortunes of the synthetic textile fiber industry further demonstrates the importance of understanding international economic and competitive factors.

Strong Synthetic Fiber Demand Pre-1973

Between 1960 and 1973 the European economy was booming, with real GNP growing approximately 6 percent per year and synthetic textile production increasing at a 17 percent annual rate. However, much of the growth in demand for synthetic fibers resulted from the increasing market penetration of this product for cellulosics and natural fibers.

As a result of this strong demand, fiber capacity grew rapidly between 1950 and 1974, with over 200 plants constructed in Western Europe. By 1974 synthetic fiber production was consuming approximately 25 percent of the output of Western European petrochemicals,

TABLE 8.4. LOSSES IN SYNTHETIC FIBERS INCURRED BY THE MAJOR EUROPEAN CHEMICAL COMPANIES (MILLIONS OF DOLLARS)

Company	1975	1976	1977	1978	Total Losses 1975–78
Akzo	161	83	46	4 (profits)	290
Bayer	57	56	86	55 (est.)	254 (est.)
Hoechst	92	72	119	55 (est.)	338 (est.)
ICI	61	19	30	26	136
Montedison	171	114	126	108	519
Rhone-Poulenc	163	116	150	111	540
TOTAL	705	460	557	355	2077 (est.)

Source: *Euroeconomics: Western European Chemicals Company Strategies and Performance—Past and Future.* U.S. Department of Commerce, Washington, D.C., 1979.

and was the second most important downstream activity after thermoplastics. In 1973 the major Western European countries accounted for 31 percent of the world's capacity for synthetic fibers, with the United States accounting for approximately 35 percent and Japan around 15 percent. Six major producers (Akzo, Bayer, Hoechst, ICI, Montedison, and Rhone-Poulenc) along with two smaller producers (Courtaulds and Snia Viscosa) made up over 65 percent of the synthetic fiber production in Europe. These producers maintained the state-of-the-art technology and their costs were competitive with American manufacturers. In 1973, production of textile fibers rose approximately 20 percent in Europe, operating rates were high, and overall economic growth was strong. European textile manufacturers, therefore, initiated another round of large capacity increases.

Decline 1973 to 1980

The slowdown in world economic growth and OPEC price increases dealt a severe blow to the European synthetic textile fiber industry. Europe became a very expensive area in which to produce fibers because of the high cost of the chemicals produced from an oil-derived naptha base. In addition, those parts of the world textile industry that were in a growth phase were mainly in the Far East, where transport costs and U.S. and Japanese competition were insurmountable obstacles for Europe. As a result, export growth was relatively flat during the rest of the decade.

European textile markets, the main outlet for synthetic fibers, were also impacted by imports of finished textile goods from Taiwan, South Korea, and Thailand. These imports accounted for the modest increases in apparel consumption recorded in the 1975 to 1980 period. Furthermore, tastes changed and consumers began to resist the increased substitution of manmade fibers for natural fibers, thus contributing to a flatness in demand for synthetic fibers. Cheaper U.S. synthetic fiber imports also undercut European producers in 1979 and 1980. In 1979 and 1980 American producers had an estimated 10 percent to 20 percent advantage in the price of manmade fibers. For example, in late 1979 American products gained a 26 percent share of the polyester market in the U.K., compared to only a 7.5 percent share in the previous year. The U.S. advantage, however, was reduced in 1981 and 1982, reflecting the decontrol of oil prices and the sharp rise in the value of the dollar. As a result of these factors, European production remained flat between 1976 and 1980, and operating rates have been extremely low (see Table 8.5).

Conclusion

The developments discussed in this section changed the fundamental strategy of the European textile fiber manufacturers. Instead of rushing to be the first to add capacity, European producers have been forced to rationalize capacity to conform with the market conditions. Monsanto, DuPont, Courtaulds and Rhone-Poulenc are just a few of the chemical companies that have reduced their capacities. Most observers continue to forecast further rationalization of capacity for the industry during the next decade.

CURRENCY

As stated in the kraftlinerboard section, the fluctuations in currency rates can severely impact a company's or country's international competitiveness. The dollar's trade-weighted movement since 1971 has directly affected U.S. competitiveness, although there is often a lag effect on exports and imports. As a result of the decline in the value of the dollar in the 1977 to 1980 period, U.S. exports increased significantly; but the strong rebound of the dollar has contributed to a widening of the U.S. trade deficit and increased competition from abroad in 1982.

Despite ambitious efforts of several professional economic forecasters, the ability to forecast exchange rates still remains an inexact science. Theoretically, exchange-rate movements depend on these factors: comparative interest and inflation rates, political stability, money supply growth, and balance of payments. Therefore, countries with low inflation rates, strong balances of payments, high real interest rates, and political stability, should have a strong currency. The recent rise in the dollar can be attributed to the currency markets' perception that the United States will maintain high real interest rates and policies that will lead to a reduction in the rate of inflation. Conventional wisdom assumes that the value of the dollar will begin to decline as the differential between the U.S. real interest rate and the real interest rates of its trading partners narrows.

Because currency rates play such a significant role in international competitiveness, corporate management must devise some method to

TABLE 8.5. WESTERN EUROPE SYNTHETIC FIBER PRODUCTION AND OPERATING RATES (000 METRIC TONS)

	1975	1976	1977	1978	1979	1980
Synthetic Fibers						
Western Europe						
Production	1,865	2,305	2,155	2,345	2,380	2,160
Capacity	3,350	3,300	3,440	3,340	3,370	3,190
Operating rate	56%	70%	63%	70%	71%	68%
EEC 9						
Production	1,605	1,960	1,775	1,915	1,905	1,702
Capacity	2,745	2,800	2,845	2,700	2,675	2,465
Operating rate	58%	70%	82%	71%	71%	69%
Cellulosic Fibers						
Western Europe						
Production	720	825	815	810	830	740
Capacity	1,050	1,000	980	990	970	875
Operating rate	69%	83%	83%	82%	86%	85%
ECC 9						
Production	500	560	535	515	525	445
Capacity	885	750	650	650	622	525
Operating rate	56%	74%	82%	79%	84%	85%

Source: Textile Organon.

adjust to the currency fluctuations that occur. Most corporations assume that over the long term currency value will be determined by the difference in national inflation rates. Short-term volatile fluctuations and exchange rates (6 to 18 months) are very difficult to forecast, but companies should attempt to develop strategies that maintain their competitiveness despite an unfavorable movement in a currency rate.

UNIT LABOR COSTS

Labor costs are an important factor for most industrial countries; countries with lower unit labor costs have a comparative advantage over their trading partners. In the leading industrial countries labor costs account for roughly two-thirds of the value-added of manufacturing. Based on a review of the labor costs of the major industrial countries, U.S. competitiveness has deteriorated significantly between 1979 and mid-1982.

Over the last decade exchange-rate movements have played a crucial role in determining the competitiveness of the United States in the manufacturing sectors. In 1980 the U.S. wage rates were fifth among the top eleven industrial countries, but in mid-1982 the U.S. compensation levels had become the highest of the industrial countries, generally by a wide margin (see Table 8.6).

When evaluating the relative international competitiveness among industries, unit labor costs (output per hour worked divided by hourly compensation) is even more important. According to a study by Professor Kurosawa of the Japanese Productivity Center in 1979, Japan held a clear edge in productivity over the United States in only two areas, autos and steel. Japan's productivity was only slightly behind the United States in electrical machinery (including electronics) but further behind in other products. Even though Japanese manufacturing productivity lags behind the United States in most areas, Japan enjoys a significant unit labor cost advantage for most of these industries.

Not enough attention has been paid to the fact that the estimated Japanese compensation per hour worked in dollar terms averaged only about 45 percent of the U.S. level. Thus, as long as the ratio Japanese to U.S. productivity exceeds approximately 50 percent, Japan would have a unit labor cost advantage. This advantage is particularly staggering for the auto and steel industries. Hourly labor costs in the newly

TABLE 8.6. ESTIMATED HOURLY COMPENSATION IN MANUFACTURING[1], SELECTED INDUSTRIAL COUNTRIES (DOLLARS, ALL EMPLOYEES)

	Annual Averages			Percent Change		Est. 1981 Compensation
Country	1970	1980	1981	1970–80	1980–81	at July 1982 Exchange Rates
Belgium	2.32	14.73	12.84	535	−13	10.11
Britain	1.66	8.57	8.57	416	0	7.35
Canada	3.71	9.15	9.91	147	8	9.36
Denmark	2.23	11.17	9.74	401	−13	8.10
France	2.05	10.55	9.59	415	−9	7.57
Germany	2.26	12.68	11.00	461	−13	10.06
Italy	2.08	9.34	8.51	349	−9	6.97
Japan	1.07	6.02	6.63	463	10	5.72
Netherlands	2.46	14.33	11.95	381	−17	10.91
Sweden	3.50	14.85	13.57	324	−9	11.17
United States	4.90	11.44	12.61	133	10	12.61

[1]Data are estimates of average compensation per hour worked for all employees in manufacturing (including the self-employed in Canada and the United States).

Sources: U.S. Bureau of Labor Statistics, Citibank estimates. Table taken from Citibank's World Outlook.

industrialized countries are also significantly below U.S. costs—approximately one-tenth in South Korea, Taiwan, Hong Kong, and Brazil.

COST OF CAPITAL—INTEREST RATES

Interest rates differ from country to country and correspondingly the cost of capital in each country also differs. For example, Japan has had the lowest interest rates, on average, among the major industrial countries between 1979 and 1982, thus enabling Japanese companies to enjoy lower interest costs and a lower cost of capital. German companies also benefited from a comparatively lower rate of interest. In dollar terms, interest charges in these countries were even lower due to the rise in the value of the dollar. To offset lower foreign interest rates, U.S. companies could borrow abroad, especially to finance local subsidiaries; but several large U.S. firms (duPont, International Paper, and Mobil) borrowed Swiss francs on the Swiss bond market at what was thought to be a comparatively low interest rate in 1972. At that time exchange rates were fixed. However, in 1973 exchange rates floated, and the Swiss franc appreciated sharply, causing the effective dollar interest rate to increase significantly. Since this unfortunate experience, most U.S.-based companies have shied away from financing general debt not related to a specific world area in other than U.S. currency.

OTHER FACTORS

Several other factors can affect international competitiveness and provide one company with an advantage over its competition in another region of the world:

Government support through subsidized credits and raw materials (energy and feedstocks), direct subsidies, preferential taxes, tariff and non-tariff protection, and development incentives.

The Japanese government has been severely criticized for targeting specific domestic industries and providing these industries with special incentives and protection from foreign competition. The steel and auto sectors were targeted in the 1960s, and the electronics industry has been targeted in the 1970s and 1980s.

Saudi Arabia and Mexico have targeted the petrochemical industry, and as a result several chemical companies have elected to participate jointly in these ventures or reduce their future exposure and development plans in petrochemicals.

Well-being of the work force—management, labor relations, education and health.

Well-developed infrastructure—such as schools, roads, transportation, banking services, and communications.

Raw material costs including land costs.

DEVELOPING AN INTERNATIONAL AWARENESS AND STRATEGY

The growth of foreign competition and the challange presented by international markets play an important part in developing marketing, investment, and research plans. Most of the leading American corporations are extremely dependent on international markets and compete directly with corporations from all parts of the world.

The sources of information for developing international competitive analyses vary from industry to industry. But consultants, bankers, trade associations, security analysts, and academicians can be helpful in assisting in intelligence gathering and in analyzing the data. However, the strategic objectives and plans should be established by the corporation to ensure conformity throughout the company.

To develop a successful strategy to compete in the marketplace, a corporation has to collect and analyze information ranging from international economics to an analysis of the sales of its major customers in various regions of the world. The strong companies such as IBM, Procter & Gamble, Toyota, and Ciba Geigy have been able to adjust to the changing world environment. Other companies that have been unable to answer foreign competitors, such as Singer's Friden Division, British Leyland, or Krupp (the famous German steel company), have either disappeared or have been bailed out by the government subsidies.

[1]This paperboard is made out of predominantly virgin pulp and is used as the exterior and interior liner for corrugated boxes.

[2]This paperboard is made out of recycled paper and is somewhat inferior in quality to kraftlinerboard.

[3]International Paper, Weyerhauser, and Union Camp are three U.S. kraftlinerboard companies that have significant foreign and domestic markets.

III

Source and Types of Competitor Intelligence

9

The Role of Market Research in Gathering Competitor Intelligence

FRED CUBA

Fred Cuba is a Senior Vice-President of Data Development Corporation, a leading national Market Research Firm.

Before joining Data Development in 1980, Mr. Cuba was Research Director, Senior Vice-President of Ogilvy and Mather where Mr. Cuba started in 1965. His prior experience includes research positions at J. Walter Thompson and Young & Rubicam.

A member of the American Marketing Association, Mr. Cuba was elected into the Market Research Council in 1978. For several years, he served as Vice-Chairman of the Business Advertising Research Council of the Advertising Research Foundation. Mr. Cuba is a graduate of the Wharton School and has a master's Degree in Statistics.

Marketing is a form of economic warfare. Just read a marketing plan, particularly one for a package goods brand in a competitive category. The terminology makes one think of a military document: "target market," "pinpoint the market," "offensive and defensive strategy," "tactical decisions," "opening campaigns," "aim the advertising," and a host of other "warlike" terms.

Marketing research may be likened to the intelligence unit. It provides information to help management fight the marketing war. It is used to spot opportunities, minimize risk, and to increase the odds of making correct ecisions.

Military intelligence resports usually focus on the strengths and weaknesses of the enemy. The enemy in marketing is, of course, your competition. Virtually all market research gathers information on competition. In some cases, the very object of the research is to learn about competition. In other cases competitive information is simply a by-product of the research process.

My aim in this chapter is to illustrate how knowledge of your competition can directly impact the marketing decision.

My aim is not to turn you into professional market researchers. Thus, I will not dwell on various techniques and methods. There are dozens of good books on the subject. However, since you will probably need marketing research assistance at some time, I would first like to offer some practical advice on:

When to call on market research.

What to look for in selecting a market research firm.

How to help insure that the research will be of maximum value.

WHEN TO CALL ON MARKET RESEARCH

There are virtually hundreds of problems where market research can be of use. Here are some of the most frequently researched problems. If one of these comes up, consider using marketing research.

New Products

Should I attempt to enter this market?

What type of product should I produce?

Which of these new product ideas should I concentrate on and which should I discard?

How can I strengthen my new product?
What volume can I expect from this new product?
To whom should I market my product?
What is the best channel of distribution, price, and packaging?

Existing Products

What are the strengths and weaknesses of my product?
What are the trends in the industry?
Are my customers satisfied with my product?
How is my product performing in the marketplace versus competition?

Corporate Reputation

How well do my customers and prospects know my company?
How is the company perceived versus competition?
What are the perceived corporate strengths and weaknesses?

Advertising and Promotion

To whom should I advertise?
What should I say in my advertising?
Is my advertising good enough?
Which advertising execution should I use?
Is my advertising effective?
Is my advertising wearing out?

WHAT TO LOOK FOR IN SELECTING A MARKETING RESEARCH FIRM

Naturally, if you have a marketing research function in your company you can simply call them in on the problem. However, many companies do not have such a function and will have to go outside.

There are literally hundreds of marketing research companies in the United States. The American Marketing Association publishes a "Green Book" that lists them and provides a brief description of each. It is 244 pages thick.

The best place to start looking for candidates is with your colleagues, especially colleagues who have had first-hand experience with a marketing research firm. If they can't help, call the marketing research director of a large package goods company in your area. Try and locate two or three candidates and call them in individually for a briefing.

Here are five suggested guidelines for selecting the research firm to work with. Select a firm that:

1. Has some experience in your industry or related industries.
2. Has a marketing orientation. The design of the research as well as the recommendations that flow from the research should be actionable. A problem-solving marketing orientation will help insure useful results.
3. Communicates well. You want conclusions and recommendations that are clearly stated. You also want a supplier that can speak in your language, not in research jargon. The most brilliant study will be of little value if the report is not well organized and the conclusions clearly stated and supported.
4. Maintains high standards of quality control. Research firms vary in the amount of emphasis they place on controlling the interviewing and tabulation process. Pick one with high standards. Study the supplier's brochure. Get the opinion of corporate research directors.
5. Is not technique-oriented. Seek a research firm that fully understands your problem before they offer a solution. Make sure they are not "bending" your problem to fit their technique.

HOW TO HELP INSURE THAT THE RESEARCH WILL BE OF MAXIMUM VALUE

Whether the research will be handled by your internal research function or by an outside supplier, there are a number of things you can do to insure that the project is successful. These guidelines will help you get maximum value for your information dollar:

1. Do research early enough in the process—before positions harden. No research can stand up to the "nit-picks" of colleagues who have already taken a fixed position.
2. Confide in the researcher. Treat the researcher like your accountant. Confide what the problem is and offer all the background necessary to fully understand the situation. Don't tell

the researcher you want to do some group sessions or a telephone survey; rather, explain what you want to learn and how you plan to use the information. Let the researcher decide how the problem can best be solved.

3. Invest in actionable research, not in "nice-to-know" facts.
4. Match the quality of the information gathered to the magnitude of the decision—the level of risk. Some marketing decisions are of major magnitude:

   Should we produce this product?

   Should we change our corporate name?

   Should we change our channels of distribution?

   Should we change our advertising campaign?

   These type decisions require a high quality of information. They are strategic in nature and can have important affects on corporate performance. Other problems are tactical in nature and will probably not have a major influence. For these type problems, judgment should often be substituted for research. If research is needed, the study should be small-scale and inexpensive.
5. Seek integrated research programs, not isolated projects. Multistage programs are particularly important for recurring and difficult problems such as new product development and advertising. In an integrated program the output of one stage serves as the input for the next. To illustrate, Table 9.1 shows

TABLE 9.1. A TYPICAL NEW PRODUCT RESEARCH PROGRAM

Stage	To Learn
Strategy study	Should we enter this market? What type of product should we market?
Concept screening	What product ideas should we pursue?
Concept testing	What level of trial can be expected?
Product testing	Is the product enough? How can it be improved?
Advertising testing	What execution should be used?
Name and package testing	What is the best alternative?
Sales forecasting simulation	How much can we expect to sell?
Test marketing	How much will we sell?

an outline for a new product research program, and Table 9.2 for an advertising research program.

6. Involve those who will affect the marketing decision. If the research is to be acted upon properly, those who will be responsible for implementing the findings should be involved in several key stages of the process. They should:

   Review the research design.

   Agree upon any evaluative criteria or action standards before the research is begun.

   Attend a presentation of results and discuss them.

   Agree or have a hand in formulating recommendations based on the research.

7. The findings should be presented and discussed. The initial presentation can be a work session. It should set the stage for a set of recommendations that flow from the findings. The recommendations along with the information that support each recommendation could form the basis for a presentation to management.

   The research report should primarily serve an archival purpose. It should not substitute for face-to-face discussions and resentations.

TABLE 9.2. A TYPICAL ADVERTISING RESEARCH PROGRAM

Stage	To Learn
Strategy study	To whom should we talk? What should we say? How should the product be thought of?
Copy development	How should we express the selling message? What are the best words to use, illustrations, spokespersons, music, etc.
Copy testing	Which advertising execution should be used? Is it good enough?
Campaign evaluation	Is the advertising meeting its objective?

APPLICATIONS OF MARKET RESEARCH IN GATHERING COMPETITOR INTELLIGENCE

Now we get to the heart of the question. As I mentioned earlier, most market research gathers some information on competition. For example, the typical consumer product or service company can answer the following questions about their market and their competitors:

How large is the market?
How many consumers use the product?
Is the market growing or shrinking, and by how much?
How concentrated is the market? Do a small proportion of buyers account for a disproportionate amount of volume?
How is the market structured?
Whom do we compete with directly and with whom indirectly?
What is our product's share of volume, and what is the share enjoyed by each competitor?
How does our product's share and competitors' share vary by distribution channel or type of outlet? Geographic region? Product line?
What are the trends in share level?
How many are aware of our brand versus each competitor?
How many have tried our brand and each competitor?
How many current and loyal users does our brand have versus each competitor?
What are the trends in awareness, trial, and usage?
What types of consumers buy our brand as opposed to our competitors?
What are the differences between brands in the demographics, lifestyles, and attitudes of their users?
How and when is the product used?
What are the most important motivations for buying the product?
What are buyers' attitudes toward our brand versus competitors on the more important motivations for buying?
What are the attitudinal trends?

For some companies, particularly consumer package goods companies, this information is considered basic and is only the tip of the information iceberg. They have far more information. The strides in market research have provided the modern marketer with almost unlimited access to information on his or her brand and competition. The only restraint is cost. Still, this type of marketing data is fairly easy to obtain. Much is sold as a package by syndicated services such as the A.C. Nielsen Company, or the data can be obtained through a custom research survey. Gathering the data is not the problem. Turning the data into marketing intelligence for better decision-making is the more difficult task, and the one that pays dividends.

The remainder of this chapter is devoted to illustrations of how data on competition can be used to make better decisions. These illustrations will focus on the most important applications of competitor data gathered through market research.

NEW PRODUCTS

Identifying an Unfulfilled Need

One of the most important applications of new product market research is identifying a need that is not being adequately filled by competitive or existing brands. This is done at a very early stage of the new product development process. The results of this type study sets the overall strategic direction for the subsequent steps in the new product process.

Typically, the research gathers two key pieces of information:

1. Importance of various product attributes in the brand-selection process.
2. The degree to which each competitive brand is perceived as delivering these attributes.

The search is for an important attribute that is not being adequately delivered by competitors. Table 9.3 gives a simplified illustration of what the key results of this type of research might look like. Given this information, the company should direct its R&D effort to developing a product that "doesn't show dirt and scuff marks." This is important and is not being delivered by existing competitive brands.

Usually, the situation is far more complex. There are often different segments to a market, each desiring different attributes. Therefore, many market research studies are designed to identify the various

TABLE 9.3. STRATEGY STUDY FOR A HYPOTHETICAL FLOOR-CARE PRODUCT

Product Attributes	Importance Index (Most Importance = 100)	Percent Rating Each Competitive Brand Positively				
		A	B	C	D	E
Lasts long	100	90	80	80	90	60
Goes on easy	95	40	70	50	70	70
Doesn't show dirt and scuff marks	90	20	30	20	30	40
Provides a good shine	70	80	70	90	90	80
Goes on fast	30	5	10	20	10	10

segments comprising a market and opportunities that exist within each segment.

Product Testing

New product prototypes are nearly always tested with consumers to determine their appeal relative to existing products, and identify their strengths and weaknesses so that the proper modifications can be made. Often the new product prototype is tested against competitive brands. To illustrate, Table 9.4 shows what the results might look like for a prototype paper product tested against the market leader. The new prototype's loss to the competitive brand can be traced to its lack of softness, the most important product attribute. Given these results, the task of R&D and marketing is clear; increase the softness at least to parity while retaining a competitive edge on all other dimensions.

Determining Market Vulnerability

A key question that arises early in the new product process is how vulnerable is the market to a new product introduction. Judgment tells us that vulnerability is to a large degree a function of the number of products already competing in the market. Consider "crowded" markets such as cigarettes, packaged cereals, and shampoo. With a parity product one can only expect a tiny share of the market. In the cigarette

TABLE 9.4. PRODUCT TEST FOR A HYPOTHETICAL NEW PAPER PRODUCT

Product Attributes	Importance Index (Most Importance =; 100)	Preferred Prototype (%)	Preferred Major Competitive Brand (%)	Difference
		30	70	−40
Feels soft	100	20	80	−60
A good value	80	55	45	+10
Easy to tear	30	60	40	+20
Attractive color	25	70	30	+40
Attractive package	10	80	20	+60

market, for example, a new brand is considered very successful if it can attain a one percent share of the market.

A mathematical model is available, developed by the Hendry Corporation, that estimates the share a new product is likely to achieve in a given market. The share estimate, which has proven very accurate, is based solely on the number of competitive brands already in the market, and the distribution of the market share of these competitive brands.

Using this model is not quite as simple as it sounds since the market must first be defined. Defining the market requires substantial information on how buyers switch between competitive brands. Given this information, a complex mathematical procedure defines the market from the point-of-view of the buyer's decision process. To illustrate, Figure 9.1 shows a hypothetical example of the market structure for a proprietary drug product. The higher in the structure the new product introduction, the higher the market share that can be achieved. In Figure 9.1, a fourth type of "form" has the potential to attain the highest market share. It would take volume from all products in the category. Once the structure is defined, the model calculates share and volume for all possible new product introductions.

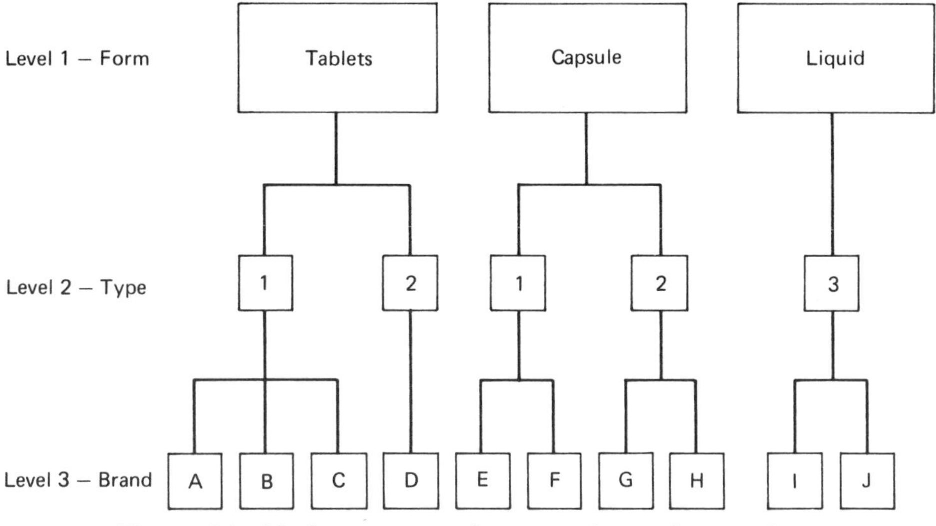

Figure 9.1 Market structure for a proprietary drug product

ADVERTISING RESEARCH

Copy Strategy

The first and usually most important step in the advertising research process is development of copy strategy—deciding what to say to your customers and prospects. The research is usually designed to screen a large number of possible selling messages on two dimensions:

1. Importance in selecting a brand.
2. Preemptability. Do buyers already associate each message with a particular competitor, or is it thought of as relatively unique, and thus preemptive.

To learn whether a message is preemptable, one must measure attitudes toward competitive brands.

Campaign Evaluation

Besides sales measures, the success of an advertising campaign is monitored by a research approach called tracking studies. This is simply repeating a number of key measures over time with different samples of the same universe. In many ways, the results of such a study are a better indicator of the effectiveness of advertising than of sales. It is a more direct measure. Sales are influenced by many things other than advertising. The typical tracking study will measure such things as brand awareness, advertising awareness, attitudes toward your brand and competitive brands on a number of dimensions, brand trial, and current brand usage.Thus, a company that uses this technique will not only have a continuing picture of attitudes and usage of their brand, but will be able to follow these trends for competitive brands. This information allows the company to learn from the success of competitive brands and avoid their failures. Here is an illustration of the latter.

A major gasoline company had tracked motorist attitudes toward their brand and competitive brands for many years. Other research had indicated that the "courtesy and efficiency of service station attendants" was of great importancein selecting a brand. The company was tempted to substitute this type of service advertising for their current product-oriented campaign. However, it was pointed out that a major competitor who had run a service campaign for many years had failed. The tracking study results indicated that the proportion of motorists who believed that the competitor's service was superior had not increased for ten years. This competitive campaign failed because while superior service was important, it couldn't be deliverd at the station level. Motorists recognized this and the tracking study picked up this failing.

The idea of substituting a service idea was abandoned, thus saving a great deal of money and time.

CORPORATE REPUTATION STUDIES

Companies often want to know how they are perceived by a particular constituency such as customers, prospective customers, suppliers, stockholders, or employees. The heart of this type of research is a set of comparisons of perceptions of the company relative to competitors in the same industry.

Table 9.5 shows a hypothetical illustration of the results of this type of corporate reputation study. These perceptions can be tracked over time to identify trends. Company A is thought of as inferior to competition with respect to its technological capability. Findings such as this should lead to a drive to improve the company's technological capability and/or a communication effort to improve the company's technological image.

TABLE 9.5. HYPOTHETICAL CORPORATE REPUTATION STUDY

	Percent Rating Each Competitor Postively		
Beliefs About Company	A	B	C
Best managed	70	20	10
Makes highest quality products	65	20	15
Gives best value	80	5	15
Has most knowledgeable sales force	80	15	5
Has best R&D capability	20	40	40
Most likely to produce major technological breakthrough	20	50	30

PRODUCT SATISFACTION CHECKS

Frequently a company conduct research to learn how satisfied customers are with its products and services and to identify any serious dissatisfactions. As in earlier examples, the results of this type of research are not viewed on an absolute basis. In a competitive situation, relative performance is what counts.

A good example is the airline industry. An airline will frequently interview people who have completed one of its flights. At the same time, they will interview flyers of competitive airlines on the same routes. This research is usually done on a continuous basis and forms a prime means of quality control. Table 9.6 shows what the results might look like. Given these results, the management of airline A should take actions to improve its luggage handling, a service on which they receive poor marks. Competitors, in contrast, do a satisfactory job.

The other area of concern is quality of food. However, in this case the competition is also rated poorly. Therefore this should be of less concern to Airline A. Nevertheless, improving food quality could provide Airline A with a competitive edge. The questions this finding could evoke are:

How much would it cost to improve food until it would be perceived as superior to the competition's food?

Would the additional cost of food improvement be more than offset by additional revenues?

TABLE 9.6. HYPOTHETICAL AIRLINE SATISFACTION STUDY

	Percent "Completely Satisfied"		
	Airline A	Competitor B	Competitor C
Leaves/arrives on time	90	80	85
Airport service	80	80	85
On-board service	80	70	80
Quality of food	30	30	30
Luggage handling	30	80	80

These questions could be answered by a well-designed testing program.

OFFENSIVE AND DEFENSIVE STRATEGIES

At the beginning of the chapter, marketing was termed a form of economic warfare. Nowhere is the militaristic nature of marketing clearer than in the test marketing of a major new product by a large package goods company.

The purposes of the test market are generally two-fold:

1. To develop an accurate sales forecast of the new product for production, marketing, and financial purposes.
2. To test various marketing tactics such as alternative advertising weights, coupon and sampling plans, media plans, advertising campaigns, in-store promotions, and price levels.

The object, of course, is to develop a marketing program that will maximize sales and profits. This maximum program will be implemented when the new product is marketed on an expanded basis, either nationally or regionally.

If the stakes are high, the existing brands, particularly the larger ones that have the most to lose, will counter by doing everything possible to cloud the results of the test market. For example, the existing brands could increase advertising, reduce price, run large coupon and sampling programs, run a variety of consumer promotions (e.g., "buy one and get one free"), and run retail promotions to increase distribution and shelf space.

Information is critical to both the new brand and existing brands. Two methods are used to gather this information. First, store audits provide on a continuous basis the sales levels for all brands, share of market, distribution levels, and out-of-stock levels. These data are provided by the type of outlet. Surveys are the second method. They provide on a periodic basis measures of consumer awareness of the new brand and existing brands, attitudes toward the brands, trial levels, repeat purchase and depth-of-repeat data, and brand-switching profiles.

The data from both sources are used in conjunction to answer a series of critical questions. The manufacturer of the new brand must know:

What is the sales trend and where is the trend heading?

Is the brand getting a sufficient level of trial?

Are sales coming mostly from first-time buyers or from repeat buyers?

How many consumers have adopted the product into their buying patterns?

Who are the buyers of the new product? Are they heavy users of the category?

Is the advertising getting through? Is it memorable? Is it influencing opinions and making consumers interested in trying the new product?

What do people trying out the product think of it? How does it compare to existing brands? Is it perceived as a good value?

The existing brands typically gather the same type of information, from a different perspective. In test marketing as in virtually all areas of marketing intelligence on your competition is vital.

10

The Financial Dimension: Penetrating the Financial Statements

ROBERT SPITALNIC

Mr. Spitalnic, Vice President-Acquisition Financing for Security Pacific Business Credit, works in the area of providing asset-based financing for acquisitions, divestments, and management and leveraged buyouts. As a Principal at Arthur Young for eight years, he consulted with clients in mergers, acquisitions, strategic planning, and growth financing. Other experience includes over five years at W. R. Grace and ITT, where in addition to being responsible for acquisitions and divestments he assisted in the competitive analysis function. Mr. Spitalnic has a B.A. in economics from CCNY and completed graduate work in Finance at the Baruch School. He has done additional work at NYU in finance.

This chapter is concerned with obtaining, developing, and analyzing financial information about competitors. While not meant to replace an accounting or financial analysis textbook, the discussion will review several analytical techniques or approaches. In most cases the accuracy obtained with competitor financial information is not the same as dealing with one's internal data. But a great deal of financial data is available from many different external *and* internal sources. This data, combined with some intelligent guesses, can be used to build a financial model.

After determining (or estimating) how well or poorly the competition is doing in terms of profitability—that is, financial ratios and growth—the differences from one's own results and industry norms must be explained. But before the explanation, the financial information has to be gathered.

SOURCES OF INFORMATION

Companies may be divided in two categories in terms of the availability of financial information:

1. Publicly traded companies for which a great deal of financial information is available, although often with little detail on divisions, particularly for product areas.
2. Privately or closely held companies for which little or no public financial data is available. Exceptions include government-regulated industries, such as trucking companies and utilities.

Publicly held companies, in addition to annual reports and required Securities and Exchange Commission filings, often provide additional detailed financial and product information oriented towards securities analysts and institutional investors. These reports can be obtained directly from the company, or from their public or stockholder relations consultants. Companies listed on major exchanges such as the New York and American Stock Exchanges are required to provide more details than over-the-counter companies.

Competitor files should at minimum contain the latest annual report, form 10-K, and prospectuses. The latter two items are particularly detailed with respect to key product areas and operating expenses. Annual reports have much non-financial information not found in other documents. However, some of the financial information in the 10-K is not in the annual report. Although the annual report may provide clues to operating costs, the additional details must be obtained from the 10-K.

Form 10-K will have sales and operating income for each business line accounting for 10 percent or more of sales or pre-tax income. Moreover, the financial statements, including footnotes, provide more detail than the annual report and other financial reports issued by the company. The 10-K provides details on such items as inventory classifications, tax accounting, and management compensation. There are summaries of the fixed assets including additions and retirements of properties, and related operating expenses such as rental expense, depreciation, and repairs and maintenance.

Although the 10-K has weaknesses—for example, the determination of business lines is quite subjective—it is the single most important financial document for analyzing publicly held competitors. The amount of detail relating to fixed assets and operating expenses is essential in the analysis or estimates of competitive advantage.

The registration statement, of which the prospectus is the first part, also includes detailed historical financial information not included in the prospectus. Part 2 of the registration contains information about the use of the proceeds from the stock being registered, and audited annual report and interm statements.

Other reports of general interest would include:

Form 10-Q—quarterly financial reports that are more detailed than shareholders' interm reports,

Form 8-K—filed when material event occurs, such as any significant purchase or disposition of assets, or a matter submitted to shareholders. When a business of significant size is acquired its financial statements are included.

Proxy statements—describe items to be voted on at shareholders meetings; also, give background of directors and officers.

Copies of all the above material can be found in the SEC's main office in Washington and in its regional offices. Forms filed with the SEC are microfiched by *Disclosure Inc.* (5161 River Road, Bethesda, Maryland; 301-951-1300) and are available from them in hard copy or microfiche. Less detailed financial information can be obtained from publications like *Moody's Corporate Manuals* and *Standard & Poor's Corporation Records.*

At the time of writing the SEC has proposed some major changes in its disclosure requirements. Their thrust is improving the format and quality of shareholder annual reports to make them consistent with similar requirements in SEC filings. The amendments to form 10-K require a revised management discussion and analysis of financial condition and results of operations, focusing on liquidity, capital resources, and a discussion of the impact of inflation on the company.

Information for individual product lines is usually not available, even in the more detailed company financial reports prepared (by some companies) for use by security analysts. These reports are still an important addition to competitor files, as they can provide additional clues to sales and operating expenses by product area. Other publicly oriented materials providing clues include management speeches to shareholders, security analysts, and trade associations, and security analysts' reports prepared for the general public and institutional investors.

The institutional reports are especially thorough and timely, but are more difficult to obtain. Older reports can sometimes be obtained directly from the investment banking firm. More current sources are insurance companies, banks, pension funds (including corporate pension groups), and large private investment groups.

The Wall Street Transcript, a weekly publication, reproduces company speeches to security analysts and shareholders, and investment banking firm reports that are more widely distributed. Each issue includes an industry round table discussion by analysts experienced within a specific industry.

FIND/SVP (500 Fifth Avenue, New York, NY 10109; 212-354-2424) for a fee provides investment banking firm research reports. It also supplies reports prepared by market research and other consulting organizations.

Although their orientation may be different, and there are SEC and ethical considerations, security analysts who specialize in an industry can provide details or intelligent guesses for divisional and product area costs. This familiarity is developed through top management contacts and on-site visits. However, as we will soon explain, more detailed information can often be developed through a company's internal staff or with retired or former employees of the competitor(s). Yet contact with analysts is a particularly good starting point.

A listing of analysts by industry specialization can be obtained from the Financial Analysts Federation (1633 Broadway, New York, NY 10019; 212-957-2860). Each year *Institutional Investor Magazine* ranks the lending analysts within each industry. The *Directory of Securities*

Research (published by Nelson Publications, 11 Elm Place, Rye, NY 10580; 914-967-9100) lists analysts covering 3000 public companies by specific company and the analysts' firms. As with obtaining research reports, the best contacts with analysts may be made through the larger institutional users of their material.

Sources of information for public and private companies are listed below. Most provide data for both types of companies, but are oriented towards (larger) public companies. However, some of the material prepared by industry trade associations or developed through multi-industry surveys of annual reports (e.g., Robert Morris Associates) can be used in developing financial estimates for private companies and divisions of public companies. The five general sources are:

General business press.

Trade press.

Trade or business association material (includes industry sponsored or oriented research studies).

Surveys of annual reports and financial Statements.

Field work—i.e., unpublished sources.

On the general sources listed, field work is often the most productive. It includes discussions with a company's own technical, marketing, and financial people, and former (including retired) employees of competitors. These organized discussions can also be used to develop and monitor non-financial information such as marketing strategies and possible technical developments, which are discussed elsewhere in this book.

Outside consultants with *specific industry experience* can also assist in estimating financial details for competitors. They can be used to obtain information through surveys and other methods without directly involving the company. Although one of the major strengths of outside consultants is aid in researching "new" (to the client) industries, these consultants working with a company's internal staff provide new prespectives on competitors (as well as on one's internal operations).

General Business Press

The general business press may be divided into newspapers and periodicals. The former includes such major business newspapers as the *Wall Street Journal* and the *Journal of Commerce*, the business section of major newspapers, and regional business newspapers. Periodicals include, but are not limited to, *Barron's, Business Week, Financial World, Dun's Business Monthly, Forbes, Fortune, Inc.,* and *Venture.* Again, these are also sources for the non-financial information.

It is hard to monitor all of these publications on continous basis. However, reference sources, such as *Predicasts F & S Index of United States* (formerly *F & S Index of Corporations and Industries*), *Readers' Guide to Periodical Literature,* and the *Public Affairs Information Service Bulletin(s),* can be used and are found in most major business libraries. The F & S Index is particularly good for developing company information, and has a seperate index for foreign companies and U.S. company overseas operations.

Trade Press

The trade press will usually provide more detailed company information including financial material. Although the degree of detail varies, many industry magazines provide particulars on operating expenses, data and indexes of plant costs (e.g., utility costs by geographical region), and in some cases the layout and listings of equipment within a specific facility. This material is important input for developing a financial model of competitors. The editors and writers at trade publications are often a useful source of information. Many provide a long-term perspective on the industry, as well as assisting in developing detailed expense estimates.

Lists of trade publications are best developed on an industry basis. Often supplier or customer oriented publications are additional sources. Detailed listings of trade publication include Ayer's *Directory of Newspapers, Magazines and Periodicals, The Standard Periodical Directory* (which lists over 65,000 publications), and *The Standard Rate & Data Service.* The New York chapter of the Financial Analysts Federation has prepared a listing by industry of the more important trade publications as well as industry statistical reports.[1]

Trade Association Material

Material from trade associations—especially surveys of membership financial statements, statistical reports, and fact books—can be very important in developing competitor income statements. Although this material is often limited to association member, it is sometimes available to outsiders. Association staff members can often provide or identify additional sources of information.

Although these industry financial surveys will not identify or provide information for individual companies, they are useful in developing estimates for specific operating expenses. Moreover, larger organizations will often list data by sales size or number of employees.

This category includes industry studies prepared for trade associations by major consulting firms such as Frost and Sullivan, A.D. Little, Predicasts, and Stanford Research Institute; and by smaller, often specialized, consulting firms and colleges. There is often multicompany, if not industry, sponsorship of these reports.

It is difficult to get an all-inclusive listing of these reports, especially the non-college publications. One should approach this on a industry basis—that is, develop as many leads as possible within an industry and attempt to contact each at least once. General listings are prepared by the FIND/SVP and Predicasts organizations already mentioned, and also in *The Marketing Information Guide* (Hoke Communications Inc., 224 Seventh Street, Garden City, NY 11535). Again, much of the industry material provides details about the marketing, technical, and other non-financial aspects. In fact, the financial information is limited or usually less detailed but can often be valuable in providing financial clues.

Industry research done each year at schools and universities, often with a regional or product orientation, is listed in *The Marketing Information Guide* and *University Research in Business and Economics* (which can be ordered from Bureau of Business Research, West Virginia University, Morgantown, WV 26506; 304-298-5837). These research organizations will often make their reports available to the public.

Among the more detailed listings of trade organizations is *Gale's Encylopedia of Associations,* which has an excellent key-word index. Publications, if any, of the specific organizations are noted. Another reference for financial information availability by industry is *Sources of Financial Information* (Robert Morris Associates, Philadelphia National Bank Building, Philadelphia, PA 19107).

Surveys of Annual Reports and Financial Statements

For a specific industry, surveys of annual reports and financial statements are often prepared under the auspices of industry trade associations. However, there are other broad surveys, including several government reports, that can be used for developing competitor financial statements. Again, individual company information is not provided. Two of the more detailed multi-industry surveys, published annually, are *Annual Statement Studies* prepared by Robert Morris Associates (Philadelphia, PA) and *The Almanac of Business and Industrial Financial Ratios* (Leo Troy, Prentice-Hall, Englewood Cliffs, NJ).

The Robert Morris book has a detailed composite balance sheet and a less detailed income statement, expressed as a precentage of total assets and sales, respectively. Selected financial ratio are also provided—upper and lower quartiles, and median—for over 300 industry categories, which are further subdivided into size groups by total assets.

Troy's book repeats some of the ratios and has less industry subgroups. Unlike the Robert Morris publication it includes banks, finance companies, and other financial institutions. Also, there are more categories in the size of assets subdivisions by industry. A more detailed income statement expressed as a percentage of sales is included.

Another annual publication is *Dun & Bradstreet's Key Business Ratios* available from Dun & Bradstreet, New York, NY. For over 800 lines of business, fourteen ratios, medians, and upper and lower quartile figures are shown.

There is a large amount of federal government material available, most of it too broad in scope for our purposes. A good reference for determining what is available, as well as for monitoring current studies, is the *Monthly Catalog of United States Government Publications.* The material is listed by issuing agency, but there is also a subject index. Most of the data has a macroeconomic orientation; however, several agencies provide industry financial statements—the IRS, and to a lesser extent the Department of Commerce and the Federal Trade Commision.

The IRS *Corporation Source Book of Statistics* is more comprehensive and detailed than other IRS publications At one time the tables, which show balance sheets and income statements for almost 300 industry group, were not published. Less detailed are the *Statistics of Income* and *Business Income Tax Returns.* Most of the publications are published yearly, and the information is usually two to three years old.

In terms of industry statistics the most comprehensive material is available in a series of reports prepared by the Department of Commerce as the result of their periodic census of U.S. Industry. Major reports include *Census of Agriculture* (farms and crops), *Census of Business* (retail, distribution, and service companies), *Census of Housing,*

Census of Mineral Industry, Census of Transportation, and the widely used *Census of Manufacturers.* This latter publication provides aggregate industry statistics such as value of shipments, cost of materials, payroll expenses, and capital expenditures. Shipments are shown by 5 and 7-digit SIC number, and 4-digit SIC for most of the other items. There are also subdivisions by geographical regions and number of employees.

The Federal Trade Commission publishes *Quarterly Financial Report for Manufacturing, Mining and Trade Corporations,* which gives interim financial and operating ratios for 22 manufacturing industries and totals only for mining, retail, and wholesale trade.

Government agencies that regulate specific industries, such as the Federal Communications Commission, Federal Power Commission, and the Interstate Commerce Commission, issue aggregate data on the industries they supervise. In addition, annual reports for companies regulated are filed, and are available to the public.

A variety of agencies at the federal, state, and local levels regulate aspects such as zoning and environmental control. Although the amount of financial information is usually limited, details as to plant layout and equipment are provided, which can be used to develop estimates of competitor costs.

Although Dun & Bradstreet reports supplemental information about public companies they are usually the only source of financial information for privately held companies. And what is available is often only a balance sheet. Much of the financial data, when shown, is old, or may reflect an estimate provided by the company itself. Changes in retained earnings may sometimes provide some estimate of profitability.

The Operation section of the Dun & Bradstreet report describes the type of goods produced or services provided, as well as details on their terms of sale. The payments section indicates how quickly bills are paid.

Some states require companies incorporated within the state to supply some financial statement information, which in turn can be ordered from the State Department or corporate regulatory agencies of about 20 states. These states include Massachusetts, Kansas, and many of the Mountain and New England states.

When companies purchase new equipment, they often finance the purchase with debt—that is, a chattel mortgage. The creditor will file a UCC Statement with the state, which will provide a description of the equipment financed.

One listing, News Front's *50,000 Leading U.S. Corporations,* for both public and private companies, has estimates of sales, number of plants, and total employees. More details are sometimes available, such as total assets, debt, depreciation, and stockholders equity. Most of the information for private companies is from questionnaires filled out by the individual companies. The News Front material is also available on tape or punched cards.

A major data source for publicly traded companies is Standard and Poor's Compustat. Its primary use is for screening purposes, but detailed financial information is available. Although information is primarily on a total-company basis, some product-line and customer data is provided based on 10-K information. Data is available on computer tape for over 6,000 companies on the New York, American, and over-the-counter exchanges.

RATIO ANALYSIS

Attempts to analyze company trends and develop intraindustry comparisons are aided by use of ratio analysis. These accounting ratios are useful because they summarize what are often complex relationships. The comparability of companies within an industry can be improved by adjusting the numbers, or at least being aware of differences, of reported figures from companies due to differences in accounting practices such as inventory valuation and depreciation.

Although no attempt will be made to describe every ratio,[2] they can, for the purpose of our discussion, be divided into three general areas: liquidity, turnover, and profitability measures.

Liquidity Ratios

Liquidity (or solvency) ratios reflect a company's ability to meet its short-term obligations. These ratios relate cash and other liquid (near-cash) items to short-term obligations. Obviously a subsidiary or division is in turn affected by the parent company's liquidity. Moreover, the division may comprise a small fraction of the total assets of the parent company.

The most widely used (and oldest) ratio reflecting a company's ability to meet its current obligations is the current ratio. It is calculated by dividing current liabilities into current assets. Current assets consist of the cash, short-term investments and notes, accounts receivable, and merchandise inventories. Current liabilities consist of all liabilities falling due within one year.

The rule-of-thumb calls for a current ratio of at least 2 to 1. However, rules-of-thumb are subject to many *exceptions.* As with all ratios one has to look at trend *and* range over time for the company and within an industry. For example, the trend has been for most companies to reduce their current ratio to under 2 to 1.

Since inventories are usually not very liquid if they have to be sold quickly, another measure to assess a firm's liquidity is the quick ratio. It is current assets minus inventories divided by current liabilities.

Interest coverage—that is, pre-tax earnings divided by interest payable in the period—is a measure of a firm's ability to remain solvent. Related to these figures are certain leverage ratios: total debt to equity, long-term debt to net worth, and long-term debt to working capital (current assets minus current liabilities). These are measures of how much capital other than shareholders' investment is being used to finance a business. Again, the operation analyzed may be a small portion of the company's total assets. In this case these ratios are less significant.

Turnover Ratios

Turnover ratios demonstrate how efficiently a firm is using its resources. Dividing sales by total assets, fixed assets, or net worth, we can measure the relative turnover of assets or invested capital.

Industry figures for asset turnover vary widely, with capital-intensive industries usually having a much smaller ratio. Again, the key thing is the trend, not the absolute numbers. Moreover, what is "normal" or within a normal range depends on the industry.

Accounts receivable turnover measures the average collection period on credit sales. Annual sales are divided by 365 days to get daily credit sales, which are then divided into accounts receivable. If the average number of days on credit sales varies widely from the industry norm, this may be an indication of poor management. Too low a figure could indicate the firm is losing sales because of a restrictive credit policy. If the ratio is too high, management may be pushing sales, increasing its chance of bad debts. Allowance also has to be made for selling terms.

Inventory turnover can be an indicator of possible trouble when the ratio is a number significantly higher than the industry. Not only is excessive capital tied up when the ratio is unfavorable, but the risk of obsolescence increases. This ratio will also be affected by inventory pricing methods.

Inventory turnover can be measured for total inventory, or may be broken down for raw materials inventories, work in process, and finished goods. The relevant equations are:

$$\text{Raw material turnover} = \frac{\text{cost of materials used}}{\text{average raw material inventory}}$$

$$\text{Work in process turnover} = \frac{\text{cost of goods manufactured}}{\text{average work in process inventory}}$$

$$\text{Finished goods turnover} = \frac{\text{cost of sales}}{\text{average finished goods inventory}}$$

$$\text{Total inventory turnover} = \frac{\text{sales (or cost of sales)}}{\text{average inventory}}$$

The relationship of value added—or revenues less purchases of raw material, components, supplies, and utilities—to operating assets (excludes non-operating assets such as investments and intangibles) is a refinement of sales to operating assets. It is calculated by dividing added value by operating assets. This approach eliminates turnover improvement which may be due to an increase in the cost of material used.

Profitability Ratios

The two key profitability ratios (i.e., measures of a company's ability to produce earnings) are return on sales and return on assets or investment. Here again there is no standard; the trend of the company, and the range within a company's industry, have to be reviewed. To avoid the distortion caused by different tax rates, these ratios are often computed on a pre-tax basis. Income should also be adjusted to exclude nonrecurring, extraordinary items.

The ratio of income (pre-tax or after taxes) to sales is a measure of the income generated by sales after all direct and indirect expenses are deducted. Care must be taken to understand the nature of accounting policies relating to income (recognition) and costing policies. This ratio, usually expressed as a percentage, is often computed on a pre-tax basis to reduce the distortion of different tax rates. Specific costs such as operating expenses, material, labor cost, and selling expenses can also be compared to sales.

Return on investment ratios relate profitability of net income to the investment—that is, assets or long-term debt and equity. It measures the firm's ability to utilize its assets or investment to a profitable position. It is calculated as:

$$\frac{\text{income before or after taxes}}{\text{total assets or investment or net worth}}$$

Several approaches are possible. One measure is the relationship of total assets (at the begining of the period, or average assets during the period or at the end of the period) to net income generated. There are many arguments for this approach. There are also arguments for using gross assets (before depreciation), or current cost or replacement cost to reduce the distortions of different depreciation policies or timing of capital expenditures. These modifications will make intercompany data more comparable.

Total assets or investment reflect the balance sheet, which, as we will bring out, is a mixture of current values and past costs adjusted for depreciation charges. The degree of financial leverage obtained through debt also distorts this figure, since interest charges on such debt have been deducted from income.

A modification would be the relationship of the total investment (total assets less current liabilities *or* long-term debt plus net worth) to net income. The reasoning is that income generation is related to the longer term and permanent capital. It is difficult to get these figures for divisions.

Often the after-tax interest cost is added back in order to remove the distortion of different debt policies. Another approach is to use income before taxes and interest. This also permits comparison between divisions of different companies, assuming the asset information is available:

$$\frac{\text{net income} + (1 - \text{tax rate})\ \text{interest}}{\text{total investment}}$$

Many consider return on stockholders' equity a key ratio. However, our analysis is concerned with divisions, often of larger companies. This fact, combined with the relatively larger distortion of equity due to certain accounting practices, causes us to focus on total assets or investment.

In analyzing return on assets it is useful to break it down into its two component ratios, the net profit margin and total asset turnover. The two ratios can be further broken down into additional ratios, which permit the isolation of specific factors that affect returns.

This is an argument for return on value added—that is, pre-tax profits divided by value added—as a better measure of a company's efficency. In addition to reducing the distortion caused by inflation, return on value added is not influenced by debt polices or the amount and timing of a company's fixed asset investment.

The Robert Morris Associates and Dun & Bradstreet books mentioned previously, which provide ratios for many different industries, are valuable for comparing a company with others within its industry. Ratio analysis is an excellent short-cut in handling masses of data required for planning, and evaluating competitors' operations. One problem is that its application is limited if only one or a few ratios are used as the basis for analysis. In comparing one's own company or other operations with industry averages, recognition must be given to differences due to the lack of uniform accounting precedures.

WEAKNESSES OF ACCOUNTING STATEMENTS

Often there is a tendency to accept financial statements without much thought. It is first necessary to differentiate between (1) internal reports—that is, statements used within the organization for planning and control, and (2) external reports, which are used by shareholders and other outside parties such as lenders. Published or external reports (which are prepared for nonpublic companies) reflect generally accepted accounting principles (GAAP) which involves a series of judgements. These judgements or accounting treatments can have significant effects on reported earnings and assets.

Since most of the information on competitors will be based on external data, we should be aware of (possible) major distortions or lack of comparability caused by different accounting treatments. For example, there are liberal and conservative procedures in recording revenue and expenses. The whole area of allocating joint product or general and administrative expenses is largely arbitrary.

Questions arise as to how sales should be recorded if sales are made on installment. Some products or projects have a long production cycle. Yet one may not know until the end of project if it is *profitable*.

Cost of goods sold is affected by the method of evaluating inventories. If there were no price changes determining costs of goods sold would present no problems.

The combined balance sheet and income statement depends upon how previous transactions such as acquisitions were handled—for example, whether the accounting used was purchase or pooling. Purchase accounting records the fair market value of the assets acquired, not the book value—that is, original cost. The value is cash paid or fair market value of the securities used. Under pooling, the acquired assets are recorded at book value. Also, the acquired firm's earnings are picked up for the entire year, regardless of when during the year the acquisition is made. Sometimes one has to reconstruct the past acquisition program of a competitor in order to really understand its financial statements.

There are three major areas that limit the comparisons between companies: (1) depreciation, (2) inventory pricing policies, and (3) the timing and treatment of capital expenditures, including mergers and acquisitions.

Some companies utilize accelerated depreciation for both tax and (external) reporting purposes. Other companies will utilize straight-line depreciation for reporting purposes, which will increase reported profits. Firms with similar assets in the same industry will often use very different depreciation techniques; moreover, identical plants will have different cost dues to the timing of the plant purchases. The point is to be aware of both the timing of significant capital expenditures and the depreciation method used when analyzing different companies.

The technique of inventory valuation influences the cost of the goods that are manufactured, and therefore profits. Choosing LIFO (last-in, first-out) in times of rising raw material prices affects valuations by placing the highest priced materials (last-in) into production and clearing them out through sales (first-out). The inventory that is left contains the lower-cost items. Since the later, higher-cost items have already been sold, reported profits and, what is often more important, cash payments for taxes, as a result are reduced. This is a major reason many companies have adopted LIFO over the last few years. It is not all one-sided though, because in times of falling prices, the reverse takes place and a business can find itself paying higher taxes.

The use of LIFO reduces the value of the turnover ratios and current ratio. Information needed to adjust the unrealistically low LIFO inventory valuation (in times of rising price levels) is often not available. Even if two companies employ LIFO the inventory figures are often not comparable because their respective LIFO inventory bases may have been acquired in years of significantly different price levels.

Under the FIFO (first-in, first-out) approach the materials purchased first are assumed to be immediately consumed and the inventory valuations left (on the balance sheet) are the most recently purchased values. This is usually in line with the actual asset-flow pattern, and the inventory figure is closer to actual market prices. The problem with FIFO is earnings are overstated during times of inflation, because the current cost of purchasing new inventory is not reflected.

There is a high degree of judgment in determining which items should be capitalized or expensed, and this impairs inter-firm comparisons. This choice can have a significant effect on profit because capital item costs must be amortized over the useful life of the assets. Expenses, on the other hand, are deducted in the year incurred. Thus both the magnitude and timing (as discussed above) of the expense are critical to profit. Judgment becomes especially important when expenses have both capital and expense aspects. For example, when a new plant is built the status of some of the start-up cost is questionable.

Because of the issues described above and the accrual orientation of accounting (the matching of revenues and expenses), it is often more valuable to concentrate on the cash flow as opposed to accounting (reported) income. Cash flow is defined as cash inflows from revenue less cash outflows for expenses. This approach may be more meaningful in determining the firm's true economic position. Some companies report high earnings but lack the necessary cash flow for day-to-day operations. A recent example of a company with cash flow problems is Baldwin-United. Expected earnings of their single-premium deferred annuities (SPDA) were taken into net income each year by what their 1981 annual report calls an "earnings model adjustment." However, expenses that had been incurred in selling the annuities, including sales commissions, are written off over ten years. This is one of many examples in accounting history where expenses related to selling (or developing) a product were capitalized—that is, not reflected immediately in the income statement. Other examples include the heavy development costs of new airplanes and the selling expenses related to real estate. The latter industry has had problems developing methods for reporting sales, and the amount to record each year. In analyzing any industry and company time must be spent in understanding how selling and development costs are handled, and their effect on cash flow.

Many people add depreciation expense to net income and call it cash flow. But sales, not depreciation, is the source of funds from operating a business. In many cases the method described will provide an answer significantly different from actual cash flow.

Besides depreciation, other expenses subtracted from net income that do not involve the outflow of cash are depletion, amortization of intangibles, and other deferred charges. Other items impacting cash flow include amortization of discount or premium on bonds payable, deferred investment tax credits, and increases or decreases in accrued liabilities.

To prepare a cash flow analysis, changes in working capital accounts other than cash are determined.[3] For example, a company sells goods, which generates revenues, but the customer does not pay the bill for, say, two months. As a result, accounts receivable rise, but not cash. Increases in accounts payable—credit purchases—or decreases in inventory, increase cash from operations; the opposite reduces cash. Remember, many expenses do not involve an immediate outlay of cash. Often one cannot develop a detailed cash flow from published statements because many of the details of accounts will not be available. Yet the attempt must be made to really understand the financial health of a competitor.

DIRECT COSTING AND BREAK-EVEN ANALYSIS

In general, it is difficult to get competitor data, especially on a product-line basis. Moreover, when available it may not be comparable with one's operations due to accounting differences, as discussed above. To address these problems competitor financial statements often have to be reconstructed. Remember, we seek not only to obtain the historical numbers, but to understand the financial aspects of competition's operations and perhaps to predict future moves.

Two related techniques valuble in reconstructing *and* understanding competitor financial statements are break-even analysis and direct costing.

Under direct costing—sometimes called variable or marginal costing—only those costs directly related to producing products are allocated to products. This system divides manufacturing costs between (1) variable costs, which are directly related to volume or output; and (2) fixed costs, which have no relation to output. The latter are often called period costs, are *not* allocated to product but written off in the period they occur.

Absorption or full costing (which is mandatory for public and tax reporting) allocates fixed costs as well as variable costs to inventory. This can result in different unit costs depending on the level of production. One of the major arguments for direct costing is the distortion caused by absorption costing. However, the allocation of overhead and fixed costs is not the key factor in our analysis. It is the ability to analyze fixed and variable costs separately, and this is what a direct costing approach provides.

In direct costing the emphasis is on the short-run and variable costs. The arbitrary allocation of fixed costs is avoided, and we can concentrate on the effects of changes in prices and direct costs. It is a valuable technique in evaluating changes in pricing, volume, product mix, or make/buy decisions, or in analyzing any changes that might affect results. Although the process has a short-run orientation, in the long run we must absorb the fixed costs of any operation. The key elements of direct costing can be summarized as follows:

$$\text{revenues} - \text{variable costs} = \text{contribution margin}$$

$$\text{contribution margin} - \text{fixed costs} = \text{income}$$

The above equations are concerned with both fixed and variable costs, not just total costs. The full impact of fixed costs on net income is clearly seen. Direct costing better compares the profitability of products, territories, and other segments of a business. It concentrates on the contribution that each segment is making to the recovery of a portion of fixed costs.

Direct costing provides details about cost–volume–profit relationships that can be utilized to prepare a break-even analysis. Break-even analysis refers to the relationship between sales, fixed costs, variable cost, and volume. It is limited to a short time period, and applies to a relevant range of output. Costs, both fixed and variable, are different for different levels of output. Some costs are semi-variable; that is, they increase with increase in output, but not directly. These costs can usually be divided into fixed and variable components.[4] An example might be maintenance, where the supply parts component increases directly with volume, but the fixed portion does not change within the relevent range. At a significantly higher level of output these cost relationships would change.

The term "break-even" refers to the point at which the company neither makes a profit nor suffers a loss. There is no question that break-even analysis, or for that matter the attempt to divide costs into fixed and varible components, requires many assumptions and simplifications of what are often complex relationships. It still is helpful to develop competitor data—one might call it a snapshot, a picture for a short period of time, within a specified range of production.

The easiest way to see break-even analysis is graphically. Figure 10.1 is a graphic presentation of cost-volume-profit relationships with the break-even point (quantity) indicated. Fixed costs are plotted as a straight horizontal line. Variable costs are added to fixed cost, providing the total cost line. The break-even point is where the total revenue line intersects the total costs line. At this volume, total revenues equal total expenses.

Note that fixed and total costs, and revenues are plotted on the vertical axis and quantity or volume on the horizontal axis. Volume may be expressed in terms of dollars, units, capacity, or other measures of output. Variable costs are the vertical distance between the fixed costs (FC) and total cost (TC) lines at a given output (Q) level.

Another format for Figure 10.1 is to plot the variable costs first and superimpose the fixed costs on the variable costs line. The total costs (TC) line would run parallel to the variable costs line instead of parallel to the fixed costs (FC) line. Both approaches assume the following:

1. Changes in sales volume or quantity produced does not affect prices.
2. Fixed costs are the same for all levels of production.
3. Variable costs vary in direct proportion to sales.
4. Inventory remains the same.
5. The product mix does not change.

In summary, the chart is an approximate linear representation of a curvelinear function. However, this restriction and all the above assumptions refer to a relevant range—a specified range of production. Outside this range a new graph—that is, a new fixed costs level—and variable expenses/revenues relationships are defined.

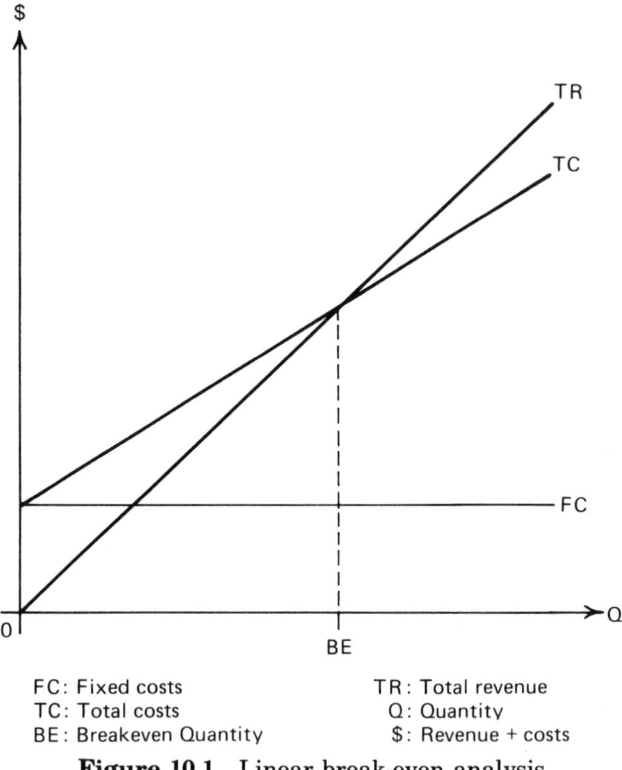

Figure 10.1 Linear break-even analysis

Although Figure 10.1 gives an easy way to see the relationship of costs and revenue, it is not the easiest way to calculate the break-even point. For this we utilize equations, developed from the relationship:

$$\text{sales} = \text{fixed costs} + \text{variable costs} + \text{income}$$

The difference between revenues and variable costs is the contribution margin. This is what is left to cover other costs and make a profit. The P/V (profit-volume) ratio or contribution margin ratio is computed by dividing the contribution margin (marginal income) by total sales; it is the complement of the variable cost ratio (variable costs ÷ sales revenue).

$$\text{P/V ratio} = 1 - \frac{\text{total variable expenses}}{\text{total sales volume (in dollars)}}$$

To find the total sales dollars required to recover fixed costs, total fixed costs are divided by the P/V ratio:

$$\text{break-even sales volume in dollars} = \frac{\text{total fixed expenses}}{\text{P/V ratio}}$$

The break-even point can also be computed in units, pounds, or other measures. For example, by dividing total fixed expenses by the contribution margin per unit, the break-even point in units is obtained:

$$\text{break-even sales in units} = \frac{\text{total fixed expenses}}{\text{sales price per unit} - \text{variable cost per unit}}$$

This information will permit us to concentrate on the key financial aspects of our competition and to determine what possible changes in strategy—for example, changes in pricing—will have on the income statement. Of course if revenue and expense data are available they can be utilized. In most cases, many of the details to do this type of analysis are not available. However, by combining the resources within our organization and the financial clues we are collecting, this kind of information *can* be developed.

RECONSTRUCTING COMPETITOR FINANCIAL STATEMENTS

The attempt to reconstruct financial statements is a valuable exercise in understanding competitors. The degree of detail required is a function both of the availability of data and the relative importance of the specific competitor. In some cases, this exercise may by performed every few years. For more important competitors we may want to do this yearly or on a shorter time basis. And for the more critical competitor(s) it will be valuable to also make an estimate of their capital investment in plant and equipment.

Most of the financial statements developed will have an absorption accounting basis, since this is how public reports and other external data are usually presented. However, there are advantages, as we discussed above, to a direct costing approach. The basic elements required to develop an income statement can be divided into six groups, as shown below. Of course, these groups can be subdivided further to provide additional details of expenses:

1. Products.
    Output level.
    Selling price.
2. Raw material.
    Annual requirements.
    Delivered price.
3. Labor Costs.
    Manpower requirements.
    Wage rates.
4. Utilities.
5. Distribution costs (including packaging costs).
6. Overhead and other fixed costs.

The sources of the information will vary both with the specific items and the type of industry. In some, annual reports and 10-Ks will be available. Some other sources are listed below. This list is not all-inclusive but may be used as a starting point in developing information.

1. Product sales.
    External reports by competitors.
    Market shares estimates.
        Outside sources—marketing consultants,
        Department of Commerce.
        Internal sources—marketing and purchasing departments.
2. Raw materials.
    Internal purchasing and cost accounting departments.
    Commodity price statistics.
3. Labor costs.
    Industry hourly rates and hours.
        Bureau of Labor Statistics—*Monthly Labor Review.*
        Internal personnel and cost accounting departments.
        Trade association and magazine surveys.

4. Utilities.

   Regional economic development agencies.

   Directly from utilities.

   Trade magazine surveys.

5. Distribution costs.

   Internal purchasing, marketing, and transportation departments.

6. Overhead and other fixed costs.

   Internal engineering, accounting, and cost accounting departments.

   Trade magazine and association surveys.

An especially valuable input is that of the internal *cost* accounting department. While we have questioned the analytical and planning uses of absorption or standard costing, the development of these standards requires detailed knowledge of both the manufacturing process and the costs of materials and services. Although it can also be said of other departments within a company, there is a particular failure to utilize the resources and experience of the cost accounting group.

For some competitors an attempt should be made to develop an estimate of the cost of the existing facilities. Internal engineering and manufacturing personnel will be of great assistance in this area. The construction costs can be developed back to the year built through the use of construction cost indexes. An example of this kind of index would be the Plant Cost Index and Equipment Cost Index published monthly in *Chemical Engineering*. Some industries such as pulp and paper have a great deal of information on company equipment and configuration reported in the trade press. Additional material can also be obtained from local zoning and environmental control agencies. It is surprising how one can often develop a figure within 25 percent or less of actual costs. A suggested format for summarizing this data is given in Table 10.1.

Another exercise that will be useful, although one can not obtain accuracy to the nth degree, is to calculate the break-even point of a competitor. As we have stressed previously, (1) the direct costing approach provides better insights into a competitor's operations, and (2) a lot of financial information is available or can be developed to obtain the estimates of the breakdown of the fixed and variable components of costs. Some items such as depreciation or research are 100 percent

TABLE 10.1. ESTIMATE OF FIXED CAPITAL INVESTMENT

Equipment and instrumentation	$________
Installation costs	$________
Subtotal	$________
Construction and related overhead	$________
Subtotal	$________
Contingency	$________
Total fixed capital investment	$________

TABLE 10.2. GUIDE FOR CALCULATION OF BREAK-EVEN POINT

		Percent of Total Cost	
	Total Cost	Fixed	Variable
Raw material	$________	0	100
Direct labor and supervision	$________	40	60
Utilities	$________	25	75
Maintenance	$________	50	50
Operating supplies	$________	30	70
Control laboratory	$________	50	50
Plant overhead	$________	75	25
Depreciation	$________	100	0
Property taxes and insurance	$________	100	0
Royalties	$________	0	100
Subtotal	$________		
Containers	$________	0	100
Packaging costs	$________	25	75
General office and administration	$________	75	25
Sales expense	$________	75	25
Research	$________	100	0
Freight allowance	$________	0	100
Subtotal	$________		
Contingency	$________	____	____
Total cost of sales	$________	____	____

fixed; other such as raw materials or royalties will usually be 100 percent variable. Table 10.2 gives a suggested format for summarizing these costs. In this case the estimates of the cost breakdown are for a chemical process plant, but the format can be changed for different industries. Also, the cost items can be subdivided even further depending on the detail required—or attempted.

The results of the above will be a more detailed knowledge of our competitors. As in the budgeting exercise, the real value may be in the process of developing the numbers, rather than in the specific numbers themselves.

---

[1]Attempts to obtain a current copy were not successful; however, the *Financial Analyst's Handbook II* (Sumner N. Levine, ed., Homewood, Illinois, Dow Jones-Irvin, 1975) has reproduced an earlier guide. This book has two additional chapters on information and reference sources.

[2]Extensive treatments of ratio analysis include Roy Foulke, *Practical Financial Statement Analysis,* New York, McGraw-Hill, 1968; Donald E. Miller, *The Meaningful Interpretation of Financial Statements,* New York, American Management Association, 1972; and Charles H. Gibson and Patricia A. Boyer, *Financial Statement Analysis,* Boston, CBI 1979.

[3]In an excellent article, "Cash Flow: Assessing a Company's Real Financial Health," in *Financial Executive,* July 1982, pp. 34–40, J. Edward Ketz and Richard F. Kochanek provide a detailed discussion of how to determine cash flow.

[4]This is usually a difficult task without internal data. Most cost accounting books review techniques for determining the fixed and varible components of costs, as well as discussing direct costing and break-even analysis. Three texts are John J. W. Neuner and Edward B. Deakin III, *Cost Accounting: Principles and Practice,* Homewood, Illinois, Irwin, 1977; Gerald R. Crowingshield, *Cost Accounting: Principles and Managerial Applications,* Boston, Houghton Mifflin, 1969; and Adolph Matz and Milton F. Usry, *Cost Accounting: Planning and Control,* Cincinnati, South Western, 1976.

11

Economics' Contributions to Competitor Intelligence in Business

DAVID I. GOLDENBERG

The president and founder of Systematic Forecasting, Inc., David I. Goldenberg is a nationally known business economist with over 20 years of diversified industry experience. He specializes in devising practical ways to analyze, predict, and plan for companies facing complex and fast-changing situations.

Mr. Goldenberg has been CEO of an industrial textile producer and an electronic products venture development firm, and has led major corporate activities in acquisitions, economic research, product development, and business planning. He has managed a successful turnaround and was responsible for a profitable divestment program. In addition, he has developed computerized forecasting systems and business segment models, and has established formal marketing planning and analysis, field intelligence, and sales forecasting systems in Fortune 200 companies.

Mr. Goldenberg taught at the Graduate School of Business of Fairleigh Dickinson University. He lectures on management, marketing, planning, finance, and economics for colleges and industry, and has published papers on business planning, textile fiber forecasting, and mergers and acquisitions. Mr. Goldenberg earned an M.A. in economics from the New School for Social Research, where he is now a Ph.D. candidate. He holds an M.B.A. in marketing from Columbia and a B.A. from Rutgers.

INTRODUCTION

Certain branches of economics contribute significantly to the gathering and interpreting of information about competitor business behavior. Industrial Organization Theory, a subcomponent of Microeconomics, is the most relevant branch of economics. Six other branches of economics which also make useful contributions are: financial economics, political economics, economic history, planning and development, econometrics, and managerial economics.

Competitor intelligence is a new topic for American firms but an old one in Europe and an ancient one in Oriental organizations. Economics enhances competitor intelligence in three distinct ways. First and foremost, economics provides the only holistic approach to this practical subject. Competitive intelligence necessarily requires a multidisciplinary treatment. Another discipline may momentarily be paramount in a given circumstance, but no other single body of knowledge applies so well across the broad spectrum of international business or shows how to integrate all the disciplines into a coherent and cogent analysis. Some other disciplines are popular starting or end points in the conduct of competitor intelligence. Finance and accounting are examples. Consider Figure 11.1. It isolates a representative firm between two sets of markets. One set of markets supplies the firm with resources. The other set of markets is served by the products of the firm. Economic tradition encourages competitive analysis to somewhat overemphasize the importance of the markets served, as is discussed later.

The second way that economics enhances competitor intelligence is through research. Economic research has produced a vast body of data on specific competitive practices characteristic of particular industries and firms. Such research is not well known within the business community. There are several reasons for this. Other economics topics traditionally provide greater rewards and recognition with less effort. Economics' contributions to competitor intelligence is also hidden by economists' use of jargon. Tradition, however, is the primary problem. Business interest in competitor intelligence boils down to imparting superior performance to an enterprise compared to its competition—in other words, getting and keeping an edge. Conventional economic studies address a very different issue. The traditional economic issue is: How can overall public welfare be maximized? Translating these differences in language and objective into contemporary and actionable English is a formidable challenge.

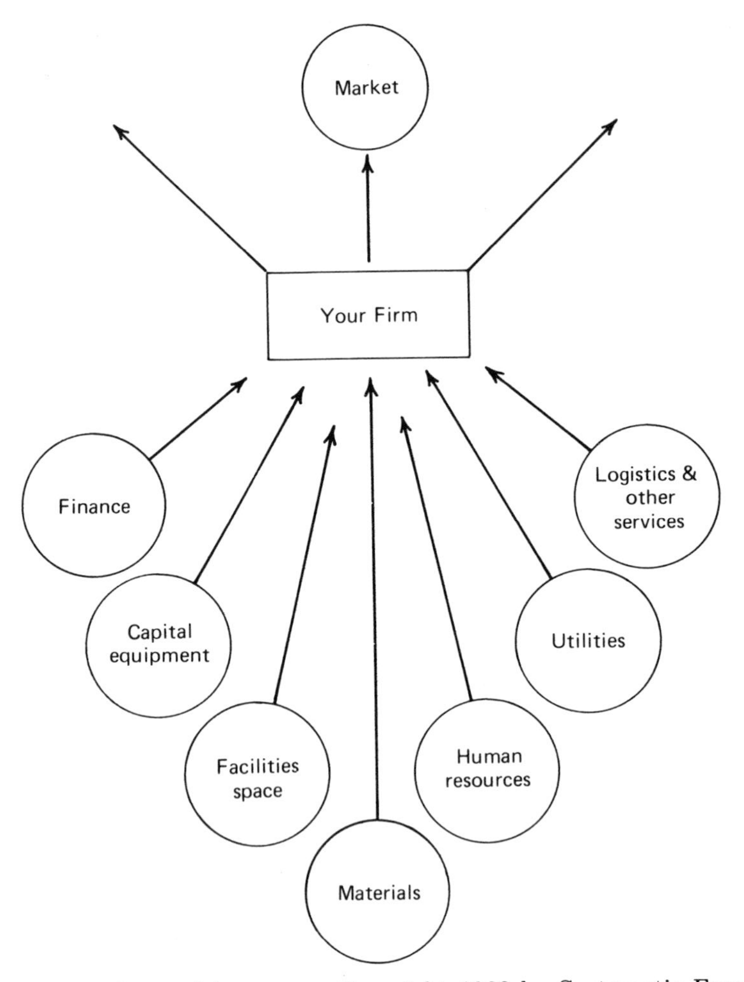

Figure 11.1 Competitive arena. Copyright 1982 by Systematic Forcasting, Inc., Fair Lawn, NJ.

The third way economics and particularly econometrics can aid competitor intelligence is by providing some potent, dramatic, and reliable tools. Many of the popular devices are, in contrast, not generally valid, unreliable, especially impractical for providing overall management perspectives, and, of course, obsolete.

Economics' contributions to competitor intelligence include posing basic questions, identifying lines of analyses to resolve those issues, devising and testing techniques for this work, and amassing and indexing a relevent body of knowledge. These points are discussed below, so that interested readers can adapt relevant concepts to their needs and avoid mistakes known to others.

FIRST ISSUE: THE COMPETITIVE ARENA AND ITS CRITICAL SUCCESS FACTORS

Effective competitor intelligence starts with a particular attitude. That attitude is: Do it right the first time. Second attempts are embarrassingly expensive.

Several assuredly wrong ways to start are known. Rushing in for a quick kill is one. Inadequate preparation and overambitious goals inevitably destroy competitor intelligence efforts. Invest the time to build rapport with management. Otherwise competitor intelligence reports will remain unused as too late, inadequately detailed, or incredible. Successful competitor intelligence requires, however, more than management rapport. Qualified people are essential.

An effective competitor intelligence system requires a multidisciplinary approach. Which disciplines are necessary? That depends upon your circumstances. Answering a deceptively simple question will point to the right areas. The question is: What are the past, present, and future critical success factors for the industry?

Only by working back up the distribution channels from the ultimate consumers through your customers, your firm, and your suppliers, can you begin to answer this first vital question. A modest survey often suffices. For example, success in an industry depends upon more than competing as a seller in a particular market against other suppliers of like products. Some industries are critically dependent upon marketing skills. Others turn upon manufacturing expertise. Still others make their money through astute purchasing. Retailers are one example of the latter situation. Consider for instance Sears' purchasing practices.

Textiles exemplify the dynamics inherent in business competition. When cotton, wool, and silk were the predominant fibers, the textile industry found it easy to make money in purchasing while maintaining parity in manufacturing and marketing. The arrival of synthetic fibers and organized commodities markets changed things for textile mills. Then they also had to compete in manufacturing and marketing.

Identifying the Critical Success Factors (CSFs) is not enough; one must also determine their relative importance, the commercially acceptable performance range of each, and how decision makers combine them.

A telephone survey of executives of major U.S. textile mills provided the information needed to construct Table 11.1. The survey answered a few questions at a point in time.

> Which factors are essential to an ongoing relationship with your fiber suppliers?
>
> What is the relative importance of those factors?
>
> How does your (primary, secondary, . . .) fiber supplier rate on each key trait?

Changes in the ratings occur over time. These are detected by repeating the survey periodically. Statistical techniques can enhance the analysis. However, a simple survey can be effective, credible, and statistically valid if it's well designed.

Eight factors were critical to success in the U.S. synthetic fiber industry in 1980, according to a survey of textile mills. Table 11.1 calls these factors "key traits." Maximum point score patterns can be tested statistically to detect major changes. Analysis of the survey's data enables adjustment of the relative importance of the CSFs. It also permits scaling them so that a perfect rating's maximum score equals 100 points.

The first basic issue does more than remind us that every industry is dynamic. Every industry has its own life-cycle. Distinct sets of strategy options are relevant and effective at different stages of an industry's life-cycle. Consequently the critical success factors change.

The U.S. synthetic fiber industry epitomized a growth industry. The first OPEC oil embargo marked the onset of a decade of transition for that industry. Today it is a mature industry whose growth rate essentially parallels that of the population. Rules for success in the U.S. fiber industry have changed markedly. Customers of the U.S. fiber industry are predominantly U.S. textile firms. The textile industry is undergoing its own life-cycle transition from a mature to a declining industry, and so the factors critical to success in textiles are also changing. These industries are interdependent. Their component firms, however, have yet to recognize—let alone address—the implications of the combined life-cycle transitions.

Identifying and ranking the industry's future CSFs describes the relevant arena and establishes its rules. This battleground's character and rules depend upon considerations outside the industry. Tracking

TABLE 11.1. DOMINANCE AND LEADERSHIP (SUBJECTIVE RANKING)

Max. Points	Key Traits	duPont	Celanese	Akzona	Eastman	Allied Chemical	Monsanto	Avtex	Badische	Hoechst
30	Volume	30	20	14	15	12	16	5	10	8
20	Pricing	15	15	10	10	10	5	10	10	5
15	Product Mix	15	10	10	5	5	10	5	5	3
15	Quality	15	12	12	12	13	8	10	10	10
5	Selling Effort	5	4	3	4	4	3	5	3	3
5	Service (Customer & Technical)	3	3	3	3	3	3	4	3	3
5	Innovation	5	2	1	1	2	2	2	1	1
5	Market Knowledge	5	4	4	4	4	3	5	3	2
100		93	70	57	54	53	50	46	45	35
	Rank	1	2	3	4	5	6	7	8	9

Source: Copyright 1980 Systematic Forecasting, Inc., Fair Lawn, NJ 07410.

these external considerations can require such specialized activities as: environmental scanning, demographic and psychographic research, macroeconomics, technological evaluation, and legal research. Various departments of a firm and such affiliated organizations as investment bankers, trade associations, auditors, and so forth, usually can provide the necessary inputs. Eliciting cooperation is a common initial problem. Coordinating and condensing the information is another. Later, these sources often can provide valuable insights about the nature, intensity, track record, and prospects of key competitors' activities in their special areas.

SECOND ISSUE: RATING THE COMPETITION

The second basic issue appears as a question. What are the strengths and weaknesses of each competitor? Some fundamental errors are common in addressing this issue. The first concerns defining one's competition.

Too many organizations act as if their competition comes only from firms already selling similar products. Figure 11.1 demonstrates that every business competes in a number of markets. It competes in some as a seller and in others as a buyer. In both roles, the rivalry focuses upon resources. Sales and marketing efforts vie for consumers' dollars while procurement activities compete for productive resources.

Certain individuals are the crucial resource, if history is any guide. They found new industries and firms and ruin old ones. Professor Carothers' research at duPont led to synthetic fibers, but who remembers the duPont executives who made the strategic decision to financially support abstract research into polymer chemistry? Inventors often become folk heroes because their discoveries establish industries. Entrepreneurs are more important as innovators. Edison was both, and a rarity. Barnum specialized in promotions rather than discoveries. Every firm owes its existence to an entrepreneur, not necessarily to an inventor. The entrepreneur frequently shapes the character of the firm forever. Today it is fashionable to refer to a corporation's culture rather than its character or ethos. Regardless of the term, some special individuals invariably set the tone by fiat or example. Harold Geneen of ITT and Edwin Land of Polaroid are but two recent cases in point.

A second error in defining competition results from mental laziness. It is convenient to concentrate upon one's product or manufacturing process. That familiar territory is where executives expend most of their efforts. Consequently, there is a tendency to say: "My competitors are those producing the same goods in about the same way." That is, however, incorrect. Your customers determine your competition. Whenever they can better satisfy their requirements with a different product or service you also compete against the suppliers of that commodity for those consumers' dollars. Cotton farmers compete with wool and several synthetic fibers, not just with other cotton farmers. Many textile products are luxuries and compete with services such as vacations, or tangible products such as home electronics equipment. Cola sodas compete directly with one another. They also compete against other soda flavors, carbonated alcoholic beverages such as beer and champagne, and even water—with or without coffee or tea flavoring.

Direct competitors seldom are as troublesome as indirect competitors. The latter are harder to identify and track, and they usually pose greater strategic threats. Market entry by indirect competitors often is unexpected and disruptive. Steel production yields sulfuric acid as a by-product. That puts steel companies in the chemical industry, too. Pharmaceutical companies not only supply drugs, but they sometimes compete with surgeons and even bed rest supplied by hospitals and nursing homes. Such organizations may not operate according to industry conventions. Their technology usually imparts atypical characteristics in terms of goals, pricing and cost structures, locations, seasonal activity, strategic inputs, and vulnerability to outside pressures such as business cycles.

One approach to identifying competitors starts by listing direct rivals. Then determine what resources are essential for a successful entry into the business. *Any* firm that has or can get the right kinds and amounts of those resources is a potential entrant. A list of potential direct entrants is more readily constructed and screened once the CSFs for direct entry are established. No one has yet devised a reliable (let alone easy) way to identify prospective but indirect rivals.

Competitive entry is common in an industry's growth phase. Deciding if and how to enter and compete in a new industry requires information. Established firms need to know who might enter and how the newcomers are apt to behave. Exxon, Apple, and IBM penetrated the small computer business very differently in terms of methods, timing, and impacts upon the industry, rivals, and themselves.

"Shake-outs" often characterize the transitions from a growth to a mature industry and from a mature to a sunset one. At those junctures, the concerns of competitor intelligence necessarily change. Essentially, they reverse. "Who'll leave the industry next?" and "When and how will they exit?" and "How will that help or hurt us?" are key competitor intelligence questions for firms remaining in the industry after its first transition. Exiting firms have to readdress the competitor intelligence issues associated with entry into other industries. The decline phase of an industry eventually compels every firm to deal with entry questions if it is to survive.

Such issues have been identified and analyzed in considerable depth in the literature of that branch of economics known as Industrial Organization Theory. Articles in leading management journals supply enough references to enable anyone interested to quickly develop an appropriate bibliography.

Experience demonstrates that six lines of approach are particularly fruitful in gathering and evaluating business intelligence about competitors' strengths and weaknesses. These lines are gap analyses, culture, strategic planning process, influences, asymmetries, and signals. Each topic is discussed in turn in the following sections.

Gap Analyses

Gap analyses were one of the earliest approaches to competitor assessment. Successful gap analyses require competitor intelligence about resources. Gap analyses seek to identify disparities by ascertaining the kinds and amounts of resources needed to successfully enter, survive, and thrive in an industry. Then one compares those requirements with the kinds and amounts of resources on hand at, and attainable by, various competitors. Such an exercise is advisable periodically, although it suffers from some deficiencies in practice.

Gap analyses depend heavily upon the particular technology assumed to be appropriate. Innovations in the technology of production, marketing, purchasing, or even management can vitiate the conclusions reached from gap analyses predicating the use of other technologies.

Mechanically performed gap analyses risk neglecting some possible maneuvers by competitors. Critical shortages of strategic resources may exist and be correctly identified by a perfunctory gap analyses. However, a superficial study may neglect the possibility of trading or selling surplus resources for the required ones. It may also define competitors too narrowly. Defining a rival as a particular division of another firm precludes the possibility of intradivisional transfers of such resources as funds, management, capital assets, expertise, and so forth.

Gap analyses can also mislead by focusing strictly upon tangible resources rather than also taking intangible ones into consideration. Threshold levels of resources must be exceeded for a firm to succeed; however, technology or skill can drastically raise or lower those minimum requirements. An industry's early technology frequently is very uncertain.

Critical resources thresholds are often rather broad bands initially instead of the microscopically fine lines implied in the literature. Hence some firms apparently function well with inadequate or even impossibly low resource levels. The productivity of a leading pioneer can so far surpass its competitors as to be literally incredible to them. DuPont seemingly achieved this enviable position in the early 1970s with its non-cellulosic filament fibers. Its output per spinning machine was almost triple that of its competitors.

Although useful in some circumstances, gap analyses are no longer sufficient on their own to adequately assess competitors' strengths and weaknesses. Ability and willingness to exploit obvious resources in traditional ways is a convenient but dubious assumption underlying all gap analyses.

Culture

The culture of an organization imposes a unique character upon a firm. Every firm has its own culture. Few, however, have consciously planned their culture or considered its implications for competitor performance and intelligence.

Some firms and even industries are extremely circumspect and unaggressive in their dealings with competitors. This is typical early in the growth phase of an industry. Everyone is too busy then trying to grow as fast as the market to seriously worry about competitors. As the industry's growth rate inevitably settles down to some proportion of the population's growth rate, competitors command greater attention because future growth comes at their expense. How will they react?

Past behavior is a major source of insight into a rival's culture and, hence, its future behavior. Each firm accumulates experience in its executive team. Each firm also builds a pattern of acceptable behavior. Some organizations will employ questionable practices unashamedly. Others categorically reject such practices in fact as well as in theory.

ITT became very adept at acquisition and divestment under Mr. Geneen's direction. It apparently was not as competent at operating its acquisitions, however. American automobile manufacturers' labor–

management practices are part of their culture. They stand in sharp contrast to those of foreign competitors relying on Theory Y or Z instead of Theory X.

A firm's culture attracts some types of people and repells others. Highly bureaucratic organizations reward conformity and personal loyalty to superiors at the expense of innovation and progress. If IBM is exempt from this viewpoint, then why did Wang and Amdahl leave? Hewlett Packard and 3M, to name but two, put innovation far ahead of conformity in their priorities.

A firm's culture can change. Typically, however, it does so very slowly over long intervals. It also experiences spasmodic and sometimes drastic revisions. The latter commonly result from new leadership within the organization attempting to make its mark and demonstrate its authority via reorganizations. Another cause of sudden cultural change within a business arises from the periodic need to play catch-up. This usually results from management's understandable preference for traditional ways of doing business despite a dynamic environment. Some corporate cultures change in response to their management's moves; other corporations' cultures are shaken into new patterns by such moves.

Historic profiles of competitors' cultural patterns help explain their past behavior. Such profiles offer vital insights into their characters. Cultural profiles can spotlight aspirations, goals, vulnerabilities, sensitivities, standards, sanctions, and so forth. Predictions about the nature, timing, and success of alterations in competitors' behavior are crucial to evaluations of the merits of strategic options for your organization. Such forecasts are greatly facilitated and enhanced by competitor intelligence based upon cultural profiles.

Strategic Planning Process

A third competitor intelligence activity investigates competitors' strategic planning processes. Every organization necessarily has a strategic planning process. Most, of course, are quite informal. The environments within and around each competitor are far more complex than is generally recognized. Figure 11.2 illustrates the management process tensor for an extremely simple business. The managment process involves at least three dimensions. One concerns the functional areas or disciplines. The resources available to managment and the limitations imposed upon it combine into a second dimension, since

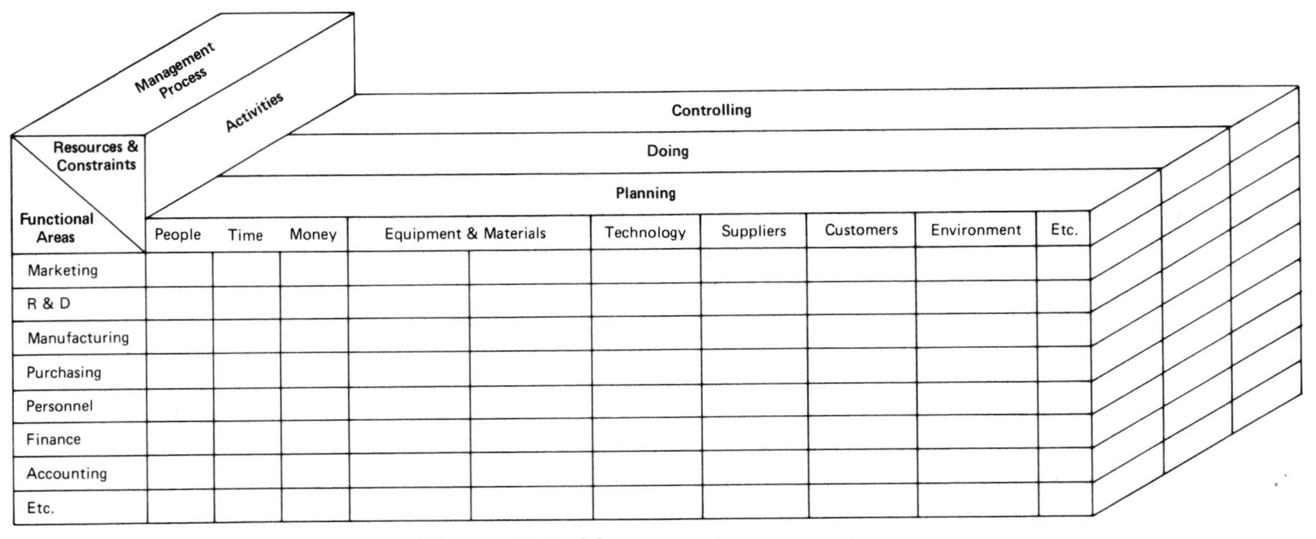

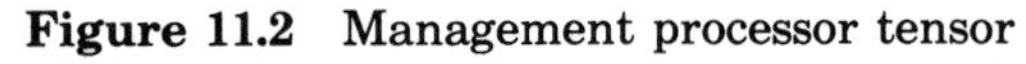

Figure 11.2 Management processor tensor

constraints can be represented as a relative or an absolute scarcity of a resource. Activities form the third dimension of the management process. Mathematically the management process is a tensor, rather than a matrix, because it includes three or more dimensions simultaneously. Using the unfamiliar term "tensor" reminds us to take a comprehensive view and be alert to the possibility of additional dimensions in a given situation. The business represented is simple because it only sells one product to one geographic market after producing its output with one production line in one plant with but a single conversion step. The organizational structure of that business is surprisingly complex, even after further simplifying assumptions are imposed.

Figure 11.2 does not detail the organizational structure of the firm it represents. That organization's structure falls out of the chart as interconnections between and within the 168 cells shown. The intracellular structure is unimportant for strategic purposes and, hence, ignored. That simplifies things considerably. Nevertheless, the remaining possibilities for intercellular connections are enormous. These possibilities can be reduced to an absolute minimum by adopting three heroic assumptions.

The most important of these strong assumptions is that each cell is directly and individually linked to all the others with an instantaneous, two-way, and noise-free communications channel. This premise reduces the required interconnections to just over 14,000. Combining any two of the three management process activities—for example, planning plus controlling—more than halves the required interconnections to almost 6200.

Lastly, one function is ignored because most firms really don't perform all of those shown. The neglected function varies by industry and firm. It might be marketing in the use of a captive subsidiary. A service business might delete manufacturing from the list. However, eliminating any single function simplifies the organization's structure to only 4608 interconnections.

Real businesses are obviously more complex than the hypothetical one charted. Therefore, some of their supposedly required interconnections are apt to be defective or missing. Those defective or nonexistent interconnections represent vulnerabilities to particular changes in the firms' environments. Suppliers to giant retailers often cut costs by eliminating or minimizing the marketing function. If the major retail account of such a firm could be persuaded to split its purchases or decided to squeeze its supplier, the latter would be vulnerable for years. Sears seems to have periodically employed this strategy.

Figure 11.2 provides a check list of functional areas and activities to probe in order to uncover competitors' strengths and weaknesses. It also indicates how to combine these explorations with gap analyses. More importantly, the management process tensor points the way to more refined forms of competitor intelligence in the abstract realm of strategic planning processes.

Every strategic planning process depends upon a series of key premises. Strategic planning processes can be distinguished and assessed in terms of the premise value patterns adopted and rejected. The premise position pattern characteristic of any given strategic planning process can be ascertained fairly rapidly. Any good microeconomics text identifies the relevant list of premises. Transforming that list to a map is easy. The map is used to contrast two patterns of premise positions. One, of course, is that for the firm's current strategic planning. The other premise position patterns can vary; usually, however, an initial comparison is made against the premise position pattern for success in the competitor's current environment. This comparison is analogous to gap analysis.

Marked discrepencies on the map may indicate profoundly different perceptions of the environments, a blunder on the part of your competitor, or use of erroneous information in mapping. Each of these possibilities can be checked. For instance, the position pattern of a strategic planning process must reasonably agree with the requirement of the future environments expected.

A key trait of any strategic planning process is the potency of the strategies it can generate. That characteristic can be deduced by studying the premises of the particular process. Are those assumptions internally consistent? Are they compatible with the firm's environment?

Each strategy has one of three levels of potency: (1) dominant, (2) vulnerable, or (3) inferior. An inferior strategy is either unworkable or self-defeating. Competitors can safely ignore an inferior strategy unless it disrupts the market. A dominant strategy cannot be defeated by any one competitor or any coalition of competitors; it is also invulnerable to inept execution. Dominant strategies obviously are extremely rare in business situations. However, no one can afford to ignore such a strategy once it is discovered. Rivals facing a dominant strategy can only hope to minimize losses by immediately withdrawing from competition. In fact, the astute possessor of such a strategy will broadcast its existence in detail. Vulnerable strategies are the norm. Their success depends upon factors beyond the strategist's control. If and only if the external environment is completely favorable, and competitive interaction is too little or too late, and the implementation is flawless, can a vulnerable strategy succeed.

Thorough examination of a strategic planning process discloses more than the potency of the strategies it produces. That study can also identify the kinds of strategies generated, and it can go further to spotlight such strategies' weak points for effective retaliatory responses.

Business intelligence about rivals' strategic planning processes usually is neglected. There are numerous reasons for that—abstruseness, unfamiliarity, and difficulty, among others. Most importantly, these efforts seldom yield fast and dramatic results. Nevertheless, their findings offer longer lead times and more profound insights at less cost than any other branch of competitor intelligence.

Influences

A quick, relatively easy, and often useful competitor intelligence approach looks for major influences. This approach researches the competition in terms of external factors with significant potential for impacting a competitor's behavior. For instance, which consultants are on retainer? Some leading American synthetic fiber producers' consulting affiliations are given in Table 11.2. Each of the consultants named in Table 11.2 recommends a particular strategic planning process. That preference facilitates predictions. Even more interesting results may appear when this sort of research is extended to cover a long period.

DuPont seems to make a point of being the first to retain consultants claiming to have novel techniques. That gives duPont a peculiar double

TABLE 11.2. STRATEGIC PLANNING CONSULTANTS IN THE U.S. MAN-MADE FIBER INDUSTRY

Firm	Present Strategic Planning Consulting Affiliation
duPont	Braxton Associates
Celanese	McKinsey Company
Tennessee Eastman	Arthur D. Little
Allied	Booz, Allen and Hamilton
Monsanto	Bain & Company, and Schleh & Company

advantage. DuPont gets a head start in understanding any new development. If the innovation is meritorious, duPont has a head start in implementation, too. The consultant leaves with a polished presentation and an impressive record. DuPont also captures some subtle advantages beyond any immediate improvements. It probably has a better understanding of the consultant's methodology than the originators. If there are flaws in that methodology, duPont knows them better than the consultant. If those weaknesses are correctible, then duPont knows what to do and how, long before anyone else. Consequently, duPont can monitor the consultant via trade talk and reasonably accurately predict competitors' progress and behavior.

A number of other major influences are almost self-evident. Where does a firm recruit? American Cyanamid's management is heavily populated with Princeton University alumni. What are the affiliations and interests of the outside directors of your competitors? Rivals have auditors, counsel, and investment advisors. They also have ties with unions, suppliers, regulatory agencies, academia, political parties, religious and charitable institutions, and so on. Such connections influence the nature, direction, and behavior of your competitors. For example, Alexander Graham Bell's work with the deaf led to the telephone. Today the Bell System still devotes considerable effort to product development for the hard of hearing.

Changes in competitor's sources of major influences can alert one to a problem within that firm or a shift in its conduct. Was a new auditor retained after the old one qualified its report? Are different affiliations being established? Revisions in corporate influences can take many forms. Dramatic shifts in influences are rare and usually publicly reported; variations in intensity of the relationship with various influential factors are more common but harder to detect and evaluate. Monitoring fees paid and the outsiders' personal areas of expertise can provide clues to these matters.

Asymmetries

A fifth line of analysis for competitor intelligence concerns asymmetries. Asymmetries essentially are uneven relationships. The hysteresis response curves of engineering exemplify asymmetries inherent in such familiar devices as automotive shock absorbers and high fidelity loud speakers. Individual and group behavior can also occur unevenly. For instance, some businesses function better as aggressors than as defenders. Martin Marietta is a recent case in point of the strong defense. Until recently, one could cite RCA or Polaroid as asymmetrical firms. Both were better innovatively than administratively or operationally. Aerospace companies were superb recruiters of engineers but relatively wasteful in using and retaining these critical personnel. On a personal basis, few individuals are naturally ambidextrous; most of us are right-handed by inclination or as a result of training.

Asymmetrical behavior confounds classical economic theorists. Firms do not act alike, nor do they behave in a smoothly balanced fashion. Strategists must deal with asymmetries rather than deny their existence or ignore them, as classical economists conventionally do. Identifying and exploiting competitors' asymmetries is a subtle matter in practice as well as theory.

Monitoring competitors' behavior frequently uncovers established asymetries. However, advantageous asymmetric behavior can be consciously acquired. Even a pacifist can learn to fight or can hire attorneys as bodyguards. Obviously the strengths represented by one's asymmetries in given circumstances transform into weaknesses when those circumstances are altered.

Idiosyncratic behavior also occurs in your firm. That's harder to identify and evaluate, but such assessments are fundamental preconditions to the development and execution of successful strategies in the business world. Knowledge of the asymmetries of your firm and each of its rivals is potentially invaluable. It sharpens the choices of strategies, opponents, and tactics. The principle is simple: Pit your strengths against others' weaknesses and don't let them do that to you. Implementing such advice is never easy, but some guidelines exist. Always assume at the outset that your competitors will detect and respond to your action in the strongest possible way. That is the Sylos Postulate from Game Theory. It can be modified in practice to: Always assume that opponents will respond in their usual fashion unless there is strong evidence to the contrary. However, one must then beware of inexperienced rivals, because they may originate a devastatingly effective response.

Communication

A last line of analysis for this discussion of competitor intelligence deals with communications between opposing businesses. Information almost inevitably flows throughout an industry via the trade press articles, standard financial reports and commentaries, and a host of semiofficial documents such as press releases, trade association reports, product descriptions, price lists, patent filings, securities registrations, speeches, articles, technical papers, and so forth. These information channels present opportunities to collect and disseminate information. Examination of the media used and messages conveyed by competitors can be quite revealing.

Competitors' advertising expenditures, media choices, timing audience targets, and information content often provide considerable insight into their marketing strategies, practices, and sophistication. Monitoring technical and trade show presentations and paricipants can be informative. This is especially the case when tracked across business cycles and geographic markets. The use of an atypical spokesperson or changes in the timing, tone, or frequency of communications alert one to the prospect of important developments.

Some industries communicate to dampen competition on price. Firms may talk back and forth via the marketplace until an acceptable price pattern is established for the next market period. Certain variants of this are legal and known as price leadership; other types of interdependent price-setting conflict with the spirit, if not the letter, of the antitrust laws. Price-making practices and communications are especially sensitive areas, since the relevant theories, data, and analytical techniques tend to be well known.

Established communications channels sometimes transmit important signals to competitors. If a press release in the chairman's name is unusual, that's a signal. If it announces that the board of directors has approved a major change, then the signal's importance is enhanced. The extent to which one's territorial interests and commitments are clearly proclaimed varies by industry and firm. Many aggressive firms have learned to look for such signals before they leap, and even then they send up a trial balloon. Many established organizations find that rattling an occasional warning is a more effective deterrent than an unannounced retaliatory attack.

Signal intelligence is a well-established commercial practice. International businesses used codes and couriers to protect their internal communications centuries ago. Security of remote access computers and data banks is a more modern concern. Computer and other technical personnel tend to talk relatively openly to one another regardless of their corporate affiliations. Careful listening to such conversations can alert technical experts to selected revisions in the capabilities and intentions of key competitors.

Every organization signals. Enterprises seldom are aware of the variety, intensity, frequency, consistency, and compatibility of the signals they emit, because most of those occur unconsciously. Trained and experienced observers can and do detect such clues and assemble them into surprisingly accurate bodies of information. Consquently, defensive commercial intelligence needs improvement. Defensive signal intelligence presents a double opportunity. It can strengthen your defenses against rivals prematurely learning your intended strategies, and it also can enhance the impact of any formal announcement upon the rest of the industry.

Outside of fictional works, there is little evidence that commercial rivalry and competitor intelligence has generally degenerated into an analogue of national and military intelligence. However, the absence of such evidence is neither conclusive nor reassuring. Leading firms in certain industries have experienced serious problems when rivals' competitor intelligence efforts became too aggressive. So called "hi-tech" outfits are particularly susceptible to such invasions of privacy; they have been targets throughout history. During the Industrial Revolution, British textile machinery designs were effectively transferred to America in contravention of English law. International piracy of chemical processes—especially antibiotics and other pharmaceuticals—was well documented in the world press two or more decades ago. Overzealous competitor intelligence activities recently appeared in the computer field. Strong competitive pressures may encourage these practices; so do the potential rewards, especially the savings from reverse engineering. There is also a further complication.

Business really occurs globally. A firm may operate within national boundaries by choice, but there is no assurance that all of its competitors will do the same. A large domestic market can attract imports and eventually domestic operations by foreign owners. A domestic firm's innovation may have great potential overseas, and hence threaten foreign competitors. Firms' thinking and behavior are conditioned by their environment. Competitor intelligence and other practices deemed normal in one environment may be barely tolerable in another, and unthinkable in a third. Consequently, there's an obligation to learn and respect the rules of the game when operating in new arenas, and, perhaps, to alert newcomers to the rules in your competitive spheres.

Defensive competitor intelligence should be standard practice. It is not. Most American companies' defenses against competitor intelligence efforts range from almost nonexistent to tokenism. That's both regretable and unnecessary. Most managements are unaccustomed to this mode of competition. Too many American organizations respond with incredible frankness, completeness, and enthusiasm to almost any judiciously phrased inquiry from anyone other than an obvious direct competitor.

Company confidential information must be identified and protected both physically and psychologically. Restrict knowledge of the existence of confidential documents to those few who must know. Forbid discussion of company business in public. Restaurants, airport lounges, taxicabs, sidewalks, bars, and golf courses are not suitable locations for conducting business. Employees have to be educated to avoid unintentional disclosures of potentially confidential information. Formal training, alas, will not suffice. Sanctions also are essential.

Some organizations pride themselves on their defensive intelligence. Whirlpool and a few other organizations with ongoing competitor intelligence functions sometimes brief outsiders on how they established and conduct such activities. Even those with nothing to hide may at least produce a useful mystique and self-esteem, provided, of course, that their efforts are not excessive. Company survival can depend upon maintaining control of truly confidential information. An effective set of policies and practices is imperative in such cases. Publicize the existence but not the details of your defenses when you have found them successful or whenever severe penalties are invoked. Conversely, keep your offensive competitor intelligence activities as much out of the limelight as possible. If discussion is unavoidable, then compliment your executives' intuition or "feel" for the market or luck. So intangible a talent cannot be acquired with certainty or speed.

SOME QUANTITATIVE CONTRIBUTIONS

Competitor intelligence has just begun to exploit quantitative methods. Game Theory is one such body of knowledge with much to offer. Econometrics, the melding of mathematics and economics, is another. Most of the techniques are publicly available. They do, however, need adaptation to work reliably. Such adjustments almost always are obvious to those sufficiently well qualified to understand the techniques and able to recognize where they would fit.

Too many of us overreact to quantitative methods. Those with an instinctive aversion may delay their firm's use of a valuable tool kit, but blind enthusiasts are a greater danger. Misuse of econometrics can endanger the firm and disrupt its industry. Attempts to apply a recently learned technique rather than the appropriate one is a common blunder. For example, superficial familiarity with simple linear regression often is misleading. Recent business school graduates almost invariably interpret the absence of a linear correlation as conclusive evidence of the lack of any causal relationship. Expertise, not familiarity, is mandatory both in applying quantitative methods effectively to competitor intelligence problems and in expressing the results so that management can act upon them with assurance.

Two quantitative techniques with competitor intelligence applications will be briefly discussed. The first will primarily be described in terms of its results, as the actual method is too elaborate and technical for this chapter. Discussion of the second econometric tool, called GREI, includes both the theory, formulas, and a brief example.

Certain manufacturing industries are worth modeling in detailed physical terms on a computer for competitor intelligence purposes. Those industries have well-understood and well-documented production fuctions. A production function is economic jargon for a precise type of recipe.

Industries with Leontief production functions are especially easy to model. Such recipes only work with unchanging mixes and proportions of ingredients. Chemical processes often satisfy these conditions. Modeling the physical flows of rival chemical firms is simplified by some real-world phenomena. The technology of each firm, its equipment, and its capacity at each stage almost always can be estimated quite accurately from public data. Each firm's degree of forward and backward integration also is ascertainable. So are its material purchases and products marketed. Consequently, this type of modeling generates two forms of competitor intelligence.

The kinds and amounts of opportunities and threats that a given rival can resist or must react to become apparent from repeated runs of the model. It also helps identify the response options available to that rival.

The materials balance model described above can be enriched with financial data. Rivals in a chemical industry buy and sell known mixes at ascertainable prices at least as a first approximation. Consequently, it is practical to modify the model to estimate rivals' internal transfer prices. Then one can gauge the intrinsic marginal profitability of particular technologies, plant sizes, and competing businesses. This sort of information is particularly useful in assessing the economies or diseconomies of sale and integration available to established or new firms. It also helps one's own facilities expansion planning and timing.

GREI is a fairly new and unpublicized tool for competitor intelligence. A Senior Science Fellow at Monsanto Company, Mr. A. W.

Dickinson, and the author of this chapter, developed GREI in 1973. GREI, of course, is an acronym; it stands for gross relative effectiveness indicator.

GREI is an overall or gross measure of performance because it captures the consequences of all functional activities. It is also a gross measure in the sense that it can be used to monitor aggregate performance at the levels of the plant, SBU, business, or the overall enterprise. GREI therefore can be used either alone or in conjunction with various functional performance measures such as financial documents.

GREI is a relative measure of performance. It shows how effective a particular firm's performance has been versus that of its competitors as a group. It does not compare actual performance against any ideal.

GREI's focus on overall performance results against competition renders it a measure of efficacy rather than efficiency. Efficiency or productivity measures require two spurious premises. To measure productivity, one must know both what can happen and be capable of comparing actual results with that theoretically feasible optimum. Those premises are too stringent whenever marketing, innovation, external shocks, and delayed responses can strongly affect performance. Consequently, GREI only claims to monitor efficacy. It does not aspire to the unattainable.

GREI also is an indicator. It reports one of two states of affairs. At worst, GREI indicates whether a particular firm has been and is likely to remain more effective, as effective, or less effective than the group of all the other firms comprising the industry. At best, GREI provides data ranking all competing firms in the industry according to their effectiveness. No one has yet proved that GREI values depict smooth, constant differences in performance. Were that the case, then GREI values would represent an index of just how much more or less effective each firm's performance was.

A given firm's GREI value results from using a formula to condense four data series into one number. The formula reflects three key premises. A couple of mathematical devices are used to keep things simple. GREI's three critical assumptions are almost but not quite intuitively obvious. They are:

The more effective the firm, the higher its average capacity utilization rate (ACUR).

The more effective the firm, the closer its actual capacity utilization rates come to its ACUR.

> Each firm competes against an artificial "coalition" of all other firms comprising the industry.

In practice, one large equation is used to find any specific firm's GREI value. That equation makes repeated use of shorter ones. The first premise requires capacity utilization data about the firm of interest in order to find its ACUR. The second premise requires data obtainable from the calculation of ACUR. That information is the standard deviation around the mean. Implementing premises one and two reduces the data series on the firm's capacity and output to two numbers, M for ACUR and E for standard deviation. The Coefficient Variation (CV) is a statistical ratio that further distills those numbers. CV = E/M. The GREI formula employs the symbol F for the firm's coefficient of variation instead of CV.

Incorporating premise three into the GREI formula imposes additional requirements and establishes the relationship between the variables. One requirement of premise three is to find the coefficient of variation for the capacity utilization of the rest of the industry. That is represented by the symbol I. Premise three implies a comparison of the firm's performance against the rest of the industry, or a relationship of F − I. It also means looking for statistically significant differences. Determination of statistically significant differences requires another type of standard error.

The missing standard error, S, is deduced in stages. The proper S is the standard error for the CV of the overall CUR. GREI, however, employs two CVs, F and I. Each has its own standard error, S_f for the firm and S_i for the rest of the industry. Two things are needed. One is a formula to find S_f and S_i. The other is a formula to deduce S from S_f and S_i. The formula for S_f is $[F(1 + 2F^2)^{1/2}]/2N$, where F was previously explained and N refers to the sample size. An English rendition of the formula to find S_f would be:

> Take the value of F and square it.
> Double that number.
> Increase that number by one.
> Obtain the square root of the result.
> Multiply the square root times F.
> Halve that result.
> Divide the result by the sample size.

The same formula works for S_i. Just replace each F with an I.

The formula that pools S_f and S_i into S is simpler. It is $S = (S_f^2+S_i^2)^{1/2}$.

The above symbols yield a short formula for GREI values or Ts. GREI values will seem peculiar because the most effective firm has the most negative "T" and the least effective has the largest positive "T". Obviously the firm with T=O is truly average. Reranking the results before reporting them obscures this source of psychological discomfort.

The strange unadjusted values of GREI are a logical consequence of the interaction of the premises. Premise one implies that the best firm will have a high ACUR, and that assures a low value of F. Pemise two implies that the best firm also will have a small standard error around its ACUR, and that assures an even lower value of F. Premise three dictates subtracting I from F. Hence, the superior firm should have a negative T value since F will be less than I.

GREI values were calculated for all U.S. man-made fiber producers. Table 11.3 reports those findings by fiber and form as well as overall for each of the nine leading firms. GREI depends upon capacity data by firm. Capacity data also is a good, independent measure of the size of a firm. An earlier table displayed the subjective ratings of the fiber producers by their clientele.

These three different overall evaluations can be compared and combined. Table 11.4 presents the results.

There are statistical techniques to test whether or not these measures really represent different characteristics. They do in the case of the U.S. man-made fiber industry through 1980.

Mathematical methods enhance competitor intelligence work. There are quantitative tools to quickly and reliably detect critical but subtle distinctions and relationships. These save time and effort by extracting information from data. Geometric techniques serve to clarify and dramatize presentations. Astute use of econometrics can impart major, long-lasting, and nearly indetectible advantages to competitor intelligence as well as operations.

UNUSUAL DATA SOURCES

Competitor intelligence relies heavily upon publicly available data. Well-stocked libraries, therefore, are an important resource. Some firms have such repositories. A highly qualified and experienced business research librarian is a treasure. Such individuals need not be in

TABLE 11.3. 1980 GREI RANKINGS FOR U.S. SYNTHETIC FIBER PRODUCERS (1 = BEST)

	Acrylics & Modacrylics	Cellulosics		Polyamides		Polyolefins		Polyester		Overall
		Yarn	Staple	Yarn	Staple	Other	Staple	Yarn	Staple	
Akzona		3	1	3	5			13	6	7
Allied				2	2			4		3
Avtex		4	4				1	8		4
Badische	4			5	6			7		9
Celanese		1	2	15	3			12	3	5
duPont	1			1	1	9		1	1	1
Eastman	2	2						2	2	2
Hoechst								5	5	6
Monsanto	5			6	4			6	4	8

Source: Systematic Forecasting, Inc.

TABLE 11.4. 1980 RATINGS OF U.S. SYNTHETIC FIBER PRODUCERS (1 = BEST)

	Overall	Capacity	GREI	Subjective
duPont	1	1	1	1
Celanese	2	2	5	2
Eastman	3	5	2	4
Allied	4	7	3	5
Avtex	5	4	4	7
Akzona	6	6	7	3
Monsanto	7	3	8	6
Hoechst	8	8	6	9
Badische	9	9	9	8

Source: Systematic Forecasting, Inc.

your employ. Top university libraries normally have superb researchers who are eager to help.

There are a number of commercial secondary research services. Most of them are in the New York City telephone directory. These organizations can perform on-going or episodic research via computerized data bases.

A few computerized data bases are particularly interesting. For instance, Economic Information Systems (EIS) of New York City has a data base on-line at Control Data's Service Bureau, of potentially great importance to competitor intelligence studies of manufacturers. EIS data was reworked and extensively analyzed industry-by-industry by the Federal Trade Commission. The results are available as a series of "Working Papers" from the FTC's Documents Office in Washington, D.C.

Doctoral and masters theses often contain significant information. There are directories of such documents. It is especially helpful to use the latest of these papers as a reference to other important material in the industry and firms of interest. Theses written by persons experienced in the industry or firms under study deserve particular attention.

Speeches and articles by competitors' employees can provide valuable insights. Care must be taken in reading such items. Superficiality is one problem. Puffery is a danger. Use of the medium to convey a signal is another. However, recently retired writers or speakers are recognized authorities with a known propensity to communicate their lore.

Another underexplored resource is experienced trade executives and observers. Union officials, financial analysts, executives at supplier and customer firms, trade association officers, analysts at various government agencies overseeing the industry, trade press reporters and editors, and educators training people for work in the industry, are sometimes particularly acute observers. Industry executives can and should be interviewed. These prospective fonts of wisdom about their competitors should not be ignored.

Any serious competitor intelligence effort should cover three more sources of information. Court cases involving competitors should be identified and analyzed. So should business-school cases; Harvard Business School publishes a cross-indexed directory of leading cases, available in any good business-school library. Perhaps the most neglected sources of information are the files and reporters or newspapers in the localities where your competitors operate.

CONCLUSION

Competitor intelligence is a multidisciplinary art. History and logic demonstrate that economics forms the core of competitor intelligence. Economics makes substantial contributions in its own right and is the only discipline offering a basis for integrating other bodies of knowledge in a coherent fashion.

Competitor intelligence deals with basic issues. What are the critical factors for success? Who are my competitors? How did, do, and might they compete? What are their individual and combined strengths and weaknesses? Adjustments in orientation and terminology make various branches of economics extremely helpful in resolving the basic issues.

Economics provides more than a central focus to and coordination of competitor intelligence. It offers detailed guidance in developing and carrying out lines of analysis. Six such approaches were discussed in some depth.

A number of quantitative tools and techniques for competitor intelligence work come from econometrics. True expertise is necessary to select, use, and interpret the results of such methods. Competitive pressures and the advent of inexpensive but powerful microcomputers and their software assures increasing reliance upon quantitative tools.

Economics covers a large body of literature. Some of it is particularly relevant to competitor intelligence, and most but not all of it is available commercially. Useful starting points in locating relevant literature include research libraries at leading graduate schools of business, trade press editors and trade association executives and economists, and government economists at agencies monitoring the industry of interest.

Those relatively unfamiliar with competitor intelligence for business typically recognize a need to impose and enforce clear boundaries with respect to the laws of the lands within which their firm operates. However, they usually err in attaining and maintaining the critical balance between information and action. Action is indeed crucial to business success. American managers seem almost paranoid in their fear of paralysis by analysis. Perfect intelligence information certainly would be wasted if unused, but action based on insufficient or incorrect intelligence is both far more common and far costlier. Successful intelligence efforts will somewhat restrict American managers' traditional freedom of action. An obvious but hopefully temporary political problem must be addressed at this point. Tact rather than concession often buys enough time for line management to recognize and accept the benefits of a better balance. Token competitor intelligence efforts often are completely wasteful, and misleading. They also can instill false confidence at first, which later turns into suspicion. Consequently, one must take considerable care when initially establishing a competitor intelligence effort.

12

Media: The Double-Edged Sword

WILLIAM MICHAELS

Mr. Michaels is manager of public relations and internal communications for Alexander & Alexander Services Inc., the world's second largest international insurance brokerage firm. He was formerly manager of news services for International Paper Company, and has worked for a number of business and technical magazines in the United States and Canada, and has taught in both countries. He has contributed articles to several publications, and coauthored a novel, *The Night They Stole Manhattan.* A graduate of Saint Michael's College in Winooski, Vermont, he holds a master's degree in Teaching English as a Second Language from the same institution, and a master's degree in journalism from The Pennsylvania State University.

An army of information-gatherers is constantly feeding material into the ever-voracious appetite of the world's media. Well-established in the United States, this army has secure beachheads in much of the industrial world—certainly in the industrialized countries of the Western Hemisphere, Europe, and the Far East. There are even outposts in the controlled economies of the third world and Eastern Europe.

Quite often, this information army is considered the adversary of business, not its ally. What makes it an adversary—something to guard against, something that at times means it is held both in fear and contempt—is exactly the same reason this army should be regarded as an ally; or as one publication puts it, as a capitalist tool. It is an impartial seeker of information and it wants to share whatever information it is able to obtain.

A journalist is schooled in the five W's: who, what, where, when, and why. To this has been added the one H, how. This is precisely what business wants and needs to know, and yet individual businesses are not always willing to publicly reveal the answers to these questions. Consequently, a dedicated journalist in order to answer these questions must often turn to other, more cooperative sources. Of course, not all journalists or publications have the same amount of dedication. So the degree to which answers are pursued and reported varies from reporter to reporter, and from publication to publication.

Historically, the press has always been interested in the workings of commerce. Early newspapers were founded to provide business with reliable information. In shipping, for instance, newspapers were a means of broadcasting the contents of the latest cargo arrived in port. They were also a way to announce sailings and to report ships lost at sea.

Trade wars provided one challenge to business, and real wars offered the chance of great profit or the risk of complete failure. So even during the birth of modern business—and even though conveyed slowly through primitive means—information was considered essential. It alerted people to opportunities and dangers, and peddling it could be profitable.

Over the years, the print-oriented press evolved into three forms that should be of interest to anyone in business concerned with collecting and analyzing information: (1) the general press, (2) the business press, and (3) the specialized or trade press. The mainstream of press development in the nineteenth century began to focus on other aspects of news, and less on business. For some businesses, the general press can still be a source of information. In some consumer businesses, local or regional advertising campaigns may be the first indication of a competitor's new product launch. A newspaper's life style or fashion sections, which are also aimed at consumers, may also provide a company with information not previously published about a competitor.

Some of the early nineteenth century business publications have survived until today, though with modifications. But while business became less of a topic of interest for the general press, some entrepreneurs saw the need for more specialized business publications. In the latter part of the nineteenth century, specialized trade publications were founded. Eventually a growing industry—for instance, steel, mining, construction, paper—might be able to support several such publications. They covered, and continue to cover, such diverse subjects as technological developments, new products available from suppliers, an industry's personalities, its expansions, and in more recent times, often its contractions. In other words, these publications cover the various events happening in an industry that are deemed newsworthy.

Specialized publications function as two-way sources of information. They offer suppliers to an industry a medium of advertising, while being a common depository of information for suppliers and everyone else in the industry or for anyone interested in it, such as security analysts, government officials charged with economic development, or investment bankers.

Although while some of these publications operate like most general-interest magazines and charge for subscriptions, many of them are sent free of charge to readers. The readers may receive them simply by the virtue of being in an industry. The publications try to maintain accurate subscription lists through various means. The publication essentially sells advertising space based on the number of readers it has, and trys to promote itself as "the" publication that reaches the right people, the ones who make buying decisions.

The best of the trade publications have staffs made up of journalists as well as people who have gained knowledge of industry by working in it. Magazines actively seek this type of person when an opening occurs, and the best will try in various ways to provide an industry's level of compensation.

Some of the trade magazines are published by technical or professional societies and associations. These are often journals of record, publishing papers delivered at technical meetings.

Another development has been the general business publication. In this category fall magazines and daily and weekly business newspapers. Often the reporters are business generalists; some, however, cover a small number of fields and gain a certain expertise that enables them to write substantive articles. These reporters establish reliable sources of information, attend an industry's meetings and conventions, and talk to security analysts who follow the business.

What information can each of these types of publications—business press, trade press, and general press—provide to people in business?

For rapid, basic information on business happenings as well as significant world events, the Dow Jones News Service (the Ticker) has no equal. It and the *Wall Street Journal,* along with Reuter's Wire Service, are used as the principal means of satisfying corporate disclosure requirements mandated by the Securities and Exchange Commission. Events that would have a material impact on a publicly held company must be disclosed to the public.

One of the wire's disadvantages—that it carries such a large volume of information that much is irrelevant to a particular industry—has been overcome by electronics and computers. Now through various computer time-sharing services and through different services offered by Dow Jones, it is possible to have only those stories of particular interest made available. In time-sharing, key words are used to search through a computer that has access to Dow Jones or other wire services such as United Press International. Wire services offer national, state, feature, and sports wires, for instance. Someone in the steel industry might want to see anything covering the industry, and might use steel as the key word. The computer will select any article with steel in it, saving tremendous amounts of time. Key words need to be carefully selected: someone in the paper industry using "paper" as the key word would get stories on the industry, but would also get stories on a multitude of subjects such as finance, newspapers, or diplomatic activity.

Other computer services can provide a tremendous amount of information. The computer makes looking for articles on various subjects an easy task, as long as the article has been put into the system. Except for some newspaper services, computer information services are best used for research where up-to-the-minute information is not required.

Wall Street Journal and Dow Jones Ticker reporters will invariably follow-up a press release to get answers to questions that are just as invariably *not* dealt with in the release. At times the reporters do succeed in getting further information, but they can strike out just as easily.

It is possible to get more than basic information from the media, however, if you are willing to wait a few days or weeks. A newsletter or trade magazine might (through other sources) find out more details about what is going on. In fact, a newsletter may even beat a company in making an announcement. This is especially true when two or more partners are involved in a deal.

In one case, for example, a company had decided to embark on a new type of financial arrangement. The investment bankers, however, were so proud of their part in this, and so eager for other companies to follow suit, that they revealed the essential details to a newsletter several days before the company was ready to release the information in fulfillment of its disclosure requirements. The newsletter came out on Monday, and the release came out on Tuesday. The newsletter carried much more information than either the release or the article printed in the *Wall Street Journal.*

Such jumping of the gun before a company is ready to talk about a development happens frequently. In one instance a business directory in a routine updating of its material was inadvertently given some details on a new production process that was being used experimentally at a company's facility. Another time, a trade publication was erroneously referred by a headquarters' secretary to an employee at a plant about to undergo some modernization work. The employee did not realize that a decision had been made at corporate headquarters not to discuss the project yet. The reporter got even more information than he had bargained on; some people like to talk. Furthermore, when later questioned by someone at the company, the reporter protected his source of information, enabling him to use that person at a later date.

Getting information from suppliers can happen any time. One trade publication was able to put together the details of a plant expansion from talking to a supplier, well over a year before all the details were formally announced. These included the capacity of a new machine, the introduction of new technology, the impact on the rest of the company (shutting down two older machines), and what would be the major characteristics of the improved product. Some two years after the article appeared, a major competitor was surprised by the announcement of the new product and forced to scurry about to meet the challenge.

The above examples are cases in which a knowledgeable reporter was able to obtain information not generally available. Reporters are human, however. Certainly the generalist confronted by specialized knowledge can make mistakes. Sometimes it is a simple thing, such as confusing capacity with production. The *New York Times*, which has interest in several newsprint mills, once reported Canadian newsprint production for one year as the industry's capacity. Since in that particular year the industry had operated at about 90 per cent of its capacity, production was overstated by one million tons. In another instance, a magazine that specialized in a parent company's operations printed several errors on a major subsidiary that operated in a different business segment; one of the errors indicated that the subsidiary had built a new manufacturing facility in Canada, when in fact the money had been spent in a modernization program. Although it might have been sloppiness in reporting or a misunderstanding of the information, it was nevertheless the type of error unlikely to be made by a journalist regularly covering the field.

Even some of the most respected publications in a particular field will sometimes hire freelance writers to do articles. Freelancers sometimes lack the specialized knowledge, and produce articles of dubious value. A lot of material passes through an editor's, hands and dedication and knowledge can get lost in the frenzy of publishing.

What all this means is that while the media can be a useful source of information, the information needs to be collected and analyzed on an organized basis. Reporters, publications, and the article's sources can all be classified as to reliability. Some publications are weakly staffed and provide little useful information. Even in these cases, however, once in a while a nugget of solid information can be found. Then it becomes a question of resources. Do you want to invest the time and money in a publication that will infrequently be of value?

Trade publications and national business publications are easy to get. Local media can also be useful, although the speed at which the material can be obtained is often slow. In most cases it is necessary to use a clipping service; by the time a newspaper is read, and the article clipped and mailed, weeks can pass. On the other hand, if you use one of the computer services a story of major significance might be carried by the state wire. In this manner it would be possible to have the story the same day the newspapers get it.

If speed is not essential, however, local papers often try to do feature articles on local businesses and the manufacturing facilities of national companies. Often because everyone treats the article as a local matter, more information may come out than if it were being handled at the corporate level. It is possible to get information on capital investment in a plant, switches in product lines, and new equipment installations from such articles. Details of industrial accidents such as fires or explosions will also be covered, often with the impact on production.

Although local journalists may not be particularly skilled in business reporting, they are usually closest to the local branch of the company. They also have knowledge of the public agencies that are likely to be current on what is going on in a community. Building and environmental permits, real estate deeds, and tax records are among the public documents that a local reporter has access to in pursuit of a story on business. In one instance, a small-town reporter got information on a large deal involving two national companies, neither of which was being specific about what was going on. The detailed story, written primarily from public documents, was printed in the small paper, and then was picked up on the state wire of one of the major services. Eventually the article ran in the major newspapers of the state. An industry trade publication that happened to have an office in the state read the story and printed a version in its weekly newsletter, which is read by security analysts, bankers, and competing companies.

The information discussed until now has shared one common denominator: it is printed (or displayed on a video screen), available to anyone who wants to find it. But sometimes solid information available to a reporter is left out of an article for various reasons. To protect a source, the reporter may generalize rather than specialize, or some elements of a story may be dropped altogether to maintain a good relationship with a source. Does that mean reporters will never discuss what they know? Sometimes. But other times, in order to cultivate another source—you—reporters will share information.

If someone wants to cultivate a relationship with a reporter in hopes of gaining information, a couple of steps need to be taken. First, explain the situation to the company's public relations department, which is charged with protecting information as well as distributing it. Even with coordination, and a careful explanation of the possible pratfalls, an employee having an independent relationship with the press runs the dangers of legal problems or company embarrassment. A press relationship is a two-way street. Information has to flow both ways. In the horse-trading, it is possible that a reporter will take information about another company, but that probably won't satisfy the reporter for any sustained time.

This discussion has concentrated on print because electronic journalism is usually a poor source of information. Television is looking for visual material, and thus far has not been eager to deal with statistics, numbers, or complex business issues. Obviously it has disadvantages. Radio is much the same. Since both are transitory in nature, it is difficult to know what has been on the air.

If something of interest is broadcast and you know of it, it is sometimes possible to obtain videotapes or transcripts. This is usually impossible, however, with local stations.

The key to using the media for information is organized collection and analysis. This will provide basic information, trends, and at times even specific technical information or secrets. But the media are only part of the overall program of collecting information. The media have weaknesses and strengths; trying to understand how they work, and who is working in them, will ensure that they supply the maximum amount of accurate and useful information.

13

Analyzing Competitive Technological Capabilities

ROBERT A. WALDE

Mr. Walde is the Corporate Technical Director for Allegheny International. Previously he was a Technical Consultant with the Gulf Research and Development Company, a subsidiary of the Gulf Oil Corporation, and President of Technology-Government Coordination. Prior to that he was General Manager of the Commercial Development and Marketing Division and Manager of Business Development for the Gulf Science and Technology Company.

After receiving a B.S. degree in Chemistry from Georgetown University in 1955, Mr. Walde was employed as a Research Chemist by Gulf Research and Development Company. During this period, he took graduate work at Carnegie Mellon University in Chemistry. In 1962, he joined Air Products and Chemical, Inc., as Manager of Chemical Research. He studied business administration at Lehigh University and subsequently became Coordinator of Market Development for Air Products' Chemical Division. In 1972, he joined American Bioculture, Inc., as Manager of Commercial Development, and returned to Gulf Oil Corporation in 1974.

Mr. Walde is Executive Director of the Commercial Development Association and has served as both Meeting and Program Chairman for recent Association meetings. He is also a member of the ACS, Metal Properties Council and Technology Transfer Society, is the holder of a number of U.S. and foreign patents, and has authorized several publications.

OVERVIEW

Technology is becoming an increasingly important factor in determining a company's competitive position. Technology is the primary determinant of product cost and performance, and the main source of new products for future growth. Technology can be acquired by a number of routes, including internal R&D, manufacturing and marketing experience, and external acquisition.

Information about competitors' technical activities can be obtained from sources such as annual reports, publications, patents, technical meetings, and business actions.

Staying competitive in the present business and using innovation for growth are keys to business success. A company can maintain its position by following the competition or, better, by leading the way and staying ahead. It is important to know your relative cost position with respect to the competition. In a slow-growth commodity market, a new entrant with a lower-cost plant or technology can push the highest-cost producer out of the business.

All technologies, products, and businesses have life cycles: they grow, peak, and decline. It is important to anticipate decline so that activities can be initiated to develop a replacement.

The learning-curve theory predicts cost declining with experience of production. It should be realized that sudden and sharp drops in competitive cost can occur when new technologies enter the environment. A good example is the impact of microelectronics on calculators.

The profitability of a business is influenced by the type of technology used and the commodity or specialty nature of the business. It is important to be properly positioned in the competitive environment in order to have acceptable profitability.

Every business has several key technologies associated with it. It is important to identify these, and focus technical effort on them to maintain a strong position relative to the competition. If the competition does a better job of focusing and using technical resources, then they will move ahead.

The best strategy for technical competitive analysis is to:

Understand your relative technical position.

Determine the key technologies for your business.

Conduct an ongoing technical effort to maintain superiority.

Monitor what the competition is doing, but don't follow them: they may be going in the wrong direction.

THE IMPORTANCE OF TECHNOLOGY TO A COMPANY'S COMPETITIVE POSITION

Technology is the basic determinant of manufacturing cost.

Technology is the basic determinant of product performance.

Technology is the source of new products.

Technology is becoming an increasingly important factor in establishing a company's worldwide competitive position, and is the basic determinant of a number of key business functions. Technology is the basic determinant of manufacturing costs. It governs the type of raw materials used to operate a process, and the quantity and quality of those materials.

The technology used determines the investment required for a particular manufacturing process. For example, if extremely high temperatures and pressures are required in a chemical or refining process, the investment will be substantially higher than for an alternate technology requiring less severe conditions.

The efficiency of a process is determined by the technology that is employed. The yield of product and the rate at which the product is produced are key elements of cost.

There are many examples of how new technologies have had significant impacts on these three cost factors. Technologies that enabled the use of refinery by-products such as propylene and ethylene to replace acetylene had a substantial impact on the cost of manufacturing intermediates for making textile fibers. Most recently, technology has had a significant impact on reducing the energy required to operate commercial processes, thereby reducing operating costs.

Technology is a key determinant of product performance. It determines the efficiency with which a product performs, or the amount required to perform a particular task. It also determines the effectiveness of a product or the degree to which it performs a desired task. By using technology to improve the efficiency and effectiveness of the products a company sells, higher prices can be obtained, thereby increasing revenue.

Technology is the primary source of the new products that a company must depend upon to facilitate future growth. Technological change can also result in the competition producing new products that enter the market and substitute for a company's existing products. Product substitution through technological evolution has had a major impact on many industries in the past few years. One of the most obvious examples has been the development of engineering plastics and their substitution for established materials such as glass, steel, and leather.

SOURCES OF TECHNOLOGY

Problem solving and idea generation.

Internal R&D organization.

Manufacturing experience.

Licensing or purchase.

Government-funded R&D.

R&D programs are only one source of technology for a business. It is important to access all sources in order to gain the greatest degree of diversification and to minimize the cost of acquiring technology.

Problem-solving and idea-generation sessions held with internal task groups can be a very effective method of developing new ideas for solving existing problems and developing new products. A company that uses techniques like this to stimulate creative and innovative thinking by its people will greatly enhance its competitive position.

Manufacturing experience is a major source of new technological ideas. Most of the ideas or technologies coming from this source relate to improvements in existing processes. It is very important to maintain a continuing effort to reduce manufacturing cost and improve quality control. The impact of Japanese use of technology to reduce the cost and increase the quality of automobiles on U.S. manufacturers has been quite obvious. U.S. auto companies are now reacting to this technological challenge and are introducing robotic systems and statistical quality control on the assembly lines.

A company's marketing organization can be a major source of new ideas for developing new products and improving on existing ones. An effective marketing organization will continually encourage its sales force to communicate with customers regarding their new needs and the kinds of new products that the competition is bringing to them. This can be a major source of information about what the competition is doing, as well as a guide to the kinds of new technologies on which a company should be focusing.

The licensing or purchase of technology is a source that can be very effective for quickly filling in gaps in the technologies needed to run a business. Many companies offer services to search for new technology, and offer a collection of technologies that others have given to them to offer for licensing. Many universities are now promoting the development and licensing of technology to gain additional revenues. University development departments can be a very valuable source of innovative new technologies.

The federal government spends billions of dollars each year on research. Much of this work is done at national laboratories and other federal laboratories run by the Departments of Defense, Agriculture, and Commerce. It is much easier now to communicate with government laboratories about the technologies they are developing, and to acquire information and gain licenses for using the technologies to develop new products and processes. It is now the policy of the government to encourage the use of government technology by industry. Most major labs have an industrial liaison office that will help to set up visits and meetings. This is a source of technology to some extent overlooked by industry.

SOURCES OF INFORMATION ABOUT COMPETITORS' TECHNICAL CAPABILITIES

Annual reports.

Technical publications.

Patents.

Recruiting and building activities.

Presentations at technical meetings.

Speeches by executives.

Corporate news magazines.

Trade magazines.

There are many sources that can be tapped to gain information about competitors' technical activities. A major source of information available once a year is a company's annual report. Most companies like to impress the investment community with things they are doing to develop future business, and will frequently give information about what they are doing on their research programs.

Most companies with major research activities produce technical publications. By keeping track of publications in areas of competitive interest, an indication can be obtained of the type of technical programs being conducted.

Patents represent another source of information about competitor activities. Unfortunately, this information is not available in the United States until the patent is issued, and this can sometimes take years. Patents are issued in some foreign countries very shortly after the application is filed. Belgium, for example, normally issues a patent about six months after filing. When competitive information is critical to a business situation, it is important to keep tract of foreign patents being issued in the area of interest.

When a company is planning on entering a new area of technology or engaging in a major technical move they will usually be recruiting new employees and building new laboratories. Maintaining contact with employment advertisement as well as building and construction plans can be another source of information about future activities.

Presentations at technical meetings constitute a more timely source of information than technical publications. The meetings also present an opportunity to ask questions and have conversations with people from other companies to gain more details about what they are doing. If having a better understanding of competitor technical activities is critical, it is important to attend all related meetings, and to have people properly prepared to ask the right questions and understand the kind of information sought.

The executives of most companies are asked from time to time to give speeches. Many of these speeches are given to members of the investment community whom they are attempting to impress. Reviewing business publications that report on these speeches can be a source of information about new directions that a company may be taking with its technical programs.

Most major corporations put out corporate magazines describing activities going on in the company. A lot of the space in these publications is filled with information about new developments the company is making in their business or technical activities. Copies of these magazines can be obtained by writing to the company or owning shares of their stock.

A good intelligence activity relies on collecting bits and pieces of information and then tying them together into a coherent pattern. If understanding competitive activities within a business segment is critical, it is important to maintain a planned effort to gain and analyze information. Usually one piece of information alone will not develop a picture, but a collection of pieces of information can produce an understanding of what direction the competition is taking to develop and use new technologies. Unfortunately, in spite of early warnings about competitive technological change, many companies and industries have ignored them until the impact was seen on their P&L statement.

HOW TO STAY TECHNICALLY COMPETITIVE IN BUSINESS

Follow what competitors are doing.
Maintain an aggressive and innovative technical effort.

Following what your competition is doing is important, but is not necessarily the most effective way of maintaining a competitive technical position. By only tracking what the competition is doing, a company will always be following in their footsteps. A more sensible approach is to maintain an aggressive and innovative technical effort so that the company leads the way rather than attempting to follow what others are doing. A key element of successful technical competition in business is to have an effective program over a broad base to acquire technology, and then to stimulate the innovative use of that technology to achieve business objectives.

There are two key phases of technological evolution. The first is the development of the technology. At this point the technology is only information derived from a creative process. The second and most important phase is the creative application of the technology to develop a new product or process, or to solve an existing operating problem. The creative application of technology to achieve an economic business objective is by far the most difficult phase. There is really no shortage of technology, but there has been a shortage of the creative application of technology. This has resulted in many U.S. businesses losing their competitive position in world markets.

RELATIVE COMPETITIVE COST POSITION

Understanding a company's relative cost position within an industry where several competitors all make the same product is very important. In this type of business, a key factor of competition is usually cost. Understanding a company's relative cost position within the cost hierarchy can be critical to long-range success. Figure 13.1 shows a representative plot depicting the way an industry might be divided with respect to cost among the various competitive companies. Total

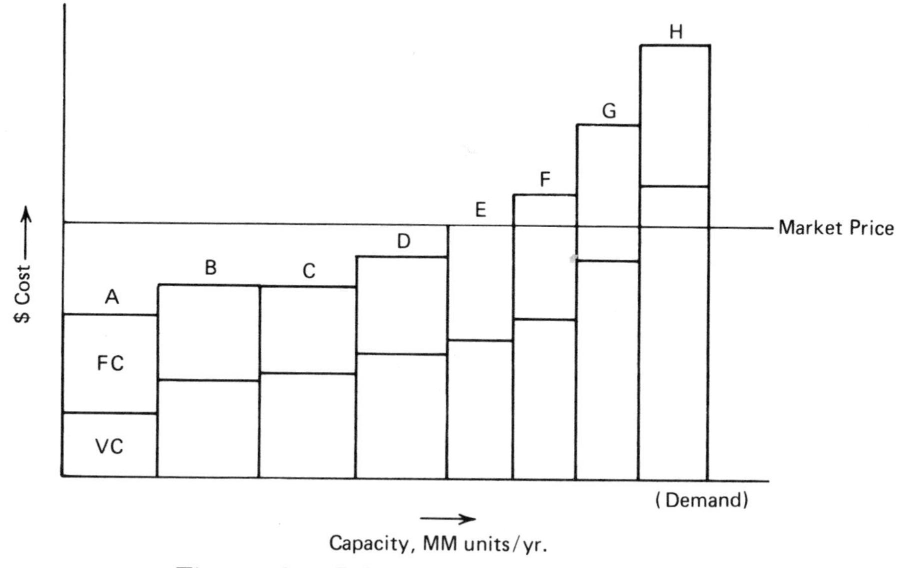

Figure 13.1 Relative competitive cost position

cost as a composite of fixed and variable costs is plotted against cumulative capacity for the industry, and companies A through H are ranked according to increasing cost. Figure 13.1 shows a typical industry distribution, where most of the competing companies produce the product at a total cost below the market clearing price and are making a profit. There will usually be a few companies who are producing at a total cost above the market clearing price, but will continue to operate because their revenues are still greater than the variable cost, and the operation will be making a net contribution to fixed costs.

When a new competitor enters the market, they usually do so on the basis of being the next low-cost producer. This is usually due to the fact that they have a new technology that gives them a definite cost advantage. In the past many companies would enter based upon having built a large plant, and thereby gain a competitive cost advantage through economy of scale. This type of new competitive entry is no longer as possible, since plant size in many cases has reached an upper limit and the markets are no longer growing fast enough to absorb large injections of new supply without serious price competitive consequences. Company A enters with a new technology and another company—for example, H—has not kept itself abreast of the technological evolution and is pushed out of the market by being displaced to a point where their total cost is greater than the market price. Preparing and understanding the distribution of competitive costs from a technological point of view can be critical to long-term success in a competitive commodity-type business.

THE LEARNING OR TECHNOLOGY CURVE

It has long been established that the cost of producing a product will decrease as more experience is gained through the production of additional units. This has been called the learning curve. The typical learning curve for a given technology can be shown as an evenly sloping curve over a period of time, showing that as the number of units produced increases, the production costs in constant dollars decreases. When we look at what happens in reality, it is discovered that the cost decline curve is not a smooth, continuous function, but over time will have periods of sharp cost decline coupled with periods of gradual cost decline. These sharp cost breaks are usually the result of a technological change having a major impact on the cost of producing a product to meet a particular need.

Figure 13.2 shows an example of a typical learning curve, and has two major discontinuities in the change in cost as a function of technological evolution. The short-run learning curves A and B are shown as straight lines, but will most likely have some slope as the point of diminishing returns is reached for reducing the cost of that particular technology. Figure 13.2 shows technology A decreasing in cost with time and the cost curve undergoing a sharp break when technology B is introduced, which then continues to show a slow decline in cost as the technology is improved upon through incremental learning. The sharp break in the cost curve is more representative of marginal cost rather than average cost due to the time lag it takes for investment in a new technology.

A good example of the impact of technological change on cost can be seen in the recent history of the electronics industry. The electron tube over the years experienced a number of improvements, which resulted in a reduction in its manufacturing cost, but this cost reduction was limited. The most significant change in electronic component cost occurred with the invention of the transistor; and subsequent further reductions occurred with the development of the microchip. This example demonstrates the significance of the concept of technological change as it relates to the learning curve.

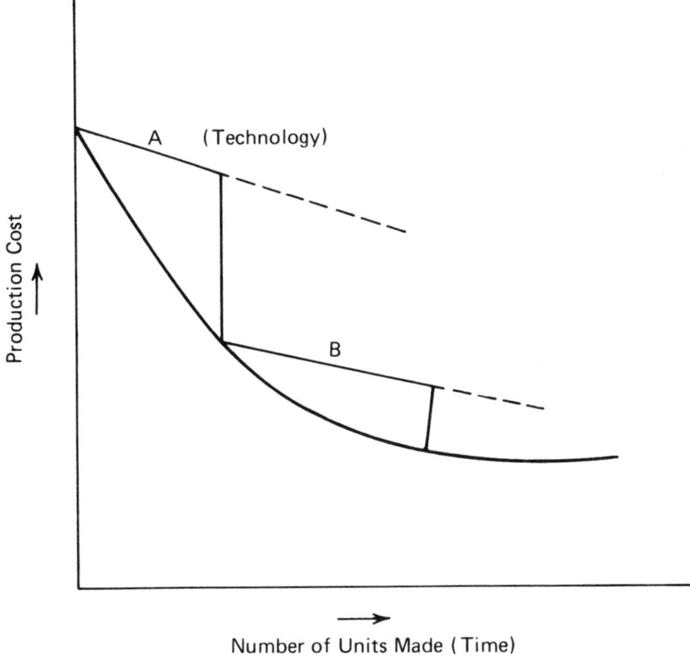

Figure 13.2 The learning curve

It is important for every company within an industry area to monitor technological change that might have a sudden impact on the cost structure of their industry. It is also important to know when to stop putting investment into old technologies and to look for a new technology for future investment. Anticipating these kinds of changes is probably the most critical aspect of competitor technological analysis.

BUSINESS/PRODUCT TECHNICAL CYCLE

It is well established that all technologies, products, and businesses go through life cycles. These life cycles can be illustrated graphically as shown in Figure 13.3 by plotting revenues as a function of time. In the early stage of a life cycle, when the new technology or product is being developed and introduced, revenue is flat. A growth period then takes place, and finally revenue growth begins to taper off, and even decrease.

Most businesses are composed of a group of products, each product being dependent upon a group of technologies.

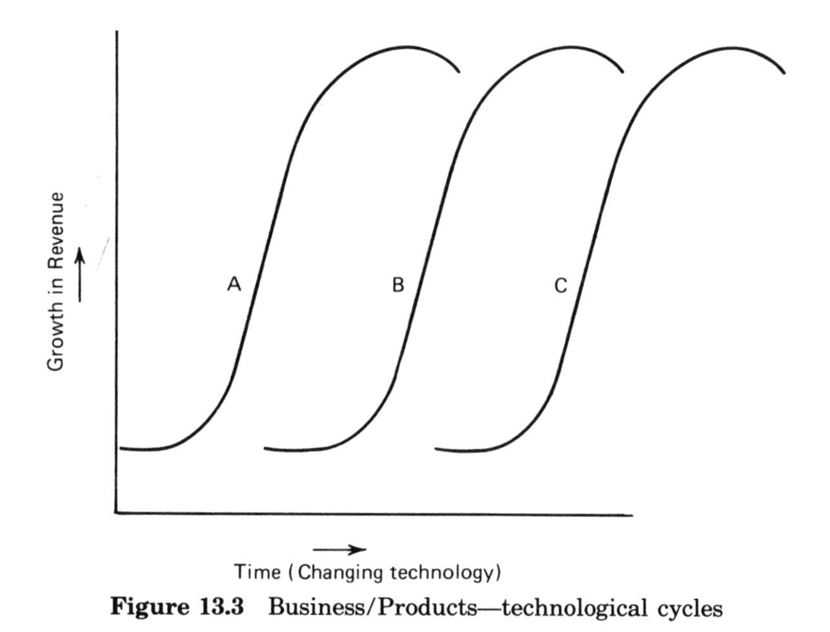

Figure 13.3 Business/Products—technological cycles

To maintain a competitive position in a business over a long period of time it is necessary to anticipate and have a series of technological evolutions. Each new technology comes into use and replaces the established one as it becomes outmoded.

It is difficult to predict when a particular technology is reaching the zenith of its life cycle. This is because in most cases when a technology reaches maturity the business revenues are also at a peak. It is hard to convince people that at this point in time a technology's life cycle is on the decline. Many companies will continue to invest new research dollars into attempts to improve existing technologies, and will do this well beyond the point of diminishing returns. One of the most difficult decisions that management must make is when to displace an old technology with a new one. In many cases this requires making new investments to displace existing investments.

The proper timing of these moves can be critical to the long-range success of a company. The decision to invest in a new technology relates to a great extent to what the competition is doing both within and outside of the business area. Many times the new technologies that make an existing technology obsolete can come from outside the established business area as well as within the business area.

The best strategy is to have the new technology in its early developmental stage and initial introduction for commercial use at the same point in time when the established technology is reaching the peak of its life cycle. For example, Figure 13.3 shows technology A reaching the peak of its life cycle while technology B is well on the way to being established as the next technical base for meeting that particular market need.

TECHNOLOGY AND PRODUCTION VOLUME VERSUS PROFITABILITY

In any given business area where there are a number of products and competitors there will be a distribution of profitability. The distribution of competitive profitability will usually depend on factors such as volume of the product produced, the type of technology being used, and the type of product being made. Figure 13.4 gives an example of a typical company/product/technology distribution versus profitability. From a competitive viewpoint it is important to try to position a

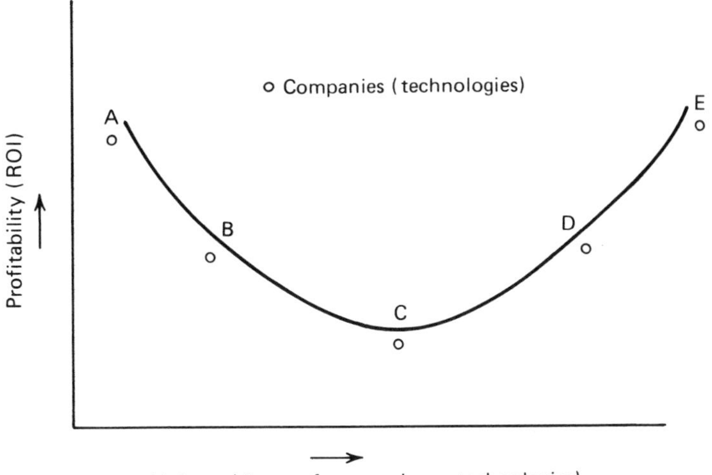

Figure 13.4 Production volume (technology) versus profitability

company's product or business to maximize return on investment. Figure 13.3 shows that product A has a high return on investment. This is most likely a technology that produces a product having a very high value added. It sells for a high price and is made in a relatively small volume. Product or technology E, on the other hand, is most likely a commodity-type product and holds the high profitability position due to the fact that it is being made using a highly efficient process or may also have high economy of scale within the industry. Product C represents a position on the curve that is to be avoided. In this case, a technology is most likely being employed that produces the product at a relatively small volume and at an uncompetitive cost. The technology being employed in this product most likely does not give it properties that merit anything other than a commodity price.

From a technologically competitive point of view it is necessary to understand how to position a product in a business with respect to price/performance and cost/volume relationships. For a commodity product it is wise to have the technical objective of being the low-cost producer, so as to be profitable at all anticipated price and demand levels. For a specialty product made in small volume it is desirable to position the product technically so that it offers superior performance in comparison to the competitive products, and thus can command a superior price or market share.

IDENTIFICATION OF KEY TECHNOLOGIES

Factors that could have future impact on business.

Problems that could impede future growth.

Ranking of factors and problems.

Technologies that could modify factors or solve problems.

Ranking of technologies for each problem and factor.

Conversion of technological objectives into R&D plans and actions.

Each business or product will have one or several key technologies. These are technologies that determine the competitive advantage one competitor has over another. One approach to obtaining a competitive advantage is to identify these key technologies as they presently exist and might exist in the future; and to focus the company's technical development effort on them.

A convenient method for identifying key technologies is as follows. All of the factors that could have a future impact on the business are identified and characterized. Every product or business will face certain kinds of problems that could impede its future growth; these are next identified and listed. After identifying each of the factors that might influence the future of the business and the problems that coud impede its future growth, these are each ranked with respect to their potential impact. Since many factors or problems may have been identified, it is convenient to select the top five, as they will have the greatest impact.

Each factor and problem will have several technologies that could influence them. The next step then is to identify the technologies that might impact the selected factors and problems. Each of these technologies, in turn, can be ranked with respect to how they would impact the selected problems and factors. The technologies can then be selected and ranked, and the highest-ranked ones converted into R&D objectives and actions.

The key technologies for a business are identified by selecting the highest-ranked technologies that will impact the highest-ranked problems and factors. These technologies can be considered as the strategic technologies for the business. These strategic technical objectives should be given a high priority for the R&D resources in the business plan for the product line or business. If a significant portion of the R&D budget is focused on developing these key strategic technologies and if they were properly selected, then a strong competitive position should be maintained.

The evaluation of key technologies is also useful for analyzing a competitive technical thrust. The question can be asked, why are they doing that? Try and identify the critical problem or factor the competition is focusing their R&D effort towards. This can serve to give a picture of how the future competitive situation may be developing.

DON'T FOLLOW—*TAKE ACTION*

Understand relative technical position versus competition.

Determine how technical change can impact existing business.

Conduct technical effort to maintain competitive advantage.

Monitor what competition is doing—but don't be led.

The most important action for developing a strong competitive technological position is to understand the relative position of a company's technology in a particular business versus that of the competition. This was demonstrated through the use of the relative costs distribution bar chart, the learning curves, and the product life cycle curves. Developing this kind of information is important to understanding where a particular business is technologically with respect to the competition. This type of information about the technological activities of competitors can be obtained by a variety of methods.

Determination of how technological change can impact a business is the next most important consideration. To the extent that a company understands how future technological change will impact its business, and takes steps to develop new technologies in a more timely way than the competition, they will gain a future competitive advantage.

The key to long-range technological success in a business is to maintain a strong and viable technology acquisition and utilization effort. This necessitates relying on all sources of technology, both internal and external, and having an aggressive effort to creatively apply these technologies to the existing and future businesses.

Stay the best in the products and business that are critical to your company's success, and maintain growth by innovation. Keep track of what the competition is doing—but *lead* the way, don't be led!

IV
Special Issues

14

Legal Implications of Competitor Intelligence

DAVID PARKER

Mr. Parker is a partner of the Manhattan law firm Olshan Grundman & Frome, specializing in corporate and securities law problems and litigation. His firm, which represents both public and privately held corporations, has been active in the mergers and acquisitions arena, having played a major role in several recent control contests.

Before joining his present firm in November 1981, Mr. Parker was with Skadden, Arps, Slate, Meagher & Flom where he was a member of the litigation department specializing in tender offers and proxy contests.

Mr. Parker was graduated from Brown University in 1969 with an A.B. in Applied Mathematics. He received his law degree from Yale University in 1973.

As businesspeople focus more closely upon the importance of assembling information about their competitors, and as the methods of obtaining that information become more sophisticated, the question inevitably arises "Is what I want to do legal?"

On the other side of the coin, as the effects of successful intelligence operations become more widely known, businesspeople must begin to ask what they can legally do to minimize their own exposure to operations of this type. These questions have become especially important in recent years as the stakes in the intelligence operations have risen and as the public has become increasingly aware of the extent to which such activities occur.

The "technology" of intelligence operations—like that of the object of the operations—is extremely fast-moving, with its limits set only by the limits of the creativity of the people designing them. It should be no wonder, therefore, that general rules of legality or illegality are hard to find. Generally speaking, there is no "fine line."

In the first place, it is likely that a planned intelligence program has not been previously tested legally. Therefore, within certain limits, a court or other determinative body called upon to evaluate the program will probably be writing on a clean slate. Moreover, as a general rule, the legal questions raised are questions of state law. As a result, rules of propriety may vary depending upon the state in which a given situation arises. Finally, the nature of the problems raised is usually very "fact-specific." Therefore, although guidance can be taken from earlier cases, it is unlikely that a given fact pattern will have a clear precedent that it can be said to follow.

THE GENERAL RULE

With the difficulties of making general statements on this subject firmly in mind, the following general rule is suggested: "If you do not want to see what you are doing reported in the front-page headlines of your local newspaper, do not do it." Needless to say, the analysis cannot stop at this point. What may be embarrassing may not necessarily be illegal. Nonetheless, this simple statement provides a surprisingly useful rule of thumb.

It is the harsh reality in this area (as with many legal issues) that cases are often decided with the benefit of 20/20 hindsight. Thus a decision that may seem quite innocent at the time it is made may be viewed later as part of a grand conspiracy. Similarly, a series of small decisions or actions, each one apparently inconsequential at the time, may later appear to be the elements of a carefully orchestrated scheme. When faced with such allegations, the people defending their actions may find it necessary as a practical matter to try to "prove a negative." That is, it may be necessary to attempt to refute the charge of conspiracy by trying to justify each of the small decisions or actions. Such a task is difficult at best—and often painful.

A related aspect of this problem is that the nature and extent of the intelligence operation may change over time. Its growth or expansion may be justifiable at any given point and, indeed, may not even have been the result of a conscious decision at the time. When attacked, however, it may be difficult to show that the whole program was not carefully conceived from the start.

Visualizing how the program would look in the local headlines therefore gives some indication of the way it would look when argued by a competitor's lawyer to a judge or a jury. (Perhaps just as important, it also enables a company to evaluate whether it wishes to risk such exposure. After all, even though publicity may have no direct legal effect upon a given situation, it may well make a company wonder why it ever got into the intelligence business in the first place.)

TWO ILLUSTRATIONS

A hypothetical example may help to illustrate this point. Suppose that a researcher for company A is out with friends at a local restaurant. At the next table, two company B researchers are having a drink and discussing their current project. Without intending to do so, the company A researcher overhears some information that will help him in his own work.

So far, the A researcher seems innocent enough (although the discretion of the B researchers is certainly subject to question). But suppose the A researcher now moves his chair so that he can hear better. Suppose his friends want to go to a movie and he decides to stay alone (or prevails upon them to stay) so that he can listen further. Say there are formulas being discussed, and he writes them down. Or what if he begins taking notes?

The plot thickens. Assume that the B researchers now discuss some information that—although it would not be useful to the A researcher himself—would surely help a co-worker at company A. Can he relay this information to his co-worker?

Now assume the A researcher decides to return the following night in the hope the B researchers will be there again. What if the A researcher had reported the incident to his supervisor, who "suggested" he return the following night? Or suppose that after a series of such events, the supervisor establishes a schedule of people to go to the restaurant to listen. Add to the scenario the ingredient that the eavesdroppers are directed to prepare memoranda of the information they overhear and to circulate them among their co-workers.

As should be readily apparent, there is a certain continuity between the two extremes of innocently overhearing a conversation and plotting to eavesdrop on indiscreet competitors. The movement from one to the other was accomplished by a series of small steps. By the end of the process, however, company B would surely want to allege that company A was engaged in a carefully orchestrated plan to steal trade secrets from company B. The A supervisor's protestations that he was only taking advantage of B researchers' indiscretion would seem weak indeed.

As another example, suppose that a researcher for company B interviews for a job with company A and inadvertently divulges useful information to the company A personnel manager. Suppose the company A personnel person passes this information on to the director of research. Now, having scored some points, the company A personnel director listens carefully to all applicants, hoping to obtain further useful information. Or what if company A decides to "hold the position open" for an extra period of time so that additional applicants can be debriefed? Perhaps it will invite a particular applicant back for further conversation, not because of any personnel-related need but rather in the hope of obtaining more information.

Now imagine that company A fills the job opening but in order to take advantage of the information flow, continues to advertise the position. What if, in addition, company A's research director gives the personnel office technical training and specific questions to ask? Suppose company A decides to have its own researchers conduct part of the interview (under the guise of evaluating the "applicant's" technical qualifications), or arranges for one of its research people to pose as the personnel director.

As with the first example, a series of relatively small steps can be seen to make a significant difference in the nature of an information-gathering program. By the end of the process, company B would have a persuasive argument that company A's activities were improper. It is important, therefore, that any program to gather competitive information be carefully structured so that it will have the best chance of standing the test of 20/20 hindsight. Legal advice should be sought at the earliest possible time to try to avoid problems before they arise. Attempts to conceive how a program will look if reported in the press will aid in this procedure (and at the very least help to protect the company from adverse publicity if the operation becomes public).

THREE SPECIAL PROBLEMS

At this point, three areas merit special mention. First, special care must be taken any time one company (even inadvertently) learns information about the prices charged by a competitor. Agreements to fix prices (which do require consensual action but need not be express agreements) are *per se* illegal under federal antitrust laws and can subject violators to extremely severe penalties, both civil and criminal. Although a discussion of the antitrust laws is beyond the scope of this chapter, suffice it to say that any intelligence operation that enables one company to learn the prices charged by its competitors must be treated very carefully, as it may at the very least expose that company to extremely serious allegations.

Similarly, the strictures imposed by the federal securities laws must be carefully observed. For example, if an intelligence operation reveals non-public information about a company of a "material" nature (such as its plan to introduce a new product, or its realization that its principal product is defective), then it could be unlawful to trade in the securities of that company while such information remains undisclosed. Clearly then, special care must be taken if there is any intention to trade in the securities of the subject of the inquiry, either for investment or to acquire control. Moreover, in the event a tender offer were made for the securities of the subject company, consideration would have to be given to the public disclosure not only of the information obtained but also of the method by which it was obtained.

Finally a legal problem is posed whenever a key employee leaves one company and joins another. Necessarily, information passes from one company to the other whenever such a transfer takes place. The attendant legal questions—almost always dependent upon the particular facts of the situation—pose a balance between the public interest in free competition and individual freedom on the one hand, and the right to protect one's business assets on the other. This balancing typically involves several factors relating to the nature of the information and the manner in which, and the reason for which, it was obtained.

The first question to be addressed should be whether the information sought to be protected is truly "confidential" or a "trade secret." An important consideration will be whether the information is already publicly available elsewhere in substantially the same form. In the usual case where it is not, the inquiry will then shift to whether the information is readily ascertainable but would have to be compiled. The difficult cases are those in which the information can be ascertained, but it would be much easier to utilize that already in the hands of (and compiled by) the subject company. In such cases, the key questions will be the amount of time, effort, and money invested by the subject company in accumulating the information.

A parallel inquiry will involve the steps taken by the subject company to protect the information. Was access to it limited? Was it kept in a secure location? Were employees advised of its confidential nature and instructed not to divulge it?

Although conceptually distinct, the question of the nature of the information will often be considered together with that of the manner in which and reason why it was obtained. As a general matter, courts are reluctant to enjoin a person from earning a living and favor free competition. However, if an employee secretly copied company documents, diverted business or opportunities, or misappropriated information for the purpose of competing with the former employer, then (as in cases of patent, copyright, or trademark infringement) appropriate remedies are available. Also, if there was an intent to injure the business of the former employer or an intent by the new employer to interfere with the former employer's contractual relationships, these motives may impact the determination. In such cases, courts may impose (at least temporary) restrictions on the scope of the employee's duties at the new company or on the new company's activities, as well as damages.

A PRACTICAL APPLICATION

As in many areas, when it comes to legal analysis of competitor intelligence, fact may be stranger than fiction. As will be seen, one court's laudable attempt to set forth general principles resulted in a highly quotable opinion that, sadly, is ultimately internally inconsistent and of little value in guiding prospective behavior.[1] The facts are as follows:

In 1969, duPont was in the midst of constructing a new methanol plant in Texas that made use of what duPont claimed was a highly secret but unpatented process. DuPont claimed that the process was the result of expensive, time-consuming research that the company had taken special precautions to safeguard and that gave duPont a competitive advantage over other producers. During the course of the construction, parts of the process (which would have eventually been enclosed within the plant) were exposed to view from the air.

Another party, presumably a competitor, hired photographers to take aerial pictures of the construction. Several pictures were taken and delivered to the presumed competitor. DuPont, having seen the airplane circling over its plant and fearing that the photographs would enable a skilled person to deduce its secret process, contacted the photographers and asked them to reveal the name of the party who had hired them. When the photographers refused—citing their client's desire to remain anonymous—duPont sued the photographers.[2]

Not surprisingly, one of the first things duPont did in the lawsuit was to demand as part of its pretrial discovery the identity of the photographers' client. The defendants again refused to make this disclosure and moved to dismiss the case. In essence, they said they had done nothing wrong: they had not trespassed, they had conducted their activities from public airspace, they had violated no government aviation standard, breached no confidential relationship, and engaged in no fraud or illegal conduct. DuPont responded with a motion to compel the disclosure of the identity of the defendant photographers' client.

The district court denied the defendants' motion to dismiss and granted duPont's to compel. This decision was appealed to the United States Court of Appeals for the Fifth Circuit, which affirmed in an extended opinion.[3]

Prior to this case, all Texas trade secret cases had involved some element of trespass, other illegal conduct, or breach of confidential relationship. In their appeal, therefore, the defendants asserted that since no such element was present in their case, their motion to dismiss should have been granted. The court of appeals, while tacitly acknowledging that none of these elements was present, disagreed with the defendants, stating "we do not think that the Texas courts would limit the trade secret protection exclusively to these elements."

Recognizing that "[t]his is a case of first impression, for the Texas courts have not faced this precise factual issue," the court of appeals held that a rule stated in the Restatement of Torts (a scholarly compendium of law adopted in whole or in part and then interpreted on a state-by-state basis in many states), which rule had been adopted by the Texas Supreme Court in an earlier case, was the correct one to apply. Included in that rule is a provision (not treated in the earlier case) stating that a person should be held liable if he or she discovered the secret by "improper means." The court thus shifted the definitional question from what is "illegal" to what is "improper." The balance of the court's opinion, then, was devoted to explaining and interpreting the meaning of the term "improper means."

Stating what it characterized as a "clear" rule, the court of appeals held as follows:

> One may use his competitor's secret process if he discovers the process by reverse engineering applied to the finished product; one may use a competitor's process if he discovers it by his own independent research; but one may not avoid these labors by taking the process from the discoverer without his permission at a time when he is taking *reasonable precautions to maintain its secrecy.* To obtain knowledge of a process without spending the time and money to discover it independently is *improper* unless the holder voluntarily discloses it or fails to take *reasonable precautions to ensure its secrecy.* [Most emphasis added.]

Despite the court's characterization, the stated rule is not "clear." Surely reverse engineering allows one—with the expenditure of a certain amount of time and money—to obtain a competitor's process without permission and at a time when reasonable precautions are being taken, while avoiding the presumably more extensive labors undertaken by the discoverer as well as without spending the presumably more extensive time and money necessary to discover the process independently. Yet the court followed a previous Texas case and acknowledged that reverse engineering was not "improper." How, then, did it distinguish aerial photography which did, after all, require the expenditure of some time and money to undertake?

Without explicitly saying so, the court once again changed the definition. Having gone from "illegal" to "improper," it shifted from "improper" to "unreasonable." It assumed that duPont's efforts to conceal its trade secret were reasonable and that those of the photographers' client to discover it were not.

It attempted to defend this assumption by quoting from the notes to the Restatement of Torts to the effect that: "A complete catalogue of improper means is not possible. In general they are means which fall below the generally accepted standards of commercial morality and reasonable conduct." Perhaps recognizing that this formulation gives little if any prospective guidance, the court added:

> In taking this position we realize that industrial espionage of the sort here perpetrated has become a popular sport in some segments of our industrial community. . . . Our tolerance of the espionage game must cease [however] when the protections required to prevent another's spying cost so much that the spirit of inventiveness is dampened. Commercial privacy must be protected from espionage which could not have been reasonably anticipated or prevented. . . . Perhaps ordinary fences and roofs must be built to shut out incursive eyes, but we need not require the discoverer of a trade secret to guard against the unanticipated, the undetectable, or the unpreventable methods of espionage now available.
>
> The market place must not deviate far from our mores. We should not require a person or corporation to take unreasonable precautions to prevent another from doing that which he ought not to do in the first place. Reasonable precautions against predatory eyes we may require, but an impenetrable fortress is an unreasonable requirement, and we are not disposed to burden industrial inventors with such a duty in order to protect the fruits of their efforts. "Improper" will always be a word of many nuances, determined by time, place, and circumstances. We therefore need not proclaim a catalogue of commercial improprieties. Clearly, however, one of its commandments does say "thou shall not appropriate a trade secret through deviousness under circumstances in which countervailing defenses are not reasonably available."

Although the court's attempt to define a general principle is laudable, it does little to provide guidance for the future. In the first place, it does not tell us what the outcome would be if the plant were complete rather than under construction, and parts of the process were still exposed from above. More to the point, it assumes without discussion that the steps duPont had taken to protect its secret were reasonable and that the overflight was not forseeable.

If the construction were taking place in the North during the winter, for example, one would expect that a temporary roof would have been constructed. Similarly, if the construction were near an airport or a tall building duPont might have been expected to have built a temporary shelter.

Moreover, it would seem that the analysis should have included a balancing or weighing of the relative value of the trade secret as against the cost of a temporary cover. If the secret were worth millions and the cost of a temporary roof or other cover rather small, then one could question the court's assumption that duPont's precautions were reasonable.

It should be noted that the court did state that to "require duPont to put a roof over the unfinished plant to guard its secret would impose an enormous expense to prevent nothing more than a school boy's trick." However the decision gives no detail regarding the size of that expense or the probability that a mere tarpaulin would have been sufficient. In any event, if a "school boy's trick" was all it took to obtain a valuable trade secret, it can be seriously questioned whether duPont could reasonably have failed to anticipate it and whether the steps it took to protect its secret were reasonable and adequate. It must be expected that duPont (and others) now do take pains to insure that sensitive construction is covered. Were the same case to be heard today, therefore, it is not at all clear that the result would be the same.

As the court itself noted, it was attempting to divine and apply contemporaneous corporate morality. Although the attempt was a good one, in the last analysis the result with respect to improper means was similar to the one that a United States Supreme Court Justice reached when discussing hard-core pornography: "I shall not today attempt further to define the kinds of material I understand to be embraced within that shorthand description; and perhaps I could never succeed in intelligibly doing so. But I know it when I see it. . . ."[4] This court tried to define improper activity, but in the end only "knew it when it saw it."

THE FREEDOM OF INFORMATION ACT

A final area of concern relates to information given to the government. This concern is especially important in regulated industries where the most sensitive information must be disclosed to government agencies. Much of this information then becomes publicly available under the Freedom of Information Act and local "sunshine laws." As a general rule, the areas in which the government agency may decline to make information available under these provisions (e.g., trade secrets, ongoing investigations) are relatively few. Moreoever, the agency may decide not to assert its right to decline, determining instead to make the information available. Of course, it may also simply err—inadvertently disclosing information by an "honest mistake."[5]

Sound practice would then suggest that information be provided to the government only on an "as-needed" basis. It may, for example, be possible to arrange for an agency to review certain filings and to return them for retention in the company's own files subject to their availability for further review. Similarly, it is often possible to arrange to receive notification before specified information is disseminated. Such arrangements will give the filing company an opportunity to take appropriate steps, including going to court, to attempt to prevent its dissemination.

Similar considerations must be made when determining whether to seek legal redress when one's own company has been the subject of an intelligence operation. In addition to the cost of litigation if, say, key employees leave to join a competitor and the difficulty of determining in advance whether the litigation will be successful, the problem of presenting the allegedly confidential information to the court without thereby making it public must be addressed.[6] In such circumstances elaborate, though cumbersome, procedures must be developed to be sure that the information in question will be protected not only while the case is in progress but also after it is over.

CONCLUSION

As should now be clear, the legal questions raised in the area of competitor analysis are many and varied with little in common other than their lack of susceptibility to easy answers. In this chapter, then, an effort has been made to illustrate not only the types of questions that arise but also the manner in which they do so. Generally, the most important matter to keep in mind when planning an intelligence operation is that in the event of a challenge, the situation will be viewed with perfect hindsight. It should therefore be structured with that thought in mind so as to place it in the best possible light.

On the other hand, when protecting one's own information, the preventive steps taken before the events have transpired may well determine the result of the actions taken afterward in the attempt to remedy (or at least to limit) the damage. In both cases, counsel should be involved in the process as early as possible, in the hope that problems can be avoided before they arise.

---

[1] The facts set forth here are based upon the case E. I. duPont deNemours & Co. v. Christopher, 431 F.2d 1012 (5th Cir.), reh. and reh. en banc denied (1970), cert. denied, 400 U.S. 1024, reh. denied 401 U.S. 967 (1971).

[2] Although the suit was brought in federal court, due to jurisdictional determinations unrelated to the facts of the case that court was required to apply the law of the state of Texas as it believed the Texas state courts would have decided.

[3] Normally federal appellate courts will hear appeals from only a final order—i.e., one that ends a case. The reasons why an interlocutory or interim appeal was heard here is not made clear in the opinion. Again, the appellate court was constrained to apply

Texas law. The effect of the affirmance of the court of appeals was merely to confirm that a cause of action had been stated and to remand to the district court for further proceedings. Presumably, one of the first items on duPont's agenda was to pursue its demand for the identity of the defendants' client. One may expect that this tactic alone may have resulted in sufficient pressure to force a favorable settlement.

[4] Jacobellis v. Ohio, 378 U.S. 184, 197 (1964) (Stewart, J., concurring).

[5] See, for example, "E.P.A. Mistake Gives Trade Secret to Rival," *New York Times*, September 19, 1982.

[6] Of course a reputation for aggressive pursuit of those believed to have misappropriated trade secrets may help to deter such occurrences. See, "I.B.M. Sues Competitor," *New York Times*, March 18, 1983; "Spinoff Suits Mount in Silicon Valley," *New York Times*, January 3, 1984; "Franklin and Apple Settle Suit," *New York Times*, January 5, 1984.

15

Competitor Analyses and Risk Assessment in a Foreign Environment

LEE F. WITTER

An independent risk analyst with over 20 years of intelligence experience in foreign cultures, Mr. Witter's assignments focus on competitor business situations in developing countries. After a long career in military intelligence, which included numerous overseas tours as a military attache, Colonel Witter served as the Chief of U.S. Government Current Intelligence in Southeast Asia. Before retiring from the Army in 1979, Mr. Witter was an assistant professor of International Relations at the United States Military Academy, West Point. In recent years Mr. Witter, who holds a Ph.D. in international affairs, has been on the corporate staff of a Fortune 100 company where he helped supervise the organization and development of an international risk assessment staff.

In his client work, Mr. Witter draws upon indigenous analysts to collect in-country information that he and his associates then develop into full country-risk analyses. They are capable of developing both indigenous and foreign competitor risk assessments in over 50 countries.

IMPORTANCE OF RISK ASSESSMENT

For many multinational companies, competitor analysis in a foreign environment is not only very difficult but is often crucial to company profits. Though it can be argued that themes in earlier chapters are relevant to competitor analysis in a foreign environment, a whole new dimension and approach must be considered.

Today multinational corporations face fierce competition abroad at a time when their power has diminished. This makes them particularly vulnerable to the actions and control of foreign competitors and countries. To minimize the negative aspects of this trend, the chief executive officers of these enterprises must increase their firms' understanding of the dynamic aspects of change occurring in foreign competitive arenas.

In spite of this critical need to better understand the character of business competition in foreign cultures, very few multinational corporations conduct a systematic and programmed risk assessment of countries where they have investments. Even fewer conduct competitor analyses of companies operating in that same foreign environment. Today many American industries are rapidly losing ground in both domestic and overseas markets to aggressive foreign competitors, and yet many American companies within these industries have been unable to respond to this new challenge. Very few strategic planning departments are designed to effectively sharpen the competitive edge of American corporations in American and European markets. These companies are even less prepared to meet the challenges in the third world.

Strategic planning, including competitive analysis and international risk assessment, should now more than ever be brought into the core management functions of multinational corporations. It should be used to identify attractive foreign markets, provide forewarning of destabilizing events, determine trends, and reinforce a firm's international competitive advantage. Rapidly changing world events and political dynamics, as well as the extent of the international operations of multinational corporations, require the continuous monitoring and evaluation of international political change, planning, and forecasting. Yet in too many multinational corporations an appreciation of the importance of foreign competitor analysis and risk assessment is lacking. For various reasons most firms have been unable to organize the rudiments of this function within the corporate headquarters.

COMPETITOR ANALYSIS

Competitor analysis in less developed, third world countries should be initially accomplished in a manner similar to the method used in the United States, Europe, and other OECD nations.[1] The manner should be similar in the sense that a systematic approach should be institutionalized which incorporates, as a minimum, the same variables analyzed in OECD nations. There all similarity ends. Business operations in non-OECD countries are distinctly different. In fact, it could be argued that competitor analysis is region-specific, country-specific, and product-specific. To insure that all factors are adequately considered, the same competitor intelligence questions asked in an OECD nation analysis should also be asked in third world nations, but the questions should be skewed in favor of the following variables.

Role of Personalities

One of the most important variables in understanding the competitor and the environment in which a company operates in a foreign country is the culture of that competitor and the role of key actors. This is particularly critical because personalities play a very significant role in third world nations. The behavior of the personalities and the third world companies are strongly affected by societal, religious, political, ethical, family, and complex associational values. For example, frequently the chief executive officer's personality, behavior, and values determine the total organizational culture and operational behavior of that company. Interestingly, this is one area that receives little or no attention in the United States. Foreknowledge of key individuals' expectations and strategies provides significant insight into the probable behavior, actions, and expectations of the competitor company. This is a basic but often overlooked factor that should be reevaluated on a systematic, ongoing basis.

In third world nations a second very important variable is the background of other key company people. They are often members of the extended family, a corporate group, tribal contacts, religious groups, a friend of the president, a clique, or even an extension of the government. Determining who the other key personalities are is not always an easy task. An evaluation of the publicly listed key officers, board of directors, or list of associates rarely discloses the power of influential secondary actors.

If the chief executive officer and his key organizational people are as important as they appear to be, the next question is how to obtain information on these individuals. If the individual being studied is a public figure and well known, that information is often available in public documents such as newspapers and periodicals. But obtaining biographic information on lesser-known figures in a foreign environment is more difficult.

There are, however, sources in most third world nations where sensitive information can be gleaned. A visit to the country might be required in order to conduct a discreet check into the individual's background and personality. The discreetness of such an investigation cannot be overemphasized, for if discovered it could lead to short-term failure and possibly long-term irrevocable retaliation.

A third important area, often ignored because it is not as important in the developed world, is to investigate and determine if there is a secret financial sponsor. In the Far East, for example, most countries have a "pariah minority" composed of wealthy Chinese or Indian residents. These silent partners are difficult to detect, yet are often the key variable that reveals how a competitor company will act in negotiations and sheds light on the competitor's capabilities, goals, patience, and dedication.

Organization

Of less significance are the history and background of the company. The initial search should identify the historical development, organizational changes, and announced strategy. This can be determined by examining an annual report or company briefs. Annual reports or company prospecti available in non-OECD countries are, however, printed more for the native audience, and as such they may have political or economic subtleties that can only be detected by the most sensitive analysis. This applies to public as well as private companies. Consequently, these company reports are often biased, "suspect" documents and should be treated accordingly. Areas where these reports are useful, however, is in developing sociometric diagrams, personal linkage graphs, and associational connections, which are important to understanding the actual, if unstated, strategies of these competitors. The annual reports usually list the directors and key executives as well as individuals in subsidiaries and associations. An analysis of this information serves as the initial framework for further research and should be expanded as new information is gleaned.

Many companies do not publish annual reports and, consequently, it is difficult to obtain answers to the above questions. A visit to the country might be required, and numerous personal sources must be queried. A reliable local agent or investigative agency is best for this task. Discretion is vital. A query of personal sources close to the personalities of the competitor company has a high probability of detection and is often counterproductive, to say the least.

There are some fairly reliable sources available in the third world countries to obtain much of this organizational data. Local banks often maintain dossiers on companies and personalities, and if properly approached are willing to share this information. The whole "approach" technique in itself requires thorough and detailed analysis to insure that the confidentiality of the request will be respected. Bankers are deeply involved with most enterprises, know many of the chief executive officers personally, and possess a wealth of information on the history of companies as well as their strategy. If handled properly, bankers can serve as a most valuable and reliable source. Remember that "quid pro quo" arrangements can often serve as the nucleus of a long-term intelligence exchange.

Two other areas that deserve attention are the organization of the company and its product lines. Organizational analysis discloses the center of power in the foreign firm and may contribute to a fuller understanding of the current strategy and future objectives of the company. In this analysis not only the present company structure should be analyzed, but the organizational changes that have occurred since the company's formation as well. Organizational analysis should also identify those divisions or sections of the company that deserve closer scrutiny. Subsidiaries may be more important than the parent. They are often the most significant profit centers, and thus earnings statements can often assist in identifying this locus of power. In this analysis the division or section that serves as the key policymaker emerges. This can be accomplished by following a decision from birth to completion, determining input, and deciding who was the most influential during certain stages of the process.

An effective competitor analysis strategy in a third world nation must go beyond the analysis of the competitor to include research into the marketing potential in the country. This research should be country-specific, product-specific, and area-specific. In risk assessments, the company should first determine the sales potential of its own product in that country. This requires that a historical analysis of foreign competitors' products be reviewed from a cultural as well as an economic perspective. Tracking indigenous products' sales by volume and value is often a useful way of depicting the relative strength of the competitor product and sheds light on the potential of a foreign product in a country.

Once the evolution of the target industry's major products has been analyzed, market and customer needs should be determined. Here it is very important to look at the precise stage of economic development in the country. Though countries do not follow a set path of development, they do follow a general cycle in the movement from a traditional or basically agricultural society to an industrial one. This is not a linear movement—not bipolar—but often a mix incorporating the dual nature of traditional and developed societies. Countries often follow a strategy for their development plans, and its analysis will add insight into the balance, identify the areas that will be receiving emphasis and attention, and underscore potential growth areas that will be receiving the greatest amount of economic emphasis, potential profits, and permanency. The development plans of a nation are useful tools in determining government goals and emphasis and the monetary commitment of the country. There is an optimum time to market one's product. An analysis of where a country is in its developmental cycle provides valuable information in determining not only if but when it will be worthwhile to market a product in a third world country.

If indigenous companies are making a profit, in all likelihood there is sales potential in that country. A look at the company's annual report might add some insight into the potential of your product. If the annual report is not available, then a thorough in-country market analysis will be necessary.

In determining the sales potential of a product in a third world country, there are other factors that affect the development of a marketing strategy. Heading the list of considerations is the culture of that country. A company must determine how the unique cultural aspects would affect the marketing and selling of the proposed product—a "cultural compatibility" analysis. A major concern is how religious beliefs and customs will influence customer receptivity and marketing campaigns. Other factors such as tribalism, ethnic concerns, family beliefs, education, and even the influence of foreign policy, can affect the sales potential of a non-indigenous product.

In some countries women are heavy users of powders and cosmetics, but because of cultural restrictions only certain types of products are acceptable. One of the reasons several Western cosmetic companies have not been successful in some third world countries is because their product has not conformed to acceptable religious requirements or cultural conventions. Even if an economic analysis concludes that there is large marketing potential for a product, unless product advertisement is in synchronization with and shows respect for the native culture, marketing will not be successful. Obviously, advertising should be developed in the vernacular and respect the culture, beliefs, and values of the people.

Another area that is often overlooked is the transfer of technology. There is a need to investigate the conditions likely to govern the transfer of technology from a parent corporation to an affiliate or joint venture. Before technology is transferred, a corporation should investigate the conditions under which the technological and managerial staffs will work in the third world nation. Methods to protect the sensitive information involved should be established. This information must be handled on a proprietary basis to assure its legal and physical protection. Such safeguards will minimize the risk that a competitor will obtain proprietary information or an independent affiliate will misuse it.

If a firm's marketing endeavors are successful in the third world nation, they will attract attention and might even encourage indigenous competition. If this occurs, a strategy must be mapped out to determine what relationships, if any, should be sought with the native competitors. This is particularly important if the competitor is public rather than private, because then opportunities are fewer and relationships far less flexible. The need to monitor the indigenous competitor field on an ongoing basis emphasizes the necessity of an intelligence section, separate from strategic planning, to provide spot intelligence based on the essential elements of information requested by regional and corporate management.

There is also a pressing need for a company doing business in a third world nation to establish a counterintelligence capability, to make it difficult if not impossible for a competitor company to obtain proprietary information about one's company. It should first be determined what information competitors would want to learn about one's company. Considerations should be given to establishing procedures for screening published documents, including annual reports as well as speeches or statements released by the company. A systematic regional audit program should be conducted to insure that all sensitive information is properly identified and protected.

It is obvious that competitor analysis in third world nations is not a simple process; it goes far beyond a normal competitor analysis conducted in most developed nations. The importance of individuals and their personalities are paramount and should be analyzed within the cultural context to determine behavioral constraints or filters. Such an analysis must be fairly precise, focusing on selective variables, and must be performed over a period of time.

THE NEED FOR RISK ASSESSMENTS

Assuming that the competitor analysis survey is favorable and the company elects to do business in a foreign country, the next questions that arise are:

What risk is there in entering the market?

Is it a tolerable risk?

Is it cost-effective to enter a country?

What are the vulnerabilities?

Risk assessment involves the appraisal of the economic, political, and social environment of a country to determine what the future trends will be and how they will affect a company's operation. But risk assessment is more than this. It should include an evaluation of a company's vulnerability in different political and economic conditions.

One common fallacy is that a pattern of revolutions, coup d'etats, and chronic political violence creates an economic environment too risky for investment. On the contrary, since revolutions and risks to a business are often asymmetrically related, a risk analyst should first ask how a company can continue to operate a profitable business in such a turbulent political environment and not simply restrict the analysis to probability measures of political stability. The hard truth is that many companies cannot be selective in choosing the country they would like to do business with. Companies that deal in natural resources, oil for example, have only a limited number of candidates available. In many countries where critical resources are located, the government appears unstable and the country may have a poor economic track record. But if the longevity of the company depends upon the continued availability of the resource, management may have no alternative but to operate in the high-risk country. Here, the likelihood of an unsettling event happening or a destabilizing scenario unfolding must first be determined. It is only through the analysis of how this will affect a company's operation (threat analysis and company vulnerabilities) that appropriate contingency actions can be developed.

The questions of how one can survive, as well as how one can maximize profits in that environment thus become the most fundamental intelligence concerns.

Foreign-competitor and country-risk analyses must focus on the total commercial environment encompassing core political, economic, and social factors that determine the parameters of business competition in third world nations. Hopefully, the risk assessment of each country captures the present and future business environment, and will assist overseas managers in their strategic efforts to protect existing investments and expand desirable markets. In short, risk assessments should help the corporation to adapt rapidly to changing regional conditions in a way that minimizes profit erosion.

Favorite strategies that have insured a firm's success in the third world over the past century must be reviewed continuously because of the challenges they are receiving from a more turbulent and informed world. For years, good relations between a chief executive officer and a head of state were considered the most reliable way to insure a firm's commercial success in a developing country. This is still important in some third world nations, but now more than ever companies must search for new marketing methods and commercial strategies to complement long-standing personal relationships as well as help cement these executive relationships. The relationship between other national corporations and third world nations has grown extremely complex, and third world nations are sharing information and becoming far more sophisticated in dealing with multinational companies.

A factor that has complicated the international economic scene is the proliferation of new third world actors since World War II and the widespread belief of their political elites that the rules of international commerce are biased in favor of the West, with the consequence that their countries can be kept dependent through the application of these rules. As the old international economic order is challenged, the "rules of the game" will be modified to accomodate some of these challenges. As third world nations become increasingly demanding in their efforts to maximize their economic benefits, minimize financing costs, and protect their natural resources, the relative bargaining power of multinational company managers is being eroded. This trend is particularly visible in the consultant area. In recent years many OECD-based consulting firms have begun to provide a valuable service to third world leaders by assisting them in negotiating with multinational companies and the Western world. Some also serve as business strategic planners in third world countries.

Recent events in Latin American and the Middle East have increased management interest in competitor risk assessments. Because of the rising incidence of political and economic instability in third world nations, which for the most part were unanticipated by multinational corporations, risk analysts have the attention of chief executive officers. Unfortunately, however, Lebanese, Iranian, and Central American revolutions have skewed the attention towards violence. Now too many companies only analyze the potential for violent change and tend to focus managements' attention on the risk of revolution or rebellion. This is a very small part of risk assessment that is often overemphasized because it assumes that political violence in a country is symmetrically related to the confiscation of multinational company property. There is no such symmetrical relationship. Multinational companies can operate profitably in countries where violence is possible, as well as in countries that appear to be very peaceful and stable. Risk assessments should tailor relationships between multinational companies and countries that would not only permit a company to survive during times of instability and crises but will also enhance commercial relationships. The company's policies and actions, no matter what happens in a country (a revolution, government overthrow, or mass demonstrations), can be compatible, insuring that resources, investments, and people will continue to be secure.

In the strategic planning sections of most corporations, very few individuals understand the dynamics of change, much less how to analyze what occurs in the third world. The specter of nationalization, revolution, and acquisition of company holdings haunts many companies, yet very few firms develop a systematic way of analyzing these threats or try to develop contingency strategies that will enable their management to operate in such an environment.

In the past, many companies assessed risk in a country by focusing on analysis of economic information such as economic growth, ability to pay, balance of payment, potential profitable market, or cost-benefit analysis. Such analyses are biased towards the economic sector and place an inordinate reliance upon economic statistics. They often ignore the more fundamental political and social factors relating to stability. Corporate risk analysts must go beyond the analysis of economics and must integrate into their business research an ability to analyze the political and social change that occurs. This requires an ability to understand the dynamics of political change, anticipate its occurrence, strength, and direction, as well as the development of effective response strategies that will enable their firm to cope with rather than run from this change.

CATEGORIES OF RISK

There are numerous categories of risk assessment, and each should be analyzed systematically to insure that the whole environment is described. Political risk includes the analysis of traditional government succession as well as abrupt change by either violent or peaceful means. Risk analysts must be capable of detecting potential civil disorders, labor disruptions, rebellion, revolution, and the possibility of marshal law. A vital concern for multinational corporations should be the ability to detect a movement towards indigenization. If indigenization is anticipated, there are numerous ways a company can cushion that movement as well as assist the country in developing acceptable procedures for placing indigenous people in management positions.

An area that is often overlooked is the foreign policy of the host country. Foreign relationships may affect the operation of a multinational company. This is particularly true if the country is a client state or a satellite of a superpower or a block of nations. For example, if a country has a close economic/military relationship with the Soviet Union, it will affect not only the vulnerability of the country but also the manner in which business can be conducted.

Economic risks that should be analyzed go beyond the balance of payment, trade restrictions, and the domestic financial situation. They should also include an analysis of the structural cost of inflation. Inflation in third world nations fluctuates greatly, often in three-digit figures per annum, and this can seriously distort the meaning and measure of earnings in these countries. Additionally, the economic policies of the government not only affect the pattern of profits but also the long-term return companies can reasonably expect. Analysis should encompass changing trends in cost of materials, as well as the probability of new price controls. Other factors to be considered in economic risks are the dangers of currency inconvertibility, devaluation, and the probability of a radical shift in a third world country's balance-of-payments status.

A multinational operation must also be capable of detecting in advance the potential seizure of its assets. Seizure can be accomplished through nationalization or expropriation or in a gradual manner. Creeping expropriation is difficult to detect unless the company has a systematic way of analyzing this specific risk. Assets can also be jeopardized by confiscation or by the mere calling of guarantees by the government. Other factors that affect the security of a firm's assets are laws that may apply not only to financial arrangements but to the internal operations of the company, such as its relationship with labor and trade unions.

One common method used by third world nations in the seizure of assets is through forced joint ventures. Some countries require that all forms of national corporations operate in the country via the joint venture. Though there are certain advantages to a joint venture, it is easier for a country to disguise confiscation by a creeping percentage of ownership as well as changing the rules of the game as the joint venture progresses.

There are numerous other techniques used and mastered by third world nations that can interfere with the contractual performance and ultimately the loss of the company's assets. Some of these techniques have been the requirement of an acceptable contractor, contract expiration, export license revocation, or export and import restrictions. It is very important if a letter of credit has been established with a local or area bank that specific rules be established governing when and by whom this credit can be drawn. It is important to identify which bank has established this letter of credit, and if they have any ties or connections with government officials. It often happens that when a company wants to draw on a letter of credit because of a situation in a country, the regional bank that provided this credit declines to issue funds for fear of offending key political officals.

One of the most important factors that must be analyzed in developing risk assessments in third world countries is the value system and anticipated behavior of the nation's political elite. Third world nations, which are dominated by fewer people with a more extended power base, often have leaders who have an inordinate amount of personal influence, and thus their personalities in many cases represent more closely the personalities of the nation they rule.

If nations have personalities and mentalities and their behavior can be anticipated, how then is one able to identify these? The most obvious way to determine this would be to conduct attitude surveys, gallop polls, and perception analyses. Governments will not, however, permit such surveys to be conducted in a country because of the sensitive information obtained by such a process. How then does a risk analyst conduct research in order to accurately describe the culture, mentality, and behavioral response to threats that could emerge from within, and the ability of the system to manage these crises?

It becomes apparent that the number of variables the risk analyst would be dealing with would be huge, but if these could be incorporated in an interactive computer program this would greatly enhance the capability of analysis. However, the number of such programs in existence are very few, and their accuracy and predictability suspect. Assuming that most risk analysts do not have an appropriate computer program available, the following list highlights critical sociopolitical concerns that should be tracked and evaluated:

- Pillars of stability analysis
  - Minor position of economic analysis
  - Political factors
  - Power linkages
  - Institutionalization
  - Informal and formal relationships
  - Societal structure
  - Cultural filters
  - Tribal relationships
  - Patron-client clusters
  - Role of village
  - Languages
  - Mentality—the way people think
  - Group formations and associations
  - Millenarianism
  - Military
  - Ethnicity
- Developmental model—social, political, economical
- Systems's maintenance
- Environment for emerging competitor
- Concentric circles of decision making
- Historical implications
- Basis and perceptions of legitimacy
  - Traditional
  - Charismatic

Legal rational
Plebiscitary
Land tenure relationships
Expectations
Societal safety valves

Analytical Focus

Obviously, if one is to make an attempt to analyze the entire culture of a nation and determine what holds it together, the basis of legitimacy, and stability during crisis management, the analysis must go far beyond the normal comparative political risk analysis that some companies perform. Using indices such as terrorism statistics erroneously assumes that trends will continue and that the number of incidences in the past provides the basis for future predictions, without being influenced by societal forces. For example, many analysts assume that if the trend of terrorism has been increasing, terrorism will continue to rise, without looking at the government capabilities and measures. If, on the other hand, one is able to determine who the terrorist is and what his motivations are, describe the culture and environment in which he operates, and investigate the cause or source of his actions, one has a better appreciation of terrorist expectations and possible future actions.

An advantage of using the risk assessment theories and methods described here is that one can determine the stability of a government over the short and long term and also define the society of the country. This develops insights on how to negotiate with indigenous people, anticipate desires and expectations of local businesspeople, and glean from these cultural studies movement towards unionization, indigenization, and economic restraints placed by the government. Analyzing these variables will educate managers in regional affiliates to monitor movement and change within a society and to be able to anticipate crises. The next step would be to analyze government capabilities in handling crises and determine what risks and vulnerabilities the affiliate may face. Local management should also anticipate the different types of crises that could appear and take measures in advance to minimize or negate the impact. Obviously, the goal is to develop strategies to avoid, minimize, and even capitalize on the potential risk.

Risk assessment is not a general description of the stability of the country and potential crisis, but it involves a detailed look at each of the countries. This should be country-specific, company-specific, project-specific, area-specific, and even individual-specific. The more specific one can be in the analysis of stability and particular threats, the more precise the conclusion will be and the more reliable its predictability.

Information Sources

Not only is it paramount that the right questions be analyzed in risk assessment, but the assessment is only as good as the information obtained. The cross-cultural and interdisciplinary assessment method described here enables the risk analyst to tap into numerous existing information sources. Unfortunately, most of the existing material on third world development was written in the West. The Overseas Advisory Council and the World Bank do publish country and topic reports that provide valuable information. Other general reports are the *Financial Times,* country surveys, the numerous U.S. Department of Commerce reports related to foreign economic trends and their implications for the United States, as well as Department of Commerce marketing publications. Of general use are the Department of State Background Notes, *Gist,* and the Department of State country-study reports. Other institutions that provide country assessments are Barclays, Dun & Bradstreet, Price Waterhouse, and bank assessments. The American University area-study books are useful for factual information on history and economics, including important dates and events. Publications such as the *Far Eastern Economic Review, African Digest,* and the *Economist* provide excellent up-to-date information and sometimes analysis of countries concerned.

In addition to these sources of general information, there are numerous other sources available to businesses. The U.S. Department of State, particularly the Office of Security, which serves as the liaison between businesses and the U.S. State Department, can often be a reliable source. Numerous desk officers in area study groups in the Department of State, INR, and in the Central Intelligence Agency will provide sanitized information to businesses. A department often overlooked as a source of information is the U.S. Treasury Department, which has numerous country experts who conduct analyses. Non-public sources include the Export-Import Bank, OPEC, the Royal Bank, international banks, and numerous private organizations with a regional focus, such as the Asian Center, where experts as well as information are available.

Another source of information is returning employees from foreign affiliates and even other non-competitor companies. Overseas managers should be queried systematically by questionnaire, and returning workers and managers should be debriefed. Companies should also determine what other non-competitor companies are in the country, and efforts should be maintained to set up a joint intelligence committee to share general and specific information.

Organizational Approaches

Every corporation should have available, either in-house or on a consultancy basis, a systematic means of conducting an analysis of political, economic, and social risks in foreign countries where they are doing business. In firms with extensive overseas investments it may be advisable to formalize the risk analysis function within the corporation. Risk analysts should have an advisory responsibility with direct access to key line managers. Often when a corporation has organized such a staff there is a need to advertise its existence and function to insure not only that home-office planners know of this important resource, but overseas managers of the affiliates as well. An economical way to operate a risk assessment group is to have the in-house analysts function as internal country-risk consultants and charge the operating divisions and foreign affiliates for service on an as-needed basis.

It is often advantageous to institutionalize a troubleshooting committee on which the risk analyst would sit as a member. On this committee should also be managers, marketing people, financial investment people, physical security experts, and economists. The committee should have a charter to conduct international risk assessment worldwide, and its chairman should be a line officer with direct access to the chief executive officer.

Risk analysts cannot operate in a vacuum; they must know the company's business in order to advise on future company decisions, and they must be thoroughly aware of corporate, divisional, and regional strategic plans. By institutionalizing a systematic risk assessment section, a company can learn about the risk in a country and also how to operate in a country of high risk while minimizing the company's vulnerabilities. This is particularly important for firms in which key resources come from potentially high-risk countries.

All country assessments must be current and widely disseminated if they are to be of maximum value to operating management. Planned appraisals should be systematically updated and then reviewed by key managers. These country assessments should at least include an evaluation of the current stability of key countries and a forecast of their probable economic, social, and political trends, particularly as they relate to internal stability and the position of foreign businesses operating within those countries. With this "country intelligence" in hand, the company's managers will be better able to anticipate change in the foreign environments in which their firm operates and thus plan for it, rather than simply react to it.

---

[1]Organization for Economic Cooperation and Development (comprises the non-Communist industrialized nations, essentially the United States, Japan, and Western Europe).

16

How to Hire a Corporate Intelligence Firm

*LEONARD M. FULD

Leonard Fuld is founder and managing director of Information Data Search, a Cambridge-based research company specializing in gathering competitor information.

With almost a decade of corporate research experience, he has designed and created a variety of intelligence tools, among them the DECS Matrix described in this chapter. In addition to the reports he has published in the intelligence field, he is also editor of a quarterly newsletter, "Intelligence Update." Mr. Fuld is a graduate of Yeshiva University and Boston University.

Intelligence has become the 1980s watchword for corporate planners and marketing executives. And like most popularly misused words, "intelligence" can conjure up a wide range of images in the reader's mind. The term has been used to describe every activity from undercover corporate espionage to above-ground, ordinary library research.

In the past five to ten years, services have sprung up to provide highly specialized business intelligence to the corporate community. These corporate intelligence firms (CIFs), whose techniques fall somewhere between detective sleuthing and traditional academic research, fill a very special need for the corporate community: they are able to provide detailed profiles on the competition.

Briefly described, a CIF is a business research group devoted to examining a competitor's detailed inner workings and activities. It applies well-defined, legal research methods to uncover a corporation's closely held plans and operations.

What are some of the methods employed? Most are common-sense approaches to a difficult problem. What makes them unique to intelligence gathering is their application. In order to find out, for example, a certain manufacturing plant's production, a field staffer might examine the number of truck or train shipments leaving the plant. Or he or she may go back to the company's box supplier to track down the number of units packed and shipped.

Assignments tackled by a CIF would confound most researchers who are used to standard survey and library research methods. Instead, a CIF might employ tools as simple as a city directory, or as unusual as an aerial photograph, to reveal a competitor's activities.

Our firm recently had a case whose objective was to estimate the total production and start-up plans of a small biochemical plant. The plant, we were told by the client, was built to manufacture a new, highly perishable product for research laboratories.

The obstacles this case presented us with were many. For starters, where was this plant located? Apparently it had not yet opened for production. How many did it employ? What would its capacity be? To find out, we had to determine the machinery it used and the amount of floor space it was using. Once known, the client needed to discover the plant's projected sales territory and target market.

After locating the plant, Information Data Search designed a strategy involving the DECS Matrix (to be discussed later in this chapter), and then undertook the following steps:

1. Sent a field staffer to the plant site to determine the plant's size and activity.

2. Contacted the architect—since the plant was recently built, this person would be aware of what the facilities were designed for.
3. Contacted the town assessor's office to gather more information on the plant's use and number of employees.
4. Based on the product's most common end uses, polled regional laboratories to see if they had been contacted and under what guise the company approached them.

The original literature search produced no information, nor did a few blind telephone calls uncover anything new. That is because the intelligence needed by the client was too recent and too specific to be included in a trade magazine. Also, because of the plant's regional purpose, no one outside the start-up's parent company would likely have heard about it.

The project was successful and met the deadline. At its completion, the investigation did turn up details on the plant's capacity, its sales and marketing strategy, and current production information. The client had his answer—collected through some highly unorthodox research methods and strategies.

The lesson to be learned from this case is that standard market research techniques are too general and often ineffective when looking for competitor intelligence. Successful competitor information requires specialized techniques and services.

HOW TO IDENTIFY AN INTELLIGENCE RESEARCH FIRM

"Intelligence" does not yet have an official heading in the Yellow Pages. Service companies that perform business research as part of their work—management consultants and market researchers, among them—fall under many categories. Yet only a few currently devote their entire energies and specialties to gathering highly detailed data on corporations.

The CIF, as opposed to a management consulting or market research firm, is geared to quick response and short-term projects, which in some cases last no more than a day or two.

Another factor that distinguishes a CIF from other research services is its concentration on supplying the right details rather than offering decisions. During the course of an ordinary research project, the CIF will deliver considerable detail—not necessarily depth—on the target company. Unlike management consultants, it will not advise the client, based on the information supplied, whether to divest or acquire the target. The CIF's job is simply to impart the intelligence gathered, analyzing the quality of the data, but not necessarily instructing the client what to do with conclusions it drew about the target's operations.

Of the thousands of marketing research firms and 3,500 or so management consultants in the United States, most offer some kind of business research. Yet only a fraction of less than one percent actually provide clients with a comprehensive intelligence research package.

Market research firms, for example, generally look at the big picture. Only incidentally will they gather details on a particular corporation. They are well-versed in gauging an audience, conducting consumer surveys, and positioning a product.

Management consultants fall into a similar slot, examining for the client how that client fits into the marketplace. Whether the problem confronting the consulting firm is one of divestiture, acquisition, or corporate restructuring, the firm's mandate is to improve the client's corporate health and well-being, not to exclusively research the competition.

Because these firms concentrate on the client's activities rather than on the competition's, they have not developed the intelligence-gathering tools to microscopically examine a competing company.

On the darker flip-side of the intelligence coin are the hired guns employed by companies to infiltrate the corridors of Washington or invade a competitor's corporate headquarters. These consultants' activities may border on the unethical if not the illegal side of intelligence-gathering. These are not CIFs. They are investigators who will get the bits and pieces of data for the client, not the whole research pie. Their ability to gather the requested information is only as good as the contacts they have in their hip pockets.

An article that appeared in Barron's (March 19, 1979) provides a good overview of this gray area of intelligence-gathering:

> Directly or indirectly, corporations deploy hundreds (thousands, by some estimates) of agents with widely divergent backgrounds and contrasting methods of operation. Here will be a Ph.D. preparing a scholarly analysis of long-range policy trends, based on private talks with government specialists. There will be a young free-lance lawyer with a phone-answering machine for an office, hustling to make it, not so much as a lawyer but as a Washington operator. Here a former newspaper reporter worming advance information or an unreleased document out of a carefully cultivated source—but for a private client now, not the reading public. And, of course, the high-prestige types—large law firms, well-

established information-gathering companies and the official Washington representatives (often bearing a vice president's title) of the nation's major corporations.

In short, many different types of companies and individuals research the competition—even if only incidentally, although most do not have all the necessary skills to provide a detailed competitor profile. Table 16.1 describes the various information service groups and what they can offer the company seeking competitor intelligence.

WHAT FEATURES SHOULD A CIF HAVE?

There are no hard and fast features or characteristics that describe the ideal CIF. Certain firms may have the expertise that would put them head and shoulders above another research firm, although they may lack some of the usually desired features.

Still, there are common features that a client should keep in mind when shopping for a CIF to meet its needs. Understand that the list provided below is made up of general statements. All of them may not apply to successfully complete your project.

TABLE 16.1 INFORMATION SERVICE GROUPS

Service Group	Primary Service	Competitor Information Incidentally Supplied
Advertising Agencies	Promoting client's products	Competitor's products
	Surveys	How competition markets products
	Researching market in preparation for advertising campaign	Competitor's advertising
		News clippings

Intelligence Weakness: Service designed to react to changes. Often does not offer research beyond depth of information published in trade press.

Research-oriented towards the entire market, not to one or two companies. Larger advertising agencies, however, may offer a CIF service in some form.

TABLE 16.1 *(Continued)*

Service Group	Primary Service	Competitor Information Incidentally Supplied
Business Schools	Teaching and research in business	School library often a wellspring of valuable competitor data
	Private consulting on part of professors	Professors contracted to research and analyze competition
	Publishing research studies on business environment	
		Off-the-shelf analyses of competition available
Intelligence Weakness: Professors hired have limited time and resources; must rely on client's backshop operation. School library may not have complete collections or current information.		
Commercial Credit Agencies	Supplying financial reports on private and publicly held corporations	Competitor's financial and credit status
	Reporting on management	
Intelligence Weakness: Financial information often estimated. Credit studies concentrate on outstanding debts, not on market or strategic information. Management profile often limited to brief biographical sketches. Credit reports frequently have little competitor data on privately held corporations and divisions of publicly held companies.		
Competitor Intelligence Firms (CIFs)	Supplying detailed intelligence on competition, often on short notice.	
Intelligence Weakness: Intelligence gathering is its sole purpose. Quality of reporting only limited by supply of field staff and depth of analysis.		

(Continued)

TABLE 16.1 *(Continued)*

Service Group	Primary Service	Competitor Information Incidentally Supplied
Data Base Suppliers	Supplying indexed data through computer time sharing Compiling data already collected by a third party Applying computer modeling to collected data for purposes of forecasting or analysis	Offer any data on competitors that has appeared in a news source
Intelligence Weakness: Limited by secondary sources used to compile data base. Often out of date. More useful for historical analysis on competition than on current or future activities. Lacks depth. Does not collect information reporting on divisional or product level.		
Government Agencies	Maintaining records on national and local activities (financial, social, and educational) Demanding reports from various groups and individuals	Regular reports on corporations, organizations, and individuals SEC filings Regulatory agencies keep records on companies that fall under their aegis Congress and subcommittees sources for corporate infomation Foreign service supplies information on foreign suppliers
Intelligence Weakness: Information on corporations often dated and lacking depth. Data is catch-as-catch-can, not on request. Companies will only report to the government what they absolutely have to report; nothing more.		

TABLE 16.1 *(Continued)*

Service Group	Primary Service	Competitor Information Incidentally Supplied
Information Retrieval Services (includes newsclipping document retrieval and data base services)	Collecting of all secondary data upon request Scanning of data bases Clipping and indexing of news articles	Delivery of secondary sources Reporting on whatever competitor information in artilces or texts
Intelligence Weakness: Information on competition often dated or misstated. Limited to secondary sources. Does not go beyond secondary sources to verify or update.		
Investment Bankers	Middleman for corporate acquisition searches Matching buyer and seller Researching marketplace for client	Informal reports on competition Reviews competitor's acquisition history Reports if competitor made any approaches to candidates of interest to the client
Intelligence Weakness: Ad hoc research methods. Little use of field staff. Relies almost exclusively on "old boy" network.		
Lawyers	Representing client legal protection Informing client of legislative changes that may affect client Patent filings	Competitor's litigation Tips on acquisition candidates
Intelligence Weakness: Concerned with client's immediate legal problems. Lawyers monitor market changes only incidentally. Lawyers generally do not actively solicit competitor data; whatever competitor news crosses their desks usually occurs only through the course of normal business.		

(Continued)

TABLE 16.1 *(Continued)*

Service Group	Primary Service	Competitor Information Incidentally Supplied
Management Consulting	Corporate strategy Identifying markets Acquisition, divestiture	Often maintains contacts with competition Regular reports on competitor activities, on request
Intelligence Weakness: Research usually centered on clients operations, not the competitor's. Often relies on contacts and news articles for competitor intelligence; little field staff.		
Market Research	Surveys Product Positioning Indentifying Markets Market Shifts	Spotting new products Passing along hearsay Reports on competition's plan for new market strategy Collecting clippings on competition
Intelligence Weakness: Little depth on competitor operations. Trys to cover entire market, not enough depth on individual companies.		
Public Relations Firms	Projecting positive image about client Measuring public feedback to client activity Planning long-term public relations for client Surveys for client to gauge public opinion	Retrieve news clippings Content analysis of client vs. competition Reports on competitor innovations and activities
Intelligence Weakness: Not prepared in staff or research skills to gather in-depth information on competition		

1. *Responsiveness.* Intelligence research may require the research firm to report to a client on a daily or even hourly basis. The CIF should have the necessary staff time to devote to the client, as well as the available communications channels. That is, the CIF should have either electronic mail, telex, facsimile, or a combination of these devices to be able to make the client aware of any changes in sufficient time.

2. *Systematic Approach.* For accuracy and efficiency, the CIF should have a structured approach to competitor research. Too often a company will seek the most convenient research approach at hand, rather than the most effective means. As often occurs, a company will hire its ad agency to do highly detailed corporate research—research the agency may not at all be prepared to undertake. In another instance, an executive may decide it is more cost effective to hire a business school student on summer vacation to undertake the research. In both of the above cases, the ad hoc researcher is likely to overlook crucial sources or too quickly dismiss an important piece of data in the quest for information.

The structured system allows clients to clearly see all the options open to them, and what they will get if they use each option. For example, should the company order a comprehensive study including extensive field interviews? Or will a simple literature scan or content analysis provide the client with all the necessary data to make the assessment? With a structured approach the client is neither overserviced nor misinformed.

3. *A Combination of Skills.* An intelligence operation has to be able to supply the client with a variety of skills from within the research organization. This means the CIF should stock in its talent inventory people who are expert data base searchers, experienced telephone interviewers, business analysts with a broad background, and the appropriate field staff to complement the back shop activities.

A company that purports to be a CIF but only staffs librarians or analysts is not likely to give the client the breadth of knowledge and experience required. Limited to only secondary information, or to a desk chair analyst, the client will suffer from narrow perspective and overlooked intelligence sources.

4. *Contacts.* Don't let anyone mislead you. A CIF without outside contacts—or the means to find them—is a firm working in the dark. Of course, no CIF can hope to maintain contacts in every industry or specialty.

To insure the CIF's credibility, the client should have the CIF describe its contact list, or its ability to locate the contacts through whatever methods it has available.

Alternately, the client can also select a CIF by its specialty, let's say chemical processing. By knowing in advance what areas the CIF has experience in, the client automatically narrows the search.

5. *No Off-the-Shelf Research.* A market research firm that specializes in producing packaged market studies is not considered a CIF. This statement is true for many reasons. First, a packaged study may touch on certain companies you are interested in, but not go into any depth. Second, these reports quickly date themselves. Especially in rapidly changing markets, off-the-shelf studies become worthless in a matter of months. You can be sure the research for a report dated January 1983 was completed at least two to six months before that date.

Almost all intelligence work is custom-designed, tailored to a particular client's needs and specifications. A client has too many highly detailed questions, far too many to ever be of interest to any general readership that might purchase a mass-produced market report.

6. *Long-term Arrangements.* Much like any other service firm, the CIF and the client benefit greatly from a long-term working relationship. Long-term assignments allow the client the time to learn what the CIF's range of services are. The CIF, in turn, learns the client's various research needs and will often develop additional expertise and services to further aid the client.

7. *Quotes and Proposals.* Research fees generally begin at $25 per hour and can exceed $100 per hour. The rates depend on level of expertise applied and the type of firm the client deals with.

For example, a management consulting firm will likely bill out its time at a rate closer to the $100 mark; while a firm strictly devoted to research can offer lower fees.

Project costs can range from $1000 or less for a single company assessment to hundreds of thousands of dollars for longer-term monitoring on a host of competitors, requiring many updates.

Whatever firm the client finally settles on, the CIF should clearly state the final dollar amount and turnaround time for completion of the project. Time permitting, the CIF should also submit a written proposal describing cost and time factors.

FINDING AN INTELLIGENCE FIRM

As already mentioned, competitor intelligence is a relatively new phrase in the business dictionary, and the executive searching for a CIF must look in a number of different areas to find one.

The first and probably the best source is a referral, a colleague who has used a service and was satisfied. If the prospective client does not know of a current CIF user, he or she can call any number of large corporations and ask to speak to their market research or corporate planning staffs. These two groups are the most likely users of an intelligence service.

Another, already mentioned source of firm names is the Yellow Pages. Although a potentially laborious task, you can expect to find intelligence research firms listed under the following headings: Business Consultants, Foreign Trade Consultants, Industrial Consultants, Management Consultants, and Market Research and Analysis.

Professional societies will also prove to be storehouses of tips and recommendations on the new consulting firms or firms that provide the research you are looking for. Many of these national societies also have local chapters that further extend this "old boy" referral network. Two professional groups the executive should contact when beginning a blind search are the North American Society for Corporate Planners (NASCP) and the American Marketing Association. Both are nationally respected with a broad-based membership. The NASCP does have regional chapters to act as a further springboard for contacts. Their addresses and telephone numbers are:

THE NORTH AMERICAN SOCIETY FOR CORPORATE PLANNERS
300 Arcade Square
P.O. Box 1288
Cleveland, Ohio 45402
513-223-4948

THE AMERICAN MARKETING ASSOCIATION
250 South Wacker Drive
Chicago, Illinois 60606
312-648-0536

Finally, if all of the above suggestions fail, turn to a number of recently published directories. These indexes were designed more as a reference work to locate library information services, not to find the broader, more complex CIF firm. Because of their orientation, these texts do not compile the information using the terms "business intelligence" or "competitor intelligence." Most probably the researcher will find the service firm under the broader heading of "information service." A closer look at the firm's description will quickly tell the reader if this group can possibly offer what is needed.

Here are a few directories that will aid the executive in the CIF hunt:

INFORMATION INDUSTRY MARKETPLACE
R.R. Bowker Company
1180 Avenue of the Americas
New York, New York 10036

CONSULTANTS AND CONSULTING ORGANIZATION SOURCES
Gale Research Company
Book Tower
Detroit, Michigan 48226

RESEARCH SERVICES DIRECTORY
Gale Research Company
Book Tower
Detroit, Michigan 48226

THE TOOLS: HOW A CIF GATHERS COMPETITOR INTELLIGENCE

Earlier in the chapter, we mentioned the DECS Matrix, a research tool specifically designed by Information Data Search to uncover minute corporate details. The DECS takes the macroscopic aspects of an industry and applies them to a particular company. It allows the investigator to zoom in on those sources and contacts most likely to reveal the desired information about the competitor.

THE DECS MATRIX

DECS stands for Distributors—External Experts—Customers—Suppliers. The DECS Matrix depicts the relationship a particular company has with its business evironment. It reveals the key access points for locating intelligence on a company.

Every company has a position in the marketplace. It has competitors, or potential competitors. It must have sources of supply, distribution channels and, most important, end-users or customers.

How a company buys, sells, and distributes its products reveals intelligence about that company. During the course of business, any one company will come into contact with its competition, supply sources, and customers. All these contacts become key intelligence sources about the company and its market. In many instances these contacts will provide a more accurate picture about the company than the company could provide about itself.

A DECS shape and how a particular company fits into the matrix will vary from product group to product group. Mature industries, such as automobiles or steel, will form an entirely different matrix than that of the personal computer industry, for example. Steel companies have relatively fixed lines of distribution. Their sources of supply and end-users are well known. The personal computer industry, on the other hand, is a new, dynamic industry. Its market is constantly being redefined, with new competitors and distribution channels opening up every month.

Based on the resulting DECS Matrix, Information Data Search will design its research strategy. A Personal Computer DECS Matrix may dictate that the research concentrate more on suppliers and competitors than on end-users, whereas steel—because of a recent surge of imports—may require a greater concentration on the consumer and external expert side of the matrix.

How the DECS Works

The key element to the DECS Matrix is the concentration ratio—that is, the ratio representing the largest percent of market shares held by the four leading companies in the industry.

The vertical axis on the grid is a list of all the possible intelligence sources that might supply information about the target company. These sources are placed on intelligence levels and range from importers to news media. The entire horizontal axis is a percent scale used for the concentration ratio. The researcher takes each intelligence source and measures the ratio for it, and then marks the appropriate locus on the matrix.

In the following example, Information Data Search examined the personal computer industry. We can see from the results, shown in Figure 16.1, that the top four companies have 60 percent of the market (that is the concentration ratio for that intelligence level). On the other hand, the ratio for overall suppliers in the industry is quite low, less than 20 percent.

How to Read the DECS

After the researcher has computed the concentration ratios for each element and mapped them on the grid, a pattern emerges. With the DECS the rule of thumb is that whatever elements appear on or to the right of the target company are the most accessible and likely the most knowledgeable sources of information about the company.

Examining the DECS Matrix for the personal computer industry, we see that the local press, trade press, computer clubs, Radio Shack, and disk and keyboard manufacturers as falling on or to the right of the target company. On the other hand, mail-order concerns, discount stores, and microchip companies fall to the left of the target.

What does all this imply about the researcher's ability to find information on the target companies? It tells the researcher to direct the most research efforts toward interviewing local newspapers and trade press, as well as the disk drive and keyboard suppliers. Likewise, it instructs the researcher to ignore mail-order firms or discount stores.

The matrix indicates the direction the research should take. It instructs the investigator where to go and which sources to omit in the research process. In short, the DECS Matrix is a time-saver, a way to zero in on highly valuable competitor intelligence sources.

Still, it is not foolproof. And depending on the segment of the market being examined and the time period being looked at, the shape of the DECS may change. Also, since the matrix is an indicator, it cannot account for strange or unusual occurances.

For instance, the DECS may tell the researcher that the trade press may be a poor source of intelligence. But in calling a reporter for one of these magazines, the investigator could discover that this same reporter used to work for one of the companies under study and can supply a good deal of information about that company.

These are the flukes, circumstances no technique can account for. Yet, as an indicator, the DECS can steer the researcher in the right direction, saving time and expense by pinpointing those sources most likely to have the needed intelligence.

DECS Matrix

Target Industry Personal Computers

Target Company/Group Apple Computer/Suppliers

Industry Group	4 Firm Concentration Ratio: 0% 50%	.	. . . . 100%
Target Group (Manufacturers)		X	
Distributors			
Retailers	X (Chain Stores) X (Independents)		
Distributors			
Independent Reps.			
Transportation			
Other (Mail Order)	X		
External Experts			
Media			X (Local Paper) X (Trade Press)
Trade Organization			
Government			
Consultants			
Other ( )			
Customers	(Computer Clubs) X		
Suppliers			
Manufacturers			
Equipment			
Materials/Components	X (Microchip co's)		X (Disk co's) X (Keyboard co's)
Other ( )			
Other (Importers)	X		

Figure 16.1 DECS matrix—target industry: personal or home computers; target company: major products

A BRIEF LIST OF NOTABLE CIFs

HARLAN BROWN & MARKOWITZ, INC.
1307 Dolley Madison Blvd.
McLean, Virginia 22101
703-821-1920
Contact: Harlan J. Brown, Chairman
Zane N. Markowitz, President

INFORMATION DATA SEARCH, INC.
The Corporate Intelligence Group
1218 Massachusetts Avenue
Cambridge, Massachusetts 02138
617-492-5900
Contact: Leonard M. Fuld, Managing Director

INFORMATION FOR BUSINESS
25 West 39 St.
New York, New York 10018
212-840-1220
Contact: James C. Burke, Director
Christopher Samuels, Director

17

The Use of Competitor Intelligence in Acquisitions and Divestments

ROBERT SPITALNIC

This book has provided approaches to gathering, analyzing, and using competitor information. This chapter will describe how these techniques can be utilized to assist in one of the most important strategic decisions corporations must make—their acquisition and divestment programs. Our concern here is not with the unplanned, unrelated megabuck deals, or the financial gymnastics of some acquirers. Our concern is with acquisitions that meet specific business and strategic objective/needs. As one investment banker observed in the *New York Times* (October 4, 1982) about the Allied-Bendix-Marietta affair, "No one was playing chess—only checkers. They could see only one or two moves ahead."

If a company is to compete successfully in a market the acquisition program can play a significant role in the attempt to further utilize one's competitive strength or to reduce competitive disadvantages. Similar approaches can also provide input for the divestment program. The techniques described are especially valuable in those cases when (planned) unrelated diversification is necessary.

A review of the literature indicates most acquisitions have not been successful. This reflects the judgements of the acquiring companies' management, not just attempts by professors to develop measures of firms' performance that compare acquiring and non-acquiring companies.

One study to determine whether acquisitions were a successful method of growth reviewed the acquisition behavior of 93 manufacturing firms over 20 years. In estimating the overall success, "acquiring firms felt that about 20 percent of acquisitions were considered outright failures, 51 percent were a full success, the remaining 29 percent were judged a partial success."[1]

Booz, Allen & Hamilton in 1960 made a survey of 128 acquisitions by companies in the Chicago area. Those companies making four or fewer acquisitions had good results *less* than half of the time; companies making five to ten acquisitions had good results 62 percent of the time. The remaining acquisitions had doubtful results, or the acquired company had been sold or liquidated.

More recently, Acquisition Horizons, a consulting firm, surveyed 1400 companies in 1982.[2] Replies were received from 537 companies, ranging in sales size from $125 million to over $2 billion. All of the companies replying had made at least one acquisition—and usually more—in the last five years. Almost three-fifths were characterized as totally or very successful. But over 40 percent were considered only somewhat successful or unsuccessful.

Of the ten primary reasons given for the shortfall in results versus expectation, at least seven reflect a failure to perform the required competitive homework—that is, to really understand the acquired company and its place in the industry. The reasons given are as follows:

1. Management was not as deep as expected.
2. Company's net profit margins were less than expected.
3. Market did not grow as fast as expected.
4. Industry profit margins were less than expected.
5. Market position of acquired company was less strong than expected.
6. Pre-acquisition research proved inadequate or inaccurate.
7. Systems of acquired company were less developed than expected.
8. Competition was tougher than expected.
9. Lack of new strategic plan for acquired company.
10. Capital requirements larger than expected.

Almost all of the reasons could have been identified through better market and competitor research. Reasons 1, 7, and 10 also reflect a failure to plan effectively for integration of the company after the acquisition.

Of course, one of the strongest indicators of the failure of many acquisitions programs is the high level of divestments. According to statistics published by W. T. Grimm & Co. (a Chicago firm that records merger and acquisition statistics), divestments accounted for more than one-third of total acquisition activity in the past ten years. This figure was as high as 55 percent in 1976.

Peter Drucker once remarked that two-fifths of all acquisitions are unsuccessful. Some analysts feel that this figure might be too low. A review of economic and financial literature shows no evidence of increased profitability for acquiring companies. In fact, several studies indicate conglomerate or unrelated acquisitions result in poorer returns and higher risks to the acquiring company and its stockholders.[3] The message is buy the stock of many companies, as opposed to the stock of one company that buys many companies.

Of course most of the research leaves much to be desired in terms of controls, survey size, definitions, and measuring profitability. The latter is often difficult to determine, especially when comparing different companies and industries. In addition, some unrelated diversification was caused by defensive measures or reactions to a declining market. Examples include cigarette manufacturers acquiring food or beverage companies, or W. R. Grace reducing its dependence on Latin America and shipping by moving into chemicals. Without these moves profitability might have been much lower.

In general terms one may still say that acquisitions have not been successful primarily due to a combination of a short-term financial reporting orientation towards acquisitions and the failure to do the *right* industry and competitor homework—particularly the qualitative analysis. The first is a result of the perception that the *reported* earnings are the key factor in determining stock prices. Accounting changes, particularly opinions 16 and 17 of the Accounting Principles Board of the American Institute of Certified Public Accountants, eliminated some of the reporting abuses. And some recent studies indicate cash flow is more important than reported earnings in determining stock prices. However, the purpose of this chapter is to address the homework problem.

Let us first review the various types of acquisitions. Throughout this discussion we are talking about the acquisition[4] of one company by another, as opposed to the side-by-side *merger* of two equal, or almost equal, companies.

TYPES OF ACQUISITIONS

Acquisitions may be divided into four groups: vertical, horizontal, concentric, and conglomerate. The last two may also be expressed as related and unrelated diversification.

With vertical acquisitions (or integration) the firm expands by acquiring companies in *different* stages of production or distribution—for example, backwards towards a raw material producer or forward towards the ultimate consumer. Examples include a steel mill acquiring iron ore reserves, or oil refineries acquiring service stations.

Horizontal acquisitions refer to acquiring companies engaged in the same stages of production or distribution process; that is, firms producing the same products (or services) in the same or different geographical markets. An example would be a steel manufacturer in the East buying a West Coast steel plant.

Concentric acquisitions are diversification moves related to the company's existing skills and strengths but applied to different customers or products. An example would include an automotive parts distributor purchasing a distributor of food products.

Conglomerate acquisitions are those unrelated to current operations. The only consistent factor, if any, is management. Of course, many acquisitions will not fall neatly into one of the four categories. Some may have two or more elements of the above depending on how the acquisition is analyzed.

The most common problem with many corporations is that they have no acquisition strategy. They react to suggestions thrown at them by investment bankers and other intermediaries. Before developing an acquisition strategy, the potential acquirer must insure that it really understands its current operations. The acquiring firm must know the following:

What do we do?
What do we really do?
What do we do well?
What do we do poorly?

These are difficult questions to answer, and will require a great deal of hard work, analysis, and serious reflection. Yet the corporation must perform this exercise, and on a periodic basis. Not only are the answers critical to developing the acquisition program, but they are essential to the company's current activities.

Techniques described in many of the previous chapters are particularly helpful in answering these questions as well as in developing additional questions. Each company has unique strengths and weaknesses relative to its competition and the industry within which it operates. Answers to the above questions tell the company where it is. As it further analyzes and understands the competition, the results can be used in developing an acquisition strategy.

One approach to corporate self-analysis is to look at each of the key functional areas—production, marketing, finance, and R&D. Questions and items to review relating to production might include:

Manufacturing cost per unit relative to other competitors.
Raw material costs and availability relative to competitors.
An analysis of plant location.
Effect of OSHA regulations.

Questions can be developed for all of the functional areas. An analysis of the answers provides a picture of the firm's competitive advantage. There are other approaches, which include a review of the total company and its particular strengths in general, and by industry. Another method could be segmentation utilizing customer needs or substitute products to define a market.[5]

The input from an understanding of the company's strengths and weaknesses can be used to develop an acquisition program. The other critical input is the environmental/industry analysis. From these inputs opportunities and (possible) threats are identified, and a comprehensive acquisition program can be developed. Companies—and for unrelated acquisitions, industries—can then be identified and analyzed.

One other factor to consider is the attitude of management—especially the board and the CEO—toward acquisitions. This is hard to quantify. Each company has a style and character, which to a large degree is influenced by the CEO. However, this input is more critical to the implementation stage of an acquisition program.

The environmental analysis can be approached in different ways. One method is to divide the analysis into three areas:

1. Macroeconomic analysis.
2. Market research/industry analysis.
3. Public issue analysis (social, governmental, cultural).

The details of environmental analysis wil not be discussed here. An excellent approach to analyzing industries is Chapter 8, "Industry Evolution," of Porter's *Competitive Strategy*. The book puts industrial organization economics in a format that can be utilized by management.

Particularly in unrelated acquisitions, but also with concentric acquisitions, it is necessary to do a great deal more analysis of the industry as well as of specific companies. The lack of success of many acquisitions is caused by a failure to understand the industry in which the company participates. On the next few pages key areas are outined that must be explored—often in great detail—if one is to be successful.

In entering a new industry some very critical questions arise: What will the new competitors do? How will they react? These questions are difficult enough to answer in an industry in which the acquirer is experienced.

INDUSTRY ANALYSIS

I. Market (demand) factors
   a. Size—total, segments

b. Growth rates—total, segments
c. Pricing trends
d. Cyclicality, seasonality
e. Sensitivity of demand
1. Price
2. Service
f. Captive market (degree of)
g. Diversity of market

II. Customer (user) factors
a. Types of users
b. Size
c. Location
d. Level of concentration
e. Buying habits
f. Product use/performance
1. Level of product differentiation
2. Does product save buyer money?
g. Product importance/image to user
1. Cost relative to final product
h. Quantity, frequency of purchase
i. Terms of purchase
j. Service

III. Competitive factors
a. Existing companies
b. Potential entrants
1. Related/unrelated
2. Customers
3. Suppliers
4. Horizontal integration
5. Unrelated diversification
6. Barriers to entry
a. Economies of scale
b. Product differentiation
c. Capital requirements
d. Switching costs (customers)
e. Access to distribution channels

- c. Substitutes/innovations

IV. Suppliers
- a. Concentration relative to industry
- b. Product specialization
- c. Substitute/products
- d. Delivery system/service

V. Other industry factors
- a. Trend setters
- b. Distribution
- c. Dealers
- d. Service
- e. Warranties
- f. Capacity
- g. Values
- h. Financial characteristics
  1. Fixed costs
  2. Profitability

VI. Social factors
- a. Values and priorities
  1. Environment/ecology
  2. Life style
  3. Social responsibility
  4. Product standards
- b. Needs/expectations
- c. Pressure groups
- d. Demographics

VII. Government factors
- a. Legislation
- b. Regulation
- c. Taxation
- d. Special incentives
  1. Production supports
  2. Exports
- e. Political issues
- f. Legal/antitrust issues

VIII. Economic factors
  a. Inflation/deflation
  b. Fiscal policy
  c. Monetary policy—interest rates
  d. Wage and price controls

IX. Technological factors
  a. Maturity and volatility
  b. Complexity
  c. Differentiation
  d. Patents/copyrights
  e. Processing/manufacturing technology

UTILIZING A COMPETITOR INTELLIGENCE SYSTEM

A competitor intelligence system will also be of great benefit to a company's acquisition/divestment activity, not only in terms of reviewing a company's position within its industries but also in providing the means to quickly review and analyze both related and unrelated acquisitions and to provide input for possible divestiture activity.

As explained in chapter 5, the intelligence cycle has four phases:

1. Direction (planning).
2. Collection (gathering information).
3. Processing (analysis).
4. Dissemination (communication of intelligence).

The first phase, *planning or determining the direction* of the intelligence activity, is as frequently ignored in acquisition planning as it is in the competitor intelligence program. As discussed above, many corporations have not initially thought out their acquisition program. Senior management must identify the business decisions and/or actions the required intelligence will support. For example, does an acquisition program seek to make better use of a company's strong research activities or its national distribution network? The acquisition program goals should—if they are carefully defined—determine the scope and time constraints of the intelligence efforts and direction.

Although there is a need for quick reaction in most acquisition situations, and although priorities will often change with the different stages of negotiation, top management must still have a continuing strategic overview. Not just a "deal-making mentality" but answers to critical questions are required. Why is the acquisition necessary? How will it fit? These questions should be reviewed *before* the acquisition program is implemented.

Because the competitor intelligence system will also be used to provide acquisition candidates, the orientation and information needs will be different. For example, key items to analyze include organizational fit and post-merger integration. The questions relating to fit and post-merger integration are often ignored in acquisition analysis. Salter and Weinhold discuss measures of strategic fit in a chapter entitled "Acquisition Screening Systems," and raise important questions relating to the organizational compatability of the potential acquisition:

> Does one merger partner possess certain administrative systems (such as purchasing or inventory management) that can help upgrade the performance of the other partner? Are the planning and control systems . . . compatible, or does the approach used in one appear either threatening or superfluous to the other? Is there compatibility in the design and administration of executive compensation systems, or are the reward systems so different that successfully integrating administrative units or transferring personnel between companies is highly unlikely? Is there compatibility in the work rules, wages, and benefits of the respective labor forces? Do the companies share common values with respect to product quality, risk taking, and social responsiveness?[6]

As the company begins to understand an industry and its competitors it will sometimes change the direction of its information needs. The analysis and dissemination phases of the intelligence cycle thus provide feedback for changing information planning and priorities.

While phase 2, the *collection* phase, is often the easiest part of the intelligence cycle, it may be (as has been pointed out) too easy. That is, an enormous amount of data is available—so much that management is often overwhelmed. This is particularly true when the seller or a representative has prepared a great deal of information, a large portion of which often avoids the most significant strategic factors; for example, competitor threats or possible technological changes.

An existing collection system greatly facilitates the development of relevant strategic data. This becomes especially valuable given the tight timing demands of most acquisition transactions. Moreover, these files can contain information on possible candidates. A format similar to the base case intelligence file described in chapter 5 will have a comprehensive description and analysis of competitors.

Use of key item checklists can be valuable but should not become a replacement for creative analysis required for each candidate. The checklist insures certain items have been covered, but often critical items peculiar to a specific industry do not lend themselves to a checklist format.

Phase 3 of the competitor intelligence system, the *processing and analysis of the information* (or recording, interpretation, and analysis of data), must also be done in a comparatively short time frame. For those acquisitions that involve vertical or horizontal integration (and to a lesser extent, concentric mergers), the established collection/analysis system can often be utilized; in fact, some of the candidates may have been previously analyzed. As the company moves into new unrelated areas, greater use must be made of outside consultants or other industry experts such as retired executives to provide the needed insights.

Again, because the acquisition aspect changes the orientation, concern should be shown with some additional areas in the intelligence system—for example, the fit of the two particular companies, and the attempt to determine how the two organizations can work together to obtain competitive advantages. Another key part of the exercise is predicting future competitor moves relating to new entry. Although answering this question is difficult enough for related acquisitions, it becomes particularly difficult for unrelated conglomerate acquisitions, and to a lesser extent in concentric acquisitions.

Phase 4, *dissemination and use,* recognizes that the short deadlines that confront management in acquisitions may cause gaps in the detail and accuracy of the material; yet this information must be available to senior management before the final acquisition decision can be made.

The format in which the material and analysis is presented is also important. Charts can be useful in summarizing points for management. Moreover, the periodic reports that are issued can be used as input to develop acquisition candidates. One technique that works with very large diversified companies is to rank each of the major business segments by some key financial ratios, such as return on assets and equity. Appropriate comments about some of the key differences including a summary of strategic advantages can explain the different returns. This can be extremely helpful in getting top management's attention toward filling gaps in a company's competitive position.

DIVESTMENTS

The growth in the level of divestments has in part been the result of the high level of acquisition activity during the late 1960s. Either the acquisitions have not worked out or the acquired companies had some operations that were not of interest to the acquiring company.

There are other factors accounting for the growth of divestments. Ten to fifteen years ago, most of the divestments were "dogs." More recently, some profitable operations have been sold off. Examples would include Esmark's sale of Vickers Petroleum and RCA's sale of Gibson Greeting Cards. These operations did not fit into the companies' long-range plans.

These companies are taking a portfolio approach to their business. Although the divested operations may be doing well, the parent feels it can do better, or is more comfortable, in other areas. Many large companies are recognizing that certain industries and specific product areas do not lend themselves to the control and planning requirements of very large companies. There is now greater use of strategic planning techniques in determining divestments, as well as in the acquisition area.

In an article in the *Wharton Magazine* that summarizes preliminary results of a research study, divestments were divided into *aggressively motivated,* which are undertaken voluntarily and reflect movement into new directions; and *defensively motivated,* which are due to "financial distress in the parent firm, weak market position of the divested unit or pressures or direct orders from government regulatory agencies. They frequently involve business units which are in the late stages of their life cycles."[7] Although most divestments were defensive, aggressively motivated divestments were becoming more common, with some firms assigning full or part-time responsibility for this activity.

Many of the techniques used in determining the acquisition decision can also be issued as input for divestment decisions. The industry and environmental information will (should be) in place. A key concern here is possible new products that might displace existing products; often one has to look several years ahead for possible industry/environment changes.

The competitor intelligence system will have much of the competitor/company material in place. However, since the end result is going to be different, there are a few distinctions. In addition to questions relating to competitor position, the direction and analysis will include developing buyer candidates for the proposed divestment. The analysis element will include some review of who are the most likely candidates and the competitive risk in discussing the proposed divestment with them.

In a recent *Harvard Business Review* article (July–August 1983), Kathryn R. Harrigan and Michael E. Porter discuss "End-game Strategies for Declining Industries" and review some exit barriers, which include the difficulty in selling specialized assets, related labor costs, and governmental concerns.

A significant problem in any analysis is the failure to be objective. Emotional factors which can come into play relating to any divestment decision can distort the analysis. For example, failure to recognize the decline in an industry can preclude realistic analysis.

IMPLEMENTATION OF THE DIVESTMENT PROGRAM

It is important, particularly in the early stages, to keep the divestment decision confidential. Not only are there the obvious effects on competitors and customers, but the emotional impact on management and labor. Yet in many cases the management of the potential divestment must or should be involved early in the planning and implementation. They sometimes are the most logical buyers, especially with the growth of equity and asset-based financing for leveraged management buyouts. Moreover, once management understands that these financing techniques are not viable for *their* unit, they may play a more positive role in the sale of the unit.

A key question relates to who will handle the divestment. Most companies do not have full-time divestment staffs. The smaller divestments are often not adequately serviced by the major investment banking firms, who have the most experience in this area.

Another broad issue is how to prevent competitors from obtaining this information. Some of the so-called buyers are really trying to obtain competitor intelligence. On the other hand, the most viable buyer candidates are often strong competitors.

If many acquisitions are poorly planned, the same can be said about most divestments. And the major weaknesses can be found most often in the implementation stage. Involve top management early, and present the financial and marketing risks if information about the divestment is prematurely disclosed.

One control technique is to provide very limited data in the offering brochure. However, if any discussions are instituted and more sensitive data is supplied, there is some loss of control despite secrecy agreements. The information may get into the hands of competitors or potential competitors, and this possibility has to be factored into the divestment planning.

Detailed checklists for the many steps involved in a divestment can be found in Fredrick A. Lovejoy's *Divestment For Profits* (New York, Financial Research Foundation, 1971). This book will also provide methods for developing alternative approaches to the handling of divestments, including who gets involved and when.

It is hoped that the level of the acquisition analysis, including competitor intelligence, will reduce the number of divestments. However, one must also recognize that we are dealing with a continually changing environment with new threats—and new opportunities.

---

[1]H. Igor Ansoff, R. G. Brandenburg, Fred E. Portner, and R. Radosevich, *Acquisition Behavior of U.S. Manufacturing Firms, 1946–1965,* Nashville, Tennessee, Vanderbilt University Press, 1971, p. 7.

[2]Letter to author from Robert H. Kenmore.

[3]See Malcolm Salter and Wolf A. Weinhold, *Diversification through Acquisitions: Strategies for Creating Economic Value;* New York, Free Press, 1979, pp. 22–33, 104–5, and 144–153.

[4]The form of the acquisition may be a merger, consolidation, or the acquisition of stock or assets.

[5]Approaches to determining competitive advantages and disadvantages are discussed in Steven E. South "Competitive Advantage; the Cornerstone of Strategic Thinking," *The Journal of Business Strategy,* Spring 1981, pp. 15–25; Peter J. Carroll, "The Link Between Performance and Strategy," *The Journal of Business Strategy,* Spring 1982, pp. 10–20; and Michael E. Porter *Competitive Strategy; Techniques for Analyzing Industries and Competitors,* New York, Free Press, 1980.

[6]Malcolm A. Salter and Wolf A. Weinhold, *Diversification through Acquisition,* p. 193.

[7]Irene M. Duhaime and G. Richard Patton, "Selling Off," *Wharton Magazine,* Winter 1980, p. 46.

Index

DATE DUE

5-27-88	JUL 17 1999		
FEB 20 1992			
MAR 12 1992			
APR 06 1992			
4-3-94			
NOV 20 1994			
5-20-96			
ALAFM			
JUL 17 1999			